AMERICAN RADICALISM, 1865–1901

ESSAYS AND DOCUMENTS

HOW AMERICANUS MONOPOLUS TAKES AN AIRING

CONNECTICUT COLLEGE MONOGRAPH NO. 3

AMERICAN RADICALISM
1865-1901

ESSAYS AND DOCUMENTS

By

CHESTER McARTHUR DESTLER

1972

OCTAGON BOOKS

New York

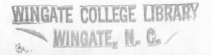

Reprinted 1963

*by special arrangement with Connecticut College
and Chester McArthur Destler*

Third Octagon printing 1972

OCTAGON BOOKS

A Division of Farrar, Straus & Giroux, Inc.

19 Union Square West

New York, N. Y. 10003

Library of Congress Catalog Card Number: 63-14344

ISBN 0-374-92128-8

Printed in U.S.A. by
NOBLE OFFSET PRINTERS, INC.
NEW YORK 3, N. Y.

TO

KATHARINE

APOSTLE OF MODERATION

PREFACE

RADICALISM has been one of the three great modes of cultural development in the United States, asserting "new meanings" and demanding "the acceptance of new forms of behavior." Throughout American history the radicals have combatted traditionalism with its staunch adherence to old forms. They have hastened the slow reorientation of "old meanings and forms to . . . new circumstances."[1] Repeatedly the practitioners of the radical method have precipitated sharp breaks with the past through innovations that have contributed to the distinctive character of the American tradition.

For nearly two centuries in the United States, folk and sophisticated thought alike have regarded native, democratic radicalism as the peculiar product of the frontier. Such undoubtedly was the viewpoint of the Virginia gentry in 1775. Three and a half decades later Timothy Dwight of Yale College attributed the levelling influences of the day to the turbulent frontiersmen with their casual regard for property rights. Subsequent experience with Jacksonian Democracy and the agrarian movements of the late nineteenth century strengthened the conviction with which this thesis was entertained by conservative easterners. It was accepted gratefully by residents of the trans-Allegheny states as evidence of the important contribution made by their section to the nation's development. Caught up by Frederick Jackson Turner, this theory of democratic origins became a major corollary of the frontier hypothesis that has been such a factor in the development of a school of *national* history in the United States. Nationalist, radical democracy, Turner taught, was the creation of the moving frontier.

Under the influence of this thesis some half century of scholarship in western history has been focussed upon the regional background of the recurring periods of unrest and radical agitation. Assuming an exclusively local origin and the unique character of these movements, and stressing their direct, practical relation to specific western problems, historians have studied western radicalism almost without regard to ideological considerations or possible indebtedness to other regions.

Shortly before John D. Hicks completed his monumental study of Populism[2] within the conceptual limits of the Turner frontier and sectional hypotheses, I undertook the study of western radicalism in terms

[1] Ralph E. Turner, *The Great Cultural Traditions*, I (New York, 1941), 20.
[2] *The Populist Revolt* (Minneapolis, 1931).

VII

of ideological interchange and conflict between western agrarians and urban radicals. This approach was suggested by seemingly unrelated studies undertaken on the instance of William E. Dodd and Avery Craven. Simultaneous investigation of the Pendleton plan of 1867 and of the labor-Populist alliance in Illinois of 1894 led accidentally to discovery of the influence of Edward Kellogg's ideas upon both urban and agrarian radicals after the Civil War. Eventually, I embarked upon a study of the career of Henry Demarest Lloyd, a radical of the first rank, which is now nearing completion. While pursuing this project I uncovered urban origins of a number of supposedly rural stereotypes and remedial proposals that Turnerians have regarded as peculiarly western. These discoveries led inevitably to the consideration of whether, out of the ideological intercourse of country and city there had not developed in the late nineteenth century West a new radical synthesis. If its existence could be demonstrated such a novel but indigenous creed would give new meaning to the bitter conflicts that characterized the short-lived labor-Populist alliance of 1894–1896.

The following papers and documents are offered in the hope of establishing the validity of this approach to the study of American radicalism. Its potentiality for the larger study of American cultural history may be suggested by the effects of attempted co-operation upon alien and indigenous systems of radical thought. The sequel to the letter from Burnette G. Haskell to August Spies, for example, offers a clear illustration of ideological conflict between two alien ideologies and a single, semi-indigenous school in which the latter rejected both imported systems as destructive of the purposes of its own agitation. A campaign address of 1894 by Henry Demarest Lloyd, the tenth number in this volume, contains perhaps the most complete harmonization attempted of Populism with the varying types of proletarian and middle class Socialism then propagated in the West. Its discovery led me to re-examine my earlier study of the labor-Populist alliance, whose initiation I had already described in a brief, published essay which is reproduced here (Chapter VIII). The results of this re-analysis, which had the advantage of materials gathered in the course of my research on Henry D. Lloyd, are presented in two long essays.

The volume is offered also in the hope that it will throw new light on the reformulation of the traditional, Jeffersonian radicalism that occurred in the age of the "Robber Barons." The felt necessities of wage-earners and farmers, the propaganda of mercantile organizations, and the proposals of radical urban publicists contributed significantly to this process during an era of intensified intercourse between farm and city. The essay on Edward Kellogg may suggest the feasibility of demonstrating folk acceptance of a radical deviation through careful canvass of the journals, pamphlet literature, and programs of successive labor and agrarian movements. It may indicate, also, the possibility of tracing the fortunes of new proposals, whether of native or alien origin, until they are finally rejected or included in a new synthesis. The co-operative, single tax, land reform, free silver, and Nationalist movements might well be re-studied from such a standpoint. Similarly, attention might be paid profitably to the secondary as well as the primary effects of the agitation of Marxian and revisionist Socialism upon the developing American radicalism.

The essay on the Toledo natural gas pipe-line controversy is included in the series because it offers an urban example of the invocation of traditional antipathies to monopoly and special privilege to justify a venture in municipal ownership of public utilities. The same city, it will be recalled, was famous a few years later as a center of the neo-democratic movement in which the Ohio reformers, Samuel M. Jones and Tom L. Johnson, appealed to the same stereotypes as a means of arousing popular support for other municipal ownership programs. The paper upon *Wealth Against Commonwealth* is republished because of Henry D. Lloyd's attempt to win mass support for a new theoretical approach to the problems of monopoly capitalism. Since this was offered as part of the ideological basis for the labor-Populist alliance, Lloyd's proposals bear a direct relation to the central problem under consideration.

I am grateful to the editors of the *American Historical Review*, the *Mississippi Valley Historical Review*, the *Pacific Historical Review*, the *Journal of Political Economy*, and the *Quarterly Bulletin* of the Historical Society of Northwestern Ohio for their courtesy in permitting me to reprint here the essays that have appeared in their journals. I am especially indebted to Alice E. Smith, Curator of Manuscripts of the State Historical Society of Wisconsin, for her encouragement of my studies in American radicalism, to Agnes Inglis, Curator of the Joseph A. Labadie Collection of Labor Materials at the University of Michigan, for permission to publish the letter from Burnette Haskell to August Spies, and to Dr. Guy Stanton Ford for his editorial criticism of my appraisal of *Wealth Against Commonwealth*. I am indebted to John D. Rockefeller, Jr., and to Professor Allan Nevins of Columbia University, for their courtesy in allowing me to use portions of the "John D. Rockefeller Conversations with William O. Inglis" manuscript in preparation of

Chapters VI–VII. The entire volume has profited from the suggestions of Professor Leonard W. Labaree of Yale University who read the manuscript. I am indebted also to my colleague, Professor Hamilton Martin Smyser, for his assistance as editor of the Connecticut College Monograph Series, to Connecticut College for financial aid in publishing this volume, and to ex-President Dorothy Schaffter and President Katharine Blunt for their interest in its completion. Finally, I wish to express my appreciation to Master Samuel B. Heminway and the Fellows of Berkeley College of Yale University for their hospitality, which has made the final stages of work on this monograph a pleasure.

C. McA. D.

New London, Connecticut
September 3, 1945

CONTENTS

ILLUSTRATIONS

CHAPTER I

WESTERN RADICALISM, 1865–1901: CONCEPTS AND ORIGINS*

IN May, 1943, President James B. Conant of Harvard University announced that for the immediate future one of America's greatest needs could be met only by the development of an indigenous radical movement. In the postwar years, he predicts, the nation will witness a bitter conflict between "American reactionaries," who will fight for the restoration of the ante-bellum or ante-New Deal business system, and a generation of "European radicals" whose agitation and collectivist policies will strike a jarring, alien note. Hinting that the activity of the imported school will be so unpalatable to the native temper that it will produce a dangerous schism in the United States, President Conant invokes the shades of Jefferson, Emerson, Thoreau, and Walt Whitman in the hope of summoning up a group of "American radicals." These, he hopes, will counterbalance the other two and do much to preserve the cherished liberties and equality of opportunity of our democratic system in the years to come.

Contemporary liberal publicists, such as Max Lerner, were quick to comment upon Mr. Conant's failure to identify a native radical tradition more recent than that produced by the transcendental flowering of New England. More recent epochs, they asserted, have produced American radicals with an outlook more directly related to the problems of a metropolitan, machine age civilization. Such were the insurgents of the Progressive era and their Bryanite rivals. The "Sons of the Wild Jackass," who disturbed the slumbers of Calvin Coolidge with suggestions of farm subsidies and a government operated plant at Muscle Shoals, though begotten, supposedly, in a cultural desert, were surely indigenous. But like Mr. Conant, his liberal critics failed to determine whether there had actually developed in the United States, after the Civil War, a native school of radical thought whose basic concepts might be identified and the course of its influence traced into the twentieth century in an attempt to determine its utility in terms of the needs of today.[1]

---

* Reprinted from the *Mississippi Valley Historical Review*, XXXI, (December, 1944), 335–368.

[1] James B. Conant, "Wanted: American Radicals," *Atlantic Monthly* (Boston), CLXXI, May, 1943, pp. 41–45; Max Lerner, "American Radicals," *PM* (New York), May 31, 1943, p. 2.

Although students of western history have long contended for the existence of a unique agrarianism in the West after 1865, they, too, have have failed to establish the existence there of a distinctive school of radical thought. Insulated by the continued influence of the frontier hypothesis from the records of contemporary or preceding urban movements within or without the region, and preoccupied largely with local sources of information, they have based the traditional story of western radicalism upon the assumption of an isolated, rural development undisturbed by external influences other than those affecting the marketing of farm surpluses. The singularly barren result, so far as knowledge of fundamental tenets or their implications is concerned, must be attributed to the conviction that radicalism in the American West was exclusively the product of repetitive sociological and economic processes at work on the frontier, which found expression in a somewhat emotional discontent or in a patchwork of remedial proposals that lacked any philosophical basis other than a desire to restore the working prosperity of a small entrepreneur, rural economy.

An escape from this *cul de sac* has been suggested by the new emphasis upon the region's participation in the technological, urban, and intellectual movements of the late nineteenth century that was urged upon historians nearly a decade ago. The late Marcus L. Hansen stressed particularly the need for study of the processes of cultural importation and acclimatization that were intensified in the West by the quickened communication and huge population movements of the period. The implied suggestion that historians take advantage of the familiar approach of the social anthropologist to the study of cultural diffusion is especially fruitful when applied to the study of western radical thought. It suggests the possibility of ideological transmission between rural and urban areas in both directions, not only of single concepts as culture traits, but of an entire complex of ideas, the limitation upon the process being the suitability of an imported thought cluster for inclusion within the prevailing ideology of the region after modification of one or both of the patterns of thought involved so as to produce, finally, an integrated product.[2]

Applied to the task in hand, this approach involves, first, identification of the fields of significant intercourse between western agrarians and preceding or contemporary urban movements; second, analysis of the basic concepts of the resulting system of radical thought; and third,

[2] Clark Wissler, *An Introduction to Social Anthropology* (New York, 1929), 356–370; Dixon R. Fox, ed., *Sources of Culture in the Middle West: Backgrounds versus Frontier* (New York, 1934), 76–87, 106.

demonstration of the identity of these concepts with those of the contributing radical and liberal movements. The indigenous character of the product, its radical deviation from the accepted canons of the period, and its significance for subsequent eras can be indicated in the course of the analysis, which may assist President Conant, possibly, to a final termination of his quest.

The existence in the Upper Mississippi Valley, in 1865, of a system of democratic thought derived from an earlier integration of urban radicalism with the coonskin democracy of the hardwood frontier, suggests that subsequent intercourse between urban and agrarian radicals occurred within a conceptual pattern common to both. William Trimble has shown how the working-class Locofocoism of the Jacksonian era was transplanted by the westward movement to the rich soil of the Middle West in the forties and fifties. There it fused with the similar but less well-defined conceptions of the Benton Democracy in neighboring upland southern areas of settlement. It was reproduced so completely by wheat farmers on the prairies and oak openings farther to the north that insistence upon "equal rights" and intense hostility to monopoly, chartered corporations, banks, and the "money power" are to this day frequently regarded as peculiar to the rural mind. The great emphasis placed upon natural rights and the social compact by the Locofocos served in the North Central States only to re-emphasize the still dominant Lockean psychology and political theory that the region had received with its population from the Atlantic seaboard. Insistence that "Democracy is the cause of Humanity" quickened there and in the Old Northwest alike the humanitarian impulse that Charles Grandison Finney and the Second Great Awakening had aroused in American Protestantism. Although much of the older liberal heritage had been institutionalized by the establishment of constitutional democracy and the development of democratic churches, it had been vitalized anew by the evangelical movement, the temperance and anti-slavery agitations, the homestead movement, and the continuous struggle against chartered banks and special privilege in the prairie states until the appeal to arms imposed an ill-kept truce upon domestic quarrels. Shared by western farmers and the laborers of East and West alike, the radical democracy of the Locofocos and Free Democrats was Abraham Lincoln's mainstay in 1860.[3]

[3] William Trimble, "The Social Philosophy of the Loco-Foco Democracy," *American Journal of Sociology* (Chicago), XXVI, May, 1921, pp. 705–715; William Trimble, "Diverging Tendencies in New York Democracy in the Period of the Locofocos," *American Historical Review* (Washington), XXIV, April, 1919, pp. 396–421; Merle Curti, "The Great Mr.

The revival of the democratic movement in the trans-Allegheny states after the Civil War was more than the resurgence of ante-bellum quarrels provoked by exclusively western impulses. It offers the first clear illustrations in this period of the effect of intercourse and co-operation between eastern and western, urban-born and agrarian movements upon the development of western radical thought and action. This is notably true of the antimonopoly sentiment that flourished in the western states in the half dozen years before the panic of 1873. Although rural grievances against a railroad and steamboat combination in the Upper Mississippi Valley furnished the initial impetus, and the Locofoco heritage supplied the intellectual foundation, the continuing antimonopoly movement of these years cannot be fully understood without reference to mercantile interests, the National Labor Union, and the activities of several propaganda organizations that operated from central offices on the eastern seaboard. Resentment against the extortions and monopolistic practices of the railroads was not peculiar to western farmers. It was shared by western merchants, eastern importers and shippers, the producers and refiners of the Pennsylvania oil region, and laboring men as well.

It is not surprising to find in 1867 a National Anti-Monopoly Cheap Freight Railway League with headquarters in New York City. Although not much is known of this interesting organization, the private papers of its secretary reveal a far-flung agitation in behalf of cheaper railroad and telegraph rates that was directed from the eastern metropolis. Distribution of pamphlet literature and a "Monthly Circular," and attempts to influence the press and bring pressure to bear upon state governors, such as Reuben E. Fenton of New York, were accompanied by successful efforts to stimulate antimonopoly conventions and recruit supporters in the East, the Middle West, and as far away as Houston, Texas. The interested support that these efforts received from John A. Gano, president of the Cincinnati Chamber of Commerce, documents the mercantile aspect of the cheap freight movement.[4]

Locke: America's Philosopher, 1783-1861," *Huntington Library Bulletin* (Cambridge, Mass.), No. 11, April, 1937, p. 133; Gilbert Hobbs Barnes, *The Antislavery Impulse: 1830-1844* (New York, 1933), Chapter I and *passim;* Frederick Jackson Turner, *The United States, 1830-1850: The Nation and its Sections* (New York, 1935), 320-322; Wilfred E. Binkley, *American Political Parties: Their Natural History* (New York, 1943), 211-234.

⁴ John A. Gano to O'Reilly, Oct. 12, 1867, Henry O'Reilly to Henry Blaney of Zanesville, Ohio, n. d., C. B. Sabin, Houston, Tex., to O'Reilly, Sept. 30, Oct. 7, 1867, O'Reilly to Josiah Quincy, Jan. 22, 1868, Henry R. Gibson of Jacksboro, Tenn., to O'Reilly, Oct. 9, 1867, Governor R. E. Fenton to O'Reilly, Sept. 27, 1867, Henry O'Reilly Papers, Public Library, Rochester, N. Y.; Frederick Merk, *Economic History of Wisconsin during the Civil War Decade* (Madison, 1916), 308-328; Howard K. Beale, *The Critical Year: A Study of Andrew Johnson and Reconstruction* (New York, 1930), 255-264.

The propaganda stimulus to the western antimonopoly movement was even more noteworthy in the case of the American Free-Trade League, whose headquarters were also in New York City. It was financed there largely by New York importers and by manufacturers' and shipping agents dealing with Great Britain, who had an immediate interest in the reduction of the war tariff. Although its technique bore a striking resemblance to that of the Anti-Corn Law movement, the leaders of the Free-Trade League were avowedly disciples of "the peculiar Free Trade doctrines of William Leggett," the prophet of Locofocoism.[5] Chief of these was William Cullen Bryant, editor of the New York *Evening Post* and persistent champion of the Locofoco creed, who was president of the League during its formative years. By 1869 the free traders had expanded their activities into an intensive, far-flung propaganda campaign among the wage earners of the seaboard and westward in the interior towns and farming districts of Ohio, Illinois, Missouri, Iowa, Wisconsin, Minnesota, and California. Its numerous tracts, circulated by over half a million annually by *colporteurs* and voluntary workers, the numerous public meetings stimulated in all the important towns of the West, and tariff reform copy supplied gratis to an extensive list of western newspapers that were supported by paid advertisements, were reenforced by branch leagues in Cincinnati, Chicago, St. Louis, and San Francisco, which were financed in part by eastern funds.[6]

The central theme of this propaganda was "equal rights" and "no monopoly." This was a deliberate, intensive appeal to the antimonopoly stereotypes of urban wage earners and the agrarian West, upon which the changes were rung by Bryant's *Evening Post*,[7] Horace White's Chicago *Tribune*, and by paid lecturers and the monthly organ of the movement, the *Free-Trader*. It was the theme of William M. Grosvenor's *Does Protection Protect?*,[8] the preparation of which was subsidized by the League and circulated as a more popular reply to the arguments of Horace Greeley and Henry C. Carey than the technical reports of David A. Wells. Colonel Grosvenor, it should be noted, was at the same time a paid agent of the Free-Trade League, and, as chairman of the Missouri Liberal Republican State Committee, the lieutenant of Carl Schurz.[9]

[5] William Allen Butler to the editor, Feb. 26, 1870, New York *Tribune*, March 2, 1870.

[6] *The League*, I (New York, 1867–1868); *The Free-Trader*, II–V (New York, 1868–1871); *The People's Pictorial Tax-payer* (New York, 1871–1872); and surviving examples of the League's pamphlet literature in the New York Public Library.

[7] Semi-weekly edition, Jan. 8, 12, 15, 22, 26, Feb. 5, 12, 26, April 17, 20, 23, July 20, 1869; especially the "No Monopoly" series of articles, May 25, 1869, to June 28, 1870.

[8] New York, 1871.

[9] Mahlon Sands per L. [H. D. Lloyd, Assistant Secretary, American Free-Trade League] to Edward A. Atkinson, May 13, 1872, Edward A. Atkinson Papers, Massachusetts Histori-

The synchronism of the propaganda of the Cheap Freight Railway League and the Free-Trade League with the continuing antimonopoly movement in the West, is in itself highly suggestive. It is obvious that the revival of Locofoco stereotypes in the Mississippi Valley was but part of a nation-wide development that was shared by all the elements that suffered from the high tariff and the abuses of railroad and telegraph management.

The central role of the tariff reformers in the Liberal Republican movement illustrates both the intersectional character of the anti-monopoly revival and the role of nonagrarian elements in it. At the outset the Liberal Republican revolt in Missouri was itself an urban movement, initiated and sustained as it was by the liberals of St. Louis of whom Colonel Grosvenor, then editor of the *Democrat*, was a leading figure. In the original Missouri movement, as in its larger extension to the Old Northwest, the urban free traders were the most active and in-fluential single element. They were encouraged by the branch Free-Trade Leagues in the region and by the home office in New York, which was deliberately stimulating a widespread movement against special legislation and the corrupt, pressure politics of the period. In Ohio the merchants and lawyers prominent in the free-trade movement furnished the leadership of the Liberal Republicans and the closely allied Reunion and Reform movement. In Illinois Horace White's Chicago *Tribune* gave the main impulse to the Liberal Republican revolt from Grantism. He was ably seconded by the president of the Chicago Tribune Company, ex-Lieutenant Governor William Bross, a free trader and railroad anti-monopolist. In San Francisco the branch of the American Free-Trade League was the means of bringing Henry George and Governor Henry H. Haight together in a state-wide crusade against tariff, railroad, tele-graph, and land monopoly.

The fiasco of the Cincinnati Convention of May, 1872, must be at-tributed to the New York free traders who, over the strenuous protests of their western allies, bowed to Carl Schurz's demand that the Greeley-Fenton high tariff faction be admitted through compromise of the all-important tariff issue. Thus the rise and decline of free-trade propa-ganda from 1865-1872 and of the closely related Liberal Republican movement furnish well-defined examples of interaction between the agri-cultural West and urban centers within and outside the region that oc-curred on the ideological plane and through political organization and

---

cal Society; General Roeliff Brinkerhoff, *Recollections of a Lifetime* (Cincinnati, 1900), 215; W. M. Grosvenor to the editor, Feb. 7, 1872, New York *Tribune*, Feb. 10, 1872.

action. Re-enforcing earlier low tariff and Locofoco sentiment, they clearly identified protectionism with the rise of monopoly in western democratic thought.[10]

Most students of western radicalism had overlooked the dual character of the Greenback agitation that spread so rapidly after the panic of 1873. Judged by its origins, Greenbackism was at once a western inflationist proposal and an eastern radical philosophy by means of which its urban working-class adherents sought to substitute a co-operative economy for the mercantile and industrial capitalism of the day. In its former capacity it originated with Henry Clay Dean, the bitter end Iowa "Copperhead," who urged greenback inflation upon a depressed, indebted West as a means of liquidating the war debt, overthrowing Radical rule, and emancipating the region from eastern financial and economic controls. It was taken up by the Cincinnati *Enquirer* in 1867 as a means of wresting control of the Democratic party from August Belmont and Tammany Hall. Toned down by George H. Pendleton into a currency stabilization, debt reduction scheme involving little or no inflation, it continued to attract support in the West for nearly a decade under the title of the "Ohio rag baby."[11]

Some of the support enjoyed by the *Enquirer's* brand of Greenbackism came from the trades unions of Cincinnati. The political spokesman of this element was Congressman General Samuel F. Cary. Along with the wage earners of Cincinnati, Chicago, and the Atlantic seaboard, he adhered to a much more elaborate economic and monetary theory. This, for want of a more distinguishing name, must be termed Kelloggism. Its author, Edward Kellogg, had been a New York merchant during the Locofoco period. Forced into assignment by the panic of 1837, he had found in the usurious manipulation of currency and credit by

[10] Carl Schurz to [?], May 9, 1872, Schurz to Horace Greeley, May 6, 1872, J. D. Cox to Schurz, Dec. 3, 1870, Mahlon Sands to Schurz, Nov. 10, 1870, Carl Schurz Papers, Library of Congress; E. A. Atkinson to Charles Sumner, May 23, 1872, Wm. M. Grosvenor to Atkinson, April 5, 1872, Atkinson Papers; J. D. Cox to C. Schurz, April 5, 1872, J. D. Cox to Allyn Cox, May 6, 1872, Jacob D. Cox Papers, Oberlin College Library; *Free-Trader*, III (May, 1870), 204; *ibid.*, IV (May, 1871), 215; New York *Evening Post*, Mar. 24, 1871; A. T. Andreas, *History of Chicago* (3 vols., Chicago, 1886), III, 858; D. C. Cloud, *Monopolies and the People* (Davenport, Iowa, 1873), 231–239; [James Dabney McCabe], *History of the Grange Movement; or, the Farmer's War Against Monopolies . . .* (Chicago, 1873), 510–511; Henry George, Jr., *The Life of Henry George* (New York, 1901), 207–218.

[11] Chester McA. Destler, "The Origin and Character of the Pendleton Plan," MISSISSIPPI VALLEY HISTORICAL REVIEW (Cleveland), XXIV, September, 1937, pp. 171–184 or below Chapter II; Reginald C. McGrane, *William Allen: A Study of Western Democracy* (Columbus, Ohio, 1925), 208–238; R. McClelland to David A. Wells, June 18, 1875, David A. Wells Papers, New York Public Library.

privately owned banks the cause of periodic depressions and of the concentration of wealth. Arguing that monetary policy and banking were strictly governmental functions, he sought to supplant private and state banks with a national banking and currency system to be operated exclusively by the central government. Its outstanding features were to be a flexible currency, loans on real estate at low rates, and interchangeability of the paper currency with government bonds. Such a system with its low interest rates, Kellogg taught, would destroy money monopoly, secure to labor its just reward, lower rents, and promote the development of rural society. His book, *Labor and Other Capital*,[12] was republished in successive editions after 1860 and became a classic of American radicalism, the "Bible" of currency reformers[13] until shunted aside by the free-silver craze of the nineties.

Kelloggism won wide support among wage earners and western anti-monopolists after the Civil War. Alexander Campbell disseminated its doctrines among the discontented farmers of the Mississippi Valley and urged them to institute the new monetary and banking system by adapting it to the greenback currency and public debt of the day. While Campbell and another Illinois Congressman seconded the efforts of General Cary in pressing Kellogg's system upon the national legislature, the Illinois Anti-Monopoly Association joined hands with noted labor leaders, A. C. Cameron of Chicago and William L. Sylvis. Together they wrote the Kellogg program into the platform adopted by the National Labor Union at Chicago in 1867, the same year in which the "Pendleton plan" emerged from the inflationary agitation initiated by Henry Clay Dean and the Cincinnati *Enquirer*.

Space is lacking to trace in detail the interaction of the two currency agitations upon each other and of both upon the agricultural West through the next three decades. It should be noted, however, that after the failure of the Labor Party in 1872, the labor reformers secured endorsement of Kellogg's monetary system from the Illinois State Farmers Association in 1874–1875. They persuaded it and the Indiana farmers to join them in the organization of an independent political party representing both laborers and farmers, a movement that culminated in the National Greenback Party of 1876. Revived in the eighties by the Knights of Labor, Kellogg's familiar monetary and land banking proposals were taken up by farm journals such as the Chicago *Express* and the *Western Rural*, and championed by W. D. Vincent, the future journalistic exponent of Populism in Kansas. Eventually the National

[12] New York, 1849.
[13] Samuel Leavitt, *Our Money Wars: The Example and Warning of American Finance* (2nd ed., Boston, 1896), Preface, 73.

Farmers' Alliance, led by Jay Burrows, a disciple of Kellogg's, embodied the land loan plan in its platform while the southern Alliance advanced from this to the noted "subtreasury" scheme as an adaptation more attractive to staple farming. Government loans of greenbacks to farmers on land or crop mortgage security became the central feature in the platforms of farm organizations from 1886–1892, of the Union Labor Party in 1888, and of the Populists in 1892. Faith in the far-reaching efficacy of such a program was a common and distinguishing feature of working-class and western agrarian radicalism until the decline of the Knights of Labor and the rising free-silver crusade pushed its advocates into the "middle-of-the-road" during the "Battle of the Standards."[14]

The co-operative movement is another example of the alacrity with which western agrarians borrowed urban formulas ready-made in their attempts to solve agricultural problems. In this case European experience was clearly drawn upon, while the influence of organized labor in America upon the farming co-operative movements seems almost indubitable. Although ante-bellum *Arbeiterbund* experiments and agitation by Horace Greeley may have suggested the feasibility of a co-operative movement, the first vigorous development of productive and distributive co-operation in the United States occurred after Appomattox in the urban centers of the East and the Ohio Valley. There workmen in all leading trades experimented with co-operative workshops and patronized co-operative stores. This movement was vigorously espoused by William L. Sylvis and the National Labor Union as "a sure and lasting remedy for the abuses of the present industrial system." The need of these co-operative experiments for adequate credit was one reason why the laborers espoused Kellogg's monetary and banking system. Western antimonopolists, whose delegates attended the congresses of the National Labor Union, learned there of the co-operative plans of the wage earners. By 1871, in the same region where Kelloggism was propagated by Alexander Campbell and the railroads and war tariff were attacked by the antimonopolists, the farmers turned also to "Co-operation" as a sovereign remedy for rural ills. Eventually the Grangers adopted the Rochdale plan of consumers' co-operation and made direct contact with the English Co-operative Union.[15] The revival

[14] Chester McA. Destler, "The Influence of Edward Kellogg upon American Radicalism, 1865–1896," *Journal of Political Economy* (Chicago), XL, June, 1932, pp. 338–365, or below, Chapter IV.

[15] Carl Wittke, *We Who Built America: The Saga of the Immigrant* (New York, 1940), 238–239, 344, 355–360; John R. Commons et al., *History of Labour in the United States* (4 vols., New York, 1918), I, 504–512, II, 53–56, 110–112, 118–119; Solon Justus Buck, *The Granger Movement: A Study of Agricultural Organization and its Political, Economic and Social Manifestations, 1870–1880* (Cambridge, 1913), 46, 52–53, 259–260.

of interest in co-operation among western and southern farmers during the eighties followed hard upon the renewed agitation of the idea by the Knights of Labor who were the greatest agency then propagating knowledge of European and American co-operative experiments in the United States.[16] Its contact with the farmers increased rather than diminished after its catastrophic defeats in 1886 since it deliberately penetrated the country towns and rural areas of the East in search of recruits.[17] Thus, while the ideological impulse to the co-operative experiments of the Farmers' Alliance movement was partially derived from surviving Granger experiments or drawn directly from British experience, a portion at least came from the American labor movement. In this period, also, co-operative creameries were introduced into the Middle West from Scandinavia by Danish immigrants.[18]

During the same period midwestern farmers made an original and important contribution to the theory and method of democratic control over corporate enterprise. Individualistic and with no previous experience in the eastern states or Great Britain to guide them, they sought a practicable remedy for the vicious practices of railroads and grain elevators. Inspired by the antimonopoly movement and by the Locofoco tradition of using the power of the democratic state to eliminate special privilege, their demands ranged from legislative rate-fixing to construction and operation of a transcontinental railroad by the national government. Eventually, they secured the adoption in a number of states of the novel method of controlling railroads and warehouses by means of independent regulatory commissions with rate-fixing powers. Although the originality of this Granger device has been called into question as recently as 1940,[19] the most careful research reveals that in neither the Atlantic seaboard nor Great Britain were strong regulatory commissions placed in control of railroads or other utilities until Illinois had led the way in 1871–1873.[20] Furthermore, the establishment of the Illinois

[16] Norman J. Ware, *The Labor Movement in the United States, 1860–1895: A Study in Democracy* (New York, 1929), 327; Commons, *History of Labour in the United States*, II, 430–438; Symmes M. Jelley, *The Voice of Labor* (Chicago, 1887), 255: "To supersede the wage system by the introduction of the co-operative industrial system has always been the goal of the Knights of Labor . . . ."

[17] *Knights of Labor* (Chicago), March, April 10, July 17, Sept. 11, Dec. 18, 1886; *Western Rural* (Chicago), XXIV, April 17, 1886, p. 245.

[18] Wittke, *We Who Built America*, 295.

[19] Joint session, Mississippi Valley Historical Association and the American Historical Association, New York, December, 1940, "To What Extent was the West a Radical Force, 1865–1892?" A symposium. Frederic L. Paxson, chairman, Robert E. Riegel, Louis Pelzer, James A. Barnes, Albert H. Kohlmeier, Chester McA. Destler.

[20] Robert E. Cushman, *The Independent Regulatory Commissions* (New York, 1941), 23–36.

Board of Railroad and Warehouse Commissioners and the vindication of the state police power in Munn *v.* Illinois by the Supreme Court was so radical a departure from the dominant theories of Herbert Spencer and Judge Thomas M. Cooley that Associate Justice Stephen J. Field delivered an indignant dissent and expressed his views privately as follows:

> I send you by today's mail a copy of my dissenting opinion in the Chicago Elevator case and in the so-called Granger cases. I think that the doctrine announced by the majority of the Court practically destroys the guarantees of the Constitution intended for the protection of the rights of private property.[21]

In this instance western agrarian radicalism perfected a governmental agency and an addition to democratic constitutional theory that were accepted eventually by eastern states and the national government as well. Yet, lest the interaction here be thought to have been exclusively from west to east, it should be observed that the legal theory upon which the power of the regulatory commission rested was first championed in the Illinois constitutional convention of 1869–1870 by Reuben M. Benjamin, a New York graduate of the Harvard Law School, who had migrated to Bloomington, Illinois, on the eve of the Civil War.[22]

Western cities made significant contributions to the radical movements of the rural West and urban East in the seventies and eighties. The wider antimonopoly movement that was directed against industrial combinations and speculative manipulation of commodity prices received its initial impetus from Henry Demarest Lloyd. His antimonopolism was derived from a Locofoco family background. It was confirmed by four years' work as assistant secretary of the American Free-Trade League. After this he joined the staff of the Chicago *Tribune*. First as financial editor and then as chief editorial writer, he campaigned for over a decade for reform of the Chicago Board of Trade, exposed the looting of western mining companies by rings of insiders, described the daily misdeeds and monopolistic practices of the railroads, and attacked the Standard Oil Company and other trusts as they emerged into public view. He lent vigorous support, also, to the agrarian demand that Congress establish a strong, national rate-fixing commission in control of the railroads and a postal telegraph to be operated by the national government in competition with the Western Union.[23] He then turned to a

[21] Stephen J. Field to David A. Wells, Washington, June 29, 1877, David A. Wells Papers.

[22] John D. Hicks, "The Development of Civilization in the Middle West, 1860-1900," in Fox, *Sources of Culture in the Middle West*, 88-89.

[23] The financial page, real estate and railroad columns, and the editorial page of the Chicago *Tribune* from 1875-1885 are the best sources of Lloyd's ideas. Cf. Caro Lloyd, *Henry Demarest Lloyd, 1847-1903: A Biography* (2 vols., New York, 1912), I, 18-81.

wider public in a series of impressive magazine articles that laid bare the implications of the combination movement for democracy in America and demanded its control through further extension of the regulatory powers of the state.[24] These articles with his editorials and other contributions in the *Tribune* initiated the antitrust movement[25] that was superimposed upon the continuing struggle with the railroads in the West. Diverted from journalism to a career of social reform, Lloyd continued the fight against monopoly by publication of his great work, *Wealth against Commonwealth*,[26] and by participation in the Populist revolt. Until after its collapse he was regarded by the western agrarians as one of their chief inspirers.

An equally notable contribution to American radicalism came from San Francisco and Oakland, California, urban centers developing within a few hundred miles of the mining and agricultural frontier of the Far West. There Henry George, another journalist, but onetime Philadelphia printer's devil, perfected the single-tax theory in the midst of a prolonged struggle with the West Coast monopolies. An admirer of Jefferson, a Jacksonian Democrat of the Locofoco tradition, he saw in land monopoly the cause of poverty. By taxing away the unearned increment in land values, or virtually confiscating ground rents, he would break up the great speculative holdings in the West, check the dissipation of the national domain, and weaken franchise monopolies of all kinds. Abolition of all other taxes would destroy the monopolies dependent upon the protective tariff. Thus a single, decisive use of taxing power would restore both liberty and equality of opportunity to American economic life while at the same time it would check the urban movement, revive agriculture, and enrich rural life.[27] After leading a fruitless land reform movement on the West Coast during the depressed seventies, Henry George moved to New York City where he published *Progress and Poverty* in 1880. Its appeal to natural rights, its indictment of the existing business system, its moral overtones and moving appeal to the traditions of humanitarian democracy, and its utopian panacea all exerted a profound influence upon public opinion in Ireland, Great Britain, and the United States.

[24] Collected in Henry D. Lloyd, *Lords of Industry* (New York, 1910), 1–147.

[25] John J. Hamilton of the Des Moines *News* to Lloyd, July 17, 1897, Henry D. Lloyd Papers, State Historical Society of Wisconsin; Fred E. Haynes, *Third Party Movements Since the Civil War with Special Reference to Iowa* (Iowa City, 1916), 147, 204–205.

[26] New York, 1894.

[27] Henry George, *Social Problems* (New York, 1886), 72–322; and *Progress and Poverty* (New York, 2nd ed., 1880), *passim;* cf. Henry George, Jr., *The Life of Henry George*, 207–218.

In a crusade for social justice that continued until his dramatic death in 1897, George exercised an unprecedented influence upon the American labor movement.[28]   He awakened journalists, intellectuals, small capitalists, and young lawyers to a comprehension of the grave economic and social problems of the rising urban world.   His system of democratic economics dealt the first shattering blow to the economic determinism derived from the "Manchester School" and to the Social Darwinism that discouraged all attempts to remedy social evils or shackle the anarchic business of the day.   Independent labor politics, municipal reform, and the development of a more public-spirited political leadershp received direct and powerful impetus from the single-tax movement in eastern and midwestern cities between 1880 and 1900, while the single-tax panacea offered to discontented workers, farmers, small capitalists, and intellectuals an alternative to Marxian Socialism that promised social justice while preserving the old individualism.[29]   Most leaders of the Farmers' Alliance movement refused to accept the single tax as "the universal solvent that will melt away the social and industrial ills that afflict our nation."   The agitation for the single tax, nevertheless, did much to increase agrarian interest in the land question, while "Sockless Jerry" Simpson, Populist Congressman from Kansas in the nineties, was an earnest disciple of Henry George.[30]   In this decade, also, the support given by George A. Schilling and the powerful single-tax bloc in the Illinois Federation of Labor was an important factor in the election and progressive administration of John P. Altgeld.[31]   Although the exact extent of Henry George's influence upon the rural West remains to be determined, the single-tax movement is an outstanding illustration of the far-flung influence of a western but urban-born school of thought upon proletarian movements and middle class liberalism in regions as far distant as the Atlantic seaboard, the British Isles and Australasia.[32]

[28] *Knights of Labor*, Jan. 15, 1887, p. 3: "No man has exercised so great an influence upon the labor movement of to-day as Henry George, although never himself connected as a leader with any of the labor organizations of the country."

[29] Henry George to John Paul, Nov. 7, 1893, Henry George Papers, New York Public Library; John Chamberlain, *Farewell to Reform* (New York, 2nd ed., 1933), 43; Fred E. Haynes, *Social Politics in the United States* (Boston, 1924), 122–136.

[30] *Farmers' Voice* (Chicago), March 9, 1889; N. B. Ashby, *Riddle of the Sphinx* (Des Moines, 1890), 264–265; John D. Hicks, *The Populist Revolt: A History of the Farmers' Alliance and the People's Party* (Minneapolis, 1931), 161.

[31] Eugene Staley, *History of the Illinois State Federation of Labor* (Chicago, 1930), 100–105.

[32] Henry George, Jr., *The Life of Henry George*, 207–218; George Raymond Geiger, *The Philosophy of Henry George* (New York, 1933), 381–475.

During the late eighties an urban, eastern, American-born socialist movement attracted interest in the cities and farming areas of the West. Known as Nationalism it developed spontaneously from enthusiasm provoked by Edward Bellamy's *Looking Backward*. Converts to Bellamy's utopia of a highly centralized, almost militarized socialist commonwealth organized Nationalist Clubs as far west as California. Members and officials of the Farmers' Alliances, trades unions, the Knights of Labor, and a few outstanding railroad executives joined the movement. The earlier antimonopoly movements and the propaganda of the Knights of Labor[33] had prepared the soil well for sowing Nationalist principles among western agrarians. It is not surprising, therefore, to find N. B. Ashby, lecturer of the National Farmers' Alliance, endorsing Nationalism "as the only true and effectual cure" for "the social question," and as the logical, evolutionary fulfillment of the nation's destiny.[34] With Nationalist clubs active in fourteen Middle and Far Western states the organizers of the People's Party were almost compelled to invite them to send delegates to the Cincinnati Conference of May, 1891, where five Nationalists helped to frame the first national manifesto of the Populist revolt. At the subsequent conventions at St. Louis and Omaha in 1892, the Nationalists joined with the Knights in giving effective support to the "transportation plank" in the revised platform. So gratified were they at its adoption that the Nationalists gave Populism such wholehearted support that Nationalism lost its identity in the People's Party. To its strength Bellamy's followers contributed especially in the eastern states, although he continued to enjoy considerable influence with the older antimonopoly element in the West.[35]

The examples of effective intercourse between the rural West and the urban world, whether within or outside the region, could be increased still further by reference to the agitation for reform of the nation's land policy, led by George W. Julian, and the free-silver movement. They are sufficient, however, to indicate something of the diverse origins and composite character of the western radicalism that burgeoned beyond the Alleghenies in the last third of the century. Western agrarian movements were influenced by at least five schools of reform or radical agita-

---

[33] For nationalization of the railroads and telegraph, see Ware, *Labor Movement in the United States*, 379; Powderly to Mrs. Alzina P. Stevens, April 11, 1893, Harry J. Carman et al., eds., *The Path I Trod: The Autobiography of Terence V. Powderly* (New York, 1940), 401.

[34] *Riddle of the Sphinx*, 255-256.

[35] Haynes, *Social Politics*, 138-148; Chicago *Tribune*, July 4, 1892, for Nationalist mass meeting at Omaha; J. Martin Klotsche, "The 'United Front' Populists," *Wisconsin Magazine of History* (Madison), XX, June, 1937, pp. 376-378.

tion originating from without the region before 1890. In at least one important field the farmers' movements of the region made a major contribution to democratic thought and action in the same period, while publicists in two western cities initiated the important antitrust and single-tax movements. Such cross-fertilization between eastern and western, urban and rural movements was but one aspect of the larger development of the West, which on intellectual, technological, business, and artistic planes was subject to similar processes of acculturation. In each field the result was a mosaic of indigenous and imported elements, all adapted in greater or lesser degree to the regional *milieu*.

This analysis suggests that in Populism may be found the system of radical thought that emerged in the West from three decades of recurring unrest, agitation, and intercourse with radical and reform movements in the urban world. Although scholars have studied it as a political movement or as the product of social and economic conditions, as a school of thought Populism has been rarely, if ever, subjected to the careful analysis that Socialism, Anarchism, or Communism have received. Yet the Populists themselves regarded Populism as a faith and a creed as well as a program. They exhibited, furthermore, a clear sense of continuity with preceding radical movements. This was illustrated at the Omaha convention by the wild cheering that greeted Alexander Campbell, the aged prophet of Kelloggism to midwestern farmers in the sixties.[36] Further continuity between Populism and its forerunners was exhibited by the leadership of the People's Party. Not only were General James B. Weaver and Ignatius Donnelly representatives of the older Greenback and Anti-Monopoly traditions in the West, but the chairman of the national executive committee, Herman E. Taubeneck, was a former Greenbacker, while the first secretary of the committee was Robert Schilling, veteran labor reformer and labor leader.[37] As secretary of the platform committee in the Cincinnati conference of May, 1891, Schilling reported and together with Colonel S. F. Norton of the Chicago *Express* undoubtedly induced the committee to base its manifesto on

[36] *The Vanguard* (Chicago), July 9, 1892.

[37] A striking example of the sense of continuity between Populism and the preceding labor and agrarian reform movements is furnished by Robert Schilling's "The History of the People's Party," *Official Souvenir of the National Convention of the People's Party at St. Louis, Mo.*, July 22, 1896 (Milwaukee, Wis., 1896). Schilling had been second president of the cooper's national union in 1871, active in the National Labor Union, in the Labor Party of 1872, in the Greenback movement, author of the Preamble of the Order of the Knights of Labor, Commons, *History of Labour in the United States*, II, 75–76, 161, 163, 241, 336. For his role in the first Populist convention, see Cincinnati *Commercial Gazette*, May 21, 1891.

Edward Kellogg's economic philosophy. Further evidence of continuity between Populism and earlier radical movements is found in the long series of conferences that began with the organization of the Union Labor Party in Cincinnati in 1887 and culminated at Omaha on July 4, 1892. There Kelloggism, Nationalism, the more limited program of government ownership proposed by the Knights, the single tax, land reform, woman suffrage, the liquor question, and the cause of organized labor were urged upon successive platform committees by reformers who had grown gray in the service of each particular "cause."[38]

At first glance the program that emerged from this process seemed like a "crazy-quilt" of unrelated and "crackpot" proposals.[39] Yet it produced a fairly durable synthesis, judging from the tenacity with which the Populists reiterated their Omaha platform on all and sundry occasions, until an era of unemployment, mortgage foreclosures, Coxey's armies, and industrial conflict had so heightened the emotional overtones of the movement that the least well-ballasted agrarians and the professional politicians in control of the party machinery sought quick relief and easy victory through free silver. It was this synthesis, under the name of Populism, which received such intense loyalty from its adherents and provoked an emotional opposition from conservative elements. Proclaimed in the Omaha platform as the official version of the Populist creed, it must now be analyzed in an attempt to identify the basic concepts that it shared with its progenitors and to determine the extent to which it presented a well-defined system of radical thought.

The continuing vitality of the equalitarian tradition among the radical movements that produced the Populist "revolt" will be apparent from the foregoing narrative. Examination of the Omaha platform, also, indicates beyond doubt that Populism, too, was consciously cast in the mold of "equal rights." Inherent in its thought lay the traditional Jeffersonian hostility to special privilege, to gross inequality in economic possessions, to concentrated economic power, and a preference for human rights when opposed by overshadowing property rights. All of this had motivated American democratic radicalism since the days of Thomas Paine and the Democratic Republican Clubs of 1793-1800. So oriented it is not surprising to find the preamble of the Omaha platform declaring in 1892 that the purpose of a government freed from corporate control would be to establish "equal rights and equal privileges . . . for

[38] Chicago *Tribune*, May 19, 21, 1891, for an extraordinary analysis of the composition and the issues pressed upon the Cincinnati Convention of May, 1891.

[39] Solon J. Buck, *The Agrarian Crusade: A Chronicle of the Farmer in Politics* (New Haven, 1920), 127.

all the men and women of this country." Coupled with this is the clearly expressed, traditional faith of American liberals in "civilization" as a liberating, elevating process, which, like human rights, must be saved from the machinations of the money power. Thus, Populism was but an extreme projection of the Jeffersonian creed.

Antimonopolism was the dynamic element in Populism. It sprang directly from the equalitarian tradition. The preamble and planks of the Omaha platform demonstrate this beyond question.[40] The pre-

SLASHING A POISONOUS BROOD

amble denounced the corruption of democratic government by privileged business, and the abuses by which a buccaneering capitalism exploited the people and created a new class of millionaires. Rather than the "sham battle over the tariff," the real issue, it declared, lay "in the formation of combines and rings," in the power of "capitalists, corporations, and national banks," "the oppressions of the usurers." The dominant antimonopoly bias of Populism was even more clearly expressed in the platform itself. This was devoted entirely to the three great fields of monopoly that had been the butt of agrarian agitation for decades: money and banking, railroads and communication, and land.

[40] Chicago *Tribune*, July 5, 1892. Cf. Hicks, *Populist Revolt*, 427-444, Appendixes A–F, for the platforms adopted by the series of conferences that culminated at Omaha, July 4, 1892.

The remedies proposed show clearly how far the Populists were committed to government intervention in business and to limited experiments with state socialism as a means of combating the great movement toward monopoly and economic concentration then under way in the business world. To destroy "the money power" and to solve the "financial question," to use terms employed by the presidential nominee of the party,[41] the platform proposed an exclusively governmental currency and a combination of government operated postal savings banks and "subtreasuries." The latter "or a better system" was to loan money to farmers on crops or land at no more than two per cent interest, while the volume of the currency was to fluctuate with the demand for agricultural credits.[42] Irrespective of the obvious indebtedness of this financial program to the earlier agitation of Kelloggism, it is plain that money monopoly was the evil for which such a drastic extension of government activity into banking was proposed. Monopoly on the railroads and in communications was dealt with in the same manner. Here again government ownership and operation was the remedy, a solution derived from the Knights of Labor and Nationalism. Land monopoly, the third great problem dealt with, was to be remedied by government action also, in this case by restoration to the national domain of alien holdings and land held by railroads and other corporations in excess of their actual needs.[43] The graduated income tax was proposed by the Omaha convention as the proper means of dealing with the giant fortunes accumulated through government favoritism to capitalists and usurers. Considered apart from the supplemental resolutions adopted at the convention, the Omaha platform, therefore, was directed almost entirely at destroying monopoly and at correcting the economic evils that it had produced.

In taking antimonopolism as its central principle Populism revealed its fundamental identity with all the varied "isms" that had agitated the West during the "Thirty Years' War," as one veteran of radical

[41] Chicago *Tribune*, July 6, 1892, address by General James B. Weaver.

[42] Restoration of the per capita volume of currency to the early Reconstruction level, plus free coinage of silver, were also demanded. They were simply designed to correct what the Populists held to be an earlier deflation that had penalized debtors.

[43] Led originally by George W. Julian, the land reform movement had sought a sweeping revision of the national land policy so as to restore the national domain, stop extravagant land grants to railroads, and commit the national government to a genuine homestead policy. By 1891 this movement had met success, save in its failure to deal with the great tracts of land that had fallen into private or corporate hands as the result of the earlier policy of favoring great enterprise and speculators at the expense of actual settlers. Paul Wallace Gates, "The Homestead Law in an Incongruous Land System," *American Historical Review* (New York), XLI, July, 1936, pp. 677–681.

movements termed the preceding decades of agitation.[44]   Populism was laid on foundations quarried from Lockean thought and evangelical Protestantism.   Upon this subtratum and in the *milieu* supplied by frontier opportunities and corporate repressions Locofocoism had erected the frame of prairie radicalism and built into it an abiding hostility to monopoly.   Buttressed and strengthened by the controversies of the postwar decades, the antimonopoly spirit had attacked railroads, the protective tariff, money monopoly, and the trusts.   Kellogg's program had re-enforced the demand of Granger legislators that the machinery of the state be turned to positive use in breaking monopolies as the only way in which a just economy could be achieved.   In the eighties this novel program of state intervention in business had developed to a point where some farmers joined the Knights of Labor in demanding a postal telegraph and a government owned and operated railroad system.   Thus in its platform, Populism fulfilled the promise of Locofocism[45] and successive antimonopoly movements although, unlike the earlier working-class champions of equal rights, the Populists sought relief through the extension of governmental action into economic life.

Populism was more than antimonopolism, therefore.   It advocated a program of economic collectivism which it urged upon the American people as the only remedy adequate to solve the problem of monopoly. Not only did the Populists propose to employ government power through actual ownership and operation of banks, railroads, means of communication, and the monetary system, but in the preamble of their Omaha platform they promised to remedy "falling prices, the formation of combines and rings, the impoverishment of the producing class . . . by wise and reasonable legislation, in accordance with the terms of our platform." But, as if this might prove insufficient, they went on to declare:

We believe that the powers of government—in other words of the people—should be expanded (as in the case of the postal service) as rapidly and as far as the good sense of an intelligent people and the teachings of experience shall justify, to the end that oppression, injustice, and poverty shall eventually cease in the land.

The full implications of this declaration were revealed two years later when, in St. Louis after the autumn election, a great conference of party leaders under the leadership of Lyman Trumbull and Henry Demarest Lloyd advanced to the extreme position of advocating government ownership of all monopolies that affected the "public interest."[46]

[44] Leavitt, *Our Money Wars*, Preface.

[45] Turner, *The United States, 1830–1850*, 125–126, 320.

[46] Number eight in a series of resolutions, attributed to Lyman Trumbull, presented by Henry D. Lloyd, and adopted by the conference.   Chicago *Searchlight*, Jan. 24, 1895.

Collectivist though the Populist philosophy was in its demand for state intervention and ownership in the field of monopoly enterprise, it would be a mistake to conclude that it was socialistic either in purpose or spirit. The object of government ownership, as desired by the Populists, just as in the case of the independent regulatory commission championed by the Grangers two decades earlier, was the strengthening of competitive capitalism and the salvation of small enterprise. As the Populists saw it, the chief danger to the American system lay in the threatened destruction of free enterprise by the rise of an irresponsible, unsocial monopoly system which rested in last analysis upon legislative, executive, and judicial favoritism.

As H. S. Person has written recently of the midtwentieth-century problems of cartels and monopoly:

Strategic regulation of basic industries through ownership and yardstick operation of a fraction of the national plant would prevent monopolies and provide basic services and materials at the lowest possible prices on equal terms to all private competitors in industry and would strengthen competition under fair conditions, promote private enterprise and eventually be the salvation of small enterprises.[47]

Such appears to have been the object of Populist collectivism,[48] which was what was to be expected from small enterprisers engaged in wheat and cotton farming. Their economic position would have been strengthened immeasurably by the low rates on credit, transportation and communication, and by the low cost of land and manufactured products that they hoped to secure as a result of government ownership and operation in the limited fields of economic activity that they designated. Their economic independence and political importance might well have been enhanced by means of it.

Populism's kinship with preceding radical movements in the rural and urban West and East was indicated, also, by the sympathy which its adherents gave to the co-operative idea. Now and then, as in Illinois, the State Purchasing Agent[49] of the Farmers' Alliance was active in organizing the new party, while the Nationalists in its ranks were eager to hasten the coming of a co-operative utopia. Despite the havoc wrought by the depression upon the underfinanced co-operative organizations of the farmers, and perhaps because of the widespread distress, interest in co-operation continued among the Populists and their sympathizers. Utopian novels such as *Altruria* by William Dean Howells

[47] "Postwar Control of Monopolies," *New Republic* (New York), CIX, Dec. 27, 1943, p. 908.
[48] Merle Curti, *The Growth of American Thought* (New York, 1943), 608, 610–611, 618.
[49] D. M. Fulwiler.

and *Equality* by Edward Bellamy were expressions in literature of an attitude in Populist ranks that led to the projection or establishment of a series of co-operative communities. Such was Mrs. Annie L. Diggs' proposed "Colorado Co-operative Colony," the Ruskin Co-operative Colony in Tennessee, whose *Coming Nation* had such a wide circulation in Populist ranks, or the Christian Commonwealth Colony established in Georgia after the collapse of the People's Party by the former editor of the *Wealth Makers* of Lincoln, Nebraska.[50] The American Co-operative Union was the product, in 1896, of a Congress convened at St. Louis by the co-operative elements within the People's Party simultaneously with its last great national convention.[51] The shattered remnants of the American Railway Union, which for two years had supported Populism, organized the Brotherhood of the Co-operative Commonwealth, a few months later, by means of which they planned to colonize a western state so thoroughly with co-operative communities that they could control it politically and use the power of the state to aid them in establishing a "co-operative commonwealth."[52] These same elements in the St. Louis convention of 1896 were part of the "middle-of-the-road" faction that remained loyal to the antimonopolism and economic collectivism of the Omaha platform.[53] Thus in supporting the co-operative movement, whether of producers or of consumers or in especially organized communities, the Populists were seeking through private, voluntary organization in the economic field to diminish "the power of the industrial empire." This might well have been accomplished by means of "a great co-operative movement in America"[54] as much as by government ownership of monopolies.

How radical the Populist advocacy of a democratic collectivism was

[50] Mrs. Annie L. Diggs was a prominent Nationalist as well as a leading Populist speaker in Kansas. Haynes, *Social Politics*, 149. For her projected colony, see Mrs. Annie L. Diggs to Henry D. Lloyd, Sept. 17, 27, 1895, Lloyd Papers. For the Ruskin colony, see Eltweed Pomeroy, "A Sketch of the Socialist Colony in Tennessee," *American Fabian* (New York), III, No. 4, April, 1897, pp. 1-2; "Ruskin Cooperative Colony," *Encyclopedia of Social Reform* (New York, 1897), 1210. For the Christian Commonwealth Colony, see *American Co-operative News* (Cambridge, Mass.), III, No. 6, Jan. 1899, pp. 2-4; James Dombrowski, *The Early Days of Christian Socialism in America* (New York, 1936), 135-170. This colony was sponsored also by clergymen of the "social gospel" movement, such as George D. Herron who frequently advocated Christian Socialism at Populist meetings.

[51] *Coming Nation* (Tennessee City, Tenn.), July 5, Aug. 1, 1896.

[52] N. W. Lermond to H. D. Lloyd, April 26, July 16, Sept. 21, 1896, Lloyd Papers; *Commonwealth* (New York), II, No. 50, Dec. 14, 1895, pp. 19-20.

[53] Lermond to Lloyd, July 16, 1896, H. R. Legate to Lloyd, May 13, June 7, 1896, Lloyd Papers.

[54] Thurman W. Arnold, *The Folklore of Capitalism* (New Haven, 1937), 220.

in the light of the contemporary historical situation can be determined easily. The emotional reaction that it provoked among conservatives was so extreme that in propertied circles it made "Populists" more "a term of reproach than was 'Red' a generation later."[55]   A comparison of Populism with the contemporary single-tax and tariff reform movements makes the point even clearer. Henry George advised his followers not to enter the People's Party, while the Populists rejected his single tax as inadequate to the task in hand.[56]   Although Henry George's gospel resembled Populism in its appeal to natural rights, its hatred of monopoly and special privilege, and to a limited extent in its proposal to right economic injustice by use of the taxing power, the Populists rejected as unrealistic the assertion that the single tax alone would destroy all monopolies, eliminate poverty, and make land available once more to the masses. Henry George was seeking to turn the hands of the clock back to the full opportunity of the frontier and to the unrestrained individualism of the competitive system. The Populists, on the other hand, believed that such liberty gave strength only to the strong, who in turn oppressed the weak.[57]

The Triumphant Plutocrats . . . believe in a civilization whose fitting coat of arms would show a hog and tiger rampant, slaying and rending, devouring and gorging, while on the shield's bar sinister . . . would be such legends as "supply and demand"; "devil take the hindmost"; . . . [58]

It was the obligation of democratic government, the Populists asserted, to extend its fostering care to the weak and to protect them from the strong lest the "producing masses" be enslaved.[59]   Only through state intervention, control, and expropriation of the greatest economic aggregations of the day, could the problem of monopoly be solved. Thus, over the issue of individualism versus collectivism Henry George

[55] Edward R. Lewis, *A History of American Political Thought from the Civil War to the World War* (New York, 1937), 303; Frank B. Tracy, "Rise and Doom of the Populist Party," *Forum* (New York), XVI, Oct., 1893, pp. 240–250; F. B. Tracy, "Menacing Socialism in the Western States," *ibid.*, XV, May, 1893, pp. 332–343; Chicago *Tribune*, July 5, 1893, address by Associate Justice David D. Brewer of the United States Supreme Court at Woodstock, Conn., July 4, 1893.

[56] Klotsche, "The 'United Front' Populists," *Wisconsin Magazine of History*, XX, June, 1937, pp. 378–379.

[57] Cf. President J. Burrows, National Farmers' Alliance, "Which is the Controlling Factor, Interest or Rent?" *National Economist* (Washington), I, April 27, 1889, p. 92, and Alson J. Streeter, presidential nominee of the Union Labor Party in 1888, letter of acceptance, July 14, 1888, Alson J. Streeter Scrapbook, courtesy of Mr. C. D. Streeter, Keokuk, Iowa; *Farmers' Voice*, Feb. 1, May 12, 1888, Feb. 1, 1890, May 14, 1892.

[58] *Vanguard*, July 9, 1892.

[59] Cf. *Farmers' Voice*, Feb. 1, 1890.

and the Populists were in direct antagonism. It is not surprising to find the single taxers on the side of Grover Cleveland in 1892.[60]

That the Populists regarded tariff reform as a mere palliative is indicative of their determination to embark upon a revolutionary use of governmental power in subjecting the corporate business system to democratic controls. Although the free trade agitation had been an important factor in the revival of antimonopolism in the West from 1867–1872, the eastern free traders from the outset had advocated specie payments and laissez faire. Such outstanding tariff reformers of the eighties and nineties as Carl Schurz, David A. Wells, E. L. Godkin, and Grover Cleveland adhered to this position. In basic interests and sympathy they were far closer to the national banks and the existing business system than they were to the western agrarians and the Knights of Labor. In 1896 the tariff reformers were found along with William McKinley and Marcus A. Hanna on the side of the railroads, the protected industries, and high finance. Men of such stamp had little to offer to western radicals who were bent upon a drastic reorganization of American economic life through collective action by the democratic state.

If more evidence were wanted to establish the radical character of Populist collectivism it could be found in a study of the contemporary schools of law and constitutional interpretation. In the late nineteenth century, as Roscoe Pound has shown, the courts and legal profession were dominated by the natural rights and historical schools of jurisprudence with their emphasis upon individual liberty.[61] Guided by such publicists as Judge Thomas M. Cooley and Christopher G. Tiedeman,[62] and by the leaders of the American bar, federal and state courts reduced the police power to a minimum and imposed judge-made restraints upon the legislative power. The fate of the federal income tax in the Pollock case, the emasculation of the authority of the Interstate Commerce Commission, and the failure of the first important antitrust suit in the Knight case show how far removed the courts and bar were from the Populist conception of the welfare state.

It is apparent that as a radical system Populism was primarily economic in character. Its contributions to political theory and constitu-

---

[60] Only the most radical single taxers, inspired by Father McGlynn, supported the People's Party in the depression years that followed, Klotsche, "The 'United Front' Populists," *Wisconsin Magazine of History*, XX, June, 1937, pp. 379–380.

[61] *An Introduction to the Philosophy of Law* (New Haven, 1922), 45, 49–51, 52–55.

[62] Benjamin R. Twiss, *Lawyers and the Constitution: How Laissez Faire Came to the Supreme Court* (Princeton, 1942), Chapter II, and pp. 122–130.

tional practice were secondary and derivative rather than of primary importance to the Populists. In order to attack monopoly, to break its hold on the government, and to apply the collectivist program, it was necessary that the government be fully and continually responsive to the public will. To accomplish this the Populists elaborated a program of direct democracy, which they offered as a corrective for the then feebly functioning system of representative government. The initiative and referendum, the Australian ballot, honest elections, and the popular election of United States Senators were accepted and endorsed at Omaha in a series of supplemental resolutions that were attached to but not made an integral part of the platform. Although they were regarded undoubtedly as desirable in themselves, they were linked in Populist eyes with the larger objective of subjecting corporate capitalism to the control of the democratic state.[63]

[63] Throughout the Populist period, the initiative and referendum continued to be the objectives of an independent reform agitation. Like other demands listed in the Omaha platform which became a part of the Populist creed the agitation for direct legislation had originated in the East. So far as can be determined its first exponent was Benjamin Urner of Elizabeth, N. J., who espoused it after defeat in the local congressional election on the Greenback ticket in 1882. In 1888 his efforts were seconded ably by Boyd Winchester, United States consul at Berne, Switzerland, who urged Americans to take up the Swiss initiative and referendum. The Nationalists took up the campaign for direct legislation in 1891. Early in 1892 The People's Power League of New Jersey, supported by wage-earners, was founded to promote this reform. It was endorsed on June 17, 1892, at the New Brunswick industrial conference that launched the independent political movement in the state. The New Jersey demand for the initiative and referendum was taken direct to the Omaha Convention by Joseph R. Buchanan of Newark.

Buchanan became a member of the platform committee at Omaha. Once he had gained the floor, during the committee sessions, he refused to relinquish it, the story goes, until he had won some concession to the New Jersey "industrialists" who demanded direct legislation as the fundamental reform. After it was included in the supplemental resolutions, direct legislation was adopted almost universally by Populist state conventions between 1892 and 1896.

The agitation for this reform continued independently of Populism as well as within the People's party. One of its noted supporters, who refused to become a Populist, was Samuel Gompers. His followers in Boston were sufficiently ardent in their demand for the Swiss referendum to attract the attention of Oliver Wendell Holmes, the jurist.

After 1894 the New Jersey movement widened out until, simultaneously with the meeting of the last great Populist national convention, the National Direct Legislation League was organized at St. Louis on July 21, 1896. As Populism declined, Eltweed Pomeroy, a Nationalist, New Jersey ink manufacturer, kept the movement for direct legislation alive as President of the newly formed League and editor of *The Direct Legislation Record* (1894–1903). It was under his leadership that the agitation won its first substantial gains.

The initial and continuing New Jersey leadership of the movement to persuade the United States to adopt the Swiss system of direct legislation; the initial eastern labor union,

If Populism as a radical system was primarily economic in character, was any concept other than antimonopolism and the desirability of a semicollectivist economy fundamental to its economic theory? Careful study of the St. Louis and Omaha platforms of 1892 indicates that there was. Closely linked with declarations in favor of an alliance with urban labor is found the statement, identical in both documents: "Wealth belongs to him who creates it. Every dollar taken from industry without an equivalent is robbery. If any one will not work, neither shall he eat."[64] This statement furnishes the second key to Populist economic thought. Its origins can be found in the early antimonopoly and Granger movements. The *Prairie Farmer's* famous cartoon of the early seventies, showing the farmer, who pays for all, surrounded by a clergyman, merchant, lawyer, legislator, soldier, railroad magnate, and doctor, expressed this theory of wealth. It had been shared by the National Labor Union, the Industrial Congress, and the Knights of Labor.[65] More remotely, the same view had been postulated by Edward Kellogg as fundamental to his new monetary system.[66] It was basic to the ante-bellum labor movements.

This third fundamental concept in Populist economic theory, which it inherited from earlier labor and agrarian movements, was none other than the "labor-cost theory of value" as the economists term it. Although it was derived ultimately from classical economics, it had been

Nationalist support for the proposal; and its subsequent adoption by western agrarians as the result of direct transmission via a noted, or notorious labor leader at Omaha, together lend strong support to the thesis of this essay. Aside from Benjamin Urner's first newspaper championship, the most effective early journalistic support for the initiative and referendum was found in Edward Bellamy's *New Nation*, the *Arena*, and the *Direct Legislation Record* which was first edited by J. W. Sullivan in New York. Sullivan's book on direct legislation appeared there in 1892.

J. W. Arrowsmith, "The Direct Legislation Movement in New Jersey," *The Direct Legislation Record*, I (May, 1894), 2–3; Sylvester Baxter, "Shall We Adopt the Swiss Referendum?" *New Nation*, I (January 31, 1891), 15–16; W. D. McCracken, "How to Introduce the Initiative and Referendum," *Arena* (May, 1893), reprinted in *ibid.*, III (May 6, 1893), 229; Mark De Wolfe Howe, editor, *Holmes-Pollock Letters. The Correspondence of Mr. Justice Holmes and Sir Frederick Pollock 1874–1932*, I (Cambridge, 1941), 50; Lloyd Papers, J. W. Sullivan to Henry D. Lloyd, May 31, 1894, which makes very clear the wage-earner support of the movement for direct legislation in New York, Massachusetts, and New Jersey that spring when attempts were being made to secure constitutional amendments or statutes for the institution of the initiative and referendum there.

[64] Chicago *Tribune*, Feb. 25, July 5, 1892; Hicks, *Populist Revolt*, 437, 442.

[65] John R. Commons *et al.*, *A Documentary History of American Industrial Society* (11 vols., Cleveland, 1911), IX, 36–42, 177, X, 39–47; Commons, *History of Labour in the United States*, II, 90, 121, 164, 173, 352.

[66] *Labor and Other Capital*, xv–xvi, xx–xxiv.

widely accepted in Europe and America in the sixties by radicals opposed
to the machine age. In it the European anarchists and American
labor reformers and agrarian leaders had found justification for their
struggle against merchant capitalists and the great corporations.

The labor-cost theory was derived from the conceptions of a pre-
industrial age. By its application small producers, whether wheat
growers and cotton farmers, or skilled laborers and small shopkeepers,

SHYLOCK'S BANK

sought to regain or bulwark an economic position that was being undermined by the factory age, the middleman, and monopoly capitalism.
The adherents of this theory regarded capital as the product of labor
alone, possessing "no independent power of production" of its own.
As such, they thought that it deserved little or no reward. The whole
value of the product should go to the producer, although a nominal interest might be allowed to the possessors of idle funds who loaned them
to productive workers.[67] Consumers and producers co-operation, the
independent regulatory commissions, a government operated banking
and monetary system, government owned railroads, telegraphs, and
telephones had been regarded by labor reformers and agrarian leaders
as the means, not only of combating monopoly, but also of establishing
an economic system in harmony with the labor-cost theory. Loyal
to this philosophy of wealth the Populists at Omaha asserted that the

[67] Commons, *Documentary History*, IX, 36.

middleman, the financier, the railroad promoters with their watered stock and monopoly rates, the bankers and mortgage holders, and the organizers of "trusts and combines" were all nonproducers. They were profiting from bad laws and the perversion of democratic government at the expense of the producing masses who, by this process, were being so impoverished that they were "degenerating into European conditions."[68]

Since urban labor suffered from these evils as much as the farmers, since it was denied the right to organize and, in addition, was assailed by hired bands of Pinkerton detectives, the Omaha convention urged it to join the agrarians in an independent political alliance. By means of the ballot box, they could promote a peaceful revolution in American government and economic life. "[T]he union of the labor forces of the United States this day accomplished shall be permanent and perpetual. . . . The interests of rural and civic[69] labor are the same; their enemies are identical."[70] Antimonopolism and the labor-cost theory of value, twin foundations in the economic theory of Populism, were thus offered to urban labor as the ideological basis of an independent farmer-labor alliance in politics.

The desirability and practicability of such a coalition had long been an article of faith for both labor reformers and leading agrarians. Their adherence to this view explains the persistence with which the consummation of the alliance had been sought over three decades. Attention has already been directed to repeated instances of co-operation between organized labor and the farmers' movements. At least two attempts had been made to organize such a political party before the Populist period.[71] Even earlier, labor reformers had appealed to antimonopolism in order to induce their followers to ally themselves with the farmers, as did Francis A. Hoffman, Jr., in his address to the Workingmen's Party in Chicago, January 25, 1874:

I hope, however, that you will enlarge the sphere of your labors beyond this narrow field, and extend an invitation to the laborers and workers of all other cities and towns to form similar organizations, harmonizing in spirit and action with your own; more particularly with a view of joining hands with the farmers, the laborers of the country, your natural allies, in one common, united effort to free this country from the shackles of monopoly . . . extend a helping hand to the farmers, the laborers of the field. They are your vanguard. . . . Aid them in their brave warfare with your common enemy, hydraheaded

---

[68] Omaha platform.
[69] "urban" in the St. Louis platform.
[70] Omaha platform.
[71] *Supra*, pp, 7, 8, 15; Commons, *Documentary History*, IX, 139, platform of the New York Labor Congress, March, 1866. The National Greenback, the Greenback-Labor, and the Union Labor parties were the results of attempts to organize farmer-labor parties before 1890.

monopoly. Workingmen, laborers, come in solid phalanx, unite with your brethern [*sic*] in the country, . . . [72]

The kindred interests of laborers and farmers as producers, and their common hostility to monopoly were emphasized by Ethelbert Stewart, editor of the Chicago *Knights of Labor*, in 1888, in his attempt to unite the labor movement with the farmers in support of the Union Labor party.[73] Alson J. Streeter, the presidential nominee, appealed to the same concepts when he justified the campaign of the party in his letter of acceptance.[74] The Populist invitation to urban labor, extended in the heated preamble of the Omaha platform, was little more than a repetition of these earlier pleas for a united front. It was based on identical concepts.

The effectiveness of the Populist appeal to urban labor depended on the degree to which the labor movement still adhered to the producers' economic philosophy with its labor-cost theory and antimonopolist creed. From 1825 until the late eighties, together with the concept of self-help through co-operatives, they had furnished the ideological foundation of working-class movements in the United States.[75] This economic philosophy, which represented the outlook of the lower middle class, instead of that of a job-conscious proletariat, made it possible for labor reformers to support the farmers in radical movements that were based upon a similar philosophy derived originally from working-class Locofocoism and elaborated on the basis of rural experience and subsequent intercourse with urban centers. Perhaps, as Henry David contends, antimonopolism was the peculiar program offered by the American workingman as his contribution to the realization of the "American dream."[76] Only with the rise of modern trades unions after 1880 did wage earners come gradually to the view that they should work for their own craft interests independently of the farmers or the middle class.[77] The story of the labor movement in the late eighties and early nineties centers upon the struggle between the new trades unionism and the older school of labor reform with its producers' philosophy that had united wage earner and farmer in a common faith over six decades.

It was entirely normal, therefore, for the leaders of the farmers'

---

[72] Undated leaflet, "Speech of Francis A. Hoffman, Jr. delivered at 12 Street Turner Hall, on Sunday, January 25th, 1874, At the Mass-Meeting of the Workingmen's Party," George A. Schilling Papers, Labadie Collection, University of Michigan.

[73] Jan. 4, Feb. 1, 1888.

[74] July 14, 1888, Streeter Scrapbook.

[75] Commons, *History of Labour in the United States*, I, 217–219, 275–276, 318, 551–555; Selig Perlman, "The Concept of Class in the Development of the American Labor Program," Meeting of the American Historical Association, New York City, Dec. 27, 1940.

[76] Discussion of Perlman's paper, *ibid*.

[77] Perlman, *op. cit.*

alliances and for agrarian advocates of a third party to confer with Terence V. Powderly, rather than with Samuel Gompers, between 1889 and 1892. Unfortunately for the Populists, the swift decline of the Knights of Labor, champions of the older philosophy of American wage earners, made them an insufficient recruiting ground.[78] The trades union leaders, on the other hand, apart from their job-conscious, autonomous outlook, were hardly conciliated by Populist preference for the leaders of the rival labor movement. Both factors, undoubtedly, motivated Samuel Gompers to write for the *North American Review*, just before the Omaha convention, that although labor would be friendlier to the People's Party than to any other, there could be no hope of a complete "unification of labor's forces in the field, farm, factory, and workshop." Because the Populists were largely *"employing* farmers" in contrast with the *"employed* farmers of the country districts or the mechanics and laborers of the industrial centers," Gompers persuaded his followers and the public that complete "coöperation or amalgamation of the wage-workers' organizations with the People's Party" was "impossible, because it is unnatural."[79]

The success of the Populists in recruiting a following from the ranks of organized labor depended, therefore, upon whether the wage earners' attachment for the older and more distinctively American philosophy of labor reform was greater than its loyalty to the newer, imported trades unionism. In 1892 the hold of the latter seems to have been stronger.[80] After the panic of the following year had plunged labor into unemployment and acute distress, however, even Gompers wavered in his devotion to a strictly job-conscious, craft program. The American Federation of Labor actually moved toward a *de facto* alliance with Populism.[81] The depression years, therefore, tended to force organized labor back into the older philosophy and justified making one more attempt to form a common front with the agrarian movement. This presented the Populists with their long-sought opportunity to recruit heavily from urban labor. It furnished the acid test of a radical creed based upon antimonopolism, the labor-cost theory of wealth, and belief in the common

---

[78] Their membership fell below 100,000 after 1890, many of whom were farmers and small shopkeepers.

[79] Samuel Gompers, "Organized Labor in the Campaign," *North American Review* (New York), CLV, July, 1892, p. 93.

[80] George H. Knoles, "Populism and Socialism, with Special Reference to the Election of 1892," *Pacific Historical Review* (Los Angeles), XII, Sept. 1943, pp. 295–304.

[81] Chester McA. Destler, "Consummation of a Labor-Populist Alliance in Illinois, 1894," MISSISSIPPI VALLEY HISTORICAL REVIEW (Iowa City), XXVII, March, 1941, pp. 589–602, or Chapter VIII below; Klotsche, "The 'United Front' Populists," *Wisconsin Magazine of History*, XX, June, 1937, pp. 380–384; Staley, *History of the Illinois State Federation of Labor*, 109–137; Commons, *History of Labour in the United States*, II, 509–514.

interests of all producers, which offered a limited but clearly defined economic collectivism as the goal of the farmer-labor alliance.[82]

Perhaps because they have been preoccupied with interpretations derived from the older Turnerism, historians are just beginning to inquire into this neglected aspect of the Populist movement. When it is given full attention it will be found that the greatest problem of ideological conflict and adaptation produced by the attempted coalition did not develop out of a clash between Populism and the half-formulated philosophy of a shattered trades unionism. It sprang, instead, from the clash of indigenous Populism, produced by decades of cross-fertilization between urban and agrarian radical movements, with an imported, proletarian Socialism which made its first great appeal to English-speaking wage earners in America in the depression-ridden nineties. At least some of the zeal with which the Populist national headquarters and Congressional delegation turned to free silver in 1895–1896 was the result of this far more irreconcilable conflict.[83] The tendency of the strong antimonopoly bloc within the party to come to provisional terms with the Socialists on the basis of government ownership of all monopolies, which Henry D. Lloyd and the Nationalists supported, motivated some of the steamroller tactics with which Herman E. Taubeneck and Senator William V. Allen deprived the powerful antimonopolist-Nationalist-labor-and-Socialist element at the St. Louis convention of effective expression in 1896 and delivered the People's Party into the hands of the free-silver Democracy.[84] This precipitated the withdrawal of the labor and left wing elements from all association with the Populists.

Leaderless, lacking a separate party organization after the turn of the century, the antimonopolist radicalism of the West survived as a vital force in American thought and politics. The Populist demand for an effective, but restricted, democratic collectivism had been the American counterpart of the "new liberalism" in Great Britain that had arisen under the stimulus of Irish land reform agitation, Henry George, and

[82] Cf. Ware, *Labor Movement in the United States, 1860–1895*, pp. 352–353, for a pessimistic appraisal of the extent to which antimonopolism or cheap money offered ground for a durable alliance between the American farmers and wage earners.

[83] H. E. Taubeneck to Ignatius Donnelly, July 27, 1892, Dec. 28, 1893, Jan. 29, 1895, indicates that an interest in insurance of continued campaign contributions from the American Bimetallic League was also a factor in the swing to free silver, Ignatius Donnelly Papers, State Historical Society of Minnesota. For influence of the anti-Socialist bias of Taubeneck and his associates upon it, see open letter from H. E. Taubeneck to S. F. Norton, Aug. 20, 1895, H. L. Loucks to Taubeneck, clipping from Aberdeen, South Dakota, *Dakota Ruralist*, H. E. Taubeneck Scrapbook, courtesy of I. D. Taubeneck, Bronxville, N. Y.; Thomas F. Byron to Lloyd, April 8, May 5, 28, 1895, F. J. Schulte to Lloyd, April 4, 1896, Lloyd to R. I. Grimes, July 10, 1896, Lloyd Papers.

[84] S. Philip van Patten to Schilling, Oct. 27, 1896, Schilling Papers; Henry D. Lloyd "The Populists at St. Louis," *Review of Reviews* (New York), XIV, Sept. 1896, p. 303.

Socialism, in response to the problems of an even more mature industrialism. Like the "Newcastle Program" of 1891, which enjoyed a temporary vogue before defeat by the conservative reaction in 1895[85] only to re-emerge a decade later as the foundation of the program of Campbell-Bannerman, Asquith, and Lloyd George, Populist antimonopolist collectivism was re-enforced in the new century in America by the social awakening of the middle class and continued as the central feature of the neo-democratic movement. Essentially American still, somewhat less extreme in the devices that it advocated as the means of governing the economic forces of the day, it produced nevertheless a new crop of "American radicals" that escaped the notice of President James B. Conant in his plea for an indigenous radical movement. Led by Robert M. LaFollette, Hiram Johnson, George W. Norris, and the Bryan brothers, they continued the old fight against the railroads, tariff, trusts, "Wall Street," and corporate exploitation of the public domain. Less extreme in their collectivism than the Populists had been, they borrowed the agrarian conception of the democratic welfare state and employed the independent regulatory commission as their chief agency in subjecting American capitalism to a system of government regulation and control that has expanded with each revival of the democratic movement. Thus the alleged radicalism with which the "New Deal" has multiplied the number of regulatory agencies and commissions and ventured upon public ownership in the electric power industry, as well as its confused and contradictory banking and monetary policies,[86] can be traced to "the general philosophy and specific ideas" of the Greenback, Granger, and Populist movements of the late nineteenth-century West. So can the now powerful co-operative movement of the mid-century which, under the aegis of the Grange and the Farm Bureau Federation and the Co-operative League of the United States of America, Inc., at last challenges monopoly capitalism at its most vulnerable point, the market. If President Conant would find "American radicals," therefore, let him visit the regulatory agencies of the federal government, follow the career and read the works of Thurman Arnold,[87] call upon Secretary of the Interior Harold L. Ickes, and invite Henry A. Wallace to lecture at Harvard University on "monopoly and free enterprise."

[85] William Clarke, "Liberalism and Social Reform," *Encyclopedia of Social Reform*, 811–812.

[86] Joseph E. Reeve, *Monetary Reform Movements: A Survey of Recent Plans and Panaceas* (Washington, 1943), 193–194, 241–242.

[87] Thurman Arnold, *Democracy and Free Enterprise* (Norman, Okla., 1942), *passim*, illustrates Arnold's application of the now traditional antimonopolism of the West to the complex restrictions imposed on American economic life by trade associations, corporations, cartels, patents, and labor organizations.

CHAPTER II

THE ORIGIN AND CHARACTER OF THE PENDLETON PLAN*

THE PENDLETON plan was the product of western sectionalism and factional politics in the Democratic party of Ohio. Within the latter, the Civil War had produced new divisions. Aside from the War Democrats, who joined the Union party in 1861, three distinct Democratic factions appeared. These were an embittered "peace-at-any-price" element, a strong conservative faction, and a moderate peace group. Between them maneuvered a ring of Cincinnati politicians. Led by Washington McLean, party boss in Hamilton County, they controlled the Cincinnati *Daily Enquirer*, a most influential Democratic journal in the Northwest. Its publishers were motivated not only by personal and partisan considerations, but also by a desire to preserve Cincinnati's river trade and southern market. After Vallandigham's defeat in 1863, the *Enquirer* went over to the ultra peace faction. In 1864, however, it came to terms with the moderates and conservatives in time to support the Democratic national ticket.[1]

Peace found the *Enquirer* somewhat discredited on account of its extreme opposition to the war. Leadership in the party passed to the conservative wing, under whom the Democrats regained much ground lost since 1862.[2] The perpetuation of war hatreds, however, and association with the "copperhead" element prevented them from carrying Ohio in 1866, when a potential majority might have been rallied to the support of Andrew Johnson.[3] In these circumstances it was obvious that the Democracy could not hope to carry Ohio with issues that revived the passions of the war. Emphasis upon questions more vital to western sentiment was imperative if it was to return to power.

A revival of sectional feeling in the Northwest furnished the opportunity. Western grievances in 1867 were largely economic, although

---

* Reprinted from the *Mississippi Valley Historical Review*, XXIV, (September, 1937), 171–184.

[1] Charles R. Wilson, "The Cincinnati *Daily Enquirer* and Civil War Politics" (doctoral thesis, University of Chicago, 1934), 258–260, 263–265.

[2] *Ibid.*, 348–349.

[3] Howard K. Beale, *The Critical Year* (New York, 1930), 388–390. The abortive effort of Alexander Long and William M. Corry to lead a bolt of the ultras failed when Vallandigham remained in the Democratic party. Cincinnati *Daily Enquirer*, September 19, 1867; Wilson, "Cincinnati *Daily Enquirer*," 347.

southern reconstruction and the centralizing policy of Radical Republicans provoked a conservative reaction.[4] The war had left the Northeast in control of the nation's banking, currency, and public debt. Since specie and state banknotes had disappeared from circulation, the West suffered a chronic scarcity of money, as paper currency moved periodically to New York in payment of the debtor section's balances.[5] Inadequate banking facilities and the introduction of short credits into business intensified the credit stringency west of the Alleghanies.[6] Hard times there, precipitated by a panic in London and general crop failures in the Northwest, increased the embarrassment caused by a centralized banking system.[7] Frontier competition with older agricultural districts, rate manipulations by railroads under eastern control, high taxation, and elevation of the war tariff swelled the chorus of discontent.[8]

Dissatisfaction with Radical fiscal policy developed early in the West. The greenbacks were popular there while the tax exempt privilege of the war bonds was criticized and national banks were regarded with hostility.[9] There the propaganda of a group of paper money and cheap credit enthusiasts appealed strongly to farmers and laborers.[10] In the face of this the Radicals undertook to fund the floating and short term debt, including the greenbacks, into long term, tax exempt bonds. By this means they hoped to secure an early return to specie payments.[11]

[4] Robert McClelland to Alexander H. Stephens, April 23, 1867, Robert McClelland MSS. (Burton Historical Collection, Detroit); Beale, *Critical Year*, 388–390.

[5] Horatio Seymour MSS. (New York State Library), scrapbooks, XII, 7–8; Simeon Nash to John Sherman, December 7, 1865, John Sherman MSS. (Library of Congress), vol. 88, p. 20464; *Nation* (New York), VI (1868), 188, 227; *Cincinnati Daily Gazette*, January 1, 1869.

[6] Edward McPherson, *A Handbook of Politics for 1868* (Washington, 1868), 373; *Congressional Globe*, 40 Cong., 2 Sess., 1876.

[7] John Bigelow MS. Diary (New York Public Library), May 12, 1866; *Cincinnati Daily Gazette*, January 1, 1867; Cincinnati *Daily Enquirer*, August 14, 17, 28, 1867; *New York Tribune*, September 13, 1867.

[8] Ohio State Board of Agriculture, *Twenty-first Annual Report, 1866* (Columbus, 1867), 48, 68, 70–75, 190–191; *Twenty-second Annual Report, 1867* (Columbus, 1868), 40–41; *Twenty-third Annual Report, 1868* (Columbus, 1869), 62–63; Solon J. Buck, *The Granger Movement* (Cambridge, 1913), 7–8; W. A. Lloyd to Sumner, July 17, 1866, William Birney to *id.*, December 3, 1866, Horace W. White to *id.*, January 30, 1867, Charles Sumner MSS. (Harv. Coll. Library, Cambridge); *Nation*, IV (1867), 81; Beale, *Critical Year*, 259–260, 394.

[9] Beale, *Critical Year*, 246.

[10] *Infra*, 56–57.

[11] Jay Cooke to Greeley, May 10, 1866, Hugh McCulloch to *id.*, March 5, 1866, Horace Greeley MSS. (New York Public Library); Hugh McCulloch, *Men and Measures of Half a Century* (New York, 1900), 201–202; Burke A. Hinsdale, ed., *Works of James Abram Garfield* (Boston, 1882–1883), I, 197.

Currency contraction, begun on April 16, 1866, failed to accomplish the desired end.[12] Instead, it provoked a western protest that broadened into an attack upon the public debt and national banking system. A huge long term funded debt was viewed with apprehension in the West. Currency contraction and a quick return to specie payments, it was argued, would greatly enhance the value and burden of public and private obligations. At the same time it would precipitate a sudden decline in the price of agricultural produce.

The *Cincinnati Daily Gazette*, a Radical organ, voiced these fears and pled for an alternative policy. Before currency contraction and resumption were attempted, it argued, all of the war debt that had been contracted in depreciated currency should be redeemed in greenbacks. Twenty years would be ample time to achieve a return to specie payments.[13] The editorials that developed this proposition were written by Samuel R. Reed. Later they were published in a pamphlet entitled, *The Currency and Finances: A Policy for the Present Expansion of Currency, Trade & Public Debt.*[14] Similar demands came from the East.[15] In the West, the extreme opponents of Radical finance were led by Henry Clay Dean, an ultra "peace" Democrat from Iowa. Dean denounced the national banks, the bondholders, and New England. He called for an immediate issue of greenbacks large enough to pay the war debt at once.[16]

To the publishers of the Cincinnati *Daily Enquirer*, this situation presented a golden opportunity. By a persistent appeal to the discontented, coupled with attacks on bondholders and advocacy of Dean's inflationary liquidation of the debt, they could capitalize sectional unrest and place themselves at the head of an irresistible movement to overthrow the Radical régime.[17] Victory would reverse the Reconstruction policy. Cincinnati's southern market and primacy in the West

[12] Alexander D. Noyes, *Forty Years of American Finance* (New York, 1909), 13-14.

[13] *Cincinnati Daily Gazette*, October 19, 21, 1865; February 2, 5, 8, 15, 1866; January 16, 17, 1867. Cf. Sherman MSS., *loc. cit.*; Cincinnati *Daily Enquirer*, December 14, 1867; Beale, *Critical Year*, 241-242, 247 n.

[14] Cincinnati, 1866.

[15] James A. Woodburn, *Life of Thaddeus Stevens* (Indianapolis, 1913), 578; Beale, *Critical Year*, 240-241, 245-246. Cf. Hugh McCulloch to Greeley, March 5, 1866, Henry C. Carey to *id.*, February 22, December 20, 1867, Greeley MSS.

[16] Cincinnati *Daily Enquirer*, July 15, 1867; Cincinnati *West and South*, September 5, 1868; Henry C. Dean, *Crimes of the Civil War, and Curse of the Funding System* (Baltimore, 1869), *passim.*

[17] Cincinnati *West and South*, November 23, 1867; July 4, August 29, 1868; *Cincinnati Daily Gazette*, February 27, 1868; Cincinnati *Daily Enquirer*, July 15, 1867.

could then be regained.[18]   Success in Ohio would restore the *Enquirer* clique to its former influence in the party.   If the Northwest followed his lead, Washington McLean could engage once more in the presidential game.   Such motives probably led the *Enquirer's* managers to abandon their conservative views upon the currency and national debt.[19]

On January 6, 1867, the *Enquirer* attacked the conservative wing of the Ohio Democratic party.   Two days later, apparently, McLean urged Henry Clay Dean's inflation scheme upon the party's leaders without success at the Ohio State Democratic Convention.[20]   Allen G. Thurman was nominated for governor under the aegis of the conservative and moderate factions.   The platform was concerned with constitutional questions to an unusual degree.[21]   When George H. Pendleton opened the state campaign in a masterly oration at Urbana, April 25, 1867, he listed the inflated currency as one of the nation's grievances against the Radicals.[22]

Undiscouraged, the *Enquirer* appealed to the people over the heads of the conservatives.[23]   During February, March, April, and May it shrewdly identified itself with current resentment against the tariff, the national banks, and the contraction policy.   Bondholders were attacked as a dangerous aristocracy and sectional antipathy to New England was played up.[24]   Henry Clay Dean's argument for immediate inflation and debt redemption was printed and discussed.[25]   In early June the editors

[18] Cincinnati *Daily Enquirer*, October 9, 1866; April 21, 1867; March 17, 1868.

[19] As late as January 20, 1867, the *Enquirer's* views upon the debt and currency were conservative.   It upheld the debt's sanctity, though it failed to see any Radical disposition to pay it (November 2, 1866).   It maintained steadily that specie was the only true currency.   Nevertheless it argued that "all attempts suddenly to return to a specie basis will not only prove abortive, but will produce great and sudden prostration and distress in all branches of productive industry. . . .   We are unhappily in a state in which to stimulate or deplete is equally hazardous" (November 26, 1866).   A return to specie payments it regarded desirable, but like the *Gazette* held it wiser to pay off interest-bearing obligations before funding the greenbacks (December 5, 1866).   Before January 1, 1867, then, the *Enquirer* held the usual anti-contraction views prevalent in the West.   It even conceded that hard times in the West were due neither to a scarcity of currency or to the paper currency.

[20] Cincinnati *West and South*, August 10, 1867.

[21] The platform was drawn up by Clement L. Vallandigham.   Two short planks dealt with economic questions, taxation, and the tariff.   *The Ohio Platforms of the Republican and Democratic Parties, from 1855 to 1881* (Columbus, 1881), 28–30.

[22] Cincinnati *Daily Enquirer*, April 26, 1867.

[23] For its sensitiveness to its loss of influence within the party, see Cincinnati *Daily Enquirer*, May 1, 1867.

[24] February 18, 21, March 13, 15, 16, 25, May 4, 20, 22, 28, June 1, 6, 1867.

[25] April 19, 24, 1867.

inveigled the *Cincinnati Commercial*, an outstanding Radical journal, into a controversy upon the merits of Dean's program.[26] This enabled the *Enquirer* to argue that Dean's scheme would not result in repudiation. Money would not be too plentiful if it were put into effect, it contended, while the people would be relieved of the burden of the war debt.[27] It then ridiculed the Ohio State Republican Convention for its failure to endorse the project. Radical solicitude was reserved for the Negro, it observed, while "white people" groaned in "servitude to debt."[28] Finally, on June 30 a long editorial urged the Democratic party to make payment of the debt in legal tender the central issue of its campaign.[29]

As anticipated, these tactics evoked a strongly favorable popular response. An alarmed attorney reported a rapidly growing sentiment in Indiana, Illinois, and Iowa that demanded payment of the debt in greenbacks. This sentiment, he wrote to Charles Sumner on July 6, 1867, was even stronger among Unionists than among Democrats.[30] The published correspondence of the *Enquirer* and resolutions adopted by local Democratic conventions indicated the strength of the public reaction.[31] The severe drought[32] that began in mid-August was undoubtedly a factor in the growth of inflation sentiment. In any case, it destroyed Republican expectations, based upon prospective bumper crops, of electing General Rutherford B. Hayes and ratifying a state

[26] June 7, 9, 11, July 2, 1867.

[27] June 9, 20, July 14, 1867.

[28] June 18, 21, 1867.

[29] " 'Pay the National debt in legal-tenders!' will soon be the watchword from one extremity of the land to the other. 'Pay the debt and save the people from the most onerous and oppressive taxation that ever existed,' will be the cry. The people—the taxpaying people—upon the one side, and the aristocratic bond-holder upon the other; and between them the struggle is to take place. In such a contest there can be but one result—the overthrow of the aristocracy. The people are determined to pay the debt immediately, and thus get rid of the army of revenue collectors, pimps, spies, and detectives, as well as of stamps and revenue taxes.

"The Democracy of the United States never had such a weapon in their hands for the complete overthrow of the destructives who have brought the Republic into disgrace and impending ruin, as this one of paying off the debt in legal-tenders. . . .

"The nigger has been the trump card of the Federalists for the last ten years, and with it they have beaten us in every encounter. But this is a very different question, and one they could not so easily handle. Seize hold, then, of this measure at once and make it the slogan of the campaign, and victory will, as sure as the earth revolves, perch upon our banners." Cincinnati *Daily Enquirer*, June 30, 1867.

[30] Charles Seitzer to Sumner, Sumner MSS.

[31] June 26, 29, July 13, 15, 16, 17, 23, 25, 28, 29, August 1, 12, 17, 18, 21, 22, 1867.

[32] Cincinnati *Daily Enquirer*, August 14, 17, 28, 1867; *New York Tribune*, September 13, 1867; Ohio State Board of Agriculture, *Twenty-second Annual Report, 1867*, 161–191 *passim*.

Negro suffrage constitutional amendment by the "usual majority."[33]

This situation made it impossible for Democratic leaders to ignore the issue raised by the *Enquirer*. The State Sovereignty Democrats might demand outright repudiation and denounce the "greenback dodge,"[34] but conservative and moderate Democrats faced a hard dilemma. To oppose it might jeopardize the chance of victory in October and forfeit a controlling position in the party. Acceptance would surrender party leadership to Washington McLean and at the same time sacrifice strong convictions on the war debt and currency. Before the *Enquirer* movement got out of hand a more conservative program had to be perfected. If skilfully drawn it might take the wind out of that journal's sails and still gain the political advantage inherent in its course.

Hon. H. J. Jewett presented the conservative substitute at Zanesville, July 5, 1867.[35] He admitted the validity of the debt but criticised its high interest and tax exemption. He proposed that bondholders be offered the alternative of accepting taxable bonds bearing a lower rate of interest in exchange for their present holdings, or of being paid off in "the very kind of currency . . . received from them" during the war. Once refunded, the debt should be paid by means of a sinking fund. The money to operate this should be drawn from two sources. The floating debt of the government should not be funded, as the Radicals planned, and the surplus revenue available to finance this should be turned into the sinking fund. Furthermore, the national banknotes should be retired and replaced with an equal quantity of greenbacks. The interest saved on the bonds then securing the banknotes should also go into the fund. Beginning with sixty million in gold annually and taking advantage of additional savings as bonds were retired, the entire debt could be extinguished in eighteen years without increasing taxation. During the period of debt reduction Jewett believed that the circulation of paper currency should not exceed $1,000,000,000 which was currently believed to equal that of the war period. He did not think it wise to expand the currency beyond that figure "at present" although he did not doubt the propriety of doing so should it be justified by the "business and wants of the country" at some future date. At any rate operation of the sinking fund for five years longer would retire the paper currency.

[33] John Sherman to Sumner, August 10, 1867, Sumner MSS.; *New York Tribune*, July 3, 1867; *Harper's Weekly* (New York), XI (1867), 419.

[34] Cincinnati *West and South*, August 10, 17, 1867; May 16, June 20, July 4, 11, 1868.

[35] Cincinnati *Daily Enquirer*, July 16, 1867. Jewett had been a leader of the conservative faction for some years. In 1861 he was the Democratic nominee for governor. Columbus *Crisis*, September 26, 1861.

Jewett's plan was based upon that offered by the *Cincinnati Daily Gazette* in 1865. General Hayes immediately exposed the plagiarism.[36] This the *Enquirer* promptly admitted, and then asked the *Gazette* why it opposed a measure now that it had once sponsored.[37] The former journal then brought pressure to bear upon George H. Pendleton, leader of the moderate Democrats. Pendleton, as General Hayes remarked that year, was "the most distinguished and perhaps the most influential Democrat . . . actively engaged in politics in Ohio."[38] His popularity with ultra and conservative Democrats, together with the vice-presidential nomination in 1864, gave him great influence throughout the Northwest. He was well-to-do, with an income approaching $10,000 a year.[39] A successful lawyer, he was actively engaged in the effort to construct a southern railroad out of Cincinnati.[40] Akin to Calhoun in his views on the nature of the republic,[41] but moderate in expressing them, he could hope for the presidential nomination in 1868 if the Democrats carried Ohio in October.

Pendleton had bitterly denounced inflation in 1862.[42] He retained these views as late as April 25, 1867, when he opened the Ohio campaign.[43] This was the man whom Washington McLean hoped to use in his presidential game. By "puffing" Pendleton in the *Enquirer*,[44] by whipping up inflation sentiment, and by private pressure, McLean forced him to take a public stand on the debt and currency issues. With great reluctance, as William M. Corry reported later, Pendleton did so.[45] But instead of endorsing McLean's plan to wipe out the debt by wholesale inflation he turned to Jewett's conservative substitute. This he adapted to his own purposes without crediting its author.

Pendleton's financial views were developed in a series of addresses. These evince his reluctance to yield completely to McLean and his search for a defensible position. At St. Paul, Minnesota, on July 11,

[36] Cincinnati *Daily Enquirer*, August 17, 18, 1867.

[37] August 18, 1867.

[38] Charles R. Williams, *The Life of Rutherford B. Hayes* (Boston, 1914), I, 296. Campaign speech, Lebanon, O., August 5, 1867.

[39] Cincinnati *Daily Enquirer*, May 27, 1867; April 3, 1868. Income tax returns for 1867 and 1868.

[40] *Ibid.*, March 9, 1867.

[41] Cincinnati *West and South*, August 31, September 7, 1867.

[42] Pendleton to an unknown recipient, February 6, 1862, Miscellaneous MSS. (New York Historical Society); *Congressional Globe*, 37 Cong., 2 Sess., 549–551.

[43] Cincinnati *Daily Enquirer*, April 26, 1867.

[44] June 22, July 15, 18, 29, August 5, 12, 19, 1867; Cincinnati *West and South*, July 4, 1868.

[45] Cincinnati *West and South*, August 29, 1868.

1867, he contented himself with the suggestion that the notes of the national banks be replaced by an equal issue of greenbacks.[46] At Lima, Ohio, on August 15,[47] he moved farther to the left. There he adopted Jewett's sinking fund but ignored the proposal to refund the debt in taxable bonds at lower interest. Pendleton stipulated, however, that the five-twenties, alone of the permanent debt, should be paid in greenbacks. This, he argued, the government had a legal right to do. Although he claimed that the sinking fund would liquidate the entire debt in sixteen years without inflation or new taxes, Pendleton urged that debt reduction be speeded up by the aid of gradual inflation. The necessities of southern reconstruction, he argued, created a legitimate demand for more currency. By extending the increase over the five years in which the five-twenties were callable, and by restricting it to the needs of business, values and business interests would adjust themselves without a shock.[48] Even then high taxation and strict economy would still be necessary for the payment of the debt. In any case, the advantages[49] to be gained by paying the five-twenties in greenbacks were so great that they would offset any predicted evil.

The Lima speech clearly contemplated a more rapid debt reduction than Jewett had suggested. It also laid Pendleton open to the charge of having joined the inflationists even if he had rejected the extreme views of the *Enquirer*. Very naturally, contemporaries asked just how great the slow and moderate increase in the currency that he contemplated would be. Would it simply re-inflate the currency up to the war level, at which Jewett had winked, or would it go beyond? At Cleveland, on September 18, Pendleton ridiculed opponents who thought he desired to pay the debt suddenly with an issue of twenty-two hundred millions of greenbacks. There would be no inflation "beyond a safe and just point,"[50] he declared.

Pendleton's program received its finishing touches at Milwaukee, Wisconsin, on November 2, 1867. There he again denied the charge that he proposed so to inflate the currency that it would lose its value. He then demonstrated in detail how he would redeem the five-twenties in

[46] Cincinnati *Daily Enquirer*, July 17, 1867. No additional issue of greenbacks was suggested.

[47] *Ibid.*, August 16, 1867.

[48] Pendleton specifically excluded the ten-forty gold bonds, issued under act of Congress, March 3, 1863, from greenback redemption.

[49] These were savings in interest on the debt and an increase in the amount of taxable property.

[50] *Payment of the Public Debt in Legal Tender Notes!! Speech of Hon. George H. Pendleton, Milwaukee, November 2, 1867* (n. p., n. d.), 14–16.

the next five years, retire the gold bonds due thereafter, call in the greenbacks and return to specie payments by 1881. All this could be accomplished, he maintained, without additional taxes or adding "one
farthing to the currency."[51] Specifically, he proposed to stabilize the
greenbacks at 140, approximately seventy-one cents in gold on the dollar, for five years. At this figure he would convert the gold in the sinking fund into greenbacks and use them to redeem the five-twenties as
they became callable. Stringent economy, savings made by not funding the floating debt, and replacement of the national bank currency
would make this possible. With taxation as of 1866, a national budget
of $372,000,000, interest on the debt and sinking fund allotment[52] in-
cluded, would save $188,000,000 annually. This sum would also be
used to reduce the debt. With $280,000,000 in greenbacks available
from the surplus and converted gold in the sinking fund for debt reduction the first year, the central government could retire the five-twenties
as they became callable. Immediately after this was accomplished, the
government could reduce taxes $150,000,000 and still be able to pay the
bonds due in 1874. Then $200,000,000 more could be cut from the tax
burden. With war taxes removed the legal tenders could be called in
gradually and resumption achieved by 1881 when the last bond issue
had to be paid.[53]

As finally developed the Pendleton plan was plainly opposed to repudiation of the debt and to extreme inflation. Actually it proposed
temporary currency stabilization at the existing level of values, abolition of the national banks, high taxation, and drastic economy as the
means of liquidating the debt. Inflation, if necessary at all, was inci-
dental to and limited by the scheme. Conversion of sinking fund gold
into legal tenders at 140 precluded any extensive inflation. At the worst,
Pendleton could be accused of having been a re-inflationist, of proposing
to restore some of the war-time circulation in order to reduce the debt
and at the same time repair political fences damaged by the *Enquirer's*
maneuvers.

Contemporary evidence supports this interpretation. The *Cincinnati
Commercial*[54] and the *West and South*,[55] also of Cincinnati, acknowledged

[51] *Ibid.*, 1–14.

[52] $66,000,000 gold plus interest on redeemed bonds.

[53] This was based, apparently, upon a detailed extract from the Bangor (Me.) *Democrat*
which the *Enquirer* reprinted October 17, 1868, alongside extracts from Pendleton's Lima
and Cleveland speeches. The extract from the *Democrat* demonstrated, in a series of
annual budgets, how Pendleton's plan could be actually carried out. The *Democrat's*
scheme, however, involved a temporary increase of $100,000,000 in the currency during
1868–1873. The *Enquirer* published this on the front page, apparently to protect Pendleton from mis-representation.   [54] February 8, 1868.   [55] August 29, 1868.

the moderate character of the Pendleton plan. The *Enquirer*, which continued its inflation propaganda until February 23, 1868, defended Pendleton against misrepresentation.[56]   General James W. Singleton of Illinois, ultra Democrat of the Henry Clay Dean school, attacked Pendleton's plan in February, 1868, because it proposed to pay the "entire public debt by taxation."[57]   The *New York Herald*,[58] the New York *World*,[59] and on one occasion the *New York Tribune*,[60] agreed that Pendleton was not an inflationist.   Horatio Seymour was Pendleton's opponent in 1868.   In 1876 he remarked that the fact that Pendleton had thought a class of bonds payable in greenbacks did not "commit him for inflation nor . . . make him an opponent of specie payment."[61]

When the Pendleton presidential boom was fully launched the *Enquirer* abandoned its inflation propaganda.   In October, 1867, it had attributed Democratic victory in the October election to the popularity of the greenback issue.   On January 8, 1868, however, the Ohio State Democratic Convention rejected the *Enquirer* inflation scheme.   Instead it endorsed Pendleton's plan as the quickest and "only safe way" of returning to specie payments.[62]   Pendleton was presented to the party as Ohio's favorite son.   The *Enquirer* accepted Pendleton's candidacy and supported it ardently.   For six more weeks, however, it continued its inflation propaganda.   This was fatal to Pendleton's chances.   Acceptance of McLean's support placed him, seemingly, in the position of advocating a moderate fiscal program in public and of secretly abetting repudiation.   The effects of this soon became evident. Already the effort to commit the party to the "greenback repudiation

[56] October 17, 1867; February 10, April 3, 16, 1868.

[57] Cincinnati *West and South*, February 22, 1868.   Singleton continued, "The leading feature of Mr. Pendleton's proposition—which those who asperse it with the silly charge of repudiation have not the gumption to see—is in the language of the Ohio convention, the shortest and safest way of reaching specie payments."

[58] June 11, 1868.

[59] February 1, 1868. The *World's* editor remarked, "Now, whatever may be said against this proposal, it cannot with truth be said that it aims to inundate the country with a new flood of paper money, and pay off the debt in a currency thus depreciated. Admit the rightfulness of paying the funded debt in greenbacks, and admit the expediency of paying it soon, and it would not be easy to devise a plan better calculated than this of Mr. PENDLETON'S to prevent a great and sudden disturbance of values. . . .   If the payability of the debt in greenbacks be conceded, Mr. PENDLETON'S scheme is cautious and moderate."

[60] February 28, 1868.

[61] Seymour to George Miller, February 28, 1876, Horatio Seymour MSS. (New York Historical Society).   Cf. Speech of Senator Doolittle, February 27, 1869, *Congressional Globe*, 40 Cong., 3 Sess., 1870.

[62] *Ohio Platforms*, 32.

hobby" had divided the Democrats into repudiators, Pendletonians, and gold redemptionists.[63]   The latter were alienated beyond hope of reconciliation.   Samuel J. Tilden and August Belmont blocked McLean's effort to control the national committee[64] and designated New York City, instead of Cincinnati, as the location of the Democratic National Convention.[65]   This was a stinging rebuke to the *Enquirer* clique.   On the next day, February 23, 1868, their journal blandly claimed that it had never advocated inflation or repudiation.   Exposed and ridiculed by the *Gazette*[66] for its effort to retreat from an untenable position, the *Enquirer* excluded the once familiar inflationist cartoons and editorials from its columns.   Although its publishers engaged actively in the campaign to secure Pendleton delegates for the national convention,[67] their candidate's hopes were already wrecked upon the rock of eastern opposition.

It should now be clear that there was, strictly speaking, no Pendleton plan.   Henry Clay Dean fathered the program agitated by the *Enquirer* in 1867–1868.   This scheme sought to repudiate the war debt and legal tender currency alike by means of immediate and drastic inflation. Offered in a frank appeal to western sectionalism, it met with a strongly favorable response.   Forced by the *Enquirer's* tactics to take a public position on the debt and currency issues, conservative and moderate Democrats sought a defensible substitute.   Pendleton's program, as finally developed, was based upon suggestions made earlier by Samuel R. Reed of the Cincinnati *Daily Gazette* in 1865–1866, and elaborated by H. J. Jewett of Zanesville, Ohio, in 1867.   Pendleton took their proposals, modified, and adapted them to his own purposes.   In all probability he drew upon the computations of the Bangor (Me.) *Democrat*, published in the summer of 1867.[68]   He offered the final product, apparently, as a moderate and practical escape from Radical deflation on the one hand and "copperhead" repudiation on the other.   To western men, who opposed repudiation but wished to escape from high taxation and eastern financial control, it made a strong appeal.

Because of the movement to make him president, sponsored un-

---

[63] *Cincinnati Commercial*, February 8, 1868; Cincinnati *West and South*, May 23, 1868.

[64] John Humphrey to Tilden, February 12, 1868, August Belmont to [Tilden], [February, 1868], Samuel J. Tilden, MSS. (New York Public Library); Cincinnati *Daily Enquirer*, January 21, 25, February 7, 8, 19, 1868; *Cincinnati Commercial*, January 30, 1868.

[65] Tilden to Seymour, March 2, 1868, Tilden MSS.; Cincinnati *Daily Enquirer*, March 2, 1868.

[66] February 27, 1868.   Cf. Cincinnati *Daily Enquirer*, February 28, March 2, 1868, for its chagrin at the exposure.

[67] Frank Blair to [Tilden], May 30, [1868], Tilden MSS.

[68] *Supra*, n. 53.

doubtedly by Washington McLean, authorship of this program was attributed to Pendleton. The contemporary *West and South*, edited by William M. Corry, denied the validity of this assumption.[69] Corry defended Pendleton from efforts to identify him with the inflationist program of Henry Clay Dean and the *Enquirer*, and attempted vainly to separate him from the unfortunate sponsorship of Washington McLean in the pre-convention canvass.[70]

The evidence here presented suggests another conclusion. Since the appearance of James Ford Rhodes's *History of the United States from 1850 to 1877*, historians have written and spoken about "the Ohio idea." This has been regarded as a set of well defined fiscal proposals upon which most Ohio politicians of both major parties agreed. The foregoing narrative suggests diversity rather than agreement. After much reluctance among Democratic leaders to capitalize Radical debt and currency policies, the *Enquirer's* tactics succeeded only in dividing the party into factions. A few remained gold redemptionists, many became inflationists, but the controlling element espoused a policy that winked at inflation but involved little or none. The Republicans were similarly divided. James A. Garfield was a gold redemptionist.[71] John Sherman upheld the legality of redeeming the five-twenties in greenbacks at their existing volume,[72] while Republican state conventions in Ohio and Indiana winked at inflation in expressions that looked forward, at most, to a return to the wartime volume of the currency.[73] The *Enquirer* and the Pendletonians both demanded destruction of the national banks. The latter based their debt reduction plan upon this measure. Upon the bank issue the Republicans were silent. All united, save possibly the gold redemptionists, in opposition to McCulloch's policy of returning to specie payments by means of currency deflation. All save the same dissenters agreed on the legality of redeeming the five-twenties in greenbacks. On how to carry this into practical effect the factions disagreed. Only in opposing contraction and in upholding the legality of greenback redemption was any great agreement revealed. On the vital questions of inflation, the national banks, and the actual method of debt redemption, serious differences appeared. It may well be doubted whether this situation justifies continued reference to "the Ohio idea."

[69] August 29, September 5, 1868.

[70] *Ibid.*, May 30, 1868.

[71] Ellis P. Oberholtzer, *Jay Cooke, Financier of the Civil War* (Philadelphia, 1907), II, 40–41; Hinsdale, *Garfield Works*, I, 321.

[72] Sherman to Greeley, August 29, 1868, Greeley MSS.; Oberholtzer, *Jay Cooke*, II, 42–43.

[73] *Cincinnati Commercial*, February 21, March 5, 1868; *Ohio Platforms*, 34.

CHAPTER III

LEGAL AND SECTIONAL ASPECTS OF THE PENDLETON PLAN

ONE of the most controversial aspects of the so-called Pendleton plan was the contention that the central government might redeem the five-twenty bonds legally in greenbacks when they became callable. This claim was combatted warmly by the champions of coin redemption. They urged that the United States was committed morally to the traditional policy of redeeming the funded debt in gold by the advertisements of its selling agents, Jay Cooke and Company and others, and by the assurances given the investing public by the Treasury Department. The contrary course, these advocates declared, at the same time would violate the public faith, impair the nation's credit, and lead inevitably to uncontrolled inflation and outright repudiation. Not a few argued, in addition, that the United States was legally bound to redeem the five-twenties in coin.[1] Strong sympathy with this position has been expressed by James Ford Rhodes, E. P. Oberholtzer, and Davis R. Dewey.[2]

The historical setting of the issuance of the five-twenty bonds and the greenbacks, and the origins of the controversy over the mode of redemption of the former, have been described well by Max L. Shipley.[3] His investigation creates a strong presumption in favor of the contention that the government might legally have redeemed the five-twenties in greenbacks as they became callable, even though they had not yet risen to par. If established, this would suggest that the contest over the Pendleton plan should be viewed solely in terms of the opposing

---

[1] E. A. [Edward Atkinson], *Senator Sherman's Fallacies: or, Honesty the Best Policy* (Boston, 1868); [W. Endicott], *The Five-Twenty Bonds* (Boston, 1867); Robert J. Walker, *Our National Finances* . . . (Washington, D. C., [1867]); "Report of Committee on Finance. On the President's message relating to the public debt. . . . In the Senate of the United States. December 17, 1867," *U. S. Doc. 1320*, 40 Congress 2 Session, Senate Reports #4, 6–8; *Congressional Globe*, 40 Congress 2 Session, p. 42; Charles H. Coleman, *The Election of 1868* (New York, 1933), 26–27.

[2] Ellis P. Oberholtzer, *A History of the United States since the Civil War*, (New York, 1917–1926), II, 160–161; James Ford Rhodes, *History of the United States from the Compromise of 1850 to the McKinley-Bryan Campaign of 1896* (new edition, New York, 1920), VI, 271–273; Davis R. Dewey, *Financial History of the United States* (eleventh edition, New York, 1931), ch. xiv.

[3] "The Background and Legal Aspects of the Pendleton Plan," *Mississippi Valley Historical Review*, XXIV (December, 1937), 333–339.

economic groups and sections that its promulgation arrayed against each other.

To date, little or no attention has been paid to the position that European bankers and their American representatives took on the question of the legal status of the five-twenty bonds. Did they believe that the United States was legally, even morally, bound to any great extent to redeem these securities in coin, as Jay Cooke and Company declared? Agreement with this contention would not necessarily decide the question. Rejection of it, however, and the admission that the United States was free to redeem the five-twenties in legal tender notes if it were so disposed, would strengthen greatly the presumption that Pendleton and his supporters were on very strong legal ground in urging the adoption of this policy.

That European investment bankers disregarded the moral aspects of the question and entertained strong doubts of the legal obligation of the United States to redeem the five-twenties in gold was made clear to John Bigelow, the American Minister to France, in December, 1865. Late that month he was the recipient of verbal and then of a formal written inquiry from the Bank of Credit and of Deposits of the Low Countries. Speaking for this house, J. B. Bamberger declared:

Whilst no doubt can be entertained concerning the payment, in specie, of the coupons of half-yearly dividends upon the obligations of the said debt of 5–20, nothing in the text, either of the obligations or in the different acts which I have read, proves that the redemption of the said debt, either at the expiration of the twenty years or in anticipation, may not be effected in paper money, provided this paper be at that time a legal tender in the United States.[4]

Bigelow forwarded this inquiry to the Secretary of State, William H. Seward, on December 26, with the covering statement that it illustrated the "inconveniences which our national securities experience in European markets for the want of a specific undertaking by the government to pay them, when they fall due, in gold." If the Secretary of the Treasury could say anything in reply to the "Messrs. Bamberger" that would "diminish this difficulty in the eyes of its clients, the effect would be shared by a large circle of influential capitalists, and by a still larger, if circumstances permitted me to give it to the publicity of the press."[5] Partial corroboration of this report of European investing and banking sentiment on the status of the five-twenties can be seen in the cautious

---

[4] John Bigelow, *Retrospections of an Active Life*, III (Garden City, Doubleday Page, 1913), 297, C. B. Bamberger to Bigelow, December 26, 1865.

[5] *Ibid.*, 296–297. No record of a reply to this inquiry is extant in the State Department Archives.

prospectuses issued by two American banking concerns operating abroad, Belding, Keith, and Company of London, and James W. Tucker & Company of Paris. The statements of the latter house, made in 1867, are particularly interesting. Nowhere do they claim that the five-twenties are payable in gold, although purchase of them is urged specifically on the ground that interest on them was paid in coin. Then, after admitting that the twenty year gold bonds of 1861 were most sought after by American capitalists, Tucker & Company predicted an early return of the United States to specie payments with a resulting increment of twenty-five per cent in the market value of its other obligations![6]

Even more important confirmation of the inference that European investment bankers did not believe that the United States was legally bound to redeem the five-twenties in specie comes from the American representative of the Rothschilds, August Belmont of New York. His opposition to the Pendleton Plan and Pendleton's presidential candidacy in 1868 has been noted in the preceding essay. Belmont's admission of the legality of Pendleton's proposal was made three years later, after the Ohio State Democratic Convention had nominated General G. W. McCook for Governor on a "New Departure" platform that contained a re-statement of Pendleton's plan of 1867–1868. This last provision provoked Belmont to write to Manton Marble, editor of the New York *World*, and to General McCook, in the hope of persuading the Thurman and Vallandigham factions of the Ohio Democracy to shelve the greenback issue in the interest of winning the presidential election in 1872. Adoption of the Pendleton Plan by the national convention in 1868 had been a "fatal mistake," Belmont declared to Marble, but "now it is actual Suicide."

In 1868 it was bad enough, but then there was some law for it, as the Bonds don't say anything about the principal being payable in Gold & the holders had only the assurances of Mr. Chase & McCulloch's letters.

Since then however, Congress *has passed a law* making the Interest & principal alike payable in Gold on all the Bonds. The Ohio Resolution is therefore actually *repudiation*, . . . [7]

In 1868, it will be noted, Belmont conceded that Pendleton had had "some law" on his side!

---

[6] James W. Tucker & Co., Banquiers Américains, *Quelques Mots sur les Obligations des Gouvernement des États-Unis d'Amérique* (Paris, Briere, 1867), 7–9. Cf. Belding, Keith, and Company, American Bankers and Merchants, 80 Lombard Street, London, *United States Bonds and Securities. What they are—their cost—and the interest they pay* (London, 1867).

[7] August Belmont to Manton Marble, June 4, [1871], Manton Marble MSS. (Library of Congress), Volume XXVIII, #6064.

In his letter to General McCook, Belmont elaborated this admission and also threw light on the character of the opposition to the Pendleton Plan in 1867–1868.

I am delighted with the platform of the "new departure" as a return of reason & sound common sense, which has been banished from our State & National conventions ever since 1860. Still, as nothing can be perfect in the world, the old Bourbon blood must show itself by rehashing again that pernicious greenback doctrine & cant about Bondholders, which as much as anything else, cost us the Presidency in 1868.

. . . but why not, with the other issues, leave also the issue of the U. S. Bonds alone?! You array (but I must not say *you* because I know that you have too much intelligence & tact to make such a blunder) or rather we array against us the whole moneyed Interest throughout the Country, & we have been made to feel in '64 & '68 what that is,—Besides, while we had in 1868 the law on our side, which made it, as I told you & all my friends at the time, perfectly just to pay the bonds *at maturity* in Greenbacks, if by that time the Country had not resumed specie payments, we cannot fall back upon that now.

Revival of the Pendleton plan now, after the enactment of the bill to strengthen the public credit on March 18, 1869, involved in Belmont's mind "*Repudiation to all those who bought our Bonds since the passage of that act. . . .* The faith of the Nation is pledged by that law, & its repeal would be *retrospective*, unconstitutional & dishonest."[8]

Belmont applied no such adjectives in 1871 to Pendleton's argument of 1867. Instead, he conceded the validity of all but that portion that asserted that the five-twenties were redeemable in greenbacks when the bonds became callable, five years from date of issue. A moment's examination of the pertinent legislation of 1862 that authorized the issuance of the greenbacks and the five-twenties[9] indicates clearly that no such distinction could be made between the obligation of the United States to the bondholders when the bonds became callable and when they became "payable" at maturity. Unwittingly, Belmont had conceded the full legality of the Pendleton plan, upon which depended the feasibility in 1867–1868 of the proposal to redeem the bonds in greenbacks as they became callable by means of the financial operations described in detail above.[10] This had been the position taken by John Sherman, Chairman of the Senate Committee of Finance, in February, 1868, provided that the scheme involved no increase in the total volume of paper money in circulation.[11] When added to the revelations con-

---

[8] *Ibid.*, August Belmont to General G. W. McCook of Steubenville, Ohio, "*Private*," June 5, 1871, enclosure in Belmont to Marble, June 7, 1871.

[9] Edward McPherson, *A Handbook of Politics for 1868* (Washington, 1868), 354–355. Cf. Bamberger to John Bigelow, *supra*, p. 2.

[10] *Supra*, Chapter II.

[11] John Sherman, *Selected Speeches and Reports on Finance and Taxation, from 1859 to 1878* (New York, 1879), 165–166, speech on the Funding Bill, February 27, 1868.

tained in Professor Shipley's study, this evidence creates a very strong presumption indeed in favor of the legal basis of Pendleton's fiscal program when it was first offered to the public.

The evidence suggests, then, that the struggle over the Pendleton plan should be re-examined in terms of sectional and economic interests. Why did Pennsylvania Congressmen uphold the legality and justice of greenback redemption of the five-twenties? Was it because they spoke for the great manufacturing interests of the Keystone State where Henry C. Carey's preference for a managed, paper currency had gained a following among businessmen? How, indeed, could Massachusetts keep in Congress both a Benjamin F. Butler who stood with Pendleton and a Charles Sumner who opposed all kinds of "repudiation"? Did dependence on support from the trades unions, who as followers of Edward Kellogg preferred greenbacks, account for Butler's position? Sumner's New England backing identified itself: when, during the debate on John Sherman's funding bill (1868), he made his plea for keeping "the public faith" with the bondholders and for contracting the currency. Amos A. Lawrence and other spokesmen of the Boston Associates wrote him instantly in approval,[12] while Edward L. Pierce assured Sumner that the address had guaranteed his re-election to the Senate.[13] Surely this identifies the interest group in New England that opposed the Pendleton plan with such vehemence in the winter and summer of 1868.

State Street in Boston then rivaled Wall Street as a banking center. Together, as the *Boston Evening Transcript* boasted on May 18, 1868, they held from a third to one-half of the "entire banking interest of this Union" and controlled "to a great extent the finances of the country." Wall Street's preference for Grant in 1868 is well known. So is that of Jay Cooke and Company, after assurances had been given in regard to coin redemption of the war debt. August Belmont's reference to the "whole moneyed Interest throughout the Country" that had opposed the Democratic party in 1868 when Horatio Seymour campaigned for the presidency on a platform pledged to the Pendleton Plan, is a striking tribute to the political power exerted by the bankers of Boston, New York, and Philadelphia, and their correspondent banks in the interior.

Attention might well be given to the business connections of the great journals whose editorial views have been relied upon by historians in examining the controversy that was precipitated by the Pendleton plan. Did the mercantile and foreign banking support which the *New York*

[12] Amasa Walker to Charles Sumner, July 13, 1868, Amos A. Lawrence to Sumner, July 18, 1868, Charles Sumner MSS.; *Boston Daily Transcript*, July 14, 1868.

[13] Edward L. Pierce to Sumner, July 31, 1868, Sumner MSS.

Evening Post enjoyed bear any relation to its sturdy opposition to the Ohio "rag baby" in all its forms from 1867 to 1876? Did the manufacturing and Pennsylvania connections of Horace Greeley account for the wavering of the *New York Tribune* on the question of the legality of Pendleton's program in 1868? To what journal or journals did the national banks and American investment bankers in the metropolis look for support? And in like fashion, what were the relationships of the specie resumption, gold redemption Democrats and Republicans of the Northwest to the national banks, the insurance companies, and the mercantile interests of both West and East? To which side did the railroad corporations throw their support? Was the struggle over the mode of redemption of the five-twenties truly sectional? Or was it rather a contest between opposing banking, investing, mercantile, industrial, labor, and agricultural interests that was fought out on intra-sectional as well as inter-sectional lines? The evidence suggests the validity of the second alternative, and with it the inference that the contest over the Pendleton plan, like the contemporary struggle over the war tariff, marked the emergence in the United States of the pressure group politics that is produced by the complex economy of the machine age.

In the continued divergence between the agrarian, business, industrial, and laboring elements whose economic interests were opposed to a policy of post-war deflation, and the investing, banking, and mercantile groups that favored contraction, resumption, and gold redemption of the five-twenties, may be found the key to the persistence with which Ohio politics were agitated by the repeated revival of the Pendleton plan. Though he was crippled by a broken ankle and thus debarred from campaigning, it brought Pendleton within a few thousand votes of the governorship in 1869.[14] It was revived in 1871, as has been seen.[15] In 1875 it furnished the substance of William Allen's "rag baby" which forced Rutherford B. Hayes and his local business backers to their utmost in order to retain control of Ohio for those who supported economic policies conceived initially in the interest of powerful eastern business and financial groups.[16] As the result of this continued agitation, the Pendleton plan's contribution to western Greenbackism was second only to the more elaborate economic philosophy which Edward Kellogg had offered in opposition to the finance capitalism of that day.

[14] *Ohio Platforms*, 34–35; Hinsdale, *Garfield*, I, 482–483, speech by James A. Garfield, Mt. Vernon, Ohio, August 14, 1869; *Cincinnati Daily Gazette*, November 1, 1869.

[15] Cf. *New York Evening Post*, May 23, August 22, 1871.

[16] Reginald Charles McGrane, *William Allen, A Study in Western Democracy* (Columbus, 1925), 233–245.

CHAPTER IV

THE INFLUENCE OF EDWARD KELLOGG UPON AMERICAN RADICALISM, 1865-1896*

THE intensification of industry in old centers, and the shift from work-shop to factory elsewhere, occurred with astonishing abruptness during the Civil War and Reconstruction. Factory hands and clothing workers[1] suffered severely in this period of transition,[2] while inflation and deflation affected skilled and unskilled labor alike.[3] Nor was the stress which this entailed diminished by periodic depression and unemployment. In the country, the effects of the new industrialism, supplemented by deflation and the pressure of Western competition, bore with almost equal weight upon the farmer. In town and country men of small means felt in-creasingly overshadowed. Faced with the progressive loss of that eco-nomic independence which had characterized pre-war democracy, and rendered class conscious by the pressure of economic change, many responded with prolonged resistance to the new industrialism. Not until 1887, with the decline of the Knights of Labor, did the industrial masses accept finally their dependent status. Among the farmers, resistance was continued for another decade until, in 1896, the agrarian movement was crushed in the "Battle of the Standards." In the interim, labor re-formers and agrarian radicals denounced similar evils, supported similar programs, and occasionally co-operated in their efforts to overthrow the new régime.

As elsewhere in the course of the Industrial Revolution, skilled labor inaugurated the movement of resistance. Turning from trade-unionism[4] in 1866, it sought through the National Labor Union[5] to unite all "pro-

---

* Reprinted from the *Journal of Political Economy*, XL (June, 1932), 338-365.

[1] John R. Commons and associates, *A Documentary History of American Industrial Society* (Cleveland: Arthur H. Clark Co., 1910), IX, 72-73.

[2] E. D. Fite, *Social and Industrial Conditions in the North during the Civil War* (New York: Macmillan, 1910), pp. 199-303.

[3] John R. Commons and associates, *History of Labour in the United States* (New York: Macmillan, 1918), II, 110.

[4] A marked revival of trade-unionism had occurred in 1863-1864; cf. Fite, *op. cit.*, pp. 205-209; Commons, *Doc. Hist.*, IX, 23-24, 89, 97, 99, 104, 109; Richard T. Ely, *The Labor Movement in America* (New York, 1905), pp. 62-63.

[5] Trade-unions and other labor organizations founded this organization at a labor con-gress in Baltimore in 1866. Ship-carpenters, machinists, carpenters, glass-cutters, coach-makers, molders, printers, curriers, blacksmiths, and plumbers led in the movement cul-

ducers" against the capitalists.[6] Not unlike similar movements in Europe during the first stage of the Industrial Revolution there, this organization turned at first to co-operative production and consumption as the "sure and lasting remedy for the abuses of the present industrial system."[7] Lacking capital or credit, however, in sufficient quantity to embark upon such a program,[8] labor leaders turned with almost complete unanimity to a panacea offered two decades before by an obscure writer on political economy.

The author, whose name was Edward Kellogg, had risen from a Connecticut farm to affluence and respectability in New York.[9] When at last the head of his own concern, a wholesale dry-goods house on Pearl Street, he was forced to suspend by the panic of 1837. Indignant at the extortions of usurers, who took advantage of the situation, he sought the cause of the calamity in which so many had been involved.[10] Having survived the panic with sufficient means to permit speculation in Milwaukee lots,[11] he became increasingly interested in his philosophical investigations. Finally, he retired from active business and devoted a considerable portion of his time to research.[12] Before this, however, he began in 1841 the publication of a series of pamphlets.[13] These culminated, early in 1849, in a volume entitled: *Labor and Other Capital: The Rights of Each Secured and the Wrongs of Both Eradicated. Or, an exposition of the cause why few are wealthy and many poor, and the delineation of a system, which, without infringing the rights of property, will give to labor its just reward.*[14]

---

minating in this congress. Commons, *Doc. Hist.*, IX, 126–128, 132–133; T. V. Powderly, *Thirty Years of Labor, 1859 to 1889* (Columbus, 1890), pp. 62–63.

[6] Commons, *Doc. Hist.*, IX, 130, 141.

[7] *Ibid.*, p. 138.

[8] Commons, *Hist. of Labour*, II, 112.

[9] Edward Kellogg, *A New Monetary System: the only means of Securing the Respective Rights of Labor and Property, and of Protecting the Public from Financial Revulsions. Revised from his work on "Labor and other Capital" with numerous additions from his manuscripts. To which is prefixed a biographical sketch of the author*, edited by his daughter, Mary Kellogg Putnam (New York, 1875), p. xi.

[10] *Ibid.*, pp. xii–xiii.

[11] John H. Tweedy MSS. (State Historical Society of Wisconsin): Edward Kellogg to John H. Tweedy, New York, November 13, 1849.

[12] Kellogg, *op. cit.*, p. xvii.

[13] *Ibid.*, pp. xiii, xv, xvi–xvii. The first of these, written by a friend at Kellogg's request from facts supplied by the latter, was published in 1841 under the title, *Remarks upon Usury and Its Effects: A National Bank a Remedy; in a Letter, &c.*, by Whitehook. The second appeared in August, 1843, under the title, *Usury: The Evil and the Remedy*, and later, in the same year, with additions, entitled *Currency: The Evil and the Remedy*, by Godek Gardwell. (6th ed.; New York, 1846.)

[14] Published privately. Extracts from the manuscript had previously appeared in Janu-

Postulating the labor theory of value[15] and the then-accepted distinction between productive and non-productive capital,[16] Kellogg called attention to the paradox presented by the rapid accumulation of wealth in the hands of a few.[17]   To him, this phenomenon was unattributable to their productive powers.[18]   It existed in defiance of the fact that "present labor," as distinct from saved labor, "is indispensable to human existence" and consequently deserves a greater reward.[19]   In his search for the cause of this condition, Kellogg developed two interrelated doctrines that profoundly influenced radical thinking of the post-war period.   The first was the legal-tender theory of money.   The second was a theory of interest.

Money, he declared, is the creature of law.   All its distinctive properties are derived from the laws creating it.[20]   These properties, namely, the power to represent value, to measure value, to accumulate value by interest, and to exchange value, may by law be given to any convenient substance.[21]   They become effective through legal-tender powers conferred by law.[22]   Money, therefore, is simply a legalized agent.[23]   Its value depends not upon the material of which it is made.[24]   Nor does the value depend upon the quantity,[25] although a substance limited in quantity, such as gold, enables its owners to extort a high price for its use.[26]   Monetary value depends rather upon the legal power to ac-

---

ary and May, 1848, in Freeman Hunt's *Merchants' Magazine and Commercial Review* (New York), XVIII, 65, 625.

[15] *Labor and Other Capital*, pp. xi, xv, xxii; cf. *Currency: The Evil and the Remedy*, p. 15.

[16] *Labor and Other Capital*, pp. xx–xxii. This distinction, as made here and by contemporary writers such as Proudhon (*What Is Property?   An Inquiry into the Principle of Right and of Government*, trans. Benjamin R. Tucker [Princeton, Mass., 1876], pp. 159, 164, 166–167), is that the tools of production, capital, are unproductive when disassociated from the productive effort of the owner.

[17] *Labor and Other Capital*, p. xviii.

[18] *Ibid.*, p. xx.

[19] *Ibid.*, pp. xxii.

[20] *Ibid.*, p. 42.

[21] *Ibid.*, pp. 42, 73.

[22] *Ibid.*, pp. 68, 72.

[23] *Ibid.*, p. 42.

[24] *Ibid.*, pp. 42, 68–69, 71; cf. *Currency: The Evil and the Remedy*, p. 4: " . . . it derives all its value as a currency from law, and law only, and pebbles or any other material would answer the same purpose as gold and silver, if law could make them a tender for debt, and control the quantity."

[25] *Labor and Other Capital*, pp. 56, 232.

[26] *Ibid.*, p. 66.

cumulate additional value by interest.[27]   The prevailing interest rate fixes the value of the dollar as a medium of exchange.[28]

Thus the power of accumulation by compound interest, which Proudhon ascribed to property as the determinant of its value,[29] was transferred by Kellogg to money, its legal representative.[30]   To Kellogg, as to Proudhon, this accumulative power was the means whereby the "whole surplus earnings" of labor were preempted by the capitalists, and labor reduced to the subsistence level.[31]   Instead, however, of seeing in it the ultimate destruction of capital itself, as Proudhon predicted,[32] Kellogg recognized in interest the all-pervading force which, by fixing rent and the use of all property, determined the reward of labor.[33]   True, "if the interest on money be too high, a few owners of capital will inevitably accumulate the wealth and products of the many."[34]   Yet, if this accumulation could be stopped, farmers and mechanics "could devote the labor now expended in the support of non-producers" to increasing their own comforts and conveniences.[35]   Thus, if excessive interest rates deprive labor of its just reward and divert its savings to the capitalists,[36] and, if accumulation by interest is a necessary function of money delegated to it by law, the evil lies in existing monetary laws and can be remedied only by legislation.[37]   The remedy lies first in determining an interest rate guaranteeing to labor its proper share of production.   This, of necessity, would be no greater than labor's "natural power of production" measured by the per cent annual increase in national wealth.[38] Finally, a new monetary system must be perfected which, by breaking the money monopoly enjoyed by the capitalists, would enforce this interest rate throughout the nation.[39]   Only by means of such a monetary system could "the distribution of products be properly regulated."[40]

[27] *Ibid.*, pp. 56, 58.
[28] *Ibid.*, p. 56.
[29] *What Is Property?* pp. 153, 155.
[30] *Labor and Other Capital*, pp. 40, 42.
[31] *Ibid.*, p. 75; Proudhon, *op. cit.*, p. 216.
[32] *Ibid.*, pp. 215–216.
[33] *Labor and Other Capital*, p. 75.
[34] *Ibid.*, pp. 74, 75–88, 151–154.
[35] *Ibid.*, pp. 88, 102.
[36] *Ibid.*, pp. 75, 90, 95, 155.
[37] *Ibid.*, p. 155.
[38] *Ibid.*, pp. 158–160; cf. *Currency: The Evil and the Remedy*, p. 16.   This Kellogg estimated at from 1 to $1\frac{1}{10}$ per cent (*Labor and Other Capital*, p. 165).
[39] *Labor and Other Capital*, pp. 235, 321.
[40] *Ibid.*, p. 250.

After rejecting the existing bank currency which, as he said, rested on a fictitious basis and supported a money monopoly in Wall Street,[41] Kellogg applied his remedy through a currency system already elaborated by Thomas Mendenhall[42] in 1816 and 1834.[43] As adapted to Kellogg's theory of interest, the plan was as follows. It provided for a paper currency to be issued from a central office with branches in the several states. This currency was to be loaned to individuals, upon real estate security, and at an interest rate uniform throughout the nation. With interest fixed by the government at that rate which would secure to labor and capital their respective rights, and representing actual property in the form of real estate mortgages bearing interest, this currency would possess a uniform value everywhere in the United States. Issued by the central government through the branch loan offices to all who offered good and permanent security, it would free property and labor "from the tyranny . . . exercised over them by the capricious power of money."[44]   Finally, to guard against an overissue, and to guarantee to all money the opportunity to accumulate value by interest, this money could be converted at the will of the holders into government bonds bearing interest slightly lower than that charged on mortgage loans. Such a currency, representing actual property, with its power to accumulate limited by a just rate of interest, would be a perfect and invariable measure of value. Through convertibility into government bonds, and from bonds back into currency, its volume would be flexible,

[41] *Ibid.*, pp. 176–236.

[42] *National Money, or a simple System of Finance; which will fully answer the demands of trade, equalize the value of money, and keep the government out of the hands of stock-jobbers. In Three Letters, Addressed by a Citizen of Washington to the Congress of the United States* (Georgetown, Va., 1816).

[43] *An Entire New Plan For A National Currency: Suited to The Demands of This Great, Improving, Agricultural, Manufacturing & Commercial Republic, With appropriate Introductory and Concluding Remarks, To which is added, A Plan for A Real National Bank* (Philadelphia: J. Rakestraw, 1834).

A plan for a convertible currency, exchangeable with bonds, which aimed to regulate interest rates by the volume of money, may be found in the following work: Thomas Law, *An Address to the Columbia Institute, on a Moneyed System* (Washington, 1828). Although Kellogg may have seen this work, it is unlikely that it influenced him, since its doctrine of interest was so different from his own. Another possible source of the idea of a paper currency convertible into bonds was an article on "Banks and Banking," in the second volume of the *London Encyclopedia* of 1833 (see James Taylor, *American Currency: The Political Issue of the Day* [Chicago, 1876], p. 25). A comparison of Kellogg's chapters on the Safety Fund with Mendenhall's second pamphlet, however, indicates the latter as the probable source of the former's financial proposals.

[44] *Labor and Other Capital*, p. 252.

and always limited to the requirements of business. Legal-tender powers would complete its qualifications as a medium of exchange.[45]

Once put into effect, the result would be a social revolution. As Kellogg said:

Useful productions would probably increase from twenty-five to fifty per cent. Wealth, instead of being accumulated in a few hands, would be distributed among producers. A large proportion of the labor employed in building up cities would be expended in cultivating and beautifying the country. Internal improvements would be made to an extent, and in a perfection unexampled in the history of nations. Agriculture, manufactures, and the arts would flourish in every part of the country. Those who are now non-producers would naturally become producers. Products would be owned by those who performed the labor, because the standard of distribution would nearly conform to the natural rights of man.[46]

This attractive but peaceful revolution would be accompanied by the destruction of the money monopoly,[47] by the elimination of land speculators,[48] of foreign capitalists,[49] and of poverty among producers.[50] Debtors would free themselves from burdensome debts,[51] and the plentiful supply of currency would benefit day laborers fully as much as property owners.[52] All these, together with the assertion that the evils complained of could be remedied only by legislation and political action on the part of farmers and laborers,[53] contained a powerful appeal to the interests and democratic traditions of those classes which were confronted by the rising capitalism of the post-war period. Equally attractive was the statement that these ends could be achieved without any infringement of liberty of contract, private enterprise, and private property in production and business.[54] Thus, in spite of its similarity to the conceptions of Marx and Proudhon, and to the financial proposals of Louis Blanc, Marx and Lasalle,[55] Kelloggism remained essentially American in method and appeal.

Such was the novel, revolutionary philosophy to which the leaders of

[45] *Ibid.*, pp. 250–271. Offices of the Safety Fund could, if desired, be made offices of discount and deposit.
[46] *Ibid.*, p. 165.
[47] *Ibid.*, p. 252.
[48] *Ibid.*, p. 287.
[49] *Ibid.*, p. 281.
[50] *Ibid.*, p. 284.
[51] *Ibid.*, pp. 259–260.
[52] *Ibid.*, p. 259.
[53] *Ibid.*, pp. xxiv, 277, 293–294.
[54] *Ibid.*, pp. xxiv, 292.
[55] For an excellent comparison of Kelloggism with current European philosophies, see Commons, *Doc. Hist.*, IX, 33–41.

the National Labor Union turned in 1867. A new edition of Kellogg's book published in 1861,[56] had been followed by a powerful and widely read[57] pamphlet by Alexander Campbell, published at Chicago in 1864. Entitled *The True American System of Finance*, it appealed to farmers to join with labor in overthrowing the national banking system.[58] After restating Kellogg's legal-tender theory, it proposed to apply his doctrine of interest by adapting his interconvertible-currency scheme to the public debt and greenbacks left by the war. With the currency under the control of the people, and the interest rate lowered to 3 per cent, the estimated rate of national saving, labor would receive its just reward, and the national debt would be liquidated with ease.[59] The work of Campbell—who was later referred to as the "Moses" of the early currency reformers[60]—was supplemented by the activity of men with considerable influence in the labor world. Such were Congressman Andrew J. Kuykendall, of Vienna, Illinois;[61] A. C. Cameron, editor of the *Chicago Workingman's Advocate*,[62] organ of the National Labor Union; William

[56] *A New Monetary System: the only means of securing the respective rights of labor and property, and of protecting the public from financial revulsions. Rev. from his work on "Labor and other capital,"* with numerous additions, ed. Mary Kellogg Putnam (New York, 1861).

[57] See James C. Sylvis, *The Life, Speeches, Labors and Essays of William H. Sylvis, Late President of the Iron-Moulders' International Union; and also of the National Labor Union* (Philadelphia, 1872), p. 371.

[58] A. Campbell, *The True American System of Finance; the Rights of Labor and Capital, and the common sense way of Doing Justice to the Soldiers and their Families. No Banks! Greenbacks The Exlusive Currency* (Chicago, 1864), pp. 16–27. Campbell gave specific credit to Kellogg for all quotations, and general credit for the doctrines and proposals included in this work, stating that they were drawn from the *New Monetary System*, which he declared to be *"the Gospel of Finance."* This he urged all laborers to read (*ibid.*, p. 7 n.).

[59] *Ibid.*, pp. 27–32, 43–44.

[60] Robert Schilling, "History of the People's Party," *Official Souvenir of the National Convention of the People's Party at St. Louis, Mo., July 22, 1896* (Milwaukee, 1896), pp. 5–6. Schilling referred to Kellogg's doctrine of usury and to his book. He called the latter "the Bible of the early currency reformers."

[61] *Congressional Globe, 39* Congress, *2* Session (1866–1867), pp. 318, 576–582. In the address supporting the bill proposed here to establish the interconvertible-currency system, Kuykendall repeats all of Kellogg's distinctive doctrines, pays tribute to Kellogg by name, and draws upon A. Campbell's pamphlet for his illustrations (*ibid.*, pp. 576–582). Both the bill and the speech were widely circulated (Sylvis *op. cit.*, p. 371).

[62] See *The Address of the National Labor Congress to the Workingmen of the United States* (Chicago, 1867), in Commons, *Doc. Hist.*, IX, 148–151. Written by Cameron, chairman of the committee on address appointed by the Baltimore Convention, it repeats the fundamental doctrines of Kelloggism. Cameron was on the committee on political organization of the Chicago congress, which reported the Declaration of Principles embodying the Kellogg system, and a resolution advocating the establishment of a National Labor party to carry it into effect by legislation (*ibid.*, pp. 175, 176–181).

H. Sylvis, of Philadelphia, president of the Iron-Moulders' International Union;[63] and Richard F. Trevellick, of Detroit. Under their guidance the Chicago Labor Congress of August, 1867, embodied in its Declaration of Principles the economic philosophy of Kelloggism. It denounced the national banking system as the parent of all monopolies, and urged the modified monetary system proposed by Alexander Campbell as the indispensable reform without which "co-operation in production and . . . distribution could not succeed." This interconvertible, exclusive, greenback currency, fixing interest at 3 per cent, it named "the true American, or people's monetary system," whereby alone "the natural rights of labor" could be secured and a fair distribution of products consummated.[64]

While independent political action was being considered by member organizations,[65] leaders of the organization sought to accomplish their ends through the old parties. After a bill introduced in Congress by General Samuel F. Cary, of Cincinnati,[66] had failed of success, President Johnson's friends were approached in an attempt to persuade him to stand for re-election upon labor's platform.[67] Later, in July, a special conference of labor leaders met at New York during the Democratic National Convention of 1868. There they pressed the adoption of labor's monetary system upon the platform committee. When it was rejected, they supported the Pendleton plan to liquidate the war debt with greenbacks, and later claimed to have exerted decisive support in getting it written into the Democratic platform.[68] Johnson was again approached early in September. Horace Day, of New York, argued that the "people's monetary system" would relieve the South, restore it to its proper relation to the Union, and "break the backbone" of the Radicals

[63] See articles on money taken from the *Chicago Workingman's Advocate* (Sylvis, *op. cit.* pp. 300–301, 355, 359, 371–372). Sylvis gave specific credit to Kellogg for originating the monetary doctrine and program of the National Labor Union (*ibid.*, p. 371), discussed their dissemination by Campbell and Kuykendall, and quoted from Kellogg in his articles. Speaking of the Chicago platform, he declared: "This document I consider one of the most important ever issued in any age of the world. It is the second Declaration of Independence, and contains the principles upon which must be fought the great battle for the emancipation of labor" (*ibid.*, p. 265). On November 16, 1868, he declared that "*when a just monetary system has been established, there will no longer exist a necessity for trade-unions*" (*ibid.*, pp. 81–82).

[64] Commons, *Doc. Hist.*, IX, 176–181.

[65] *Ibid.*, p. 183: proceedings of the Chicago convention.

[66] *Globe, 40* Congress, *2* Session, pp. 779, 3885.

[67] Andrew Johnson MSS. (Library of Congress), CXLV, 22552: Horace H. Day to President Johnson, New York, September 7, 1868.

[68] *Ibid.* Cf. Commons, *Hist. of Labour*, II, 125–126.

in Congress.[69]   Finally, after the election, John Maguire wrote to President Grant from St. Louis, urging upon him the program of the National Labor Union.[70]

In the interim, the Annual Convention, representing over six hundred thousand organized workers,[71] met in New York City in late September. It resolved upon "the immediate organization of an independent labor party"[72] to accomplish the fulfilment of its program, and reindorsed Kelloggism as the sovereign remedy for labor's ills.[73]   In the following year President William H. Sylvis pushed the organization of the reform party vigorously.   Once its monetary system were put into effect, he urged, there would be no need of trade-unions.   "Such a social revolution as the world has never witnessed" would follow its adoption; "honest industry in every department" would "receive its just reward, and public thieves . . . compelled to make an honest living or starve."[74]   His tour of the South,[75] and speeches made in Congress by General S. F. Cary,[76] Benjamin F. Butler,[77] and J. T. Deveese of Raleigh, North Carolina,[78] marked the high tide of this phase of Kellogg's influence.   New editions of his[79] and Campbell's[80] works were published in 1868.   In the previous year Peter Cooper had been won to the support of the interconvertible-currency system.[81]

The culmination, in 1870–1872, of the movement to organize an inde-

[69] Day to Johnson, *loc. cit.*   See pamphlet inclosed with the same.

[70] Sylvis, *op. cit.*, pp. 86–87.

[71] Commons, *Hist. of Labour*, II, 126.

[72] Commons, *Doc. Hist.*, IX, 204; Powderly, *op. cit.*, pp. 92–93; cf. Letter from William H. Sylvis, quoted by Powderly, *op. cit.*, pp. 78–79.

[73] Commons, *Doc. Hist.*, IX, 206.

[74] Sylvis, *op. cit.*, pp. 86–87, 226–227, 228–229, 330; circular to member organizations of the National Labor Union, Philadelphia, November 16, 1868; cf. Powderly, *op. cit.*, pp. 78–79.

[75] Sylvis, *op. cit.*, pp. 80–82.

[76] *Ibid.*, p. 86.   Cary's speech circulated widely along with his bill in pamphlet form and contained a complete exposition of Kelloggism.   See *The Rights of Labor: Against Land and Money Monopolies; and an Argument in Favor of an American Monetary System. Speech of Hon. Samuel F. Cary, of Ohio, delivered in the House of Representatives, January 5, 1869* (Washington, 1869).   Cary had been supported successfully for re-election to Congress by the National Labor Union (Commons, *Doc. Hist.*, IX, 205).

[77] *Globe, 40* Congress, *3* Session, pp. 303–310; cf. Sylvis, *op. cit.*, p. 86.

[78] *Globe, 40* Congress, *3* Session, Appendix, p. 215.

[79] New York, 1868.   Title the same as that of the second edition.

[80] This appeared under the title, *The True Greenback, or the Way To Pay the National Debt without Taxes and Emancipate Labor.*   See Commons, *Hist. of Labour*, II, 120.

[81] Peter Cooper, *Ideas for a Science of Good Government in Addresses, Letters and Articles on a Strictly National Currency, Tariff and Civil Service* (2d ed.; New York, 1883), p. 10.

pendent labor party, was marked by the withdrawal of the trade-unions from the National Labor Union. Aggressive in these years of prosperity, more interested in collective bargaining than they were in the accomplishment of a revolutionary program, they broke with the organization over the question of political action.[82] This left it controlled by the older leaders, now "primarily political agitators," and by intellectuals, such as Horace Day.[83] In spite of the collapse of the organization, these "labor reformers" succeeded in creating the Labor and Reform party, whose only national convention met at Columbus, Ohio, on February 21, 1872.[84] This body adopted as its own the platform of the National Labor Union —Kelloggism with "improvements"[85]—only to find that it had been made the tool of politicians striving to control the nominations of the major parties.

The labor reformers attempted, also, to win the liberal Republicans over to Kellogg's new monetary system. A letter in the Schurz papers from Horace H. Day of New York City, April 8, 1871, urged the Missouri liberal to champion Kelloggism in the Senate just as he was breaking irrevocably with President Grant. This letter describes the interchangeable bond and currency system that the labor reformers still regarded as indispensable. It indicates more than a little of their sense of power, as well.

There is one fact of deepest import to the people and as we are getting to look to you— as one of the peoples leaders—(parties are failing to meet the popular wants)—I want to [illeg.] it out—The people have their property in Lands & Houses & workshops, and want to pledge their possession of this for money to aid them in their pursuits—*under our present financial system they cannot obtain money upon this their property*, unless at such exorbitant rates as to ruin them—I see an remedy—viz. Let the U. S. issue 1500 millions of 3.65 Bonds. Sell them on the market to the highest bidder and with proceeds pay off the 5.20 bonds. Wipe out all present Banks and allow those who wish to do lending of money to the people—to receive from the government its certificates of Indebtedness Corresponding with Bank of England notes. Then 3.65 bonds payable Principal and Interest in gold, & free from Taxation and at all *times convertible into bonds or notes*— . . . .

The nation looks in vain for a great Statesman bold enough to defy the money power, and speak for the people and propose a remedy. Plant yourself right here, *bring in a Bill now*, make a short speech which can be published in all the press of the country and we will put you on the course for President in 1872. . . .

I am a Labor Union man and have something to say & much to do.

---

[82] Schilling, *op. cit.*, p. 7; Commons, *Hist. of Labour*, II, 151–153.

[83] Commons, *Hist. of Labour*, II, 153.

[84] *Ibid.*, pp. 154–155.

[85] Ellis B. Usher, *The Greenback Movement of 1875–1884 and Wisconsin's Part in It* (Milwaukee, 1911), p. 11; Edward Stanwood, *A History of the Presidency from 1788 to 1897* (Boston, 1924), I, 336.

The next year, after Judge David Davis was nominated for President at the Labor and Reform Convention, the labor reformers sent a delegation to push his candidacy at the Liberal Republican convention in Cincinnati on May 1. Although the Davis delegates were manipulated in the interest of Horace Greeley, another attempt was made during the Convention to win Carl Schurz to the financial program desired by organized labor. As Permanent Chairman, his conversion to the "American System of Finance," which O. H. Pollock of New York urged him to adopt, might have influenced the platform committee. In any case, it should be observed that, in the final stampede of delegates to Greeley, the Davis following voted for the "White Hat," whose friendship to trades unions and co-operation made him a far more congenial candidate for labor support than either Lyman Trumbull or Charles Francis Adams, whom the mercantile middle class tariff reformers desired.

After the panic of 1873 Kelloggism revived in popularity in labor ranks. The industrial congresses of 1873 and 1874 adopted in revised form the declaration of principles of the defunct National Labor Union, in spite of opposition to the monetary plank made by a few trade-unionists.[86] The "preamble" adopted by the second of these congresses became, in 1878, after some modification, the "preamble" of the Knights of Labor.[87] In the latter, however, the interconvertible feature was dropped. There the demand was simply for a legal-tender national currency, issued by the government direct to the people.[88]

In the meantime, seed sown by the labor reformers had taken root in the country.[89] An early interest in Kelloggism had been evidenced by the antimonopoly associations of Illinois, owing to the influence of Alexander Campbell.[90] This was revived in the second annual meeting of the Illinois State Farmers' Association, the "most radical and aggres-

[86] Schilling, op. cit., pp. 7–9; cf. Commons, Hist. of Labour, II, 161; Usher, op. cit., p. 9; Powderly, op. cit., pp. 119–120.

[87] Schilling, op. cit., p. 10; cf. Powderly, op. cit., pp. 396–397: "Those who read the platforms of the National Labor Union and the Industrial Brotherhoods will find that the men who attended the conventions of these associations considered the currency question the most important of all that came up for consideration."

[88] Powderly, op. cit., p. 367. Of this, Powderly said: "No other section of the preamble has attracted less attention than that, and none other is more important to the people" (ibid., p. 398).

[89] Schilling, op. cit., p. 9.

[90] Both the state and the Eden Auxiliary Anti-monopoly associations were represented in the Chicago Congress of the National Labor Union in 1867. Alexander Campbell was one of the delegates. To these should be added, perhaps, two Land and Labor Reform leagues from Grand Rapids. The delegate from one of them, William A. Berkey, later wrote a book based upon Kellogg's ideas (Commons, Doc. Hist., IX, 170, 175).

sive" of agricultural organizations formed during the Granger movement.[91] There the National Labor Union's monetary system was presented in a paper sent by Horace H. Day, of New York.[92] M. M. Hoon-
toon, of Centralia, a vice-president of the Association, presented Alexander Campbell's views,[93] while a member from Jo Daviess County urged
the adoption of Kellogg's land-loan plan as a means of freeing the producing classes from "vassalage to the money power."[94] The inter-
convertible-bond and currency scheme was included in the platform.[95]
A year later, at the third annual convention, after an independent political movement sponsored by the Association had gained seventy-five
thousand votes in Illinois,[96] Kelloggism was again presented to the
Association, this time by Richard F. Trevellick, former president of the
National Labor Union,[97] and by A. O. Grigsby of Piatt County.[98] The
platform again supported the interconvertible-currency system. It also
endorsed the coming independent political reform convention at Cleveland, to meet on March 11, 1875, to which it sent delegates.[99] A year
later the Illinois reform party merged with the Independent or Greenback
party at Indianapolis in May, 1876.[100] In these years the farmers'
party of Indiana had also adopted "greenbackism." It had taken the
initiative in the organization of the Greenback party on a national
scale.[101] The invitation extended to labor reformers—A. C. Cameron,
Richard F. Trevellick, H. W. Wright, and Horace H. Day—to attend
the first national conference at Indianapolis on August 12, 1874, indicates the recognition of the existence of an identity in principle between
agrarian and labor radicals.[102] For this their common support of Kelloggism must have been in part responsible.

[91] Schilling, op. cit., p. 9.
[92] Proceedings of the Second Annual Meeting of the Illinois State Farmers' Association
Held at Decatur, Dec. 16, 17 & 18 . . . . (Chicago, 1874), pp. 44–55.
[93] Ibid., pp. 86–95.
[94] Ibid., pp. 59–67.
[95] Ibid., pp. 101, 109.
[96] Illinois Blue Book, 1899 (Springfield, 1899), p. 264. Cf. Solon J. Buck, The Granger
Movement (Cambridge, 1913), p. 96; Proceedings of the Third Annual Meeting of the Illinois
State Farmers' Association Held at Springfield, January 19, 20, and 21, 1875 (Chicago, 1875),
p. 7.
[97] Proceedings, etc., p. 56.
[98] Ibid., pp. 50–56.
[99] Ibid., p. 57.
[100] Commons, Hist. of Labour, II, 170. At this convention S. M. Smith of the Illinois
State Farmers' Association was acting chairman (Buck, op. cit., pp. 98, 101–102).
[101] Ibid.; Commons, Hist. of Labour, p. 168.
[102] Ibid.; Schilling, op. cit., pp. 10–11.

In these years Kelloggism spread rapidly. In the East, Horace Greeley and the *New York Tribune* had come to support the interconvertible currency.[103] H. C. Carey, of Philadelphia;[104] William D. ("Pig-Iron") Kelley;[105] and Francis W. Hughes, leader of the Pennsylvania democracy,[106] also accepted it. Pamphlets appeared at widely scattered points propagating Kellogg's legal-tender theory and advocating the interconvertible currency system. A few added his land-loan plan.[107]

THE CURSE OF THIS COUNTRY

Important among the former were Joseph Root's *Catechism of Money*, of Wyandotte, Kansas;[108] Jesse P. Alexander's *Money for All*, of Kansas

---

[103] *Proceedings of the Second Annual Meeting of the Illinois State Farmers' Association*, p. 47. Paper presented by Horace H. Day of New York. Cf. *New York Tribune*, November 9, 1871.

[104] H. C. Carey, *Currency Inflation: How it has been produced and how it may profitably be reduced. Letters to the Hon. R. H. Bristow, Secretary of the Treasury;* . . . . (Philadelphia, 1874), p. 15.

[105] *Ibid.*, p. 15; William D. Kelley, *Money and National Finances: An Address Delivered by Request of Citizens of Philadelphia,* . . . *January 15, 1876* (Philadelphia, 1876).

[106] William A. Berkey, *The Monetary Question: The Legal Tender Paper Monetary System of the United States* . . . (Grand Rapids, Mich., 1876), pp. 263–264. Quoting address delivered by Fr. W. Hughes at Scranton, Pa., October, 1875.

[107] R. C. Wolcott, *Solution of the Money Question* (New York, 1875), pp. 23–24. The *New York Advocate*, published by Peter Cooper, also supported this. See C. F. Sherman, *How I Become a Greenbacker* (Milwaukee, 1882), pp. 19–20.

[108] *Catechism of Money: A Hand-Book On Finance, in the interest of Honest Money for the People of the United States* (Wyandotte, Kan., 1876). For extract from an address by Alex. Campbell, see pp. 213–216.

City, Missouri;[109] William A. Berkey's *Monetary Question*, of Grand Rapids;[110] and R. C. Wolcott's *Solution of the Money Question*, of New York.[111] All repeated the fundamental principles of Kelloggism. The first three paid specific tribute to Kellogg or Alexander Campbell. Also, in 1875, a fourth edition of Kellogg's book appeared.[112]

"Brick" Pomeroy's *Democrat* in Chicago[113] and Cooper's *Advocate* in New York supported the interconvertible system. This had become the leading plank of the Greenback platform and continued as such until 1877.[114] Throughout the preliminary conferences which led to the final organization of the Greenback party, the labor reformers, erstwhile members of the National Labor Union, played a prominent part.[115] The Greenback nominee for vice-president in 1876 was the brilliant General S. F. Cary, early proponent of Kelloggism.[116] In Washington, Congressman Alexander Campbell of Illinois expounded Kellogg's principles of interest, money, labor, and capital, in support of a bill to establish "the American monetary system."[117]

By 1877, approaching specie resumption, falling prices, and growing hostility to the national debt had lent added strength to inflation sentiment. More and more emphasis was placed upon the argument that the stamp of the government and full legal-tender powers were the sources of monetary value. The legal-tender theory had been propagated first by

[109] *Money For All: or the Economic Science of Money, National banknotes retired—Legal tenders the only paper money—prosperity of every industry* (Kansas City, Mo., 1875; 230 pp.). For reference to Kellogg and A. Campbell see p. xiii.

[110] For reference to Kellogg, pp. iv–v; for quotations from Kellogg, pp. 30–31, 37, 39–41, 309–312, 342, 383–384. Berkey was a delegate to the Chicago Congress of the National Labor Union in 1867 (Commons, *Doc. Hist.*, IX, 170, 175).

[111] See n. 107. This short pamphlet of but thirty pages contains no references to Kellogg. The theories of interest and money, however, are obviously derived from his book (*ibid.*, pp. 3, 24).

[112] New York, 1875. Title that of the second and third editions. A biographical sketch of the author written by his daughter, Mary Kellogg Putnam, is attached.

[113] January 1, 1876; May 12, 1877. For a repetition of Kellogg's theory of money and his theory of interest, *ibid.*, February 3, 1877.

[114] *Ibid.*, May 12 and July 7, 1877; *Joliet Morning News* (Joliet, Ill.), October 10, 1877; *Prairie Farmer*, February 21, 1891; L. C. Zachos, *The Political Opinions of Peter Cooper* (New York, 1877); George Easterly, *Proposed Act to Aid in Solving the Labor Question . . .* (Whitewater, Wis., 1878). This demand had been incorporated in the party platform at Indianapolis on May 17, 1876 (Stanwood, *op. cit.*, I, 367–368).

[115] Schilling, *op. cit.*, pp. 10–14; Commons, *Hist. of Labour*, II, 168–170.

[116] Stanwood, *op. cit.*, I, 367; James B. Weaver, *A Call to Action: An Interpretation of the Great Uprising, Its Source and Causes* (Des Moines, 1892), p. 439.

[117] *Congressional Record* (44 Cong., 1st sess.), IV, 739–746: address dated January 29, 1875.

Kellogg and his followers among the post-war radicals. Now the growing strength of "fiat" money sentiment divorced it from his dictum that money must represent actual value.[118] The emphasis now placed upon the relation of the quantity of money to the price level entailed the abandonment of his doctrine that the interest rate determines the value of the currency. This change in monetary theory was evidenced by the dropping of the interconvertible scheme during the winter of 1877–1878.[119] Instead, there appeared a demand for a larger per capita volume of money.

Many turned to Britton H. Hill's *Absolute Money*. This pamphlet, published at St. Louis in 1875, advocated openly a "fiat," irredeemable, legal-tender currency, deriving its value from the sovereign act creating it.[120] The inclusion of Kellogg's doctrine of interest in the platform adopted by the Toledo Convention of February 22, 1878,[121] and the Convention's failure to demand the immediate payment of the national debt precipitated a split in the National party.[122] In the spring and summer that followed, Pomeroy's *Democrat* and *Good as Gold* led the opposition, bitterly attacking General S. F. Cary, the *New York Advocate*, and the "bond advocates" as "trimmers" "and paid agents of an Eastern money power." Pomeroy demanded a flood of "absolute money" with which to pay off the national debt and destroy the national banks.[123] As early as June, 1878, state Greenback conventions substituted "absolute money" and demands for speedy payment of the national debt for the Kellogg planks in the Toledo platform.[124] Before the fall election, the "fiat" wing of the party had definitely gained control. Some conven-

---

[118] *Labor and Other Capital*, pp. 42–50.

[119] Pomeroy formally repudiated the interconvertible-currency scheme in the *Democrat* on July 1 and 8, 1877, because it did not provide for the retirement of the national debt. Cf. Commons, *Hist. of Labour*, II, 241, 244; Appleton, *Annual Cyclopedia and Register of Important Events of the Year 1878* (New York, 1879), p. 807; Cadmus (John C. Zachos), *Our Financial Revolution: An Address to the Merchants and Professional Men of the Country, without Respect to Parties* (New York, 1878), p. 4.

[120] Britton A. Hill, *Absolute Money: A New System of National Finance, under a Cooperative Government* (St. Louis, 1875), pp. iii, v, vi, 46–48, 76. Hill rejected the interconvertible-currency plan (*ibid.*, pp. 50–51). His system was outlined two years earlier in a work entitled *Liberty and Law*.

[121] Appleton, *op. cit.* (1878), p. 807.

[122] *Good as Gold* (Chicago), June 10 and 17, July 15, 1878. For a contrary view see Schilling, *op. cit.*, p. 14.

[123] *Good as Gold*, June 10 and 24, July 1 and 15, 1878.

[124] *Ibid.*, June 17 and 24, 1878; Appleton, *op. cit.* (1878), pp. 682–683, 442, 560, 514, 577, 622–623, 613, 533, referring to the state conventions of Pennsylvania, Indiana, Michigan, Maine, Missouri, New York, New Jersey, Massachusetts, respectively.

tions, however, tried to reconcile Kellogg's doctrine of interest to the new demands,[125] and the Missouri platform added a plank requiring government loans to local governments at 2 per cent to enable them to pay off their indebtedness.[126] Everywhere, seemingly, Kelloggism had given way before the demand for inflation.[127] Naught but his legal-

SWEEP BACK THE RISING TIDE IF YOU CAN

tender theory remained. Even then, B. S. Heath, one-time associate of Pomeroy on the staff of the *Democrat*, and later proprietor of the *Pekin* (Ill.) *Legal Tender*, drew upon Kellogg's legal-tender theory by reference

[125] *Ibid.*, pp. 682–683, 442, conventions of Pennsylvania and Indiana.
[126] *Ibid.*, p. 577.
[127] *Joliet Morning News*, July 9, 1879; Alson J. Streeter Scrapbook, letter from A. J. Streeter to the *Aledo Record*, New Windsor, Ill., January 17, 1878; John S. Bender, *Money, Its Definition and Tests* (Plymouth, Ind., 1879); *National Greenback and Labor Shot and Shell, Original and Selected*, catechism by J. H. Randall, songs by W. S. Lurton (Clyde Ohio, 1878), Cadmus, *op. cit.* n.p.

and quotation in constructing his system of "absolute money." This he elaborated in a work entitled *Labor and Finance Revolution* which went through six editions between 1880 and 1891.[128]

Changing conditions, however, robbed the "Greenback song" of "its ancient charm." Successful resumption was followed by an increase in the volume of currency and by higher prices for agricultural produce. This brought quick collapse to the inflation movement.[129] Although the "fiat" theory of money remained ingrained in the radical philosophy of agrarians and labor reformers, greenbackism was of diminishing importance in the eighties. The radicalism of the "producing" classes, which intended to revise the distribution of wealth and by destroying "non-producers" restore economic independence to farmer and laborer, found refuge in the Knights of Labor or the Alliance movement.

Direct heirs of the labor philosophy of Sylvis, Trevellick, and Cameron,[130] the Knights of Labor undertook the destruction of "wage-slavery." Like the National Labor Union, they first sought to accomplish this by a system of productive and consumptive co-operation.[131] Hampered by lack of credit, however, and still regarding interest as the great oppressor,[132] they turned to Kellogg's proposal that the national government lend legal-tender currency to producers at an interest rate less than the annual rate of increase in national wealth. Already, in 1881, this had been advocated by pamphleteers, one of whom was Richard Trevellick.[133] Another was J. H. Severance, of Milwaukee, who proposed a subtreasury system whereby the government would lend money to the people and accept deposits. By this means, Severance declared, "interest, bonds and the whole speculating power that now owns and runs the government" would be destroyed.[134] Continued in-

---

[128] *Labor and Finance Revolution—Together with a Biography of the Author* (6th ed., Chicago, 1891), pp. xxvii, 54–56, 104–106. Like the *Joliet News*, July 9, 1879, Heath was still interested in the problem of usury and in Kellogg's doctrine of interest (*op. cit.*, pp. 199–201).

[129] *Chicago* (weekly) *Express*, June 14, 1881; Commons, *Hist. of Labour*, II, 248–249.

[130] Commons, *Hist. of Labour*, II, 354.

[131] Powderly, *op cit.*, pp. 458–459, 460. They also sought to free the land from monopolistic control and thus to give "men the chance to become their own employers" (Powderly, quoted by Nathan Fine, *Labor and Farmer Parties in the United States, 1828–1928* [New York, 1928], p. 120).

[132] *Ibid.*; *Knights of Labor* (Chicago), April, 1886; March 12, 1887; *John Swinton's Paper* (New York), April 12 and 26, May 3 and 17, 1885; S. M. Jelley, *The Voice of Labor* (Chicago, 1887), pp. 68–69, 81.

[133] *Money and Panics* (Detroit, 1881), p. 15. See *Chicago Sentinel* (S. F. Norton, proprietor), November 29, 1883, for reference to Louis Bristol of Vineland, N. J.

[134] *A Lecture on the Industrial and Financial Problem* (Milwaukee, 1881), pp. 25–26. This, the author declared, would relieve every indebted western farmer (*ibid.*, p. 26).

terest in Kellogg's philosophy produced a fifth and cheap edition of his book in 1883.[135] Finally, in the General Assembly held at Hamilton, Ontario, on October 5, 1885, the Knights of Labor formally accepted Kellogg's land-loan plan as its own. The petition to Congress, presented in support of this proposal, is a classic expression of Kelloggism, containing Kellogg's theories of value, money, interest, and distribution. It repeated also his belief that the concentration of wealth in the hands of non-producers was due to the "want of proper legislation" fixing a just and invariable rate of interest.[136] This petition was readopted at the Cleveland General Assembly, June 1, 1886. There given to the press,[137] it was indorsed by such farmers' papers as the *Chicago Express*[138] and the *Western Rural*.[139] This land-loan plan had been an issue in the local election in Wayne County (Detroit), Michigan,[140] the previous autumn, and was included in the platform of the independent labor party in Wisconsin in 1886.[141] It was supported by W. D. Vincent, of Clay Center, Kansas,[142] and later by John Davis, well-known Knight of Labor from the same state.[143]

While the Knights of Labor experienced an abrupt decline after their venture into politics in 1886, agrarian radicalism revived and flowered luxuriantly. Child of agricultural depression and farm-mortgage indebtedness, the Alliance movement turned to the philosophy which taught that "usury" and "money monopoly" were fundamentally responsible for trusts and millionaires. Perhaps the first agrarian advo-

---

[135] Edward Kellogg, *Labor and Capital: A New Monetary System . . . Lovell's Library*, III, No. 3 (May 15, 1883).

[136] Quoted in full in *Labor: Its Rights and Wrongs . . .* (Washington, D. C., 1886), pp. 217–220.

[137] *Ibid.*, p. 217.

[138] June 12, 1886.

[139] XXIV (Chicago, July 3, 1886), 424.

[140] J. H. Eakins, *Address to Knights of Labor and the Producing and Distributing Classes* (Detroit, October, 1885), pp. 2–4. The author, a member of the Knights of Labor, was candidate for sheriff on the Greenback ticket.

[141] Commons, *Hist. of Labour*, II, 462; see also the second of the three resolutions offered by the Knights of Labor to the resolutions committee of the St. Louis Industrial Conference, February 24, 1892 (*Chicago Tribune*, February 24, 1892).

[142] Jelley, *op. cit.*, pp. 64–85.

[143] *The National Economist*, IV (Washington, D. C., December 27, 1890), 238. Earlier, in 1886, Mr. Davis was opposed to the land-loan plan. See article by him on "Finance" in the *Weekly Labor Bulletin* (Decatur, Ill.), August 26, 1886.

This demand for land loans at low interest rates gives added meaning to the fourteenth plank of the "Preamble" which reads: "The establishment of a National monetary system, in which a circulating medium in necessary quantity shall issue direct to the people, without the intervention of banks . . . " (*Knights of Labor* [March, 1886]).

cates of the revived Kelloggism were the leaders of the expiring greenback movement. Of these, Colonel S. F. Norton, editor and proprietor of the *Chicago Sentinel*, was outstanding.[144]   On November 29, 1883, the *Sentinel* reversed its previous position and came out flatly for the land-loan plan.   In the same number Norton offered the cheap edition of Kellogg's book as a premium for a year's subscription.   The comment accompanying the offer is illuminating.

LABOR AND CAPITAL

This is the well-known work of Edward Kellogg. It is indeed another most remarkable book. A few years ago it could not be obtained for less than $1.50 per volume. It is quite as well known by the title of "Kellogg on Finance" as by that of "Labor and Capital." It always has been and still is a standard work among Greenbackers. . . .

"Usury," "Old Shylock," and the national banking system received their due share of attention in the *Sentinel*,[145] while Norton maintained that government loans to farmers would ultimately wipe out rural indebtedness and abolish usury.[146]   He declared, "unless this is *done* our boasted Republic is a ruin; our freemen are paupers, our farmers mere tenants."[147]

Late in 1885 B. S. Heath followed suit in the *Chicago Express*,[148] and gathered signatures to a petition to Congress in support of the land-loan plan.[149]   At the same time he carried an advertisement of Kellogg's work, recommending that it be "read by all, regardless of class."[150]   In his columns he preached the labor theory of value and emphasized the dangers arising from the accumulative power of interest.[151]   On September 18, 1886, the *Express* published a series of plans advocating government loans to the people on landed security.   The first of these was "Edward Kellogg's Plan," of which the rest, offered by the *Irish World*, Peter Cooper, O. A. McGuinn, Leonard Brown, Charles Sears, and B. S. Heath, were but adaptations.   Before this the *Iowa Tribune* had come to support the land-loan plan.[152]   At this time, also, Rev. D. Oglesby, of Richview, Illinois, began his career as a serialist.   Articles of his sup-

---

[144] Norton's *Sentinel* was the best Greenback paper in the country, according to the *Sunday Gazette* of Washington, D. C. (extract in the *Sentinel*, March 27, 1884).

[145] *Ibid.*, November 29, December 27, 1883; January 24, May 29, 1884.

[146] *Ibid.*, November 29, 1883; May 15, September 11, 1884.

[147] *Ibid.*, October 30, 1884. In the number of April 17, 1884, Norton quoted a long extract from Kellogg's *Labor and Capital* in support of his argument for a legal-tender irredeemable paper currency.

[148] December 5, 1885.

[149] *Ibid.*, December 5, 1885; January 9 and 16, 1886.

[150] *Ibid.*, December 26, 1885; February 20, 1886.

[151] *Ibid.*, January 9, March 13, 1886.

[152] Extract published in the *Express*, May 22, 1886.

porting the plan appeared in the *Express* in 1886,[153] and later in the *American Nonconformist* of Winfield, Kansas.[154] In Kansas, by 1888, the idea of government loans to the people was widely held.[155] Previously, in 1886, the Farmers' and Laborers' Co-operative Union of America had placed this demand in the first plank of its platform.[156] In 1888, the Union Labor party, whose first national chairman had been B. S. Heath, included it in the "money" plank of its platform as an essential portion of "a national monetary system in the interest of the producer."[157] Scores of letters in support of the land-loan plan were published in the *Farmers' Voice*, an outstanding advocate, and in the *Western Rural*,[158] *National Economist*,[159] and *Prairie Farmer*[160] as well. Such were those from Norman Cowdoin, of Chester, Nebraska,[161] and others written by J. Burrows, of Filley, Nebraska, president of the National Farmers' Alliance in 1889–1890.[162]

Finally, at the annual convention of the National Farmers' Alliance meeting at Des Moines, Iowa, January 10–11, 1889, a memorial to Congress in behalf of the land-loan plan was adopted. In it we find Kellogg's doctrine that the interest rate determines the distribution of wealth offered as the fundamental principle justifying the proposal.[163] The source of this theory of interest is fully revealed in an article published in the *National Economist* by J. Burrows, the president, in refuta-

[153] *Ibid.*, beginning with February 27, 1886.

[154] *American Nonconformist and Kansas Industrial Liberator*, January 26, 1888. See extract quoted by Raymond C. Miller, *The Populist Party in Kansas* (Ph.D. dissertation, typewritten, University of Chicago, June, 1928), p. 149.

[155] *Ibid.*, pp. 149–150.

[156] *Chicago Express*, June 17, 1886: letter from G. Campbell, Mound City, Kan.

[157] *Ibid.*, April 25, 1891; *Western Rural*, XXVI (July 21, 1888), 457; Stanwood, *op. cit.*, I, 461–462. The text in the latter should read "and loaned" instead of "or loaned." For the place held by the land-loan plan in the reform program advocated by A. J. Streeter, candidate of the party for president, see letter dated April 30, 1888, to the *Farmers' Voice*, May 12, 1888. Cf. Letter from "Union Labor," Walnut, Crawford Co., Kan. (*ibid.*, July 7, 1888).

[158] XXV (January 29, 1887), 69: letter from a committee of the Farmers' Alliance of Lowry City, St. Clair Co., Mo.; XVII (September 7, 1889), 569.

[159] I (June 29, 1889), 329, W. Hunt of Ancora, N. J., on "The Impending Crisis"; II (November 23, 1889), 159, Clark Orvis, "The Basis of Union"; II (January 11, 1890), 293, extract from the *Butler* (Mo.) *Local News*; II (February 1, 1890), 315, extract from the *Indianapolis Leader*.

[160] August 2, 1890.

[161] *Farmers' Voice*, June 9, July 21, 1888; April 2 and 20, 1889.

[162] *Ibid.*, February 4, October 13, 1888; July 13, September 7, 1889.

[163] *National Economist*, I (March 14, 1889), 10; *Western Rural*, XXVII (April 6, 1889), 217; N. B. Ashby, *The Riddle of the Sphinx* (Des Moines, 1890), pp. 316–322.

tion of the theories of Henry George.[164] Entitled "Which Is the Controlling Factor, Interest or Rent?" it refers the reader thrice to Kellogg's *Labor and Capital* (Lovell Library), which it urges all to read. From the latter the argument is obviously drawn.

The land-loan plan remained the chief reform sought by the northern alliance until after the organization of the Populist party. The interest rate of 2 per cent on government loans, together with the maximum rate of 3½ per cent on other loans, which it advocated, were to be fixed according to Kellogg's principle of the average rate of increase in national wealth.[165] This plan was indorsed by the National Grange[166] and by the Farmers' Mutual Benefit Association.[167] Bills to enact it into law were introduced in the Senate by Leland Stanford[168] and S. M. Cullom,[169] the latter acting on petition from the Farmers' Alliance of Illinois.[170]

In the meantime, Dr. Macune, president of the Farmers' National Alliance and Co-operative Union, was working out his own solution of the money problem. In the *National Economist*, which he edited, successive editorials appeared on the accumulative power of interest and on the power of money through interest to enslave.[171] These were followed by an extract from Kellogg's book which predicted that his monetary system would make the United States economically independent.[172] Then,

[164] I (April 27, 1889), 90–92.

[165] *Proceedings of the National Farmers' Alliance at Its Eleventh Annual Meeting, Held at Omaha, Nebraska, January 27, 28, and 29, '91* (Des Moines, 1891),n.p .; *Chicago Express*, September 5, 1891, extract from the *Alliance Farmer* (Lincoln, Neb.).

[166] Ashby, *op. cit.*, p. 322; *Prairie Farmer*, March 29, 1890; letter from Mortimer Whitehead, national lecturer, Patrons of Husbandry, *Western Rural*, XXIX (July 18, 1891), 467.

[167] *Joliet Daily News*, November 21, 1890; *Western Rural*, XXVIII (May 10, 1890), 293. The land-loan plan was supported by the *Ord* (Neb.) *Independent* (*Knights of Labor*, January 17, 1891), the *St. Louis Monitor* (*National Economist*, VI [December 5, 1891], 190), and advocated in letters received from Amherst, Wis., Kansas City, Mo.; Mound City, Kan. (*Farmers' Voice*, November 22, 1890; April 18, July 28, 1891); Texas; Williamsburg, Mich. (*Chicago Express*, April 4, December 19, 1890); and Yankton Co., S.D. (*Western Rural*, XXII, 331).

[168] *National Economist*, II (March 15, 1890), 408. Of Stanford's bill the *Economist* said: "The proposition itself is not original. . . . There is not an original idea either in the preamble, the resolution, or the explanation given. Each and every one has been placed before the American people hundreds and thousands of times . . . during the past fifteen years. It is simply the old doctrine of Peter Cooper modernized."

[169] *Ibid.*

[170] *Congressional Record*, 51st Cong., 1st Sess., pp. 2328, 2875, 4228; *Weekly Illinois State Journal* (Springfield), April 24, 1890. A third bill to establish the land-loan plan was introduced in the House of Representatives by Congressman Featherstone of Arkansas (see *Chicago Express*, April 11, 1891).

[171] I (June–August, 1889), 167, 188–189, 211, 344.

[172] *Ibid.*, II (September 28, 1889), 24.

after a discussion of the interest burden of the South, Macune proposed government loans on crops as well as farms.[173] Viewed from this background, the subtreasury plan offered a few weeks later to the St. Louis convention of the National Farmers' Alliance and Industrial Union in December, 1889,[174] seems little more than an adaptation of the principles behind the land-loan plan to the peculiar needs of the South. The merging of the crop and land-loan plans in the Ocala platform of December 7, 1890,[175] strengthens this inference.[176]

In the *Mississippi Valley Historical Review* for September, 1944, Professor James C. Malin suggests that the origin of the subtreasury plan may be found in certain French and Russian experiments in agricultural finance. Then, on the basis of a presumption in favor of these sources, established by C. W. Macune's report to the St. Louis Convention of December 3–7, 1889, Mr. Malin urges disciples of the Turner school to re-examine the possibilities of a genetic approach to American agricultural history in terms of European precedents. Macune's probable indebtedness to the French revolutionary policy of making loans on farm produce in 1848 can hardly be denied in the face of his reference to this in the report. There is certainly a possibility that he was familiar with the Russian plan of 1888 to provide warehouses and crop loans at low rates to the peasants. This should not, however, preclude the possibility of a domestic origin as well.

Failure to examine the *National Economist* has led Professor Malin to overlook Macune's preoccupation with Kellogg's theory of interest in the summer and autumn of 1889. Macune then argued that the peculiar interest problem of southern farmers made it necessary for them to secure

[173] *Ibid.*, II (October 5, 1889), 39; *ibid.* (October 19, 1889), p. 82.

[174] *Ibid.*, II (December 21, 28, 1889), 216, 226–227. "The sub-treasury plan is the fullest recognition of the economic truth, that labor creates all wealth, ever proposed in a legislative body" (*ibid.*, III [June 7, 1890], 182).

[175] *Ibid.*, IV (December 20, 1890), 216.

[176] *Farmers' Voice*, January 18, 1890. Here John S. Maiben, in a letter to the editor, notices the indebtedness of the sub-treasury plan to Kelloggism:

"Let any one read the outcome of the late Farmers' Alliance at St. Louis, and they will see that the main trouble with the farmer is, not how to raise corn, but how can we find a market for it after it is raised. And strange to say, the logic of Edward Kellogg has been most emphatically endorsed.

"More money at a low rate of interest. . . . God grant the time is not far distant, when we will be so enlightened that usury will be utterly abolished and those vampire [*sic*] of our monetary system, the National Banks will be scorched out of existence never able again to fasten themselves as leeches on the body politic."

For a similar analysis of the Ocala subtreasury plank see *ibid.*, April 18, 1891; letter from George C. Ward, Kansas City, Mo.

loans on crops if government credit facilities in aid of agriculture were to have the desired effect in the cotton belt. Furthermore, Macune intended to unite the southern alliance with the National Farmers Alliance, which had already endorsed the land-loan plan with acknowledged indebtedness to Kellogg. This made it imperative for Macune to pave the way for the subtreasury plan in advance of the St. Louis conference by an appeal to doctrines that the midwestern farmers had already accepted. Ideologically, therefore, Macune clearly was justifying the subtreasury in advance in terms of Kelloggism, whatever may have been the alien sources of the crop loan, warehouse scheme. This would suggest, then, the value of a genetic approach to agricultural history in terms of the American past in addition to possible borrowing from Europe, in the search for the origins of basic concepts and remedial proposals that have been featured by agrarian movements in the United States. Finally, a government subtreasury system to lend money direct to the people and free them from dependence on the money power had been proposed eight years earlier in Milwaukee by J. H. Severance, to whom reference has been made above.

Kellogg's influence upon the agrarian movement seems not to have diminished in the years 1889–1892. Aside from the continued circulation of books written by Berkey,[177] B. S. Heath,[178] and Freeman O. Willey,[179] radical papers and new pamphlets continued to disseminate his doctrines. Of the former, the *Farmer's Voice*, the *Chicago Sentinel*,[180] the *Chicago Express*,[181] and the *Alliance* of Lincoln, Nebraska,[182] at least were under his direct influence. The *Voice*, claiming one hundred thousand weekly circulation before Lester C. Hubbard's dismissal in 1892, was an early advocate of a new third party.[183] Its conception of

---

[177] *The Money Question*. For citations of this work during these years see Mrs. Marion Todd, *Pizarro and John Sherman* (Chicago, 1891), pp. 28–29; *Western Rural*, XXXII (January 4, 1894), 36; Gordon Clarke, ed. *Historical Political and Statistical Handbook of Money* (Alexandria, Va., 1896), pp. 39, 53–54; *Chicago Express*, June 27, 1891.

[178] *Labor and Finance Revolution*. The sixth edition of this work, of which there were two printings, was published in 1891.

[179] *Whither Are We Drifting as a Nation? and The New Era in Republican Government* (St. Louis, 1891). Originally published in separate volumes in 1882 and 1883, respectively, each advocated the land-loan plan and restated Kellogg's theory of interest.

[180] *Chicago Express*, January 6, 1892, extract from the *Sentinel*.

[181] *Express*, June 20, 1891. This paper was now owned by Colonel Norton.

[182] *Farmers' Voice*, September 19, December 13, 1891. The *Alliance* was edited by J. Burrows, whose indebtedness to Kellogg has been noticed above.

[183] *Farmers' Voice*, March 22, 1890; March 29, 1890; letter from H. L. Loucks to L. C. Hubbard, Clear Lake, S. D.; May 24, 1890; letter from J. Burrows; *ibid.*, letter from Loucks.

the significance of Kellogg's book was displayed not only in an editorial review,[184] but also by the publication of a long series of column extracts from this work.[185] These were entitled "Political Economy. Financial Science. Extracts from Labor and Capital, by Edward Kellogg."

Of the early Populist pamphlets, the most widely circulated, perhaps, was Colonel S. F. Norton's *Ten Men of Money Island*. Written by a famous greenbacker, whose paper had early championed the revived Kelloggism of the eighties,[186] and who was credited "with having given the Populists their creed" as "the author" of their "financial plank,"[187] the pamphlet itself cited Kellogg as an authority, and apparently drew its inspiration from a chapter of his book.[188]

Jesse Harper, another populist from the greenback "fringe," drew upon Kellogg's monetary theory, and adopted his doctrine of interest as the distributor of wealth.[189] In an article on "The Heroes of Our Thirty Years' War," the *Chicago Sentinel* placed Edward Kellogg at the head of the "strong money-reform writers" of the radical movement.[190] W. A. Peffer, noted Alliance and Populist senator from Kansas, laid down Kellogg's doctrine of interest as a fundamental Populist demand,[191] a contention which a cursory examination of the literature of the period

[184] February 16, 1889:

"We cannot condense Mr. Kellogg's masterly arguments into a brief notice of the work. He would have Government issue all legal tender money and loan the same at a low and uniform rate of interest to the people . . . taking as security productive land that would promptly . . . sell for double the amount loaned.

"This, and the limitation within reasonable bounds of the amount of land which corporations or individuals may own, would, without doubt, save America from the dangers that otherwise threaten to overwhelm us."

[185] *Ibid.*, February 16, 1889—January 4, 1890.

[186] See above, p. 68.

[187] *Chicago Times-Herald*, cited in *Joliet Daily News*, July 28, 1896.

[188] *Ten Men of Money Island* (rev. ed.; Girard, Kan., 1902), p. 32; *Labor and Other Capital*, Part II, chap. ii.

[189] "The Origin of Money and Its Uses"; letter to Hon. S. D. Noe, Danville, Ill., August 11, 1890; article written for the *Chicago Sentinel*; in A. C. Barton, *Life of Col. Jesse Harper of Danville, Illinois* (Chicago, 1904), pp. 260, 172, 205, respectively.

[190] Extract quoted in *Chicago Express*, June 27, 1891.

[191] Namely, that the rapid transfer of wealth from producers to non-producers could be stopped only by a reduction of the interest rate "to the level of average net profits in productive industries." See W. A. Peffer, "The Mission of the Populist Party," *North American Review*, CLVII (New York, December, 1893), 666, 673–674, 674–675; H. E. Taubeneck Scrapbook, W. A. Peffer to J. D. Holden, Topeka, Kan., July 27, 1895. Senator Peffer was an ardent advocate of the land-loan plan, and introduced a bill in the Senate to establish it (*Vanguard*, June 11, 1892). Colonel S. F. Norton (*Express*, September 5, 1891), John Davis, congressman from Kansas (*ibid.*, February 22, 1896), and others supported Peffer's theory of interest.

substantiates.[192]   B. G. Bernardi, anarchist, found it necessary to attack Kellogg's proposals before agitating the principles of the labor exchange,[193] while Thomas E. Hill, of Prospect Park, Illinois, felt constrained to deny any indebtedness to Kellogg for his own Hill Banking System.[194]   Finally, *Our Money Wars*, written by Samuel Leavitt, formerly managing editor of Peter Cooper's *New York Advocate*, and attached successively to the editorial staffs of the *Irish World*, the *Chicago Sentinel*, and the *Joliet Daily News*,[195] hailed Kellogg as the originator of the "American system of money," and his book as "a text-book and guide for labor and currency reformers ever since."[196]

The first manifesto[197] published by the national committee appointed at Cincinnati on May 21, 1891, demonstrates conclusively the influence of Kelloggism on the Populist program and philosophy.   After a long arraignment of the nation's ills,[198] this document concluded that their fundamental cause lay in the existing monetary system.   The remedy advocated was government loans "on approved security" to the people at 2 per cent per annum.   With a self-regulating currency "equal to first mortgages on real estate" that no clique could control, and with the interest rate lowered to the proper level by government credit operations,

---

[192] Letters in the *Farmers' Voice*, May 3, 1888; June 15, 1889; July 18, 1891; January 6, June 23, July 21, 1894; October 26, 1895; editorials, *ibid.*, February 23, April 6, 1889; *Western Rural*, XXIX (August 15, 1891), 524; *Vanguard*, October 22, 1892, "Usury is the tap-root, the essence, the soul of oppression.   It is the great central pillar upon which capital stands. It is the father and mother of all monopolies."   *American Federationist*, II (Indianapolis, August, 1895), 107, editorial; *Age of Labor* (Chicago, July 1, 1892).

[193] *Trials and Triumphs of Labor.   The Text Book of the Labor Exchange* (Independence, Mo., 1895), p. 121.

[194] *Farmers' Voice*, October 10, 1891.   The Hill Banking System found considerable support in the early years of the Populist movement.   The *Farmers' Voice* (March 21, 1891); the *Vanguard* (*ibid.*, June 4, 1892; cf. Lloyd MSS. (Madison), A. P. Stevens to Lloyd, Chicago, January 13, 1894; the Henning (Minn.) *Advocate* (Stevens to Lloyd, *loc. cit.*; *American Nonconformist*, January 28, 1892, Frank Hoskins, Henning, Minn., to the editor); L. C. Hubbard (*The Coming Climax in the Destinies of America* [Chicago, 1891]); and Mrs. Marion Todd (*op. cit.*) were all advocates of the Hill Banking System.   For its provisions see L. H. Weller MSS. (State Historical Society of Wisconsin), Thomas E. Hill to Weller, Prospect Park, Ill., April 8, 1891; Thomas E. Hill, *Money Found: Recovered from Its Hiding Places, and Put into Circulation through Confidence in Government Banks* (rev. ed.; Chicago, 1894); *Farmers' Voice*, March 14, 1891.

[195] Lloyd MSS. (Madison), circular and newspaper clipping attached to letter from Leavitt to Lloyd, July 3, 1896.   The clipping, probably taken from the *Joliet Daily News*, called *Our Money Wars* the standard Populist authority on the money question.

[196] *Our Money Wars: The Example and Warning of American Finance* (Boston, 1896; 1st ed., 1894), Preface and p. 73.

[197] *Chicago Express*, July 25, 1891; *Western Rural*, XXIX (August 15, 1891), 521.

[198] These included agricultural indebtedness, fear of rural serfdom, and the dominance of British capital in the United States.

"unproductive capital would never draw a greater increase than two
per cent. . . . " The "money now exacted as unjust usury would remain
in the hands of producers and foreign capitalists being unable to compete
with the people represented in the government would be driven from the

Designed and Engraved expressly for "The Farmers' Voice."

THE EASTERN MASTER AND HIS WESTERN SLAVES

country, and industrial independence thus secured." In Kelloggism,
therefore, lay the solution of that problem presented by the monetary
system which "the People's Party" considered "the most pressing reform."[199]

[199] *Ibid.* See also *Express*, January 17, May 9, 1891; Leavitt, *op. cit.*, pp. 306–307;
Miller, *op. cit.*, pp. 160–161; *St. Louis Monitor*, quoted in *National Economist*, VI (December 5, 1891), 190; *Farmers' Voice*, June 27, 1891.

In view of the fact that the leaders of the party organized at Cincinnati controlled the succeeding conferences held at Indianapolis[200] and St. Louis,[201] and since the financial plank of the Omaha platform[202] was taken bodily from that adopted at the St. Louis Industrial Conference,[203] it is difficult to avoid the conclusion that Kelloggism continued as an essential ingredient of Populism.   So important, in fact, was the financial plank in Populist eyes, that many proposed it as a one-plank platform for 1892.[204]   Nor is it without significance that old Alexander Campbell, "the Moses" and interpreter of Kelloggism to the West in the sixties and seventies, was wildly cheered by the Omaha convention when he was introduced by Colonel S. F. Norton.[205]   Four years later, when Populism met under the cloud of free silver at St. Louis, the "middle-of-the-road" contingent included the modified Kelloggism of the Omaha platform in their financial proposals.[206]

Enough has been said to indicate the continued influence of Kelloggism upon that defensive movement of "producers" which resisted for three decades the industrialization of America and sought by monetary experiments to counteract the falling price level of the post-war era. Essentially a "producers' " philosophy, with its emphasis upon the labor theory of value and its distinction between producing and non-producing capital, it gives meaning and unity to otherwise disconnected elements of radical thought observable in the literature of the period.   Repeated references to an unfair distribution of wealth, to the labor theory of value,[207] and to "producing" and "non-producing" classes suggest of themselves the presence of an economic radicalism fundamentally hostile to the industrial world.   So, likewise, do the prolonged attack upon the national banking system and the extravagance with which "Usury," "Shylock," and "Millionaires" were assailed.   In Kellogg's theories of

---

[200] Ignatius Donnelly MSS., Box 46, H. E. Taubeneck to Donnelly, Marshall, Ill., November 6, 1891; Taubeneck Scrapbook, clipping from the *St. Louis Chronicle*, February 28, 1892; F. G. Blood, *Hand Book and History of the National Farmers' Alliance and Industrial Union* (Washington, D. C., 1893), p. 41.

[201] Taubeneck Scrapbook, clipping from *St. Louis Chronicle*, February 28, 1892.

[202] *Chicago Tribune*, July 5, 1892.

[203] *Farmers' Voice*, March 5, 1892.   This plank was in turn but a modification of those included in the Cincinnati (*ibid.*, May 30, 1891) and the earlier Ocala (*ibid.*, December 20, 1890) platforms.

[204] This proposal reminded one E. O. Ball, of New York, that "this plan was urged twelve years ago by one of the clearest voices in this city, a co-worker with Kellogg, the author, and a merchant, as was Mr. Kellogg" (*American Nonconformist*, January 28, 1892).

[205] *Vanguard*, July 9, 1892.

[206] *Chicago Times-Herald*, July 20 and 24, 1896.

[207] For an example see above, n. 174.

money, interest, and credit, we can find the key to the then-asserted relation between these phenomena and the currency and financial proposals of the period, proposals admittedly the heart of the radical program. The legal-tender theory, the interconvertible currency, and the subtreasury plan all find an explicable origin or justification in his system. His theory of interest explains the insistence that only financial reform could remedy the unequal distribution of wealth and restore to labor its lost independence. Likewise, the emphasis upon political action, so characteristic of these radical movements, received added force from his declaration that through legislation alone could complete reform be obtained. The justification which his utopian scheme offered to the inflation sentiment of an indebted, depressed agricultural West, and the lure of its promise of an equitable distribution of wealth to rural and urban classes vexed by the economic and social maladjustment born of the industrial revolution, offer some explanation of the continued influence of Edward Kellogg upon American radicalism during the years 1865–1896.

CHAPTER V

SHALL RED AND BLACK UNITE? AN AMERICAN REVOLUTIONARY DOCUMENT OF 1883*

WRITING of the congress of "Anarchists, semi-Anarchists, and Revolutionary Socialists" that was to be held in Pittsburgh on October 14, 1883, Benjamin R. Tucker announced regretfully that "circumstances" made it impossible for him to attend. "We regret this the more," he declared, "because an elaborately-developed plan of reconciling the various schools of Socialists is to be presented by delegates acting for the San Francisco section."[1] Tucker was the leading exponent of individualistic, philosophical anarchism in the United States. This was the only type of anarchism that seems to have exerted, then or later, "a genuine influence on Americans of the older stock."[2] Derived originally from Josiah Warren and other writers of the antebellum era, this indigenous school had been re-enforced by the imported doctrines of Pierre-Joseph Proudhon and the individualism of Herbert Spencer. Since 1881, in *Liberty*, Tucker had drawn upon these alien sources to strengthen the peaceful insistence of American anarchists upon absolute individual liberty, full equality, and abolition of the state.[3]

This school of radical thought, derived originally from eighteenth century liberalism and American agrarian society, was now challenged in the United States by two alien, proletarian philosophies of revolution. A comparatively recent importation was communist-anarchism. Its champion, Johann Most, had brought to New York in December, 1882, the "semi-mystical doctrine of violence" of Michael Bakunin and the conviction that the outright terrorism of dynamite was the most effective way of arousing the masses and preparing for the revolution. Within eight months, Most had established his ascendancy over the revolutionary socialist clubs in the cities of the eastern seaboard and Middle West.

The leaders of these groups had already been stimulated into half hearted activity by the organization of the International Working People's Association, the Black International, at the London Congress of

---

* Reprinted from *The Pacific Historical Review*, XIV (December, 1945), 434-451.

[1] "On Picket Duty," *Liberty*, II, No. 14 (Boston, October 6, 1883), 1.

[2] Oscar Jaszi, "Anarchism," *Encyclopedia of the Social Sciences*, II (New York, 1930), 49.

[3] Peter A. Kropotkin, "Anarchism," *Encyclopedia Britannica*, I (14th ed., New York, 1928), 876; Paul H. Douglas, "Proletarian Political Theory," in Charles Edward Merriam and Henry Elmer Barnes, *A History of Political Theories. Recent Times* (New York, 1932), 198; Henry David, *The History of the Haymarket Riot* (New York, 1936), 73, 75-76.

1881. In the same year an abortive attempt had been made to unite the revolutionary wing of the Marxian socialists in America with the native anarchists upon the basis of a federation of autonomous groups, an Information Bureau, and the qualified approval of force. This effort to form a united front introduced a period of confused thinking upon fundamental principles, as the leading revolutionary socialists of the East and Middle West sought to facilitate a union of all extreme leftist groups by indicating their sympathy, despite their basic Marxism, with the concepts of both the American and Bakunin anarchists. The dynamic leadership and the bold insurrectionary message that Most preached in *Freiheit* galvanized this somewhat moribund revolutionary movement, with its small following of immigrant laborers and a few English-speaking converts, into activity that alarmed the police and won him a relatively strong following among proletarian extremists.

Most employed his influence to drive the shattered Socialistic Labor Party, composed of peaceful, evolutionary socialists, to the wall. Once this obstacle was removed, he set out to unite all the completely intransigent, leftist elements in the United States into a single revolutionary movement. In this enterprise he had the aid of August Spies, a revolutionary socialist of Chicago and head of the Information Bureau that was set up belatedly there in April, 1883. It was through this agency that "The Socialists of North America" were invited to send delegates to the Pittsburgh Congress the primary aim of which was to achieve "a uniform, practical, and effective organization and agitation."[4] This invitation went not only to the groups already under Most's influence in the East and Middle West, but also to Benjamin Tucker's following and to the revolutionary socialists of the Far West, who had developed an agitation along lines of their own.

The moving spirit of this third movement was a young, American born lawyer, Burnette G. Haskell. Brilliant but erratic, Haskell was secretary of the Pacific Coast Division of the now decadent International Workingmen's Association, the Red International. He had organized this division on July 15, 1881, after corresponding with Henry M. Hyndman, the leader of the Social Democratic movement in Great Britain. This Branch of the I. W. A. developed a centralized organization and an elaborate, effective propaganda technique which gained a modest following among the workers of the west coast and Rocky Mountain region. Repudiating acts of terrorism in favor of "scientific conspiracy," it won over such labor leaders as Joseph R. Buchanan, editor of the Denver *Labor Enquirer*, who became head of the Rocky Mountain Division of the I.W. A. while remaining on the National Executive Board of the Knights

---

[4] David, *op. cit.*, 90, quoting the invitation circular, and *passim*.

of Labor. There he was an outspoken opponent of the conservative policies of Terence V. Powderly, the Grand Master Workman. It was to Haskell, the leader of this revolutionary movement of the Far West, with its growing following among the Knights of Labor there, that the invitation to attend the Pittsburgh Congress came.

Haskell replied to Johann Most's bid for a union of forces with an elaborately developed plan of his own. It was designed to reconcile the doctrinal differences of the various schools of socialists and anarchists that were invited to the Pittsburgh gathering. It was intended, also, to provide the basis for the "effective organization and agitation" that Most sought. Since it was impossible for Haskell or his associates to attend the Congress, he sent his plan to August Spies with the request that he present it in behalf of the west coast socialists. Then, thinking possibly that it would be advisable to approach a representative of the American anarchists in advance of the meeting, Haskell sent the letter-press copy of his letter to Spies to Joseph A. Labadie of Detroit, with the request that he urge the plan's adoption at Pittsburgh also. It is from this copy, which was found in the Joseph A. Labadie Collection of Labor Materials at the University of Michigan, that the following extracts are reproduced. Labadie, apparently, loaned the document to Benjamin Tucker, who promptly declared to the readers of *Liberty* his opposition to Haskell's plan.

This document, which has been sent to us, does not reconcile in the least, but simply places Liberty and Authority side by side and arbitrarily says: "These twain are one flesh!" We will be parties to no such marriage. Every friend of Liberty who may go to Pittsburgh is hereby urged to examine this document carefully before giving it his adhesion. Great Pains has been taken in its preparation; it is specious and plausible; but it is perhaps the most foolishly inconsistent piece of work that ever came to our notice.[5]

Inconsistent the document certainly was when examined in the light of the principles of the three opposing schools of radical thought invited to the Congress. Although this may be regarded by some as typifying the intellectual confusion of the little band of alien revolutionaries of the period, others will be interested in the document as presenting the most elaborate attempt then made to work out a synthesized revolutionary creed that would not only harmonize the views of the individualist anarchists, the communist-anarchists, and the revolutionary socialists but also to develop an ideology that would appeal to the native-born wage-earners. The American workingmen were still dominated by eighteenth century ideas. At the time of Haskell's writing they were deeply stirred by Henry George's doctrines and proposals, which were based upon these concepts. So vigorous was the single tax movement, in

[5] *Loc. cit.*

fact, that Henry Hyndman had actually proposed to Henry George in April that they unite their forces in "a definite *international action . . .* clear enough, strong enough and noble enough to find an outlet to enthusiasts who otherwise may rush into dynamite" under the "notions that Bakunin, Kropotkin . . . and others have made popular."[6]

To conciliate the single-taxers and Tucker's following, and to develop an ideology with a potential appeal to the American born workers, Haskell drew in succession upon Thomas Jefferson, the older anarchism of Josiah Warren, Proudhon and Tucker, the doctrine of Henry George, and Bakunin's concept of a co-operative utopia of autonomous communities. These contributions Haskell sought to harmonize with the labor theory of value, the contempt for the ragged masses, and the revolutionary technique and organization of contemporary, left wing Marxism. Numerous clippings from *Truth*, which Haskell edited, were included in the latter part of the letter to Spies and Labadie. These indicate that the proposal was in reality an attempt to get Tucker and Most to adopt the organization and propaganda technique that were proving so effective in the Far West.

Tucker was antagonized, apparently, by the centralized revolutionary organization and the temporary, revolutionary dictatorship proposed by Haskell. It was certain that the followers of Johann Most would resent the repudiation of terroristic acts that the plan also contained. When Haskell's proposals were presented and debated in secret session at the Pittsburgh Congress, they met decisive opposition from the delegates, whose most influential figure was Johann Most himself. The program of the Pacific Coast Section of the I. W. A. was rejected "for substantial reasons" by the Congress.[7] Instead the delegates organized the International Working Peoples Association in the United States upon the basis of fully autonomous groups. Its Manifesto justified a proletarian revolt by arguments derived from Bakunin and Proudhon, as well as from Marx, rather than by an appeal to the rights of man.[8] Thus the "Black" internationalism of Bakunin triumphed over the "Red" internationalism of the I. W. A., which like Tucker's following, remained aloof from the new organization.

The failure of the Pittsburgh Congress to unite all the revolutionary forces was particularly unsatisfactory to the vigorous leaders of the

[6] Henry George MSS. (New York Public Library), Henry M. Hyndman to Henry George, April 3, 1883.

[7] *Freiheit*, No. 42 (New York, October 20, 1883), 1–2.

[8] *Plan of Organization, Method of Propaganda and Resolutions, adopted by the Pittsburgh Congress of the "International Working-Peoples Association," In Session from October 14th to October 16th 1883* (n.p., n.d.).

I. W. P. A. in Chicago, among whom were August Spies and Albert Parsons. As their agitation developed rapidly in the next few years and they became convinced of the imminence of the social revolution, the *Alarm* began to seek recruits from the English-speaking workers by appeals to natural rights and natural law such as Haskell was employing so effectively farther to the West.[9] As Chicago businessmen and the police showed themselves increasingly on the alert, talk revived of a union of forces between the I. W. P. A. and the I. W. A., which was then at the height of its influence. Whether because of hostile police action in San Francisco and Chicago in the winter of 1885–1886, or because of doctrinal differences, the union of forces was never consummated. The Chicago revolutionaries went on to exploit the McCormick Reaper strike and the Eight-Hour movement in such a manner as to invite police intervention and furnish an opportunity for the "propaganda by deed" at Haymarket.

Haskell's proposal for a union of forces, therefore, proved abortive. Its significance lies chiefly in the light that it throws upon the history, tactics, and ideology of the revolutionary socialists of the Far West, where the old American faith in natural rights was grafted upon the Marxian program. Its fate illustrates the extent to which Bakuninist conceptions of terrorism and of group autonomy had already come to dominate the eastern and mid-western social-revolutionary movement in 1883. Its failure revealed, also, the determination of the indigenous philosophic, individualist anarchists to yield "Liberty" neither to the "Authority" of the "Red" nor to the violence of the "Black International."

TRUTH—A JOURNAL FOR THE POOR

Burnette G. Haskell,   Charles F. Burgman,
     Editor   Business Manager.

San Francisco, Cal., Sept. 12 1883

J. A. Labadie Esq.

DEAR COMRADE:

I enclose you a copy of the letter from the I. W. A. here to the Pittsburg Convention. I have sent the original to Spies at Chicago. He will present it on our behalf. I send you copy and ask you to urge its adoption also.
                              Yours for Unity and Action,
                              (signed) BURNETTE G. HASKELL[10]

[9] Albert Parsons, "The Committee of Safety," *Alarm* (Chicago), April 1, 1885.

[10] Joseph A. Labadie MSS., Labadie Collection, University of Michigan, Ann Arbor, Michigan, by the courtesy of Miss Agnes Inglis, Curator.

Sept. 1st. [188]3

To J. A. Labadie
    and[11]

August Spies, Esq.

(To be presented by ~~him~~ them [sic] to the Socialistic
(Congress[12] which will meet in the City of Pittsburg
(about the middle of
(October 1883.

COMRADES:

We, the Executive Body of the Pacific Coast Division of the International address these words to you in earnestness and with the sincere hope that the suggestions contained therein may be adopted by you and made the basis for all future action in our great cause.

But while advocating this system which we now lay before you, we beg to say that if you shall not deem it best to adopt the same, that nevertheless we will work in harmony with you and will fraternally aid your work and plans as adopted by you. We trust you will pardon the length of this letter and the many trite things it must contain. We have endeavored to be as brief as possible without a sacrifice of clearness.

The majority of our Division Executive which consists of nine members were and still are members of the Socialistic Section in this City. It at one time numbered some two or three hundred members. But these were drawn in at the time of the Workingmen's Party here and came in because they understood (ignorantly) that the Socialists were at the bottom of and able to control that party. So they joined the Section and claimed to be Socialists without understanding even the first principles of Socialism and merely for the purpose of being on the inside of the political movement so they could secure a place at the public crib. When Kearney[13] sold out the W. P. C.[14] and it disbanded the Section dwindled down to some twenty or less men who were real Socialists and whose whole lives were devoted to the Cause. These few men agitated for some years by holding meetings, taxing themselves heavily to issue tracts, etc., as "Socialists" and met with but little success. Finally the Knights of Labor was started here and the Socialists perceived that its provision allowing the discussion of labor in all its phazes [sic] would permit them to propagate their doctrines there. So they joined the

---

[11] Inserted.
[12] "Congress of Socialists of North America," scheduled to meet on October 14.
[13] Denis Kearney.
[14] Workingmen's Party of California.

Knights,[15] aided materially to build them up and in the Assemblies did their best to spread the truth. This work is being kept up faithfully even to the present day. But we found that there were many obstacles in the way of effective work through the Knights. We had by this time become convinced of the futility of political action under present conditions and had at last arrived at the belief that the capitalistic system of competition would eventually bring about a physical conflict between the workers and the drones, and had further become convinced that liberty was forever doomed unless we could win in the conflict. So believing and preaching with the aim of making the Knights of Labor take a front rank in the work of preparation for the coming revolution, we encountered several obstacles within that organization.

First: We found that the masses of working men were densely ignorant, cowardly and selfish, and thus disinclined to learn, to act or to aid others in acting.

Second: That even if they did listen to us and applaud us that by the next meeting they had forgotten half we had said, our words having slipped out of their minds as water does off a duck's back.

Third: We found in the Knights the same class of designing politicians and "would-be-politicians" there to secure a little political popularity or influence to use in getting themselves a fat place.

Fourth: We met there the active and undisguised enmity of church people and masons who denounced us as bloodsuckers and rascals.

We found in brief after careful consideration, that the Knights of Labor was perfectly useless save and except as a recruiting ground for some other organization. We said to ourselves: "Why should we build up and sustain an organization in the interest of someone else? Why should we not rather form one of our own which we can control and direct as we think proper?"

Upon that thought we opened communication with M. H. Hyndman[16] of London. From him and some others abroad we learned enough to justify us in establishing a branch of the International.[17] We desired that organization for the following reasons:

1. It had acquired already a world wide reputation and such as to enlist all the enthusiasm and appeal to all the romance and devotion possible.

---

[15] Knights of Labor.

[16] Henry Mayor Hyndman, founder and leading figure in the Social Democratic Federation.

[17] International Workingmen's Association, now virtually defunct.

2. Its reputation was secret and mysterious—influences not to be disdained.
3. It was still in existence with powerful branches throughout the world.
4. Its London Congress of 1881[18] had agreed to the doctrine of physical force and had foreseen and prophesied the coming Social Revolution, both of which we firmly believe in.
5. It had announced the fact that this Social Revolution ought to be SIMULTANEOUS, INTERNATIONAL, and WORLD WIDE in order to ENSURE success. And to our knowledge it was the only organization so proclaiming. These also were our views.
6. The London Congress while recommending the propaganda of deed yet left it to each individual or local organization to act as it might seem best at the moment. This action permitted us legitimately to organize to put into operation our own peculiar ideas.

Thus much for our reasons. Our Division here was established and we set to work with the aim of picking out the *best* men in all other organizations and allying them with us. That work has been prosecuted with some success. We now submit to you (1st) our doctrines (2nd) our principles and (3rd) our plan of organization. We believe Them all eminently adapted to America where proper educational work is so much needed and we urge you to most carefully consider them and if you find them true and right to adopt and make them national. We urge you *not* to refer this to a "committee" but to have it read and examined and debated carefully in session before all of the delegates to the end that if there be any false reasoning or conclusions in it, that they may be corrected and amended before it is too late.

OUR DOCTRINES

1st. We hold first of all that the great mass of the people are *always* ready for revolt and revolution if they are properly led and played upon. We adduce in proof of this the fact that the despots and bourgeoisie rulers of every land have only to pull the proper strings and straightway peoples aim against peoples and workingmen of one land go out with cheers to cut the throats of their brother workmen. We adduce in further proof the fact that in 1650 in England, 1776 in America, 1789 in France, 1848 in other parts of Europe, 1861 in America, 1871 in France[19]

[18] Essentially anarchistic in composition, to which the "social-revolutionary" wing of the American Socialistic Labor Party sent delegates.
[19] The Paris Commune.

and 1877 in America[20] (All periods of revolution and popular uprising) that the people came out gladly when called upon by their leaders. That some of these uprisings were not successful was in our opinion due to the fact that the *leaders* were either not united enough nor heroic enough, nor farseeing enough. We affirm now that in our opinion revolutions should not be precipitated until capital commits some infamous act that arouses the attention of the people. Capital is doing these things almost monthly. After we shall have established throughout the world concord of thought and solidarity of action among all our *leaders* throughout the world we will then be prepared to *act*. And if we guide our action by brains and not bombast, if we go into the fight thoroughly prepared, we are *sure* to win. Any pretext will do (when the time comes to strike) that will rouse the people. They will not know *what* they are fighting *for*[21] but once embarked in the contest provided radical leaders assume and *hold* control they will fight to death and die in the last ditch. This is because of the mania inbred in the people from their birth, which makes them savage for blood and slaughter when once roused. There is no great trouble in our opinion about starting the revolution. It will come of itself fast enough. But to prevent it being guided by the bourgeoisie or by conservatives to impotent and unsatisfactory results and to prevent on the other hand it being suppressed by a new Napoleon founding a despotism, it is necessary that we educate in *true principles* to select a *few* of able, daring, heroic and noble men in every little hamlet —men who will be qualified and willing to take the lead in the movement at the start of the Revolution and hold the helm *with an iron hand* until the desired results shall be accomplished.[22] These men must understand that life and death are nothing and they should be pledged by all the balance of us a niche in the temple of Memory and Fame of future generations whether we win or lose. We can honestly offer to our comrades, no other reward than this. If it is not sufficient, then they are not the material with which we can do any effective work.

We urge most solemnly this theory. We believe it is the true one. We could present scores more of facts going to show its truth if we deemed it necessary. Bretheren! [*sic*] We appeal to you by all that we hold sacred to consider these words well and carefully. We have made far too many mistakes in the past. We have followed will o' the

---

[20] The great railway strikes and their accompanying mob violence of July 16–31.

[21] Haskell betrays here his contempt for the masses, and the influence upon his thought of the critical Marxian comments upon the *Lumpenproletariat*.

[22] A dictatorship by the revolutionary *élite*, in behalf of the proletariat, as in Soviet Russia, today?

wisps. We have gone astray in blind confidence and enthusiasm. We have spent time and money and the richest and noblest blood of Europe, that of our brothers, has vainly deluged the ground where in times past our forces have made daring but foolish stands for battle. Oh, we urge you to now aid in starting the movement again upon principles of state-craft, of policy and of reason. Let us mark our course out plainly, prove each step in the plan by reason and then pursue that plan piti-lessly, fearlessly and without disheartening, and success is sure and in the nearest future!

In brief,—with but ten men in every city of this Union who feared neither life nor death and were prepared to sacrifice *all*—with but these men guided intelligently the Social Revolution could be accomplished and the New Era would dawn. And if these ten men cannot be found or *made* then the people are too corrupt for lib[erty]. But they *can* be made! Aye! A thousand of them in every city (within three years) instead of ten, if a SCIENTIFIC system is adopted like the one we now propose to you. This is our first point. Let us recapitulate: 1. The people are always ready for revolution. It only needs leaders who are able, heroic and self-sacrificing in order to fan the slumbering spark of discontent into a flame. Let us therefore concentrate our energies upon the task of providing such *leaders* rather than in vainly trying to educate the whole sluggish world before we strike.

2nd. We hold that all existing forms of organization are inefficient and ineffectual to properly *organize, seggregate* [*sic*], *classify* and *utilize effectively* and harmoniously these same leaders. The Knights of Labor, the Trade Unions, the Socialistic Labor Party,[23] the groups as you in the East have organized them of the I. W. A. we believe have in their form of organization the germ of destruction and defeat. These are our reasons: In Trade Unions, Knights of Labor and Socialistic Labor Party the following objections apply: First more than 75 per cent of the money paid in by members goes to keep the organizations running in routine expenses of hall rent, pay of secretary, advertising, picnics, routine print-ing, reliefs, tickets, etc., etc. Thus members are drained of money which could be used to better effect and the propaganda makes no ad-vance. Second, fully 90 per cent of the time spent in meetings is utterly wasted, it being frittered away in routine business, hearing reports or listening to various members carried away by their desire to "spout" about irrelevant matters. These two things tire and disgust men and drive them away. Thirdly, there is no organized effort made to spread

[23] Frequently referred to as the "Socialist Labor Party," but actually the predecessor of the party of this name in the United States that was active after 1890.

our doctrines.   If by chance some true man is present and speaks the truth he has to do so hurriedly and brokenly, he cannot present the whole subject, he cannot do it justice.   And when he concludes, in nine cases out of ten some conservative or spy gets up with glib tongue and lawyer-like sophistry bogs and beclouds the issue and leaves the impression upon the minds of the hearers that the true man is either a fool or a knave.   And this kind of hasty public opinion sticks to a man for a long time and hampers his usefulness to the cause.   Fourthly, there is even no scientific method in use by which recruits can be gained for the organization.   This the most important work of all is left to blind chance. All members are told to bring in what members they can.   Some few do a good deal of work others are indifferent or lazy and will not lift a finger.   The result is that the men brought in by one man are liable to be used by him as the nucleus of a faction which endangers and retards the work of the organization if he is a bad man.   If he is a good man then after a while he gets tired of doing all the work and getting no thanks for it and so he gets disgusted and draws out.   Fifthly, the organization consists of *too many*; generally numbering from 20 to 800 or so.   They elect a president and other officers.   This creates rivalry, petty ambition, factions and discord.   If the president is invested with much power or the secretary receives a salary the bitterness of the contest is enhanced and finally internal commotion and discord either entirely destroy or make useless the organization.   Sixthly.   In every organization are generally one or two good talkers.   These monopolise the talk.   If they are bad men they use the organization for personal advancement only. It is a case of one talker and 50 listeners.   The listeners sometimes listen and sometimes don't.   They rarely remember exactly *what* was said but if it suited their fancy at the time when the ideas expressed grow vague and indistinct with time, there remains upon their mind *only a favorable bias* toward the *speaker;* this serves to induce them to depend upon *persons* and not *principles* and which is *WRONG.*   From this arises the possibility of the speaker becoming a little "boss," a self-constituted in-carnation of the society, making in its name all sorts of arrangements, bargains and compromises.   Sixthly [*sic*]; Under this form of organiza-tion when recruits are brought in they are brought in hastily.   They are presented in batches, referred to committee, hastily (and in 9 cases out of 10) passed upon ignorantly.   They are then elected.   And then they are left alone without instruction or information to pick up their ideas as how they can!   What wonder that every one of such organizations swarms with ignoramusses [*sic*], spies, traitors, and fools?

Now for the Groups as you have them organized with you. We believe they lack a few essential elements of success. As we understand your form of organization it is as follows:

We judge that each of your groups is composed of men who are supposed to be sufficiently advanced to do—what? Has it ever been presented to them that they ought to form the leaders of the Social Revolution when it breaks out? No. Do they understand when and how or where it will break out? No. Are they armed or prepared for it when it does come? No.[24] You may reply that they are formed for the purpose of urging the propaganda of deed, for the purpose of blowing up and removing now our tyrants, that such removals may awaken the people and induce the people to study the social question. But have they done this? No. And will they? No. Because they see plainly even if they do not admit so to themselves that this would be the childish course of dreamers and impractibles [sic],[25] rather than that of sober, scientific cool-headed conspirators. It is this latter that we must be. We do believe that your groups as at present organized serve only two purposes: First they allow the true men of our cause the pleasure of meeting and talking with friends who think as they do and second they serve (and badly so) to keep alive factional differences between Socialists, Revolutionary Socialists and Anarchists. You do not limit the membership in each group and this leaves it open to the objections made concerning other organizations. You have no guards regarding membership and in time of conflict you as well as the other organizations would not know upon whom you could safely call; nor would you know when that call was made whether or not it would be obeyed or not. You have no guards or securities that would prevent capital on the first signs of outbreak seizing and jailing every prominent leader and by this *Coup d'État* leaving you powerless and disorganized.[26]

Gentlemen! We believe that the day for unconsidered, hasty, undigested, and childish planning and talk has gone by, and that we should address ourselves soberly and earnestly to the most careful consideration of the means necessary to *ensure* success. Our cause will not *necessarily* succeed because we are right. Now as ever before, Heaven is upon the side of those who have the heaviest artillery. And we have intellect enough on our side of the house to provide means that will defeat the

[24] This fails to take into consideration the armed *Lehr und Wehr Verein* and similar groups maintained in Chicago and elsewhere by labor organizations and the revolutionary socialists.

[25] This was in flat contradiction of the views of Johann Most and many of the I.W.P.A.

[26] A shrewd prediction of what actually followed the throwing of the Haymarket bomb.

enemy if we only wake up and use it.   What we need is a complete and scientific scheme of action, flawless, to be followed unitedly and regardless of obstacles to the uttermost end.

As a conclusion we claim (1), that our present forms of organization are radically wrong, (2) and that at present we have no definite plan or scheme of action.   Hence we conclude that it is a necessity

1—That a right system of organization be prepared.
2—That a definite plan of action be agreed upon and followed.

We have at present in the labor movement three radical bodies who differ slightly in their belief but who continually waste time and effort in fighting among themselves.   These bodies are:

1. *The Anarchists*—who believe in the abolition of all government and (as we understand it) the prosecution in future of work requiring co-operation, by voluntary association.

2. *The Revolutionary Socialists*—who believe in the establishment in the future of a government styled State-Socialism in which the whole people (government) shall co-operate as manufacturers or producers and [as] merchants or distributors to the exclusion of the present burgeoisie. And who also believe that this can only be attained by forcible revolution.[27]

3. *The Political Action Socialists*—are those who believe in State Socialism but falsely hope that it may be attained by the ballot.

These three classes are the leaders of the labor movement.   They ought to be united.   That is the first and foremost duty of all of us; to seek some basis upon which we can all combine for effective work against the common enemy.   We suggest here that the following declaration of the Rights of Man and enunciation of principles is one upon which, *if each faction will yield a little*, all three may honestly and worthily combine.   We urge this action as a necessary preliminary to any work that may be done or any plan that may be adopted.   The *"Rights of Man!"* has of itself a heroic sound and when put forth by us as our guiding principles will rally many who are not with us now to our glorious Scarlet standard of war.

[27] Haskell was correct in emphasizing the difference between the revolutionary and the orthodox socialists as springing primarily from their respective reliance upon and opposition to the employment of physical force as the proper method of achieving socialism. There was, however, an accompanying hostility and friendship to trades unionism that distinguished the two factions in the order named.   Haskell failed to distinguish between the communist-anarchists, who favored terroristic actions as necessary and effective propaganda for the awakening of the masses, cf. note 25, and the revolutionary socialists of the J. W. A. The reliance upon "propaganda by deed" was stressed particularly by Johann Most.

Our Principles

We believe that we ought to adopt a grand declaration of principles formulated under the name of the "Rights of Man" and that our educational work should be directed towards securing those principles firmly in the hearts of the people. By long labor and research we have collated and composed what we believe to be a complete declaration and we insert it here. It has no duplicate that we know of in existence.

Declaration of the Rights of Man
PREAMBLE

We hold these truths to be self-evident to all people who have the welfare of humanity at heart: That all men and women are born free and with equal rights. That they were endowed, by such birth, by their Creator and as necessary incidents of their existence, with certain inalienable rights, rights of which even they themselves cannot divest themselves; and that among these rights are the right to life and the means of living, liberty and the conditions essential to liberty, and the right to the pursuit of happiness. That especially enumerating the subordinate rights flowing naturally and reasonably from the establishment of these truths, and the principles necessary for their perpetuity, we do publish and declare:

I

That the just end of all political associations and the only permissible [sic] reason for their existence at all, is the maintenance of the natural and imprescriptible [sic] rights of man and the development of all his faculties.

II

Whatever rights belong to one man belong to all men equally whatever difference may be in their physical [,] mental or moral force. Equality of rights is established by [N]ature. Society, so far from invading it, ought justly to constitute its security against the abuse of force which would render it illusory.

III

If ever it shall be found after careful trial thereof that any form or system of government or society fails to maintain the rights of man that then it is not only the right but the most sacred duty of the whole people to alter or abolish the said system by any and all possible means.

IV

Liberty is the power which belongs to a man of exercising all his faculties at pleasure. It has justice for its rule; the rights of others for its boundaries, Nature for its origin and the law for its safeguard.

V

The right of life which belongs equally to all men carrie[s] with it the right to the means of a living. Chief among these subsidiary rights is the right of each individual to receive the full product of his own labor without tithe, tax, or diminution upon any pretext.

VI

Every individual is entitled to an equal proportional share of all of the natural advantages of Earth. The whole people should hold the land, light, air and water together with other of Nature's resources, as the natural heritage in common of all mankind, and of his proportion thereof no man should ever be deprived.

VII

Every individual is entitled to an equal proportionate share of all the accumulated wealth created by past generations and that wealth should be held by Society as the natural heritage in common of all mankind.

VIII

["Society can deny to those who do not consent to this system of Society any share of the benefits produced by the co-operation of those who do consent. . . . "]

IX

Debt, profit, interest, rent and the competitive system of industry are hereby declared proved instruments of degradation and tyranny and cancers upon the Social body. So also are the present methods of punishing crime rather than preventing it; the present monetary system; the present method of suffrage; the present method of education; and the present systems of jurisprudence, church and military.

X

[A statement of the traditional rights to freedom of assemblage, press, religion, bearing arms, security of person, and absolute freedom of thought, speech and association.]

XI

[The "right of private property" rests solely upon production by the owner or rendering the "full equivalent" to the producer.]

XII

So long as members of society shall fulfill their portion of the social contract they have a right to demand of society that it provide to them the means necessary to provide for their subsistence.   Society is bound also to ensure the means of subsistence to those who are incapable of labor.

XIII

["Absolute justice is the right of every being. . . .   Every law which violates . . . the imprescriptible rights of man is void."]

XIV

In every just government the law ought above all to defend public and individual liberty against the authority of those that govern.   Every institution that does not suppose the people good and the magistrate corruptible, is vicious. . . .   Every act against the imprescriptible rights of man . . . is arbitrary and void.   The very respect due to law forbids the submission to it. . . .   Resistance to oppression is a necessary consequence of the other rights of man.   There is oppression against the social body whenever one alone of its members is oppressed.   When the government violates the rights of the people, insurrection is for the people and for every portion of the people the most sacred of rights and the most indespensible [*sic*] of duties.   When the social contract fails to protect a citizen he resumes his natural right to defend personally all his rights.   In either of the two preceeding [*sic*] cases, to subject to legal forms the resistance to oppression is the last refinement of tyranny and is both infamous and void.

XV

[The functions of government should be kept at a minimum, and officials should be selected in such manner as to ensure their being real "and not pretended microcosms of their constituents."]

XVI

[Men of all countries are brothers and should render to each other "mutual aid" while kings, aristocrats, and tyrants of all kinds are "beasts dangerous to the welfare of mankind" against whom every hand should be raised.]

XVII

The conditions which will establish universal happiness upon earth consist in the free enjoyment of the natural rights of man combined with the exercise of all his faculties upon the highest plane of mental, moral and physical worth.   The best guarantee of the existence and perpetuity of these conditions is the loftest [*sic*] possible elevation of humanity.   There will arrive a time, if progress be not impeeded [*sic*] when governments will be useless.   To advance that time education seems to be the main factor.   Hence what prevents or constrains the spread of intelligence is tyranous [sic] and unjust.

XVIII

Governments as at present existing are machines used for the purpose of enslaving the people.   Such machines should be abolished and society be permitted to reorganize upon principles of equity.   The people being too much governed all statute or common law except broad and simple declarations of principles and rights should be abolished.   These principles should be interpreted not by infamous precedent, but by the light of common sense to secure justice to all.

XIX

Neither sex, age, color nor condition should ever be made barriers against equal and exact justice.

XX

Suppress the *right of increase* claimed by the proprietor over anything which [he] has stamped as his own (property) while maintaining *possession*, and by this simple change law, government, economy and institutions will be revolutionized and evil be driven from the face of the earth.*

* *Proudhan.*   [sic]   This author in using the word "property" always means it as defined above (i.e. rather *profit* than *property* as Americans understand words).   He is wrongly understood by the State Socialists as desiring to abolish individual *possession*.

Declaration:

We believe firmly, that as a necessary step in advance to that condition of perfect "an-archy" when governments shall be no longer needed, it is imperative that the present competitive system of industry and the social structure dependant [sic] thereon be abolished and that in its place shall be substituted a system of governmental co-operation in all matters of mental, moral and physical construction and elevation.

We believe in the fact that the present system necessarily is prophetic of a future revolution which must either result in a greater and freer condition or will plunge our present civilization back into barbarism.

We affirm that believing this it is our duty to prepare for the impending conflict, to lead it when it shall break upon us, and to bend every energy to so direct it as to secure as its result the establishment of a proper system of governmental co-operation.

We affirm furthermore that all of the resources of science should be enlisted in the battle to ensure success and the welfare of the peoples of the world. We declare further that action ought to be both international and simultaneous.

It will be remembered that in 1872 at the Congress of the International held at Hague first arose the dissentions [sic] which have since divided our ranks. It was at that session that Bakounine[28] [sic] was expelled and carried with him 30 of the delegates with the aid of whom he established what has since been called the Black International as opposed to those who remained, the Red. The belief of the Reds was in the gradual education of the people and in taking no forcible action until all the world was prepared: the belief of the Blacks was in the total abolition of all present forms of government by force.

The news of this division when/ brought to Bismark [sic] provoked from him this historic remark:

"Crowned heads, wealth and privilege may well tremble should ever again the Black and the Red unite!"

There exists now no great obstacle to that unity. The work of peaceful education and revolutionary conspiracy well can and ought *to run in parallel lines.*

The day has come for Solidarity. Ho! Reds and Blacks, thy flags are flying side by side! Let the drum beat out defiantly the roll of battle: "Workingmen of all lands! Unite! You have nothing to lose but your chains. You have a world to win!"

Tremble! Oppressors of the World! Not far beyond your purblind sight there dawns the rose scarlet and sable lights of the JUDGMENT DAY!

[sic]

Plan of Action

We have shown that it is not a necessary adjunct to the success of the Social Revolution that the whole people shall be educated into a belief in Governmental-Socialistic Co-operation. We have shown that the people will follow leaders whenever those leaders are heroic enough to lead them. The only problem then presented is to provide:

(1) A sufficient number of brave and devoted men in every centre of action qualified and prepared to act as leaders in the social struggle.

[28] Michael Bakunin.

(2) Means which will place them as near as possible upon an equal
footing regarding resources of combat with the enemy.

Our present band will serve as a nucleus of this army of leaders which
we must secure.   If any dissentions [*sic*] exist among these it is then our
first duty to heal them.   Our second duty is to march upon the enemy.

We need men in every city, town and hamlet of the United States who
will be prepared when the hour of revolt shall come, to assume leadership,
rally and organize the people, inflame them with revolutionary fire and
point out to them the road to success.

These men must be unselfish, brave, able, virtuous and educated in a
knowledge of the wrongs of the old and the benefits of the new system.
Such men are hard to find.   But they *can* be found if properly searched
for; and what is better they can be *easily created* if a sensible, practical
course is adopted.[29]

First let us deal with the question of finding them.   After that we will
touch upon the means of creating them.

The organizations of the Knights of Labor, the various Trades' Unions
and the Liberal leagues which exist more or less in almost all centres of
population furnish good recruiting grounds.   Our present members
should visit these places often, they should there provoke discussion upon
social topics and those men who would make good material will be sure
to show themselves.   They will be known by their desire for knowledge.
These organizations well serve their purpose when out of 100 wages-
slaves they develop one man of thought capable of becoming one of us.
This process is of course slow. . . .

[Another method is publication of newspapers, but this and agitation at meetings "are
inefficient" and would take 100 years to secure necessary leaders for the revolution.]

We ought to adopt a method of creating revolutionists.   Why not
begin to proselyte among the young men of America? . . .

[What are needed are unselfish, brave, able, enthusiastic, virtuous young men.]

Gentlemen we say to you that if you will take the voting register of
each city and pick out from it the names and addresses of all the young
men between the ages of 21 and 25.   If you will then call them together
in meeting and provide your best speakers to address them—if these
speakers will paint the wrongs, shames, misery and hell of the present
system and picture the beauty, glory, happiness of the coming one and

[29] Such a statement indicates how far Haskell's preoccupation with radical theories and
revolutionary conspiracy had separated his thought from any realistic appreciation of the
fundamentally conservative, procapitalistic outlook of the American masses.

will point out what the students of Paris, Russia and Italy are doing and will then call upon the young men of America to follow in their footsteps, if then and there the names of the roused and enthusiastic audience are taken and the young men enrolled in groups,—then the success of the movement will astonish you all. After having organized these groups a complete system of education including such books as Karl Mark's [sic] manifesto,[30] Douais Better Times,[31] Stetsons "People's Power,"[32] Stepniak's[33] "Underground Russia" (and some new pamphlets clearly and briefly stating our doctrines which ought to be written) should be devised and the group carefully and systematically educated up to our level. This will give a starting point for the group organization which will be an immense advance over present methods.

Add to this—our best scholars should prepare treatises upon our cause and see that they are placed in the hands of educated men who are not directly identified with the wage-working class but who are humanitarians. Let us strive to interest the good men of all classes in our struggle. The movement abroad is aided by heroic men of the propertied class who sacrifice all their possessions for the cause (like Losogub[34] & Kropotkine[35] of Russia—Hyndman of England). Why should it not be so in America? There is no reason save our own indifference and our sloppy way of going to work.

Now for *our* modification of the group system. In brief it is as follows:

Let the North American Continent be divided for convenience of organization into divisions.

Let the British Possessions be divided into two divisions.

1. The Canadian Division.
2. The British Columbian Division.

---

[30] Karl Marx and Friedrich Engels, *The Communist Manifesto* (1848).

[31] Adolf Douai, *Better Times* (Chicago, 1877, 2nd ed. New York, 1884). Douai was a German Forty-niner, a revolutionary socialist, and editor of the New York *Volkszeitung* in 1883.

[32] Simeon Stetson, *The People's Power: or, How to Wield the Ballot* (San Francisco, W. M. Hinton, 1883).

[33] Sergius Stepniak, pseudonym for Serge Michaelovich Kravchinskii, the noted Nihilist and leader of the Russian underground resistance to the Tsarist autocracy.

[34] Dimitri Andreevich Lizogub (1850–1879), a large landowner from the Government of Chernigov and Poltava, who gave all his property for the revolutionary movement. Although not a terrorist, he was active in the St. Petersburg revolutionary circle. He was arrested in Odessa in the fall of 1878 and executed there with two friends on August 10, 1879. *Novyi entsyklopedicheskii slovar'* (Petrograd, 1914? vol. 24, column 518), by courtesy of Dr. John T. Dorosh, Library of Congress.

[35] Peter A. Kropotkin.

Let America (the U.S.) be divided as follows:
   3. The Eastern States Division.
   4. The Middle States Division.
   5. The Western States Division.
   6. The Rocky Mountain Division.
   7. The Pacific Coast Division.
   8. The Southern States Division.
Let Mexico be given one division.
   9. The Mexican Division.

Let each of these Divisions be presided over by a Division Executive of nine Persons the best possible material that can be selected in the district.

If this idea should be adopted it will be found that the Mexican, the Rocky Mountain and the Pacific Coast Division are already organized. That the Southern and British Columbian division are in process of organization and that correspondents and friends exist in all the other localities named, sufficient to begin the movement without delay.[36]

Let a secretary be selected to reside in some central city who can receive and forward correspondence, etc.   But let each Division be self regulating and have full charge over its own territory.   At stated periods let a convention be called of the Districts.

Let these various Division Executives begin the work of organization from themselves downward.   Let the Division Executive be composed of 9 members only.   Then let each one of these nine go out and organize a group of nine including himself.   His work is then ended as an organizer but each member of his group goes out and also organizes a group among his friends.   As soon as these groups are filled then in each group commences a regular system of education.   After this education which should be systematic, has progressed so as to make each group member intelligent concerning the movement [,] then secretly from the membership of the groups should be selected the best material and they should be given instruction and practice in scientific warefare [sic].   This will result gradually in the formation of a corps of men able to give us victory.   We believe that confining the membership of any group to 9 in number makes it of the proper number for educational purposes.   Then

[36] Haskell here describes the scope of activity of the I. W. A. and literally offers to turn over its organization to the revolutionary movement in the United States.   This was tantamount, of course, to offering to admit all other revolutionary and radical elements into the I. W. A. on the basis of the doctrinal compromise and plan of action offered above. The scope of the contemporary, subversive activities of the I. W. A. is plainly indicated, also, in the preceding passages.

again the organizing of the subordinate groups proceeding as they do from groups already organized and educated, has an advantage over in- dicriminate organization. Then again a man in one group is a mere member. Here he receives his instructions and then goes out and or- ganizes a group of his own. Of this he is the chief and instructor. It becomes a matter of pride to him to have his group active and intelligent. Then again here in these groups no one knows the full membership of the association except the District Executive. A subordinate member knows only 16 men: The 8 in the high group and the 8 in his own group. He consequently cannot acquire any "political influence" nor can he sell out or betray us. By providing a schedule of education by book and by discussion members are really made intelligent. This is *work* for them. They see that they are doing *something* and hence do not get discouraged. Then again they can be put to work to secure information of our enemies, etc. Besides the organization permeates everywhere. For instance we have here in one of our groups the assistant minister of one of the most aristocratic churches. We took him in—he was an enthusiastic young man—educated him, made him a socialist and he is now secretly but vigorously carrying on the socialistic propaganda among the daughters of the wealthy monopolists who have pews in his church! The results of this can be exceedingly good for our cause.

We have all our group meetings held every two weeks at the private houses of the members. The scheme has been in operation some time and it works admirably thus far. We believe you would find it practical and that its favorable results would astonish you. We think you could hardly do better than to adopt it.

For the purpose of showing you that our system conforms to the rules laid down by the Central Congress of the International we append the following an account of a late session thereof. From an inspection of it you will see that *methods* of orgranization are left to the individual judgment of the various localities.

[Newspaper Clippings][37]

In addition to this we think best to send you a few exhibits containing information concerning the workings of our division here. The exhibits will be found upon the succeeding pages. A careful scrutiny of them will doubtless enable you to understand thoroughly the system. . . .

[37] A lengthy account of the London Congress of July 15, 1881, that established the I. W. P. A. clipped from *Liberty*, followed by the resolutions adopted at the Congress, de- scribing its principles and method of organization clipped from *Le Révolté*. Pages 22–23 of the original manuscript in the Labadie MSS.

["Statutes of the Pacific Coast Division suitable with slight alterations for use by any other Division," and a "Circular," clippings from *Truth*, the organ of the I. W. A. in San Francisco (pages 24-25 in the original manuscript). "Circular" shows the advantages of the new group method.]

Brothers! Hoping that you will carefully consider the matters herein set forth we beg to close.

Salut et Fraternité!

(signed) BURNETTE G. HASKELL

Division Secretary

By Order Division Executive

[A postscript describing pamphlets published by the Pacific Coast Division, I. W. A. and commenting on educational methods has been omitted.][38]

AUTHOR'S NOTE

After the preceding document went to press in the *Pacific Historical Review*, additional material came to light that makes it possible to reconstruct in outline, at least, the next phase of Burnette Haskell's machinations. It also casts a little additional light upon his earlier attempt to unite the communist-anarchists and the Marxian revolutionaries.

The most significant data was found in an anonymously contributed article, "Revolution in 1889," in *The* (Chicago) *Knights of Labor* for April 30, 1887, and a covering editorial entitled "Haskell's Second Attempt to Fuse the Reds with the Blacks." Both bear unmistakable evidence of having been written by Ethelbert Stewart, who wrote also several subsequent editorials bearing on the subject as well. Collateral evidence has been gleaned from the skilfully edited Marxian contemporary, the (Chicago) *Labor Enquirer* that had been launched in late February, 1887, by Joseph R. Buchanan. This labor journalist, it will be remembered, had recently been the chief executive of the I. W. A. in the Rocky Mountain Division, editor of the Denver, Colorado, *Labor Enquirer*, and fomenter of strikes on the Gould railroads while a member of the general executive board of the Knights of Labor.

Stewart's article and editorials were the product of a vigorous and successful attempt to defeat Haskell's plan to shift the center of his revo-

[38] Some indication of the increasing influence of the I. W. A. in the Knights of Labor in the next few years can be gleaned from the following statement by H. M. Hyndman to Thomas Davidson, July 14, 1886: "Several of our men are on their Chief Council & we are capturing their branches one after another in the States." Thomas Davidson MSS. (Courtesy of Charles M. Bakewell, Yale University, New Haven, Connecticut.)

lutionary movement to Chicago in the winter of 1887 following the judicial condemnation of the outstanding leaders of the I. W. P. A. there. For reasons that may only be surmised, Stewart gained access to the secret instructions that Haskell had prepared from the district executives of his organization. These Stewart published together with other data that made Haskell's purposes plain to the Knights of Labor, and also to the rank and file of the I. W. A. from whom the insurrectionary character of their movement had been kept secret. The story of Haskell's second attempt to unite the "Reds" and "Blacks" can now be briefly told.

First, however; Stewart revealed that the presentation of Haskell's first proposal for a union of forces at the Pittsburgh Congress of October 14, 1883, had precipitated "a fist fight in the convention."[39] This suggests that it had received more serious attention there than *Freiheit's* cryptic reference to the rejection of Haskell's scheme would lead the reader to suppose. This would indicate also that the interest in a union of forces manifest by the Chicago leaders of the I. W. P. A. in the autumn of 1885, which Henry David's excellent *History of the Haymarket Riot* describes,[40] had dated in all probability from Haskell's letter to August Spies in September, 1883. The revival and serious reconsideration among the Chicago communist-anarchists of the advantages of such a union so shortly before the Haymarket Riot must have entered into the formulation of Haskell's subsequent plans.

Thinking, no doubt, that the shattered and persecuted "Black" international in Chicago would at last welcome the twice considered fusion, and willingly join in a revolutionary stroke of revenge against the constituted authorities, Haskell sent Joseph R. Buchanan to Chicago. In a short time, Buchanan presented to the wage-earners of the mid-western metropolis his skilfully edited *Labor Enquirer*. This obviously sought to bring the "Blacks" and "Reds" together while at the same time it played on the outraged feelings of the Knights of Labor who had been for ten months subject to a bitter anti-union drive of the employers backed by hired Pinkertons, the Chicago police, and the state prosecuting attorney of Cook County. Finding San Francisco rather remote from this new field of activities, and possibly embarrassed there by the attention of the local police, Haskell moved his headquarters to Denver where he took over the editorship of Buchanan's old paper. At about the same time, apparently Haskell circulated the secret instructions that he had pre-

[39] "Haskell's second attempt . . . ," *Knights of Labor*, II, No. 12 (April 30, 1887), 8. This dates the convention as having occurred in 1884, an obvious error.
[40] Pp. 146–149.

pared two years before to the district executives and the inner ruling board of the I. W. A., ordering them to prepare for the revolution which he set tentatively for 1889. The red card holding rank and file, the novitiates, of the I. W. A. were assured, according to Ethelbert Stewart, that the purposes of the I. W. A. were peaceful although they were given a course of education that included the works of Bakunin and Kropotkin. The district leaders were to bore within the Knights of Labor and the American Federation of Labor to bring them to radical views. They were to encourage government interference with business. Haskell instructed them also to fit themselves for leadership in the revolution and for the subsequent organization of "the new society." An especially picked body of blue card holders was set aside to serve as "the revolutionary force" while in the interim the white card holding members of the central committee of the I. W. A. were to formulate carefully drawn plans for revolutionary strategy and social reconstruction.[41]

In April, 1887, while the fate of the doomed Haymarket anarchists still hung upon the outcome of their appeal to the highest courts, Haskell appointed a committee to arrange the details secretly for a convention that should finally consummate the long sought union of the I. W. A., the I. W. P. A., and the Socialistic Labor Party. On this committee he put Joseph R. Buchanan, and Dyer D. Lum, whom Stewart dubbed "the most confirmed anarchist" and "at the same time the most wily diplomat" that the I. W. P. A. possessed.[42]

At this juncture, the *Knights of Labor* published Ethelbert Stewart's article, "Revolution in 1889," and a withering editorial denunciation of Haskell that put all members of the Order on guard save those in the inner circle of the conspiracy. This bold exposure must have been most interesting to the Chicago police, and to Terence V. Powderly as well. The Grand Master Workman of the Knights of Labor may well have taken warning from Stewart's prediction that if Haskell were permitted longer to tacitly recruit wage-earners for his "idiotic" plot, it could have no other result than to "frighten the ruling classes into the passage of repressive laws, that will grind the people down worse and worse, and set back the progress of industrial civilization a hundred years." Stewart recalled, also, how at the Hamilton convention of the Knights in October, 1885, Haskell's first attempt to oust Powderly's moderate faction from control of the Order had placed Buchanan on the general executive board. Although Haskell's lieutenant still held this position in

[41] These secret instructions are quoted *in extenso*, although almost in microscopic type, in "Revolution in 1889," *Knights of Labor*, II, No. 12 (April 30, 1887), 4.

[42] *Ibid*, p. 5.

the spring of 1887, Powderly saw to it that Buchanan was debarred from the approaching General Assembly on the ground that his local had failed to pay its dues. Although Buchanan denied this in helpless fury, and denounced Powderly, and Haskell issued a manifesto calling on the Knights to overthrow the Grand Master Workman or withdraw from the Order,[43] the game was up.

Buchanan held on in Chicago, taking a prominent place in the movement to secure amnesty for the condemned anarchist leaders, until after the execution of four of them on November 11, 1887. Then, when an attempt was made once more to capitalize on the sympathy for the dead to win a following once more for the revolutionary movement, Ethelbert Stewart denounced this in the *Knights of Labor* in scathing terms.[44] The ballot, he declared, was the one effective means available by which the wage-earners could secure a redress of grievances.

Stewart's fearless and discriminating journalism, the more noteworthy since the Knights of Labor were being rapidly decimated in Chicago as the result of the reactionary movement, had much to do undoubtedly with Buchanan's failure to consummate the union of "Reds" and "Blacks" that he had come to accomplish. The exposure of Haskell's revolutionary purposes to the rank and file of the I. W. A. must have accounted partially, at least, for the rapid decline in its membership the following year. Haskell discreetly retired from Denver to the newly founded Kaweah Co-operative Colony that he and his intimates established below Mt. Whitney in the remote foothills of the Sierra Nevada Mountains in California.[45] Thence he emerged in 1889, not to lead a revolution, but to take part prominently as an advocate of political action in the burgeoning Nationalist movement on the West Coast that had been inspired by Bellamy's *Looking Backward*.[46] In Chicago, Buchanan had failed to win any substantial number of the Knights to the I. W. A. despite his skilful journalism. He was more than outwitted by Ethelbert Stewart, who had the public support of courageous Chicago liberals, William M. Salter and Henry D. Lloyd, who had joined with the *Knights of Labor* in condemning both revolutionary conspiracy and the flagrant injustice of the procedure in Judge Gary's court, and in seeking a mitigation of the death sentences of the doomed anarchists before November 11, 1887.

[43] *Ibid.*, II, No. 13 (May 14, 1887), 10.

[44] *Ibid.*, II, No. 27 (November 19, 1887), 8.

[45] *The* (Chicago) *Labor Enquirer*, II, No. 27, July 7, 1888; J. J. Martin, "The Kaweah Colony," *The Nationalist* (Boston), I, No. 6 (October, 1889), 204–208.

[46] Burnette G. Haskell, "A Plan of Action," *ibid.*, II, No. 1 (December, 1889), 30–32; *ibid.*, I (September, 1889), 171–172.

Early in 1888 the Chicago *Labor Enquirer* found it politic to co-operate with Salter in supporting the series of Economic Conferences, whereby this lecturer of the Ethical Culture Society sought to promote a *rapprochement* between the bitterly antagonistic laborers and employers of Chicago.   So successful was this venture, and so rapid the decline of the I. W. A., that Buchanan criticized Bakunin editorially and declared that the time was not yet ripe for a political socialist movement in mid-August, 1888.   Instead he urged all labor and agrarian parties to unite in demanding government ownership of railroads and the telegraph.[47] Thus he abandoned revolutionary Marxism for the traditional anti-monopolist radicalism of the orthodox Knights of Labor.   This recantation brought down upon him the wrath of *Die Sozialist* and the New York *Workman's Advocate*, while the local socialists and anarchists withdrew their support from Buchanan's paper.   It promptly collapsed. Buchanan disappeared from mid-western labor circles.   He re-appeared four years later in Newark, New Jersey, where he was associated with Samuel Gompers in advocating the adoption of the initiative and referendum as noted above.[48]   Thenceforward, Buchanan continued to be an eminently respectable labor leader.   Eventually *The Outlook* solicited and published his autobiography, which has done so much to obscure the true character of Buchanan's own career and of the left-wing movement within the Knights of Labor before 1887.[49]

[47] *Labor Enquirer*, II, No. 33, August 18, 1888.
[48] Supra, p. 24, note 63.
[49] *The Story of a Labor Agitator* (New York, 1903), *passim.*

CHAPTER VI

THE TOLEDO NATURAL GAS PIPE-
LINE CONTROVERSY*

In the closing years of the last century Toledo was the scene of an important experiment with municipally supplied natural gas. The attempt to secure support for the enterprise split the city into bitterly hostile factions. It plunged Toledo, also, into a contest with the Standard Oil Company that attracted nation-wide interest. From it both parties suffered severely. The Standard interests witnessed the premature exhaustion of their large gas reserves in northwestern Ohio. Toledo's municipal pipe-line failed completely after a few years of limited success. This left a heritage of debt and of distrust with municipally managed enterprises that may have had some influence in defeating S. M. ("Golden Rule") Jones' program of municipal traction,[1] although this is somewhat doubtful.[2] The failure, however, was publicized later by private utilities as an example of the incompetence of municipal business management.[3] Today the episode is forgotten by all but elderly Toledoans whose recollections may be stimulated by the huge pipe-lines laid to meet the demands of global warfare.

The original impulse to the Toledo experiment came from Findlay.[4] This sleepy country town was the scene of great excitement in 1884–1888, as the result of the unexpected discovery of huge natural gas reserves in the underlying Trenton limestone. High pressure wells with millions of cubic feet capacity were blown in in swift succession and Findlay was

* Reprinted from the *Quarterly Bulletin of the Historical Society of Northwestern Ohio*, XV (April, 1943), 76–110.

[1] John D. Rockefeller Papers, Conversations with William O. Inglis (Courtesy of John D. Rockefeller, Jr.), pp. 1166D–E, M. B. Daly, President of the East Ohio Gas Company, to William O. Inglis, December 2, 1918. Miss Ida Tarbell in her history of the Standard Oil makes no mention of the Toledo gas controversy. John D. Rockefeller told Mr. Inglis that the Standard Oil was joined by outsiders in its Toledo investments; and that he personally had nothing whatever to do with the affairs of the Toledo companies. No evidence that he had has ever been presented. See Allen Nevins, *John D. Rockefeller, The Heroic Age of American Business* (New York, 1940), II, 336.

[2] See Brand Whitlock, *Forty Years of It* (New York, 1914), 133, 177, for other reasons.

[3] A. R. Crum and A. S. Dugan, *Romance of American Petroleum and Gas* (American Petroleum & Gas Co., New York, 1911), I, 42–44.

[4] Russell S. McClure, "The Natural Gas Era in Northwestern Ohio," in *The Historical Society of Northwestern Ohio: Quarterly Bulletin*, XIV, 83–105. This gives the story, here briefly outlined.

soon supplied with a super-abundance of cheap fuel.   The city was piped
at once by private companies, competing for the favor of a public thoroughly aroused to the advantages of natural gas.   When the companies
merged the citizens felt that they had fallen into the "clutches of a
monopoly," and resented the reasonable rates charged as extortionate.[5]
This feeling was intensified by the belief the supply of gas was inexhaustible since supposedly it was generated underground by chemical
processes as swiftly as it was withdrawn at the surface.[6]

"Free gas" was regarded as a natural right which corporate monopoly
was denying the public.   If gas was dispensed instead by the municipality at the cost of drilling and piping, it might be sufficient to attract
industries to the city and promote a rapid growth in wealth and population.   Accordingly, an act was secured from the legislature authorizing
the city to drill wells and sell the product to its citizens.   A rate war
followed hard upon the laying of the city's pipes that soon forced the
private company to sell out at a loss to the trustees of the municipal
plant.   Outside factories were drawn to the city by the promise of free
fuel, which the city guaranteed in some cases for five years.   Free plant
sites and at times other inducements were granted.   About a dozen glass
factories, and iron industries, lime kilns, and brick yards soon became
consumers of the new fuel.   The seductive theory that the gas was inexhaustible led to the wasting of vast quantities.   The city set an example
by illuminating its streets with some 200 torches burning day and night
that consumed at least 15,000,000 cubic feet of gas a month during 1887.
Factories and private residences were equally reckless, while occasionally
the wells themselves were ignited to entertain visitors.   Rapid growth
and a wild speculative boom accompanied these developments.   The
city limits were extended from four square miles to include the entire
township, land prices rose to exorbitant figures, and the population of
Findlay increased in five years from 4,500 to over 18,000.   As salt water
appeared in the first wells, new gas territory was leased in 1889, and an
ample supply was again secured.[7]

The Findlay boom soon produced reverberations in other towns of
northwestern Ohio.   Fostoria, a short distance to the northeast, em-

[5] John Adams Bownocker, "The Occurrence and Exploitation of Petroleum and Natural
Gas in Ohio," *Geological Survey of Ohio, Fourth Series, Bulletin No. 1* (Columbus, 1903),
34–35; McClure, *op. cit.*, 88–89.

[6] Edward Orton, *First Annual Report of the Geological Survey of Ohio* (*Third Organization*) (Columbus, 1890), v; Bownocker, *op. cit.*, 36.

[7] Bownocker, *op. cit.*, 35–36; Edward Orton, "The Trenton Limestone as a Source of Oil
and Gas in Ohio," *Ohio Geological Survey*, VI (Columbus, 1888), 141–150; Orton, *First
Annual Report*, 113–116.

barked upon a similar venture in municipal gas when the services of the Northwestern Ohio Natural Gas Company failed to produce the desired boom. Legislative authority and funds raised by private citizens to supplement municipal bonds were followed by the leasing of gas territory and the dispensing of gas to local industries, chiefly in glass, that soon came to consume 7,000,000 cubic feet a day. Bowling Green, twenty-four miles north of Findlay, Tiffin, and North Baltimore also embarked upon municipal gas experiments in which free gas attracted a number of glass factories and produced a boom whose life was shortened by reckless waste.[8] In Tiffin, as in Fostoria, the Northwestern Ohio Natural Gas Company had been first in the field, only to be shouldered roughly to one side by a municipal enterprise interested primarily in "free gas."

Popular excitement resulting from the discovery of the rich Lima petroleum and Findlay gas territory was such that virtually all parts of the state were affected. In northwestern Ohio every township in whole counties was tested by drilling. The belief that the gas was generated spontaneously underground was widely entertained, despite stern warnings from the State Geologist, Edward Orton, that the supply was limited and should not be wasted. Although Orton urged that Findlay institute measures for the conservation of the priceless fuel, his own statement that the new "horizon . . . bids fair to be the most prolific single source of gas and oil that has yet been discovered in this country"[9] must have contributed to the extravagant expectations of Ohio municipalities. Hundreds of thousands of dollars were spent drilling down to the Findlay gas-rock throughout Ohio,[10] Indiana, Kentucky, and Michigan. Indiana developed a gas field of her own in this horizon that was much greater in extent than the Findlay field in northwest Ohio.[11] One result of the discovery of the Indiana field was the organization of a Consumers' Gas company to supply Indianapolis in competition with private companies already in the field there.[12]

Meanwhile, the best gas territory in northwest Ohio was becoming increasingly well defined. The heart of this field was "a few hundred

[8] McClure, op. cit., 92–97; Bownocker, op. cit., 38–39, 44–45.

[9] Orton, "Trenton Limestone," op. cit., 155, 306.

[10] Ex-President Rutherford B. Hayes, writing at Fremont, April 18, 1887 observed: "Business is daily more and more active. This is especially true of the newly discovered oil and gas region near here in the counties next west of us. We shall share to a *limited extent* in this new prosperity. We find here gas enough for domestic fuel and lighting. It is a great comfort." C. R. Williams, (ed.), *Diary and Letters of Rutherford B. Hayes*, IV (Columbus, 1925), 230.

[11] Orton, "Trenton Limestone," op. cit., 307.

[12] *Toledo Blade*, December 20, 1889; May 1, 1890.

square miles, distributed through portions of five counties" some forty miles southwest of Toledo. Hancock and Wood counties were the best of the five, and in Wood, Bloom township possessed the best gas territory of all. Over forty wells were drilled there before 1890. The Simons well, the largest of these, produced initially over 12,000,000 cubic feet per day.[13]

Popular imagination in Toledo was already inflamed by the gigantic wells opened up in the Findlay district. There the great Karg well, or the Tippecanoe that produced 32,000,000 cubic feet the first day, symbolized to laymen the "inexhaustible" riches of the field. A number of wells were drilled to the Trenton limestone under Toledo in the hope of securing an independent supply of the matchless fuel. Only one, in South Toledo, resulted in a fair flow of gas, but its title was so involved in litigation that it was unused for years.[14] As a result, attention was turned increasingly to Wood and Hancock counties as the most convenient source of abundant gas.

Toledo business men were already investing in gas leases in this area, while real estate operators were fully cognizant of the advantages to be secured from "free gas." The Toledo Rolling-Mill Company was on the market for cheap fuel after its test wells had produced only a feeble supply.[15] The Business Men's Association was eager to secure gas in quantity and at a price that would attract outside industries to the city and precipitate a boom matching that of the towns in the gas territory. Judge John H. Doyle, a prominent and highly regarded attorney, tried in vain to interest citizens of means in organizing a company of their own to bring natural gas to the city, while the Findlay boom was in its first year. Captain M. J. Enright, President of the Business Men's Association, and his friends tried to get the Brice-Thomas syndicate to pipe gas to Toledo, only to have them decline the invitation after an investigation cast some doubt on the prospects of the enterprise.[16] Judge Doyle then went East to interest New York capitalists in gas for Toledo, only to find that ex-Governor Charles Foster of Fostoria, President of the Northwestern Ohio Natural Gas Company that Doyle had helped to organize in 1886, was there before him. Foster had already laid the project of piping gas to Toledo before the Standard Oil interests. Seconded by Judge Doyle and the Toledo Business Men's Association,

[13] Bownocker, op. cit., 35. See map in McClure, op. cit., 90.
[14] Orton, "Trenton Limestone," op. cit., 208–209.
[15] Ibid., 208.
[16] Toledo Blade, January 13, 1888, "Merchant" to Editor.

apparently, he induced them to enter the field and apply for a franchise.[17] Meanwhile, another company, the Toledo Natural Gas Company, had been organized, and its president, L. H. Smith, sought a similar franchise. The Standard Oil men soon acquired an interest in this company,[18] although for several years it appeared as an independent concern. At the same time they financed a rapid expansion of the activities of the Northwestern Ohio Natural Gas Company, now a Standard subsidiary. This corporation rapidly acquired control of the best gas territory in Wood and Hancock counties, piped lines to towns and cities in the gas region that had failed to secure gas for themselves, and planned to lay pipe lines to Sandusky, Toledo, and Detroit.[19]

Franchises were granted by the Toledo City Council to the Northwestern Ohio Natural Gas Company and the Toledo Natural Gas Company on the same day, September 6, 1886.[20] According to a champion of the municipal pipe-line, several years later, there had been some opposition to granting the franchises without compensation to the city. This was overcome, according to him, by statements from President Foster and Judge Doyle that if the city felt mistreated by the gas companies, it was always free to bond itself and enter the business in competition with them.[21] The prospect of competition between the two companies undoubtedly contributed to the same end. The franchises, under which the two companies began to lay their pipe-lines, provided that the price of gas in Toledo should be fixed by agreement between the Common Council and the companies.[22] Before the lines were completed, however, a quarrel developed between them over rates. The Standard Oil interests ordered construction of the Northwestern Ohio Natural

---

[17] *Ibid.*, November 2, 1887, speech by Judge Doyle; *Ibid.*, February 7, 1889; *Ibid.*, January 13, 1888, letter from "Merchant"; Rockefeller Papers, Conversations with Inglis, p. 1166L.

[18] John M. Killits, (ed.), *Toledo and Lucas County, Ohio*, I (Chicago, 1923), 574–575. Judge Doyle, some years later, said "It is true that the Standard Oil interests owned a majority of the stock of the Toledo Company as well as the Northwestern Company. The Toledo brought its pipe lines to Toledo and commenced furnishing gas in the territory set apart to it." It is not clear whether the Standard Oil interests controlled this second company from the beginning. If they did, they preferred obviously that the citizens of Toledo should think they were going to enjoy the benefits of competition between the two companies, whatever they might be. Rockefeller Papers, Conversations with Inglis, pp. 1166L–M, statement by ex-Judge John H. Doyle, made at Toledo, January 24, 1919.

[19] Bownocker, *op. cit.*, 45.

[20] Killits, *op. cit.*, 574–575.

[21] *Toledo Blade*, May 27, June 13, 1890, "C. W." (Clark Waggonner) to the Editor.

[22] Rockefeller Papers, Conversations with Inglis, pp. 1166L–M, statement of Doyle.

Gas Company's line stopped, and for a while contemplated going elsewhere only to be persuaded by Foster and Doyle that the business interests of Toledo would see that they were treated fairly, as President Daniel
O'Day of the National Transit Company asserted later.[23]   Whether it
was the assurances of Doyle and Foster, or the acceptance by the City
Council of the schedule of rates dictated by the Standard Oil managers
(as asserted later by the city pipe-line advocates)[24] that closed the breach
cannot be determined.   At any rate, construction was resumed after the
adoption of the schedule of rates and on September 7, 1888, gas was
turned on in Toledo.

This was the occasion for a spectacular "natural gas jubilee" in the
city.   Thousands of sight-seers strolled "from point to point to view
the standpipes, each tipped with a huge banner of hissing, roaring flame,
lighting the city as if by a conflagration."   A "mighty throng" attended
the mass-meeting that, as the city's leading newspaper put it, gave convincing proof of the interest taken in the new era of Toledo's progress,
inaugurated by the advent of the new fuel.

Ex-President Rutherford B. Hayes, of Fremont, Ohio, headed the list
of speakers who congratulated the city.   He gave particular attention
to what he termed "the gravest question touching the future.   Will this
beautiful, this delightful, this matchless fuel last?   Has it come to stay?
Will it be exhausted in ten years . . . will it out-last the present generation of men?"[25]   On this crucial issue he was able to quote at length
from a letter from the State Geologist.   Orton argued that although
"Natural Gas . . . has not come to stay—forever," the geological structure and rock pressure in the gas rock of the Trenton Limestone was such
as to promise a supply longer than the "gas of any other known horizons
or fields."   Although such a supply was not great enough to "make the
careless use or wanton waste of its accumulations a matter of indifference
to us [it was great] enough to amply repay the capitalists who are bringing it in . . . to the cities and towns who so greatly desire and need
it . . . enough to confer inestimable benefits on the few and favored

[23] The National Transit Company was the Standard Oil pipe-line subsidiary that laid
the pipe-line of the Northwestern Ohio Natural Gas Company to Toledo.   O'Day's statement was made in a meeting between the Mayor's committee investigating the natural
gas question and the representatives of the Northwestern Ohio Natural Gas Company.
Toledo Blade, February 7, 1889.

[24] *Toledo Blade*, February 8, 1890, "C. W." to editor.   The ordinance, however, speci-
fied that no "exclusive rights or privileges" were thereby granted that would "prevent
any other company from furnishing natural gas" to the city.   Quoted in Henry D. Lloyd,
Wealth Against Commonwealth (1894), 317.

[25] *Toledo Blade*, September 8, 1887, Address by Rutherford B. Hayes.

communities that are able to avail themselves of it.   It is the best fuel
known to man . . . ."[26]   This statement was welcomed by the *Toledo
Blade*, the most influential city daily, which observed "that there are
many scientists who believe that the production is continuous, and the
supply will be perennial.   But if [it] be limited, our reservoir is greater
than any other."   It went on to urge the Business Men's Committee to
advertise this and bring the great advantages of Toledo "as an industrial
center to the attention of those interested," prophesying that "With her
unrivaled system of transportation, and with natural gas as fuel, our
city should become the great manufacturing city of the West."[27]

The rates charged by the two gas companies during the three years
were decidedly lower than those levied on consumers in Pennsylvania.
On the other hand, they averaged about ten per cent more than those
charged in the smaller Ohio towns, and were decidedly higher than those
in the cities where the municipal authorities furnished gas at cost to
householders and factories.   Monthly charges for large cooking stoves
from November 1 to May 1, were $3.00, from May 1 to November 1,
$2.00.   The largest furnaces for heating were supplied on an annual net
contract for $75.00.   After a little over a year of service, it was estimated
that the citizens saved on an average some forty per cent over the cost
of coal.   Some consumers complained that they did not save anything and others admitted a saving of one half of former fuel bills.
A local rolling-mill asserted that it saved $20,000.00 on its fuel bill.
Glass furnaces were supplied with power and fuel at a flat rate of
$30.00 a pot.   Within three years after commencing operations, the
Northwestern Ohio Natural Gas Company alone was supplying two
glass furnaces, a large rolling-mill, a large number of miscellaneous industries, and two-thirds of the city as well.[28]

Dissatisfaction with the services of the gas companies developed, however, almost from the day of the "natural gas jubilee."   This can be
traced to a variety of causes.   Undoubtedly some resentment had been
produced by the stoppage of construction prior to the adoption of a rate
schedule by the City Council.   The city boosters must have been dissatisfied with rates ten per cent higher than those charged in the smaller
towns of the interior.   Such a schedule would make it difficult indeed to
attract industries in competition with Findlay, Fostoria, or Bowling

[26] Rutherford B. Hayes Papers (Hayes Memorial, Fremont, Ohio), Edward Orton to
Rutherford B. Hayes, September 2, 1887.

[27] *Toledo Blade*, September 8, 1887.

[28] *Ibid.*, December 31, 1888, "Natural Gas is King"; Orton, *First Annual Report*, 144–
146.

Green, whose municipally operated plants were offering "free gas" for a period of years in addition to concessions of other kinds. Under such circumstances, a boom that would accelerate the city's growth and elevate real estate values could hardly materialize in Toledo. Since the public accepted the theory of the perennial supply of natural gas, propagated by the "real estate school" of geologists, as Edward Orton called the speculators in the gas region, it was hardly to be expected that Toledo would be satisfied for long with the relatively limited advantages obtained from the services of the Northwestern and the Toledo companies.

Under such circumstances the public relations of these companies should have been a matter of first concern to their managers. Such was far from the case. No special inducements were made to factories to take the edge off the complaints of the boosters. The absence of competition between the companies soon became apparent to all, since they divided the city between themselves and refused to bid against each other for business. Eventually the control of the Toledo Gas Company by the Standard Oil interests leaked out, and many citizens came to feel that they were now at the mercy of the most unprincipled corporation then in existence.[29] While such a feeling would give a formidable weapon to agitators for municipally supplied natural gas, the treatment dealt out by the companies to their customers poured oil on the flames of public discontent. Such a friend of the companies as the State Geologist criticized them for inequitable rates given to different branches of the Toledo glass industry.[30] Customers were treated rudely by officials who exhibited little regard for the public interest. The companies felt from the beginning, apparently, that the city authorities had treated them churlishly in the initial negotiations over franchises and rates.[31] This resentment must have been intensified by the early development of agitation for a municipal pipe-line and by the recollection, probably, of losses sustained in Tiffin and Fostoria by the Northwestern Ohio Company when the municipalities entered the field. At any rate, where steps should have been taken from the beginning to offset the inevitable dissatisfaction with the inability of the companies to supply "free gas" to all and sundry and precipitate a wild boom in the interest of Toledo, if not of their stockholders, both corporations played into the hands of

[29] Bownocker, *op. cit.*, 39–40; Rockefeller Papers, Conversations with Inglis, pp. 1166A–C, M. B. Daly to Wm. O. Inglis; *ibid.*, pp. 1166L–N, statement of Judge Doyle.

[30] Orton, *First Annual Report*, 144.

[31] *Toledo Blade*, October 18, 1889, F. J. Scott to Editor. Scott at this time was a leader in the movement against the Standard Oil interests, but said frankly that in the beginning of the controversy he had felt that Toledo had done the gas companies an injustice, and "may have treated them churlishly."

the opposition by showing "no consideration for the ordinary citizen."[32]

The Standard Oil interests put a stenographer named Corwin from 26 Broadway in charge of the Toledo office of the Northwestern Company. One Saturday Corwin threatened to shut off the gas in the local Catholic church unless it paid its bill, due that day. "Pay at once or he'd close the church, was his ultimatum," despite the promise of the pastor to pay the bill Monday out of the Sunday collections. Judge Doyle, the company's attorney, had to call 26 Broadway by long distance telephone in order to secure an order letting gas be used in the church on that Sunday. A Toledo bank president was rudely addressed as "Old Man" by one of the clerks of the Northwestern and kept waiting a long time when he went in to see about some business. When the conflict between the companies and city was at its height in 1889, M. B. Daly, Superintendent of the Buffalo Natural Gas Fuel Company, a Standard Oil subsidiary, was sent to Toledo to investigate the situation for the Standard interests. He reported to Daniel O'Day that "the lack of courtesy on the part of the Company and its representatives was responsible to a very large degree for the feeling that existed against the Company itself. Its officers seemed not to recognize the fact that they were employed to direct the rendering of, literally public service, and were acting, in a sense, as stewards of the people." The superintendent of the Toledo Natural Gas Company was worse than Corwin in dealing with the public. As Judge Doyle said years later, "I never could guess how such men came to be put in such positions." Such management, unchanged for several years, gave a legitimate basis for public discontent with the service offered by the Standard Oil subsidiaries. It proved to be the decisive factor that brought victory to the movement for a municipally owned and operated pipe-line to the gas region to the south.[33]

Long before the character of the management of the gas companies became fully apparent, however, a formidable agitation was launched in Toledo for the construction of a municipally owned natural gas plant. Less than two months after the "natural gas jubilee" it became obvious to the city booster element that the Northwestern and Toledo Natural Gas companies were not going to offer the special inducements to attract the outside industries necessary to produce a boom.[34] A powerful and energetic faction within the Toledo Business Men's Association set out

[32] Rockefeller Papers, Conversations with Inglis, p. 1166N, statement of Judge Doyle.

[33] *Ibid.*, statements of Doyle, interview with Martin B. Daly, and letter from Daly, December 3, 1918, pp. 1166B–C, G–H, and N–O. Also statement of Mayor J. K. Hamilton, in a meeting with representatives of the gas companies early in 1889, reprinted in *Toledo Blade*, May 10, 1890.

[34] *Toledo Blade,* October 27, 1887.

at once to achieve this much desired end. Its leader was Captain
M. J. Enright, President of the Association, with whom the project of a
city-owned gas plant originated.[35] Other men such as Washington I.
Squire, W. S. Thurstin, and Sam T. Fish figured actively on the Natural
Gas Committee of the Association or as effective propagandists. Addi-
tional leadership emerged as the movement developed.

Enright began his agitation in October, 1887, only six weeks after
the companies had turned on the gas for their first Toledo customers. A
city pipe-line, Enright argued, was necessary to enable the city to "offer
special inducements to manufacturers." He proposed that the City
Council memorialize the Legislature to authorize the issuance of bonds
to finance the project. Once completed, the "pipe-line . . . would furnish gas at one-sixth of the prices now charged by these companies"
while the "revenue thus obtained would not only pay the interest on the
bonds but would be sufficient to create a sinking fund by which we could
redeem the bonds as they mature," and

We could offer such inducements to foreign manufacturers that there would be a strife
as to who could get here first. We would no longer be playing second fiddle to all the one-
horse villages surrounding us, but could meet their propositions and go them several per
cent better. . . .

But the great feature of the enterprise is the boon it would be to the poor man. Today
natural gas is a luxury . . . a city pipe-line would enable them to keep a fire the year around
for $5.00. Every poor man in Toledo could have gas and every one of them would be
in favor or the project. . . . We are in shape to get all the territory we want, and right in
the heart of the fields, too, . . . of the very richest gas lands, . . . and can bring all the gas
to this city that she will want for centuries to come.

When asked if he were afraid of opposition from the Standard Oil
Company Enright admitted that this would have to be guarded against.
He asserted, however, that there were "plenty of good men in this city"
who could not "be bought up by any monopoly, and we shall be very
careful that no others have any part in the matter."[36] In a public
meeting held by the Business Men's Association to discuss the project
a few days later, he made much of the fact that if the field were left to
the gas companies some $50,000.00 a month would be drained out of
Toledo to 26 Broadway. He had no desire to make war on the gas companies, he said, but he was determined to go ahead with his program
regardless of them. "No one will claim that the Standard Oil Company,
of all companies, is possessed of a very large soul or that it is worthy of
very much consideration." The entire project would cost under $1,000,-
000.00, and should be embarked upon without delay.[37]

[35] Rockefeller Papers, Conversations with Inglis, pp. 1166M–N, statement of Doyle.
[36] *Toledo Blade*, October 27, 1887.
[37] *Ibid.*, November 2, 1887.

These arguments were widely discussed and received, in the beginning, almost unanimous approval. The *Blade*, which later opposed the project, declared that there was "but one sentiment among the people concerning the proposition that Toledo shall build a pipe-line to the natural gas fields and supply nature's fuel to manufacturing establishments practically free." This, it declared, "would give the industrial interests of the city a boom that no other thing can possibly do. . . ." Given this one thing—free fuel for her factories—and "Toledo would at once enter upon a growth so rapid, so enduring, that the past dreams of her greatness will not only be realized but surpassed in the enormous extension of her industries. She will become a mighty hive of industrious workers, a city of wealth and power, and the great industrial metropolis of the West."[38]

The *Blade* denied that previous entrance of outside capital into the business and the construction of pipe-lines by the gas companies should militate against another pipe-line. "No vested right has been created, no exclusive franchise has been given," and the argument that 600 men were on the pay-rolls of the companies was "really no argument for allowing the present companies to monopolize the gas supply of Toledo."[39] It was useless for Judge Doyle to plead in the public meeting held by the Association that the companies with millions invested were vitally interested in the city, that the people were still crowding the offices of the companies clamoring for gas, and that the managers were too busy at the moment to go out in search of new industries, or to urge that the cry that Toledo was "in the toils of an octopus" be stopped. The *Blade* replied:

There will have to be stronger arguments than any adduced last night to convince the people that a city pipe-line will not be of vast advantage to Toledo. The friends of the plan must watch the legislature. The candidates for senators and representatives in this district and county should be placed on record at once. Toledo cannot afford to elect tools of a monopoly to the General Assembly.[40]

Three weeks later, W. S. Thurstin, of the Association's Natural Gas committee, reported on the probable cost of a city pipe-line, basing his estimates upon the city's experience with the municipally operated water works. Thurstin estimated that $725,000.00 would be adequate for the enterprise, including $60,000.00 for gas wells and leasing of gas territory, and some $531,000.00 for pipes of all kinds. Even if the project should cost twice the estimates, Thurstin argued that two years' gas rentals would pay the whole debt and leave the city with free gas. The real

[38] *Ibid.*, October 27, 1887.
[39] *Ibid.*, November 2, 1887.
[40] *Ibid.*

issue, he contended, was whether it was best for the citizen to "burn his own gas" or to buy from the private companies.[41] With these estimates on hand, the Toledo investors in gas territory and the men who wished to reap a harvest of money by a boom in the values of real estate such as Findlay, Fostoria, and Bowling Green were then experiencing,[42] set out to secure the necessary enabling act from the State Legislature.

Despite the "strong popular appeal" of the proposal to make Toledo a great manufacturing center by furnishing gas for little or nothing to large concerns, sober second thought developed increasing opposition to the pipe-line project among the business and professional men of the city. Within a month after Captain Enright had initiated the movement, "a very respectable portion" of the citizens were arrayed against it.[43] Some said they would have favored the plan were it not for the flings against the gas companies and an apparent desire to punish them. Others doubted the feasibility of constructing the city pipe-line for as low as $750,000.00 and feared that the tax-payers would be saddled with a large addition to the municipal debt. Some conservatives charged that the leaders in the agitation were acting from personal motives, out of a desire to unload on the city worthless gas lands and leases. To this the pipe-line advocates replied that the strongest opponents of the city line were financially interested in the natural gas companies and their motives, too, were purely personal. The general charge of "Standard Oil Monopoly" was raised against any one who opposed the plan to bring the gas boom to Toledo.[44]

After several months of heated debate the *Toledo Blade* undertook to confine the discussion to the question of the practicality of the proposed municipal pipe-line. It also launched a sweeping inquiry into the state of public knowledge on the subject. By that time the Business Men's Association was circulating petitions in support of the enabling act which they wished to secure from the legislature. Reporters were sent to interview the signers. When interviewed, the *Blade* reported the petitioners lacked

any clear idea of the cost; . . . where it is proposed to obtain gas, or whether it will be necessary to pipe it twenty miles or forty miles; there were as many opinions as there were persons interviewed as to the number of wells, . . . no one could give anything but a guess as to the cost of obtaining control of land or wells, . . . [or] a clear idea as to the cost of piping the streets, or what price will have to be charged to consumers.

[41] *Ibid.*, November 23, 1887.
[42] Bownocker, *op. cit.*, 41.
[43] *Toledo Blade*, November 26, 1887.
[44] *Ibid.*, November 25, 1887; January 12, 23, 1888. Enright expressly denied holding any gas land or leases, or any urban real estate of sufficient size for industrial purposes, or any personal ambitions or interest in the promotion of a boom.

It then called upon the city pipe-line champions to supply detailed estimates of costs, and a statement of the source and quantity of the prospective gas supply together with the number of consumers anticipated and the expected surplus that could be applied to liquidation of the bonded indebtedness. Any attempt to push the project through on the "hurrah plan" would fail, it predicted. "Its feasibility and economy must be demonstrated." This it termed the "kernel of the whole matter" and it agreed with Wm. H. Maher, the leading public opponent of the scheme, that "free gas" alone could be expected to attract few outside industries of importance to Toledo when the towns of the gas regions were offering free sites and tax exemptions.[45]

While Enright attempted to furnish the particulars called for by the *Blade*,[46] its editors made an elaborate survey of business and professional opinion on the widely discussed pipe-line project. It reported its findings in extenso, on January 14, 1888. A careful analysis of these reveals that 117 of the leaders on the produce exchange, in wholesale and retail business, in the professions, and in "other branches of trade" were opposed to the municipal natural gas plant while only fifty favored it, eight were conditionally for it, and fifteen were listed as doubtful. Even Captain Enright conceded the fairness of the survey. Those opposing the project did so for a variety of reasons. Some felt that in honor the city could not now build a line after inviting the private companies to enter the field, others that the gas companies should first be given sufficient time to earn a return on their investment. Some feared the heavy taxes that would result if the city were bonded "for so uncertain a thing as this natural gas." Several men said pointedly, "There is no use bucking against the Standard Oil Company. . . . If anybody supposes for an instant that the Standard Oil Company would permit the city to construct a pipe-line for free gas, that person has a very limited knowledge of the extent and power of the gigantic monopoly." Thus the speculative character of the natural gas business and the hazards of entering the field in competition with the powerful Standard Oil interests were fully comprehended long before the city finally embarked upon the project. The business and professional men who favored the municipal pipe-line did so because of the prospect of cheaper fuel, or of getting "gas for nothing," because it would boom the city, or because citizens rather than the Standard Oil Company should profit from the "gas fields of the city." A prominent lawyer, A. E. Macomber, urged that

[45] *Ibid.*, January 12, 13, 14, 1888.

[46] *Ibid.*, January 13, 16, 1888. Enright concluded his estimates by the declaration that the city could acquire gas lands, lay the pipe-line, and pipe its streets for a total cost not exceeding $750,000.00.

the example set by cities in England and Germany in the management of gas plants justified the belief that a similar project could be managed efficiently by Toledo. There, assuming an ample supply of natural gas available, it could be supplied at cost to consumers at a saving of at least half. With no complaint to offer against the gas companies, Macomber believed that it was the city's duty to enter the business if it could assure such a saving to its citizens.[47]

As viewed by the *Blade*, however, the strong opposition among the business men to increasing the city's indebtedness was decisive. It urged those who favored the project otherwise to join hands with the pipe-liners and establish a consumers' company like that of Indianapolis. It argued that if Captain Enright's estimates were correct such a venture would be highly profitable and useful to the city.[48] On the other hand, it gave publicity to the industries which the Toledo companies had induced to come to the city,[49] and opposed attempts to secure an enabling act for the municipal pipe-line from the Legislature.

As the tide of public opinion turned against them, the city pipe-line advocates transferred the struggle to Columbus, where the Legislature was in session. A sub-committee of the Business Men's Association prepared an enabling bill and, without reporting it to the Association for approval, in January, 1888, secured its introduction in the House of Representatives by Charles P. Griffin, a member from Toledo. A hot contest ensued, as the pipe-liners attempted to push the measure through the Legislature. The *Blade* expressed its doubts of the city's ability to finance the proposed pipe-line with the $750,000.00 in bonds the Griffin bill authorized and demanded numerous changes in the measure. Mayor J. K. Hamilton of Toledo wrote a letter of protest to the Municipal Affairs Committee of the House of Representatives, which was seconded by statements from the City Auditor and the President of the Sinking Fund Trustees. Representatives of Toledo business men and property holders presented their objections to the bill and the methods employed in its introduction, while Judge John H. Doyle pled skillfully the case of the Toledo gas companies. These, he declared, merely asked for "fair treatment" after having been invited into the city, instead of being taxed "to bring them into competition with themselves."[50] Despite this opposition, the amended bill passed

[47] *Ibid.*, January 14, 1888.

[48] January 16, 1888.

[49] February 23, 1888. These were the "Cochran mill works, the Libby glass works, the McLean glass works, and several minor enterprises."

[50] *Toledo Blade*, January 18, 23, 24, 27, 31, 1888.

the House of Representatives in March,[51] only to be smothered in a committee in the Senate.   The gas companies, aided by the great majority
of large tax-payers and business men, had won the first contest.

During the next nine months the pipe-line agitation died away.   In
this interval the Northwestern and Toledo gas companies were given
their first opportunity to win over their customers by tactful dealing and
favorable rate adjustments.   Their policy, unfortunately for all concerned, was contrary to what a sane appraisal of the situation would
have demanded.   Embittered, perhaps, by the previous contest and
deluded by the victory at Columbus both companies continued to exhibit
a lack of courtesy and consideration that developed increasing indignation among the general public.[52]   An even greater mistake, possibly,
was the failure to reduce rates to small domestic consumers to a level
proportionate to those charged others, as the presidents of the two companies admitted later and then failed to carry into effect.[53]   Meanwhile,
new discoveries of gas in the Findlay field suggested that the Toledo
companies would be unable to control the supply as they had claimed,
while an abrupt increase of twenty-five per cent in gas rates in Pittsburgh alarmed the *Blade* and caused it to revive its agitation for a
"Consumers' Pipe-Line"as a means of protecting Toledo's industries.
Attempted as a "Consumers' Trust," the venture failed to attract sufficient support.[54]

As the next meeting of the Legislature approached, the leaders of the
city pipe-line movement prepared to renew their agitation supported by
a newly organized Citizens' Board of Trade.   Its president, L. S. Baum-
gardner, was a leading pipe-liner with large interests in gas leases.   The
Board of Directors recommended that the organization take immediate
action to promote the passage of the Griffin bill now pending in the
State Senate.[55]   Just before the public meeting scheduled to receive the
joint report of the three committees[56] to which this scheme had been referred, the influential *Toledo Blade* swung over to the support of the
municipal natural gas project.   In a powerful editorial of December 1,
1888, it argued that if Toledo's industries were to develop properly in the
future, it was useless to rely upon the gas companies.   If the city was to
attract factories of the largest class, it must arrange to furnish natural

---

[51] *Ibid.*, March 7, 9, 1888.
[52] *Supra* pp. 111–112.
[53] *Toledo Blade*, May 10, 1890.
[54] *Ibid.*, April 12, December 1, 3, 1888.
[55] *Ibid.*, December 4, 1888.
[56] Natural Gas, Manufactures and Legislation.

gas "as cheaply as Findlay and the other towns of the gas area do" and "relieve men who are looking for locations for new plants from the fear of being placed at the mercy of the natural gas corporations" once they had become established locally. Under these circumstances, the city must either forego "the advantages she might reap from cheap gas, or she must do the work of supplying it at the public expense. . . . Cheap gas is a necessity," and the *Blade* pledged its support to the city pipe-line movement, although it recognized frankly the dangers of excessive expense and of wasting city funds on gas leases and drilling.

Judge John H. Doyle, counsel for the Northwestern Ohio Natural Gas Company, replied at once to the *Blade* in a public letter that widened the breach between his clients and the public. He declared that what the city needed most and had "not the slightest danger of getting" was "more of that deliberation and judgment in public affairs that successful men give to their own business." Although he went on to offer cogent reasons against the Griffin bill and any municipal venture in natural gas, they were offered in a tone that must have infuriated disinterested Toledoans. If more were needed to antagonize the city it was supplied by President L. H. Smith of the Toledo Natural Gas Company. In a heated session with the county commissioners, several weeks later, occasioned by an overcharge to the county of $127 above the rates fixed by the City Council, Smith said, hotly,

The people of Toledo don't appreciate natural gas, and we had better pull out of here and take it to some city where they do. Detroit, for instance.

I know of $5,000,000 of capital that would have been invested in Toledo had the council not fixed the natural gas price.[57]

Thereafter the breach between the city and the gas companies was virtually complete, and the conservative business element opposed to the city pipe-line was left helpless.

A well attended public meeting, held December 4, the night after the publication of Judge Doyle's letter, voted unanimously in support of the Griffin bill.[58] Mayor J. K. Hamilton, hitherto opposed to the measure despite the prominence of his brother-in-law in the movement, now appointed a committee at the request of some prominent citizens to investigate the feasibility of the proposal. Thenceforth, he gave his support to it, antagonized, apparently, by the strictures of Doyle and Smith.[59] The *Blade*, on the last day of the year, declared that "Natural Gas is King" and predicted that the Legislature, Common Council, and

[57] *Toledo Blade*, December 3, 19, 1888.

[58] *Ibid.*, December 4, 1888.

[59] Doyle could not understand why the Mayor changed his position on the municipal pipe-line question. Rockefeller Papers, Conversations with Inglis, pp. 1166N–Q.

citizens of Toledo would devote their attention "during the entire winter" to "the problem" presented by the monopolistic combination between the two gas companies, both of which it asserted were "practically Standard concerns."

Conservative opposition to the admittedly imperfect Griffin bill before the Legislature was handicapped severely by the tactics of the gas companies. The State Senate sent a special committee to Toledo to investigate the question, only to report that "a large majority of the citizens of Toledo desire an opportunity to vote on the question." Despite the telegraphed protests of one hundred leading business men of the city against the bill, the Senate passed it under strong pressure from the large lobby maintained by the pipe-liners. The *Blade* declared that the battle had been fought on fair lines with ten dollars spent by the citizens interested in the project to one spent by the Standard Oil company.[60] Two days earlier at a mass meeting held in Memorial Hall in opposition to the Griffin bill, President Smith of the Toledo Natural Gas Company had announced that he wouldn't oppose the city if it wished "to pipe gas here. . . . We want it understood, we can take care of our business, and don't want anybody to tell us how to run it."[61] Doyle had said earlier that the Standard was willing that the bill should pass and a popular vote be taken on the pipe-line project, although it did not believe it would be carried. The gas companies contented themselves with securing amendments to the Griffin bill before its final passage. The chief of these provided that before the city could bond itself for a natural gas plant the venture must be approved by sixty per cent of the voters at the next general election.

The gas companies, however, were determined to defeat the Griffin act at the city election, which was scheduled for April 1, 1889, although they refused to modify their policies to conciliate the public. Instead, they complained of mistreatment by the city authorities, threatened to withdraw entirely from the city, and refused to open their books to verify the construction costs that they submitted to the Mayor's Committee. The figures that they gave, if taken at face value, must have given pause to many a propertied citizen, since each company asserted that the cost of its lines and gas properties approximated $2,000,000,[62] whereas the Griffin Act empowered the city to bond itself only to the extent of

[60] *Toledo Blade*, January 17, 18, 1889.

[61] *Ibid.*, April 22, 1890, "C. W." to the Editor.

[62] *Ibid.*, February 7, 9, 1889; May 10, 1890. Mayor Hamilton told Daniel O'Day, Governor Foster, and Judge Doyle in a meeting between them and the Mayor's Committee, that unless the companies altered their policies the Griffin act would be adopted at the coming election.

$750,000 for its natural gas plant. Once carried in a municipal election the Gas Trustees authorized by the measure were obliged to go ahead with the project, and of course would have to ask for more funds if the initial bond issue proved inadequate. This prospect alarmed the *Blade*, which first hedged and then entirely abandoned its support of the city pipe-line, asserting that it would cost the city at least $2,000,000. Instead, it began to urge Toledoans to reconsider the entire question.[63] Then it set out to inform them of the experience of city after city with natural gas, whether supplied municipally or by private enterprise. Its reporter visited Indianapolis, Wheeling, Pittsburgh, Jamestown, New York, and Bowling Green, East Liverpool, Youngstown, and Findlay, Ohio. The early exhaustion of natural gas wells, the inevitable increase in gas rates as the nearest supplies were exhausted, inability to supply factories with cheap gas for any length of time, the small results obtained by the most extravagant inducements to outside industries, and the failure of the Citizens' Trust in Indianapolis to promote a boom there were presented with great force to its readers.[64] The *Blade* declared flatly that the city could not afford to speculate in natural gas and that if the citizens adopted the Griffin act they would have lost their last chance to withdraw from such a hazardous enterprise.[65]

The detailed reports submitted by the Mayor's Natural Gas Committee left the *Blade* unmoved in its opposition to the measure. The various sub-committees submitted conflicting estimates on the cost of the pipe-line, including wells and city connections. The one controlled by ardent pipe-liners put it at $766,923.00 including a large main line, or $678,-425.00, for a main line somewhat smaller. Another sub-committee, dominated by Wm. H. Maher, persistent foe of the project, estimated the total cost at the much higher figure of $1,559,782.00. On the question of the duration of the gas supply, a sub-committee headed by Dr. W. W. Jones was able to quote the State Geologist against himself, showing that at one time he believed that the gas was produced by the oxidization of petroleum when reached by the drill, while just two months previous he had written that the life of a gas well at Findlay was but three years and that the business had best be left to private enterprise. Accepting Orton's earlier views and citing other authorities, Jones reported that the gas wells would last thousands of years. A fourth sub-committee accused the existing companies of having employed "credit mobilier" methods in constructing their lines, and revealed that the Northwestern

[63] *Ibid.*, February 8, 11, 1889.
[64] February 21, 23, 28, March 2, 5, 7, 16, 1889.
[65] March 12, 18, 29, 1889.

lines to all the towns and cities it supplied had been laid by the National Transit Company in return for $2,000,000 in stock. The Toledo line of the Northwestern was estimated to have cost only $700,000.00 and stock watering by both Toledo companies was frankly charged.[66] The *Blade* replied to all this by accepting Maher's estimates of costs and by attempting to expose the geological fallacy upon which estimates of the future gas supply were based.[67]

Then, as the election approached, the *Blade* lent vigorous support to an executive committee that was set up by five hundred and forty-eight leading business men to defeat the Griffin act at the polls. This group urged that the city's chances of refunding a large section of its municipal debt in the next four years would be jeopardized by embarking upon a natural gas project that would cost from a million and a half to two million dollars. The *Blade* also set out to expose the interested motives of the leading pipe-liners. A reporter was sent to examine the books of the county recorders in Hancock and Wood and discovered extensive holdings listed as under lease to outstanding pipe-line advocates in Toledo or assigned by them to companies in which they were interested. This, it declared, gave added meaning to the assertion of the Mayor's sub-committee that "really choice [gas] land can be obtained by the city at a reasonable figure." The *Blade* opened its columns once more to the strictures of Wm. H. Maher and repeatedly sought to counteract the slogans of the pipe-line movement. Just before the election it charged that the enabling act, if adopted by the voters, would set up gas trustees in perpetuity and pave the way for a gigantic steal.[68]

All of this was of no avail. Unknown to the *Blade* and the Business Men's Committee, the pipe-liners had established a secret campaign committee that completely out-generalled them. Headed by E. S. Dodd it hired halls, furnished orators, and put out effective propaganda.[69] It enjoyed, furthermore, the consistent and able support of the *Toledo Commercial*, which favored the pipe-line as in the "best interests of the city," and charged after the election that "All the power of the Standard Oil Company . . . all the money that could be used—were industriously employed" to defeat the enabling act.[70] "Free gas" and "The city against the Standard Oil" were effective slogans. So were proposals to

---

[66] March 20, 1889.

[67] March 21, 1889.

[68] March 22, 23, 25, 26, 27, 28, 30, 1889.

[69] *Ibid.*, April 5, 1889.

[70] Quoted by "C. W." from the *Toledo Commercial*, April 2, 1889, in *Toledo Blade*, April 3, 1890. No file of the *Commercial* for 1889 has been found.

boom the town and utilize the enabling act as a club in dealing with the Standard Oil Company.[71]

Endorsement of the municipal pipe-line was secured from the Central Labor Union, and the strictures of the *Blade* were nullified by charges that it had been purchased by the Standard, which the *Blade* hotly denied, and by assertions that the leases it had exposed were for oil and not for gas.[72] In April 1889, the Griffin act received sixty-two per cent of the votes cast, a close margin though sufficient to give a clear-cut victory to the municipal pipe-line project,[73] despite the strenuous efforts and a last minute appeal from the Business Men's Committee.

All that remained, seemingly, was the selection of Gas Trustees, the acquisition of gas lands, and the construction of the city natural gas system. Toledo was to discover, however, that the Standard Oil Company had just begun to fight. No sooner had Governor Joseph B. Foraker appointed the Trustees from the ranks of the pipe-liners, with minority representation for the large property interests in Toledo,[74] than Judge John H. Doyle commenced an action in *quo warranto* before the Supreme Court of Ohio to test the constitutionality of the enabling act.[75] At the same time, an application was made for an injunction from the United States Circuit Court of the Northern District of Ohio against the sale of the natural gas bonds on similar grounds. On June 7, 1889, Judge Howell E. Jackson heard the suit in chambers in Nashville, Tennessee. In a sweeping decision, he upheld the enabling act and the right of Toledo to use its taxing power, if necessary, to support its natural gas pipe-line.[76] Then, when this enabled the Gas Trustees to market $75,000.00 in bonds at a premium and begin the purchase of gas lands and leases, the Northwestern Ohio Natural Gas Company, which now absorbed the Toledo Natural Gas Company, bid up prices and paid large sums in a futile attempt to prevent them from securing sufficient productive territory to commence operations.[77] When this failed, suit was brought by the Standard Oil Company in the Hancock County court in

[71] *Toledo Blade*, March 25, 28, 1889.

[72] *Ibid.*, March 16, 28, 30, 1889.

[73] *Ibid.*, April 2, 1889. The *Blade* asserted that in some wards the regular Republican ticket was "openly traded to secure votes for the pipe-line!" The *Blade* announced, however, that it would not oppose the verdict at the polls.

[74] Clarence Brown, Thomas H. Tracey, John E. Parsons, Abner L. Backus, W. W. Jones, two lawyers, an insurance agent, a retired merchant, and a physician, all of whom were to serve without pay. *Toledo Blade*, April 12, 13, 1889.

[75] Rockefeller Papers, Conversations with Inglis, pp. 11660–P, statement of Doyle; State *ex rel. v.* City of Toledo, 48 *Ohio State Reports* 112–142.

[76] Fellows *et al. v.* Walker, Auditor, *et al.*, 39 *Federal Reporter* 651–654 (St. Paul, 1889); Orton, *First Annual Report*, 148.

[77] *Ibid.*, 137.

September for an injunction against the Toledo, Findlay and Springfield railroad to prevent it from laying its tracks across lands under oil
or gas lease without consent of the lessee. If the injunction had been
granted, it would have enabled the Standard to block the city pipe-line
to Toledo in addition to denying access to Lake Erie to the independent
oil men of the Lima field.[78]

When the day approached for opening bids on the remainder of the
pipe-line bond issue in Toledo, "a determined, vigorous and implacable"
campaign was begun to prevent their sale. This was launched by an
anonymous printed letter, dated at New York, mailed from Pittsburgh,
and sent to leading investment agencies. Entitled "Caveat Emptor,"
it exploited the pending suit before the Ohio Supreme Court and the
appeal from Judge Jackson's decision to attack the validity of the bonds,
and went on to assail Toledo's credit, the financing of the municipal
pipe-line, and the adequacy of its gas supply.[79] The Toledo Commercial,
the only morning daily and long the friend of the municipal pipe-line,
changed hands at this juncture and executed a back somersault in its
editorial policy. Patrick C. Boyle, ex-oil scout and better known for his
Oil City (Pa.) Derrick, was brought in to edit the Commercial "in the
interest of the gas companies." At once he began a vigorous and scur-
rilous attack upon the city pipe-line, its sponsors, the municipal government, and the city's credit. Boyle's prejudiced editorials and articles
on Toledo circulated throughout the country either through insertion in
metropolitan financial journals or over the wires of the news association.[80]
As Judge John H. Doyle wrote later:

He [Boyle] was the worst of all. I don't know what kind of journalism they had in Oil
City, where he came from, but he acted as if Toledo were some wild west town and he began to ride rough-shod over everybody who dared to oppose the gas companies or favor
municipal gas ownership. The vile abuse he published in his editorial columns of every-
one he deemed in opposition to the gas companies made votes for the opposition every day.
If ever concerns should pray to be delivered from their friends, the gas companies were in
that fix.[81]

[78] Toledo Blade, September 28, 1889.

[79] Annual Report of Mayor Hamilton, April 27, 1890; Toledo Blade, April 28, 1890;
Editorial, "An Anonymous Letter," of the Detroit Free Press, reprinted in Toledo Blade,
October 5, 1889. Described in detail in Lloyd, op. cit., 328–330.

[80] Toledo Blade, October 7, 1889; Annual report of Mayor Hamilton, Toledo Blade, April
28, 1890; Lloyd, op. cit., 317–318.

[81] Rockefeller Papers, Conversations with Inglis, pp. 11660–N, statement of Judge
Doyle. Clark Waggonner of Toledo, prominent Republican and former editor of the
Blade, asserted that he had been asked to undertake the journalistic defense of the gas companies by a "prominent representative" of the Standard Oil Company. Clark Waggonner
to R. B. Hayes, April 9, 1890, Waggonner Papers, Letterbook VIII (Toledo Public Library), pp. 306–307.

The more immediate effect of the attack upon the gas bonds, however, was evident on October 9, when no outside bids materialized for the sale of the remaining $675,000.00 of natural gas bonds.[82] With their funds exhausted, the Gas Trustees might well have felt themselves checkmated despite their success in securing six hundred and fifty acres of gas lands in the most promising township in the gas field.[83] This property was composed in part of small holdings surrounded by the lands of the Northwestern Ohio Company and had been acquired at top prices during the competitive bidding alluded to above. Although the Gas Trustees could report October 30, 1889, that their wells had a capacity of 138,000,-000 cubic feet,[84] these had to be capped pending completion of the pipeline to the city. Meanwhile, the Northwestern Company commenced protective drilling in its holdings adjacent to the city's wells. A long delay in the completion of the city line would, under these circumstances, be accompanied by swift depletion of its gas reserves, and if it was able to begin operations later, the operation of competing sets of wells threatened a premature exhaustion of whole districts in the Findlay gas field.[85] Ultimately, both sides to the controversy would lose heavily, if the city completed its line, but in the meantime, all the advantages of delay inured to the subsidiary of the Standard Oil Company. Delay in construction of the city lines would strengthen also the position of the Northwestern Oil Company when it should apply for a renewal of the rate franchise from the Common Council before July 1, 1890.

The attack on Toledo's credit, meanwhile, precipitated an outburst of popular indignation that united many former opponents with the champions of the municipal pipe-line in an attempt to float the bonds and vindicate the city. A hasty canvass of local capitalists resulted in subscriptions to $100,000 of the gas bonds for the continuation of the pipeline. Then a great public meeting, called by Mayor J. K. Hamilton, was held on October 18, to arrange for the disposal of the remainder of the bonds and to reply to the attack on Toledo. It appointed committees to canvass the city for additional subscriptions and to prepare and circulate a pamphlet containing the facts on Toledo's municipal finances and on the soundness of her venture in municipal gas. The Common Council was requested, also, to send a committee to eastern financial centers to further the disposal of the gas bonds there. The resolutions appealed to the people of Ohio and the United States

[82] *Toledo Blade*, September 30, 1889.
[83] Orton, *First Annual Report*, 148–149; *Toledo Blade*, October 30, 1889.
[84] Orton, *First Annual Report*, 137, 142–143.
[85] *Toledo Blade*, October 10, 1889.

to observe that the Standard Oil Company, or its agents, not content with destroying individuals, and associations which stand in the way of its monied interests, now rises to grap-
ple with and destroy the rights of cities and states,

and asked them to "make common cause with us in the defense of the
community against the aggressions of colossal power."[86]

Within three weeks, a committee had published *The City of Toledo
and Its Natural Gas Bonds*. This able pamphlet presented Toledo's case
to the investing public. Reviewing the history of the natural gas controversy in the city and of municipal gas experiments in the United States
and Europe, it demonstrated beyond cavil the soundness of Toledo's
financial position and presented facts and figures on the proposed municipal pipe-line and its gas supply that had been furnished by the Gas
Trustees.[87] With this in hand, the committee of four, headed by Mayor
Hamilton, was sent east by the Common Council to market the gas
bonds. It found, as the Mayor reported later, that not only was "the
air poisoned by hostile charges" but that the special efforts of the committee were defeated by a system of espionage that kept the "Standard
people . . . informed of our movements" and by the influence which
they brought to bear upon "proposed purchasers."[88] The third committee was no more successful in its canvass of Toledo investors, and a
substitute plan for a "Natural Gas Bank" to finance the city pipe-line
was equally abortive.[89]

Thus, by December of 1889, although the municipal pipe-line had received the approval of the voters and the Gas Trustees had obtained
seemingly an adequate supply of gas, attempts to finance the project had
been defeated by the boycott in the money markets. Settlement of the
law suits pending, including one enjoining the city from issuing the bonds
already sold, was an essential condition to any further attempt to market
the gas bonds, as Mayor Hamilton advised the Trustees, but one that
promised indefinite delay. Meanwhile, many supporters of the project
lost heart and demanded a compromise, or a manufacturer's pipe-line
or some settlement of the controversy with the gas companies.[90]

At this juncture, Daniel O'Day, who was in charge of the Standard Oil
gas interests, came to Toledo and offered a plan of settlement to the Gas

[86] *Ibid.*, October 9, 12, 18, 19, 21, 1889; *The City of Toledo and its Natural Gas Bonds*
[Toledo, 1889], 32, 33–36; Orton, *First Annual Report*, 151.
[87] Prepared largely by A. E. Macomber, Attorney, in collaboration with Frank J. Scott,
a former opponent of the city pipe-line, and David Robison, Jr. This rare pamphlet is an
important source of information on the pipe-line controversy.
[88] Report of Mayor Hamilton, *Toledo Blade*, April 28, 1890.
[89] *Toledo Blade*, December 12, 1889.
[90] *Ibid.*, December 12, 31, 1889, "The Perfect Fuel."

Trustees and the city government after President H. S. Walbridge of the Toledo Rolling Mills had paved the way with an inspired but unofficial proposal and an offer of mediation. O'Day asked that the Common Council accept an ordinance that would fix the price of gas at twelve cents a cubic foot to domestic consumers and much lower rates to factories, all on a meter basis, for a period of not less than five years. In exchange O'Day hinted that the Standard Oil Company would be willing to buy out the city's gas lands and leases and its right of way, but he bluntly threatened to withdraw from Toledo by next July when the initial contract expired if this offer were not accepted. Despite the dilemma facing the city and strong pressure from the *Blade* to accept the Standard's proposal, it was rejected by the Trustees and Common Council, owing in part, at least, to popular opposition to introduction of gas meters and the necessary economizing on gas which Nature, supposedly, generated free in the Trenton limestone for the benefit of the gas companies.[91]

At this moment, when the supporters of the municipal gas plant were discouraged and without press support, Clark Waggoner took up cudgels in their behalf. Formerly editor of the *Blade*, and also of the *Commercial*, and later the best United States Collector of Internal Revenue that the Toledo district had ever had in the estimate of ex-President Rutherford B. Hayes,[92] he was well known as the champion of "lost causes" in the city. Late in 1889 he had been approached by both Judge John H. Doyle[93] in behalf of the gas companies and by T. H. Tracey of the Gas Trustees,[94] each seeking his journalistic support in the bitter controversy, with a view, apparently, to the election of the next Common Council and one of the Gas Trustees on April 1, 1890.

[91] Rockefeller Papers, Conversations with Inglis, pp. 1166A–B, Martin B. Daly to Wm. O. Inglis, December 2, 1918, and *ibid.*, pp. 1166P–Q, statement of Doyle; *Toledo Blade*, December 28, 1889. Walbridge's unofficial proposal had included the offer to reimburse the city entirely for its expenditures on its pipe-line project and a pledge to extend the new low rates for as long as an adequate supply could be secured in Wood and Hancock counties. *Ibid.*, December 18, 1889. Standard officials later thought that such a contract would have entailed heavy loss to the gas companies in view of the early exhaustion of the Findlay field. It may be doubted, however, if exhaustion of the gas deposits there would have come so rapidly had competitive drilling stopped and the Northwestern Ohio Natural Gas reverted to its earlier policy of conserving the supply by proper spacing of its wells and other measures.

[92] Williams, *Diary and Letters of Rutherford B. Hayes*, IV, 455–456.

[93] C. Waggonner to John H. Doyle, November 1, 1889, Scrapbook VIII, Clark Waggonner Papers; *ibid.*, Letterbook VIII, pp. 306–307, C. Waggonner to R. B. Hayes, April 9, 1890.

[94] *Ibid.*, Letterbook VIII, p. 161, Clark Waggonner to T. H. "Trac[e]y," October 5, 1889.

Declining to write on the side of the question opposed to his personal convictions, despite his own pecuniary embarrassments, Waggonner undertook singlehanded a journalistic campaign in behalf of the now dormant municipal pipe-line, with little prospect of financial reward.[95] Securing access to the columns of the *Blade*, whose editorial policy was now one of silent opposition to city Gas Trustees, Waggonner commenced the publication of a series of ninety-five letters that in ten months[96] reviewed the history and covered every phase of the controversy between Toledo and the Standard Oil Company. The violent personal abuse showered upon him by Patrick C. Boyle in the *Toledo Commercial* bore immediate and continuing witness to the effectiveness of Waggonner's arguments and did much to revive the popular support of the city pipe-line.[97] Over the signature of "C.W.," Waggonner defended the Gas Trustees from the attacks of the *Commercial* on their purchases of gas leases and gas bonds, and compared the attack upon the credit of Toledo with that which had been made by the Standard Oil Company upon the bonds and record of the Consumers Gas Trust Company of Indianapolis. He made cutting references to the earlier statements of Charles Foster and Judge Doyle that they would not oppose future competition if the city became dissatisfied with the services of the gas companies, and exposed the exorbitant price paid by the Standard for a single acre of gas land in order to acquire a well within two hundred feet of one of the city's wells that was located in a seventy-acre tract leased by the Gas Trustees.[98] Then as the date of municipal election drew near, "C. W." asked, "Shall Toledo be the First Subjugated Municipality?" and reviewed the exposure of Standard Oil business

[95] *Ibid.*, Letterbook VIII, p. 306–307, Waggonner to R. B. Hayes, April 9, 1890. Waggonner said that he had little personal interest in the pipe-line question, but that his neighbors had and that was reason enough for him. *Ibid.*, Letterbook VIII, p. 275, Waggonner to G. H. Hartupel, January 31, 1890; Letterbook VIII, pp. 277–278, C. Waggonner to his son, Ralph H. Waggonner, February 8, 1890. Waggonner apparently expected no pecuniary return from the discouraged pipe-liners, when he began, although he may have thought that he might improve his prospects of being restored to the collectorship of the Toledo district if he were successful. Later, the friends of the city pipe-line paid him $350.00 which he tried in vain to treat as a loan. *Ibid.*, Letterbook VIII, pp. 369, 393, C. Waggonner to A. E. Macomber, July 14, 1890; memorandum dated October 21, 1890.

[96] *Ibid.*, Letterbook IX, p. 69, memorandum entitled "95 Pipe-Line Articles" by C. W. in *Toledo Blade*, January 4 to October 4, 1890.

[97] See *Toledo Commercial*, February 2, March 2, 4, 5, April 10, 1890, for libelous cartoons of "C. W.", clippings in Waggonner Papers, Scrapbook VIII; and Waggonner's letters to his son Ralph for the public effect of the *Commercial's* abuse in reviving the popularity of the municipal gas experiment, *ibid.*, Letterbook VIII, pp. 269–270, 272–273, 277–278.

[98] *Toledo Blade*, February 6, 8, 13, March 10, 18, May 27, June 13, 1890.

methods made by J. F. Hudson in his *Railways and the Public*.[99] At the same time he charged that the *Commercial* had been bought by the Standard Oil interests to end its support of the city pipe-line and ride down all popular support of the measure by means of the libelous assaults of P. C. Boyle upon Toledoans.[100] Boyle was so enraged by Waggonner's attacks that he declared that the *Blade* had been bought by the pipe-liners and went on to make a sensational and libelous attack upon the Gas Trustees on the eve of the city election.[101] This last assault subjected him and his editorial assistant to libel suits immediately after the election.[102] These completed the destruction of the *Commercial's* influence in the city. Eventually it was sold to H. C. Vortriede of Toledo, who restored it to the channels of *"legitimate iournalism."*[103]

Meanwhile, Boyle's tactics had so alienated Toledoans that both political parties united in the re-election of the retiring Gas Trustee, Dr. W. W. Jones. Every member elected to the new Common Council was "an *avowed opponent of The Standard*" and of a "Toledo Ripper Bill" that had been introduced into the State Legislature in order to limit Toledo's control of her municipal government. Not a single Toledo daily had supported the city pipe-line during the preceding campaign, and Waggonner rightly regarded the result as a personal triumph.[104] He thanked Patrick C. Boyle, ironically, for the *Commercial's* assistance,[105] and continued his articles until early in October, exposing the obstructionist tactics behind the law suits initiated by the Standard Oil interests and their continued purchases of territory while attempting to discourage the city line with the argument that the supply was un-

[99] *Ibid.*, March 28, April 1, 1890. See Hudson, *op. cit.*, Ch. III, "The History of a Commercial Crime" which was circulated in Toledo as a campaign document.

[100] *Toledo Blade*, March 20, April 3, 1890.

[101] *Ibid.*, April 12, 1890; *Toledo Daily Commercial*, March 25, 1890, clipping in Waggonner Papers, Scrapbook IV. See also the attacks on the Gas Trustees in the only number available in the Toledo Public Library, *Toledo Daily Commercial*, February 28, 1890.

[102] Waggonner Papers, Letterbook VIII, p. 315, C. Waggonner to R. H. Waggonner, April 16, 1890; *ibid.*, Scrapbook IV, clipping from *Toledo Daily Commercial*, April 17, 1890.

[103] *Ibid.*, Letterbook IX, p. 170, C. Waggonner to H. C. Vortriede, August 27, 1892.

[104] *Ibid.*, Letterbook VIII, pp. 301, 303, 304–305, C. Waggonner to Senator John Sherman, April 4, 1890, C. W. to J. F. Hudson, April 18, 1890, C. W. to Ralph H. Waggonner, April 8, 1890.

[105] *Ibid.*, Letterbook VIII, pp. 308–309, C. W. to P. C. Boyle, President, Toledo Commercial Company, April 14, 1890: "I deem it due to truth here to say, that no Toledo paper did as much toward consolidating the people of the city in emphatic protest against the Standard Oil monopoly and outrage, as did the *Commercial* under your special direction."

certain.[106]   He also laid responsibility for the billingsgate of the *Daily Commercial* squarely upon the shoulders of Judge John H. Doyle, attorney for the gas companies and a director of the Commercial Publishing Company,[107] and appealed to Charles Foster, President of the Northwestern Ohio Company, to protect Toledo from "the vicious methods of those employing him."[108]   Doyle, as we have seen, did not approve of Boyle's methods.

Rallied by Clark Waggonner's stream of articles in the *Blade*, indignant at Boyle's peculiar brand of oil region journalism, Toledo determined to complete its pipe-line and free itself from the toils of "the Standard octopus."[109]   Popular subscriptions and the city's sinking fund took up the unsubscribed gas bonds.   An occasional eastern investor purchased a block despite Boyle's abuse, after the stigma upon the bonds was removed by successive decisions against the Standard in its litigation against the city.[110]   The line from the gas fields to Toledo was laid during the spring and summer of 1890, and part of the city was piped by a contractor who accepted gas bonds in payment.   Other contractors were paid from the income from the city's gas sales, and in other cases customers advanced part of the cost.   The gas was turned on late in 1891.[111]

After two years of delay Toledo had completed its municipal pipe-line. The long delay, the endless litigation, the expensive competition for gas lands and leases with the Northwestern Ohio Natural Gas Company, and the depreciation of the gas bonds resulting from the attack upon the city's credit had inflicted a loss upon Toledo "estimated at more than a million dollars."[112]   Legislative authorization of $400,000.00 more bonds for construction and to take up the floating debt incurred by the city in its support of the Gas Trustees was secured at the expense of another

---

[106] *Toledo Blade*, June 13, May 6, 1890.

[107] *Ibid.*, May 6, 8, 1890.   In this article "C. W." quoted the terms, "Snot Rag," "Bladder," that the *Commercial* was applying to the *Blade*, and the vitriolic attack upon one of the most prominent newspapers of Ohio, probably the *Dayton Journal*, and its editor: "That aged, sedulous addleplate, the monkey-eyed, monkey-browed monogram sarcasm, and spider-shanked pigeon-witted public scold, Majah Bilgewater Bickham, and his back-biting, blackmailing, patent medicine directory, the *Journal.*"

[108] *Ibid.*, June 13, 1890.

[109] *Ibid.*, April 27, 1890, Mayor J. K. Hamilton's annual report to the Common Council, and *ibid.*, June 6, 1890, "C. W." to Editor.

[110] *Ibid.*, May 6, 1890, "C. W." to Editor.   State *ex rel v.* City of Toledo, 48 *Ohio State Reports* 112–142, decided in favor of Toledo on Feb. 24, 1891; Lloyd, *op. cit.*, 315.

[111] Lloyd, *op. cit.*, 359; Killits, *op. cit.*, I, 464–465.

[112] Bownocker, *op. cit.*, 42.

contest at Columbus and additional litigation.[113] Meanwhile, the systematic drawing off of the city's gas reserves through the wells of the Northwestern Ohio Company had helped to reduce the pressure in the city's main to a point where it became difficult to supply both manufacturers and domestic consumers.[114] The installation of a pumping station in 1892, after additional litigation, and the acquisition of more gas territory enabled the city to supply domestic consumers. Sabotage of the line from a giant well during the first winter of the municipal plant's operation, and suspension of service by the private company to municipal institutions before the city's line was completed were but belated incidents in the attempt to prevent its satisfactory operation. By December 31, 1893, the Gas Trustees reported that they owned 5,433 acres of gas lands, with eighty-five wells, seventy-three miles of pipe outside and ninety-one miles within the city at a total cost of $1,150,-000. Its revenues to date had enabled it to meet operating expenses, absorb $67,000.00 advanced for piping the streets, and pay $60,000 into the sinking fund, while charging ten cents a cubic foot less for gas than charged by the Northwestern Ohio Company to domestic consumers.[115]

The victory of Toledo in its long and bitter contest with the Northwestern Ohio Natural Gas Company and its Standard Oil owners was destined, however, to be short lived. Beginning in 1896, failure of the gas supply in the Findlay field, precipitated undoubtedly by competitive drilling and wasteful consumption, soon affected the operations of the Gas Trustees and their competitors. A new supply developed in Ottawa County enabled the municipal plant to meet its requirements for an additional year, but when this failed the city authorities declined to spend the large sums required for the location and development of other and more distant fields. With a dwindling supply, the municipal plant lost nearly all of its customers. Finally, in 1899, the city sold its outside pipe-lines for junk and leased its city lines for the insufficient sum of $6,500 a year to the Toledo Gas-Light and Coke Company.[116]

[113] Killits, *op. cit.*, I, 464; Lloyd, *op. cit.*, 354–356.

[114] Some of the decline in gas capacity of the city's properties may have been the result of unloading of supposedly "high pressure" wells upon the Gas Trustees by Toledo speculators (Bownocker, *op. cit.*, 41–42) and some of it was probably due to the inevitable decline in capacity as the wells flowed into the city pipe-line.

[115] Bownocker, *op. cit.*, 42; Lloyd, *op. cit.*, 358–359; Report of the Gas Trustees summarized in Lloyd, *op. cit.*, 367–368, note.

[116] Killits, *op. cit.*, I, 465; Bownocker, *op. cit.*, 42–44. $100,000 only of the revenues of the municipal natural gas plant were applied to the extinction of the bonded debt, the remainder going to maintenance and the extension of its gas lands and pipe-lines.

Popular discouragement after the second failure of the natural gas supply was the undoubted reason for the complete abandonment of the municipal system with such a heavy capital loss to the city. The possibility of utilizing the natural gas pipe-line system within its limits by erection of a municipally owned, artificial gas plant seems not to have been considered. Even if attention had been called to the success of numerous European cities in operation of such non-speculative gas utilities, it is doubtful if the discouraged Toledoans would have developed much interest in such a proposal. Final disposal of the city's natural gas plant, it should be observed, occurred during the administration of Samuel M. ("Golden Rule") Jones whose interest in municipal ownership of utilities was already well developed.

Despite the heavy capital loss incurred in the final sale and lease of the municipal natural gas system, its brief operation had secured substantial savings to its own customers as long as it was able to supply them. The potential and then actual competition that it had offered to the Standard Oil subsidiaries had produced additional savings to domestic and commercial consumers. Henry D. Lloyd estimated, after an elaborate contemporary investigation into the history of the controversy between Toledo and the Standard Oil, that the reduced rates wrung from the latter between 1889 and 1894 were such that the municipal line had been a good investment on this count alone. Added to the savings from still lower rates of the municipal system, the total savings in lower gas costs to business concerns and home owners resulting from the municipal enterprise would have exceeded $1,000,000. On the other hand, the municipal gas line had at no time been able to offer "free gas" to manufacturers or to "boom the town," nor had it been able to avoid increasing its rates annually as the supply of natural gas declined, although these were kept below those charged by the Northwestern Ohio Company as long as the supply lasted.[117]

For only a short period, therefore, Toledoans were able to enjoy the satisfaction of having defeated the most hated and feared "trust" of the day. Eventually an expert accountant estimated that the total loss to the city to 1919, including interest paid on gas bonds liquidated or still outstanding, resulting from its venture into the natural gas business had been in the neighborhood of $2,000,000.[118] This, it is interesting to note, tends to corroborate Lloyd's estimate of 1894, when he contended

[117] Lloyd, op. cit., 359–361, 367–368, note; Rockefeller Papers, Conversations with Inglis, pp. 1166A–B, M. B. Daly to Wm. O. Inglis, December 2, 1918.

[118] Killits, op. cit., I, 465.

that the three-year delay in the completion of the municipal system had imposed "a loss of not less than two million dollars on the city."[119]   The final failure and heritage of debt, together with the creation of a popular antimonopoly party that was rallied later by S. M. Jones and Brand Whitlock, were the more enduring results of the pipe-line controversy in Toledo.

Failure of the Toledo experiment left the Northwestern Ohio Natural Gas Company in sole possession of the field.   In 1891, the Standard Oil interests changed its management for the better, sending Martin B. Daly from Buffalo to take charge and heal the breach between the public and the Company.   In this he was entirely successful,[120] aided no doubt by the return of Patrick C. Boyle to Oil City, Pennsylvania, where his *Derrick* was for years to come an outstanding champion of the Standard Oil viewpoint on the petroleum business and the advantages of large-scale corporate organization.   As a result, when the Northwestern's gas supply also failed, it retained its Toledo market, despite having to shift from one to another Ohio field and finally to lay lines in 1902 to West Virginia, from which it secured gas for Toledo during the next two decades.[121]   Ultimately, the Standard Oil interests disposed of their holdings in the company.

[119] *Op. cit.*, 367.

[120] Rockefeller Papers, Conversations with Inglis, pp. 1166C–E, M. B. Daly to Wm. O. Inglis, December 2, 1918.

[121] Killits, *op. cit.*, 575; Judge John H. Doyle in later years felt that the Northwestern Ohio Company would have been ruined by this early exhaustion of the Findlay field had Toledo accepted the generous five year ordinance proposed to the city in settlement of the pipe-line controversy in December 1889. Rockefeller Papers, Conversations with Inglis, pp. 1166O–P, statement of Judge John H. Doyle, January 24, 1919. Compare *supra*, note 91.

Chapter VII

WEALTH AGAINST COMMONWEALTH, 1894 AND 1944*

THE closing years of the nineteenth century brought the American people as a nation consciously face to face with problems of which it had been uneasily aware since the Civil War. In the decade before the Spanish-American War left us fumbling toward a new orientation in world affairs, two outstanding books had surveyed the domestic scene and probed searchingly the nation's political and economic structure. Both authors, one an Englishman and the other an American with an equally penetrating mind, were friends and defenders of the best they found and fearless critics of the weaknesses they discovered. Both writers lifted national thought above the pettiness of contemporary squabbles over tariffs, pensions, free silver, and the tag ends of Reconstruction and focused attention on basic political and economic issues that were never again obscured.

The Englishman was James Bryce, whose *American Commonwealth* appeared in 1888. With objectivity and disarming friendliness he measured our institutions and political mores. Where other foreign critics had infuriated, Bryce won a hearing because we felt that at heart he was one with us in our hopes, and we heard willingly the warnings that seemed but echoes of our own unexpressed fears. Amid all the pages of praise and blame there was one passage that fell on the sensitive ear like an alarm bell in the night. A few sentences selected from this forecast of things to come are an appropriate introduction to the work of his American contemporary:

There is a part of the Atlantic where the westward speeding steam-vessel always expects to encounter fogs. On the fourth or fifth day of the voyage, while still in bright sunlight, one sees at a distance a long low dark-gray line across the bows, and is told this is the first of the fog-banks which have to be traversed. Presently the vessel is upon the cloud and rushes into its chilling embrace, not knowing what perils of icebergs may be shrouded within the encompassing gloom. So, America, in her swift onward progress, sees, looming on the horizon and now no longer distant, a time of mists and shadows, wherein dangers may lie concealed whose form and magnitude she can scarcely yet conjecture. . . . In fact the chronic evils and problems of old societies and crowded countries, such as we see them in Europe, will have reappeared on this new soil. . . . It will be the time of trial for democratic institutions.[1]

* Reprinted from *The American Historical Review*, L (October, 1944), 49–72.
[1] *American Commonwealth* (2-vol. ed., London, 1888), II, 700–701.

Although near the close of this passage Bryce suggests that the time of reckoning lies "not more than thirty years ahead," he goes on to predict that the next few years "or even decades" will be preoccupied with popular attempts to regulate and curtail the powers of the great corporations and with even more strenuous attacks upon the "Trusts."[2] In 1894, six years after the publication of the *American Commonwealth*, there appeared a volume entitled *Wealth against Commonwealth*. In incisive and vigorous prose, English exposition at its best, the American author Henry Demarest Lloyd marshaled the scholarship of many years to show that the time was here and now to challenge the misuse of accumulated wealth and to break the grip of certain great corporations, like Standard Oil, upon the economic life of the nation. Lloyd, a man economically well-advantaged himself, was preaching no formulated socialistic doctrine. He was challenging corporate power and wealth and irresponsibility in the name of the commonwealth of democratic institutions. His work, which well merits mention in the same bracket with Bryce, was acclaimed in its day and echoed in the literature of the next decade. What Lloyd treated fully and cited by book and candle, the muckrakers publicized in fields he did not cultivate. Those Lloyd pilloried were the originals of Theodore Roosevelt's "malefactors of great wealth." The pat phrases of later writers rattled off the armor of great corporations, but Lloyd's spear had found the weak spots and from his thrusts, weighted with scholarship, they have never freed themselves. The attack upon Lloyd and *Wealth against Commonwealth* comes in cycles. It is sharpest when, as in recent years, the papers of some of the capitalists of an earlier day are opened by families to the use of historians writing official and definitive biographies. All of them, especially those who deal with the Standard Oil coterie, must reckon with Lloyd, and each has. In the name of Lloyd and of historical accuracy, I propose to deal with one of these critics in as impersonal a manner as a long interest in Lloyd permits.

It may be well, however, to recall the main facts about the author of *Wealth against Commonwealth*. There can be no doubt of his fitness to undertake a study of the Standard Oil and the trusts. Trained in the law and the rules of evidence under Francis Lieber and Theodore W. Dwight in the Columbia Law School,[3] he had acquired in subsequent

---

[2] *Ibid.*, II, 705.

[3] Columbia University Alumni Office Records. Lloyd was admitted to the bar in 1869 and did not graduate with his class. For the quality of instruction, see Oscar S. Straus, *Under Four Administrations* (Boston, 1922), pp. 30–31; Frederick P. Keppel, *Columbia* (New York, 1914), p. 9.

years an extraordinary theoretical and technical equipment for such a
task.   After a thorough grounding in the theories of orthodox economics
he had abandoned them, after serious study, for the historical school.
This was before Richard T. Ely returned from Germany to introduce
the historical approach into academic circles.[4]   He was equally familiar
with the philosophical and religious movements of the period, especially
with Social Darwinism and the "gospel of wealth."   While assistant
secretary of the American Free Trade League, he had learned the importance of that exhaustive, meticulous research to which was attributable
much of his success throughout a distinguished journalistic career.
Seven years as financial, real estate, and railroad editor of the then independent and liberal *Chicago Daily Tribune* had given him an almost
unequaled firsthand knowledge of business practices and railroad management at a time when the Standard Oil was perfecting its alliance
with the railroads and completing its monopoly.   He had employed this
in making the first sustained, penetrating, and comprehensive study of
corporate and speculative capitalism in America, in the course of which
he paid full attention to the petroleum monopoly.   Published during
the course of a decade (1874–1885) in the *Tribune*, the *Atlantic Monthly*,
and the *North American Review*, his findings established his reputation
as a leading American authority on the combination movement, market
manipulations, and railroad management.[5]

During the same period Lloyd worked for a higher standard of business
ethics.   He fought for public control of the railroads, discovered the
labor movement, and dedicated his life to economic reform.   Searching
for principles that could serve as the foundation for such a program, he
turned to Emerson, the philosophy and ethics of Thomas Davidson and
Mazzini, the Ethical Culture movement, and Christian and Fabian
Socialism.   From them he distilled an ethical theory and an ideal of
human brotherhood broad enough to include the working class, whose
elevation must be a major object of "The New Conscience."   In fact,
Lloyd came to regard economic problems as fundamentally ethical in
character, and the labor movement as an ethical revolt that would over-

---

[4] An early illustration of Lloyd's abandonment of the classical school can be seen in an
editorial, "The Vanderbilt-Gould Combination," *Chicago Daily Tribune*, Nov. 28, 1879.
Cf. Lloyd, "The Political Economy of Seventy-Three Million Dollars," *Atlantic Monthly*,
LI (July, 1882), in *Lords of Industry* (New York, 1910), pp. 47–54; Richard T. Ely, *Ground
under Our Feet* (New York, 1938), pp. 121–146.

[5] The financial page, real estate section, and railroad columns of the *Chicago Daily
Tribune*, 1874–1880, its editorial page for 1878–1885, occasional special articles in the same,
and magazine articles republished in *Lords of Industry*, pp. 1–147, notably "The Story of a
Great Monopoly" and "Lords of Industry."

throw classical economics, democratize labor relations, end monopolistic exploitation of the masses, and vitalize the churches with a truly social gospel.[6] To further these ends, he vainly sought the collaboration of others in the preparation of a factual, carefully documented "Bad Wealth Series." These books were to reveal with infallible accuracy the brutal, unethical methods by which great fortunes and the control of American economic life were being concentrated in the hands of ruthless monopolists. They were intended also to expose the fatal consequences of this process for free enterprise in business, for labor, for democracy itself. Lloyd believed that when presented with these facts the American people would abandon the success fantasy and pioneer in a new democracy based on brotherhood, a finer social ethics, and social control of the great corporations.[7]

Wealth against Commonwealth was the second volume in the "Bad Wealth Series," a fact that establishes its true character beyond dispute. Although it took the trust movement as its subject, it was not a formal economic treatise or simple economic history. Its first object was to make a realistic study of the pathological aspects of corporate capitalism. Furthermore, Lloyd intended to employ the results of his analysis in a formidable attack upon Social Darwinism and laissez faire economics. His ultimate purpose was to secure a hearing for a new social philosophy that should supply the theoretical basis for effective democratic action in opposition to prevailing economic trends. On the one hand, he was preoccupied with the monopoly movement as an emerging system of power. On the other, he hoped to stimulate the development of a more than countervailing democratic power, which, once in the ascendancy, would harmonize and subordinate large scale economic organization to the ideals of freedom, equality, and humanity in the great society.[8] Such purposes elevate the book from a mere muckraking tract, as some have supposed it to be,[9] to a social document of high potency.

[6] "The New Conscience," *North American Review*, CXLVIII (Sept., 1888; 3d ed., London, 1893), *passim;* William M. Salter to Lloyd, Feb. 6, 1888, Lloyd MSS. (Madison).

[7] Lloyd to C. B. Matthews, May 20, 1889, Lloyd MSS. (Madison); Lloyd to Ethelbert Stewart, Oct. 17, 1890, Ethelbert Stewart MSS. (Courtesy of Miss Margaret Winfield Stewart, Washington, D. C.).

[8] "We must know the right before we can do the right. When it comes to know the facts the human heart can no more endure monopoly than American slavery or Roman empire. The first step to a remedy is that the people care. If they know, they will care. To help them to know and care; to stimulate new hatred of evil, new love of the good, new sympathy for the victims of power, and, by enlarging its science, to quicken the old into a new conscience, this compilation of fact has been made. Democracy is not a lie." *Wealth against Commonwealth*, pp. 535–536.

[9] John Chamberlain, *Farewell to Reform* (2d ed., New York, 1933), p. 53; Allan Nevins, *Grover Cleveland: A Study in Courage* (New York, 1932), p. 607.

They explain, also, the peculiar organization and style of presentation that distinguish the book. With the objects that he had in view, it was possible for Lloyd to concentrate on the main action, to pay but limited attention to the historical setting, and to ignore chronological sequence when convenient. His discussion of the trusts, of their methods and policies, of the Standard Oil as their prototype and initiator, was presented therefore in a series of dramatic episodes replete with piercing epigrams, employing antithesis in telling fashion to heighten contrasts that in turn are pointed up by striking summaries. It disregarded or took for granted the normal, legitimate aspects of competitive business and focused attention upon the methods that had produced the trusts. "Bad wealth" rather than good was the subject because, as Socrates had said to Callicles, "the greatest are usually the bad, for they have the power."[10]

Upon the truth of his narrative and the correctness of his conclusions rested Lloyd's hope of gaining acceptance of his system of social thought. He did his utmost, therefore, to place his factual frame of reference beyond controversy, so that public attention might not be distracted from the main issues. Regarding sworn testimony, adjudicated issues, and official reports as the most reliable of all data, he based his book upon the proceedings of courts, Interstate Commerce Commission, and official investigations wherever possible. These were supplemented by use of the daily press, by counsel with such noted investigators as Simon Sterne and James F. Hudson, by information drawn firsthand from participants in the struggle against monopoly. Cognizant of the fact that the oil trust destroyed its records and guarded its secrets with almost terrifying taciturnity, Lloyd drew upon the sworn testimony of its managers, official apologies published by S. C. T. Dodd, newspaper interviews of John D. Rockefeller, and such unofficial Standard Oil organs as the Oil City *Derrick*. In describing litigation he almost invariably followed the evidence that won the case, although not neglecting to state the side of the defense. Before going to press he compared his quotations and accounts of litigation with the official records and listened to the criticism of lawyers familiar with each important case.[11] So far as its factual

---

[10] Quoted in *Wealth against Commonwealth*, p. 506.

[11] Lloyd to C. B. Matthews, May 20, 1889, *loc. cit.;* Adelbert Moot to Lloyd, Apr. 16, May 15 and 25, 1894, Lloyd MSS. (Courtesy of William Bross Lloyd, Winnetka, Ill.); Lloyd to Roger Sherman, May 23, 1893; Roger Sherman to Lloyd, June 5, 1893, *ibid.; Wealth against Commonwealth*, p. 7. John D. Rockefeller's statement to William O. Inglis, "Conversations" (Courtesy of John D. Rockefeller, Jr.), p. 903, implying that, if Lloyd had inquired at 26 Broadway, information on the Standard Oil would have been given him, is contradicted not only by the oil monopoly's well known policy of secrecy in the nineties but also by the abrupt termination of the investigation of its affairs by a group of

framework is concerned, therefore, the presumption is that *Wealth against Commonwealth* makes a faithful, accurate presentation of available data. Heavily documented, it was long regarded as a work of painstaking accuracy.

Scholarly interest in *Wealth against Commonwealth* has increased ever since Charles and Mary Beard associated its shattering effect upon American complacency with the milder shock administered previously by the *American Commonwealth*. Although a noted student of Populism dismissed Lloyd's work as a "famous tract"[12] the tendency among historians was for some time to emphasize its historical accuracy. In a single year, the authors of three outstanding books vied with each other not only in paying tribute to Lloyd's influence but also in emphasizing the reliability of his account of the development of the Standard Oil monopoly. To John Chamberlain, it was a "daring and first-rate" book of facts . . . bolstered by all future investigation." John T. Flynn's widely read work on John D. Rockefeller termed Lloyd's narrative "thoroughly faithful and authentic," "a specific, an able, a serious, and a disinterested indictment," whose publication rendered a "historic service," while more than one passage in *God's Gold* corroborated Lloyd's earlier findings. Finally, the Pulitzer Prize winning biography of Grover Cleveland, published by Allan Nevins, described *Wealth against Commonwealth* as "a searching exposure, amply buttressed by detail" and paid tribute to the accuracy with which it described "the iniquities of the trusts," the history and "sordid record of business piracy" of the Standard Oil, all of which "was laid bare in more than five hundred calm, unemotional pages." "Nothing," Nevins declared, "escaped Lloyd's keen eye."[13]

The verdict of these scholars on the accuracy of *Wealth against Commonwealth* would, in all probability, have remained unchallenged had not the last of them reversed his earlier judgment. After wide investigation, in which he had been given access to the private papers of John D. Rockefeller, Allan Nevins published a biography of the great oil magnate that painted his portrait in softer, more friendly colors than had previously

prominent clergymen that had been invited by S. C. T. Dodd to undertake such an inquiry after the publication of *Wealth against Commonwealth*. The inquiry was abandoned when the ministers concerned demanded that Lloyd be included in the investigating group, a fact that is made perfectly clear by the Lloyd MSS. (Madison). This is overlooked in Allan Nevins, *John D. Rockefeller: The Heroic Age of American Enterprise* (New York, 1940), II, 341.

[12] John D. Hicks, *The Populist Revolt* (Minneapolis, 1931), p. 322.

[13] Chamberlain, p. 54; John T. Flynn, *God's Gold* (New York, 1932), pp. 253, 255–262, 327–328; Nevins, *Grover Cleveland*, pp. 606–607.

been exhibited and that stressed the constructive achievements of the Standard Oil. In this work, Professor Nevins asserts that the excessively harsh popular indictment of both must be attributed "particularly" to "the attacks of Henry Demarest Lloyd." Then, after tilting repeatedly in his own narrative against *Wealth against Commonwealth*, Nevins subjects it to a withering attack. As "industrial history" he declares it to be "almost utterly worthless," not to be trusted "at any point," prejudiced, one-sided, omitting the case for the Standard Oil, even dishonest. Lloyd, Nevins charges, was an incompetent investigator, a rhetorical and hysterical journalist without "high literary gifts," dishonest, though admittedly earnest and sincere.[14] So detailed and sweeping is this indictment that if it stands *Wealth against Commonwealth* must be regarded as an unfounded polemic, its author classed with William Lloyd Garrison.[15]

To scholars interested in the career and influence of Henry Demarest Lloyd, the contradiction between this last evaluation of his book and the earlier estimates of his reliability raised a historical problem of first importance. So fundamental were the issues involved that, until the conflict was resolved, no reappraisal of Lloyd's character and career was possible. Upon the final adjudication of the question, also, depended the survival of the now almost traditional story of the rise of the Standard Oil and its contemporary monopolies, a story that originated with Lloyd's disclosures, or the acceptance of the narrative offered in *John D. Rockefeller, The Heroic Age of American Enterprise.*

When this work appeared, a rather random checking of footnote references to *Wealth against Commonwealth* uncovered some startling discrepancies between its contents and Nevins' account of them. Discovery of five or six instances of this character,[16] and of Lloyd's superior

---

[14] For the complete bill of particulars, see *John D. Rockefeller, passim,* but especially II, 331–342, 708.

[15] Allan Nevins to C. M. Destler, Sept. 8, 1940.

[16] According to Nevins, Lloyd invented a "fable of a prosperous oil industry in 1872 thrown into confusion and depression by the South Improvement Scheme" (*John D. Rockefeller,* I, 335, n. 47, II, 523). The account of the early history of the oil industry in *Wealth against Commonwealth,* though couched in general terms, is careful to state that the development of the Oil Region and of the refining industry was blighted increasingly after 1865 by artificial disturbances (pp. 42–44). Lloyd made no attempt to describe these in detail and began his story with the South Improvement Company, on which the first official evidence was available. His papers show that he was aware of the activities of the "Erie ring" and other manipulators of oil prices and freight rates, and of their effect in undermining the profits of many producers and refiners before 1872. He was entirely correct in regarding the South Improvement Company as the climax of this development. See "Fourth Annual Petroleum Report," Titusville *Morning Herald,* Feb. 26, 1872, for evi-

accuracy when one controversial point was referred to the sources used by both authors,[17] made me doubt the validity of the sweeping attack that had been made on both Lloyd and his book. This led to a careful investigation, the object of which was to test the truth of the numerous counts in Mr. Nevins' indictment. Lloyd's qualifications, his motives in writing, the purpose and character of the book, the accuracy of its narrative when checked carefully against its sources, and the degree to which its findings were accepted by competent, contemporary scholars have all been considered. Lloyd's publications and private papers, and primary and secondary historical materials related to the petroleum industry and the trusts have been examined. My secondary purpose in making the entirely independent investigation of the Toledo "gas war" of 1887-1899, of which the primary fruits appear in the preceding chap-

---

dence that oil production, the chief interest of the Oil Region, was still profitable in 1871.

Wealth against Commonwealth does not describe the agreement between the Standard Oil and the General Council of Petroleum Producers, that resulted in the great shutdown of 1887, as a crime, but rather as a shrewd move to prevent the producers from building a competing pipe line to the sea (Nevins, II, 336; Lloyd, pp. 152-159). Nevins is completely mistaken in saying that Lloyd blamed the Standard Oil for the destruction of derricks during the great producers' shutdown of this year (Nevins, II, 337, n. 17; Lloyd, p. 154). There is an extraordinary discrepancy between Nevins' account of the receivership and final sale of the assets of the Buffalo Lubricating Oil Company and the passage in *Wealth against Commonwealth* describing the same event, which Nevins cites as his sole authority. Lloyd's account, incidentally, is completely verified by the sources. (Nevins, II, 87; Lloyd, pp. 292-294.) Contrary to Nevins (I, 211), Lloyd was careful to show that before 1872 the refining business required only small investments and was entered by many poor men (pp. 40-41). Nevins (II, 102, n. 22) attacks a statement of Lloyd's as descriptive of the majority report of the Ohio legislative investigating committee, while Lloyd was actually summarizing the charges presented in behalf of Ohio to the United States Senate's Committee on Privileges and Elections (Lloyd, pp. 376-377) in support of the request for a senatorial investigation into the election of Henry B. Payne.

[17] Nevins makes a major issue out of a poorly worded statement in *Wealth against Commonwealth* (p. 383) regarding the inadequate investigative powers of the Ohio Legislature in the case of the allegedly corrupt election of Henry B. Payne to the United States Senate in 1885. Nevins asserts (II, 102, n. 23) that Ohio's authority was greater than that of the Federal Senate over "Ohio witnesses." This is an evasion. The documents that both Lloyd and Nevins relied upon state clearly that the Standard Oil men suspected of corruptly procuring Payne's election had absented themselves from Ohio during its legislative investigation and were therefore beyond its jurisdiction. The narrow scope of the resolution that had authorized the investigation, furthermore, had made it impossible for the Ohio committee to compel testimony on the general question of whether Payne had been corruptly elected. In any case, as Lloyd asserted and Nevins denies, only the Federal Senate could have compelled the attendance and testimony of the missing Standard Oil officials. *Report of the Select Committee . . . to Investigate . . . Henry B. Payne, Journal of the House of Representatives of Ohio,* Vol. 82 (1886), pp. 367-368; "Views of Mr. Hoar and Mr. Frye," 49 Congress, 1 Session, *Senate Report,* no. 1490, pp. 2, 34-35, 38-39.

ter, was to evaluate the account contained in *Wealth against Commonwealth*. To make sure that the Standard Oil viewpoint was not overlooked, I sought and secured permission to make use of parts of the manuscript "John D. Rockefeller's Conversations with William O. Inglis" for this broader appraisal,[18] subject to no restriction other than a promise of fairness and of making an accurate description of it in the text.

These "Conversations" were a major source cited by Mr. Nevins in his biography. They were dictated by the elder Rockefeller after his seventy-ninth birthday (1917–1918), as he listened to the reading of passages from *Wealth against Commonwealth* and Ida Tarbell's *History*. Although the oil magnate was not conducting a debate with either author, his lengthy statements contain as full a reply to the charges made by them against him and the Standard Oil as he was then able or willing to make. Their significance is increased by the fact that they were intended for his son rather than for publication. On the other hand, they were dictated without reference to documents or other primary sources. The manuscript, therefore, must be classed in the field of reminiscences, subject to the customary reservations in regard to reliability in treating incidents that had occurred from thirty to fifty years before. It should be observed, furthermore, that the story told here of the origin and development of the Standard Oil is similar in theme and character to that related by the great oil monopolist, after careful coaching by his lawyers, on the witness stand in November, 1908,[19] and to the short volume of published reminiscences that appeared in the following year.[20] All or parts of the "Conversations" that bear upon chapters VI to X, XII to XIII, XXII to XXVI, and XXIX to XXXV of *Wealth against Commonwealth* have been used in this appraisal. Excerpts from the missing sections of the manuscript, however, have been found in Nevins' *Rockefeller*.

This investigation has established beyond hope of effective denial that *Wealth against Commonwealth* was the product of six years of patient, exhaustive, and remarkably farflung investigation and research.[21] The

---

[18] Through the courtesy of John D. Rockefeller Jr., and of Allan Nevins.

[19] U. S. *vs.* Standard Oil Company of New Jersey *et al.* Nevins, II, 597–598.

[20] *Random Reminiscences of Men and Events* (New York, 1909).

[21] Nevins II, 331–332, to the contrary notwithstanding. Lloyd's quest for material bracketed the United States and reached into Canada, Great Britain, France, and Germany. A series of elaborate notebooks at Winnetka list documents sought and consulted, and scores of letters there and dozens at Madison attest to the industry with which Lloyd followed leads to material. Six years of research and writing, three or four drafts of the manuscript, and his surviving research notes all attest to Lloyd's painstaking industry and accuracy in research.

sources drawn upon and Lloyd's careful verification of the narrative create a presumption that the book makes a faithful, reliable presentation of the facts. To test the validity of this presumption, an extensive verification was undertaken of its footnotes, undocumented statements, and quotations. Of the 648 footnotes citing source materials in the book, 420 have been checked against the sources. In 410 of the 420 notes traced, the sources bear out the statements of the text.[22] In ten only, none of great import, do the citations fail to support the narrative. In addition, 241 unsupported statements were traced back to the sources. Of these 229 were completely verified, eight partially so, only four were actually incorrect. Here again the mistakes modify the narrative only to a slight degree. Scores of quotations checked in like manner were found to be accurate to an unusual extent. Since the book has been called one-sided by defenders of the Standard Oil viewpoint, it should be observed that of the 649 footnotes and unsupported statements verified, at least 170 of them came from spokesmen and officials of the oil monopoly, while at least thirty more were made by railroad officials friendly to it. Many of these present the side of the Standard Oil, although others, it should be observed, were admissions that Lloyd incorporated in his indictment of the oil combination.

When attention is turned to specific chapters and episodes in the book, verification yields positive results to a surprising degree. The account of the anthracite coal monopoly (chapter II) stands supported by subsequent investigations.[23] The criminal activities of the whiskey trust depicted in chapter III are fully supported by the sources, the description of its evolution verified by comparison with contemporary scholarship.[24] The account of the beef trust (chapter IV) reproduces accurately the report of the Senate investigating committee of 1893 and stands unreversed by subsequent revelations. The lengthy account of the activities of the Standard Oil, through supplemented now in great detail by

---

[22] In some of the 410 notes traced and verified, there were errors in page references, but in each of these cases the original passage drawn upon was located with relative ease and clearly identified.

[23] Report to the President on the Anthracite Coal Strike of May–October, 1902, by the Anthracite Coal Strike Commission, 58 Congress, Special Session, Senate Document no. 6 (Washington, 1903), p. 255, and passim; William W. Ruley, "Pennsylvania Anthracite," in Edward W. Walker, Production of Coal in 1901 (Washington, 1902), pp. 147–152; William J. Walsh, The United Mine Workers of America as an Economic and Social Force in the Anthracite Territory (Washington, 1931), passim.

[24] Jeremiah W. Jenks, "The Development of the Whiskey Trust," Political Science Quarterly, IV (1889), 296–319, reproduced in William Z. Ripley, Trusts, Pools, and Corporations (Boston, 1905), pp. 22–45, with supplemental note by the editor.

later scholarship, has been verified to an extent that is amazing in light
of the sweeping criticisms of Allan Nevins. Three chapters (XV–XVII)
that describe the attempt of George Rice, Marietta, Ohio, refiner, to
compete with the oil monopoly in the South and West are astonishingly
restrained in the use they make of damaging admissions on the witness
stand by the Standard Oil's wholesale distributor for the South and by
railroad officials in league with him.[25] The five chapters that describe
the Toledo "gas war" of 1887–1894 have been substantiated in very
large measure by the independent investigation alluded to above, a
study that drew upon all pertinent material including sections of the
"Inglis Conversations." Its findings have been published in the preceding chapter,[26] and may be compared with *Wealth against Commonwealth* at leisure.[27]

A most careful examination of the sources cited (chapter XIII) has
verified almost line for line Lloyd's description of the collusion between
John D. Archbold of Standard Oil and the attorney general of Pennsylvania in a tax suit, and Archbold's bribery of Elisha G. Patterson into
betrayal of the petroleum producers while still under contract to the
state in the same tax suit.[28] The account of Standard Oil's shabby

[25] F. B. Carley, of Chess, Carley, and Company, the exclusive Standard Oil distributors
for the South, is the witness referred to, while the railroad agents were J. M. Culp, General
Freight Agent, Louisville and Nashville Railroad, Frank Harriot, General Freight Agent,
Baltimore and Ohio Railroad, A. J. Massett, General Freight Agent of the (steamboat)
Southern Transportation Line. *Investigation of Certain Trusts . . . by the Committee of
Manufactures, House of Representatives*, 50 Congress, 1 Session, *Report* no. 3112 (Washing-
ton, 1889), testimony on the Standard Oil Trust, pp. 517–519, 524–536, 397–398, 410–411,
442–443, all of which is cited in *Wealth against Commonwealth*.

[26] Also in the *Quarterly Bulletin of the Historical Society of Northwestern Ohio*, April, 1943,
XV, 76–110.

[27] Chapters XXII–XXVI. Although this account of the struggle between Toledo and the
natural gas subsidiaries of the Standard Oil is highly accurate, Lloyd errs in not detecting
the interested motives of some champions of the municipal pipe line, in failing to recognize
the highly speculative character of the city's natural gas venture, and in failing to detect
the fallacious geological theories that underlay popular support of it and that led Lloyd himself to charge that the state geologist was in league with the Standard Oil.

[28] Cf. Nevins, II, 61–63, for a grudging admission. Lloyd's account commits several slight
errors in chronology and fails to note that the affidavits relied upon in the tax "settlement"
were supplied by Lewis Emery, Jr., a leader of the producers in their fight against the
Standard Oil. It overlooks the fact that it was customary to take tax suits before the
courts on an agreed statement of the facts. Lloyd might have observed that the initial
"settlement" of $3,145,541.64, as the amount due the state, was probably exorbitant, and
that recovery of more than the $22,000 awarded by the courts to the state, if the attorney
general had followed a different procedure, might have been defeated by removal of the case
to the Federal courts. Of the veracity of Lloyd's indictment of Archbold, Patterson, and
the attorney general, however, there can be little doubt.

treatment of Samuel van Syckel, inventor of the process of continuous distillation as well as builder of the first successful petroleum pipe line, has also been verified adequately. Neither Mr. Nevins nor Rockefeller's "Conversations with Inglis" disputes the facts in chapter VI, which describes how the Standard Oil used rebates secured from the Lake Shore and Michigan Southern Railroad to force Scofield, Shurmer, and Teagle of Cleveland into an admittedly illegal refiners' pool in 1876.[29] Lloyd's account of the South Improvement Company and how it was used by the Standard Oil to gain control of the refining industry in Cleveland, his description of the building of the Tidewater Pipe Line, the struggle between it and the railroad-Standard Oil combination, and the latter's final triumph, his story of the rate war between the Pennsylania and the northern trunk lines in 1877 that forced the former to sell the Empire Transportation Company to the Standard Oil, all stand the test of verification.   So does the account of how the oil monopoly employed its own long-distance pipe lines to throttle the railroads and use them in maintaining the monopoly that it had just established with their assistance. Equally well established is the account of the railroad rate and service discriminations imposed in the eighties in the interest of Standard Oil, of the great producers' shutdown of 1887-1888, of the ruthless means employed by the oil combination in stamping out competition.   Miss Tarbell, John T. Flynn, and Mr. Nevins add details that fill out the narrative and alter from time to time the interpretation of men and motives. But when all allowances are made, Lloyd's pioneering report on the methods by which the oil monopoly was established and maintained remains substantially unaltered, although later authorities emphasize more the role of economy and efficiency in the rise of the Standard Oil. Lloyd's condemnation of the South Improvement scheme; the account of the refineries of the Oil Region dismantled by the oil combination; the description of the heavy concentration of its capital investments in pipe lines, of the widespread espionage directed at competitors, of the decisive role of freight-rate favors in competition between refining companies, of the brutal coercion of competitors when they resisted amicable persuasion to sell out or enter the combination, of the use of bogus independent companies, and of destructive local price-cutting; and to a limited extent the assertion that the Standard Oil

[29] Nevins, II, 45-49; "Inglis Conversations," pp. 75-92.   Cf. Ida M. Tarbell, The History of the Standard Oil Company (New York, 1904), II, Appendixes 42-45, for reproduction of portions of the court record of the two suits in question, and of some of the affidavits now missing from the Cuyahoga county clerk's archives.

marketed inferior products—all were corroborated by Nevins' *Rockefeller*.[30]

Some of the more important cases of alleged inaccuracy in *Wealth against Commonwealth* must now be considered. On the highly controversial issue of whether the South Improvement Company ever did any business, Lloyd's well-supported assertion that it did is true under a fair definition of the phrase.[31] Lloyd did not assert that the Standard Oil Company was simply the South Improvement Company resurrected.[32] But he did establish beyond dispute a significant continuity between the two in personnel. Further continuity was shown in the repeated application of the idea of forcing a monopoly upon the refining industry by means of an alliance with the railroads. As applied by the Standard Oil this entailed not only exceptional rate and service favors but also, on several occasions, drawbacks on rates paid by competitors, use of the pooling device as a means to ultimate absorption of competitors, railroad assistance in espionage, and rates on oil shipments from Cleveland and Pittsburgh to the seaboard equal to or lower than those given the Oil Region, to the ruin of the refining industry of the latter.[33]

In dealing with Standard Oil's development, Lloyd's zeal in discovering its misdeeds led him occasionally to overlook or minimize evidence that would have modified his narrative. This is true of his brief treat-

[30] I, 322, 325, 335, 377–378, 402 quoting Flagler, 462, 464–472, 490–491, 497–502, 503, 514–515, 518–519, 566–568, 582–597, 652, 663–664.

[31] Lloyd, p. 59. This included, he declared, securing and organizing under a charter, collecting 20 per cent on stock subscriptions, making and executing contracts with the railroads for extraordinary rate concessions designed to force competing refiners out of business, receiving the rate increases, and the sale to the members of the South Improvement Company of such competing plants at panic prices. Only when the ground is taken that "doing business" meant only shipment of oil and receipt of the rebates and drawbacks promised in the contracts with the railroads can a plausible case be made in defense of the oft repeated declaration of the participants in the scheme that it had never actually gone into effect. Even this ground may prove untenable, since there is some evidence that some oil was purchased by or in behalf of the South Improvement Company before the railroads canceled its contracts and that in at least one instance the higher freight rates were collected by the railroads from an independent shipper. Titusville *Morning Herald*, Feb. 22, 27, Mar. 14, 15, 16, 19, 23, 1872; New York *Tribune*, Mar. 7, 1872; *History of the Rise and Fall of the South Improvement Company* (1872), pp. 33, 36–37, 56–57; *The Derrick's Handbook of Petroleum* (Oil City, Pa., 1898), pp. 168–169, 170, 174–176, 183; Lloyd MSS. (Madison), M. N. Allen to Lloyd, Oct. 18, 23, 1899. The statement of Nevins, II, 336, in the light of the foregoing would appear to be mistaken.

[32] Cf. Nevins, II, 336.

[33] Lloyd, pp. 50, 58–59, 85, 200, 206–208; Tarbell, I, 196–197; Nevins, I, 458–464, II, 73–75, for substantial agreement with Lloyd.

ment of the "immediate shipment" controversy of 1879.[34] Here he fails to note that the basic problem was the lack of tankage for storage purposes that was precipitated by the tremendous increase in production of the Bradford field. This situation the Standard Oil was doing its utmost to meet by building additional tankage.[35] Lloyd's chivalrous attitude toward women and his distrust of John D. Rockefeller as the "gentleman pirate" of the oil industry[36] led him to do the oil magnate less than justice in describing the purchase of the Bachus Oil Company of Cleveland by the Standard Oil in 1878. The original affidavits used in the preparation of this account have long since disappeared from the archives of the Cuyahoga county clerk at Cleveland, Ohio. A certified copy of one affidavit in the Lloyd Papers and the reproduction of other documents by Ida Tarbell[37] make possible verification of this chapter (VII). These and extracts from an affidavit and a letter by John D. Rockefeller quoted in *Wealth against Commonwealth* make it apparent that, once the widowed proprietor of the Bachus Oil Company had been induced to sell out, she was shown rather large consideration. Lloyd's sympathies had led him to accept uncritically the ex parte statements of Mrs. Bachus.[38] He was off guard, too, when he accepted without careful

[34] Presented simply as a part of the background for the highly reliable account of the Tidewater Pine Line, Lloyd's facts here have been verified, but they do not give enough of the general background for a full picture of the situation.

[35] Lloyd, pp. 104–107. Lloyd's failure to draw upon the newspapers or to search for the Standard Oil's side of the question leads him into this error. However, the Titusville *Herald*, July 30, 1879, makes it plain that the oil monopoly was taking full advantage to profit from the situation for which the *Herald*, June 21, 23, 1879, had declared that the producer alone was responsible. Cf. *Derrick's Handbook*, pp. 314, 315, 320.

[36] Pencil MS. "Fanatic S. oil. J. D. Rockefeller before the Interstate Commerce Commission. Nov. 26, 1887," Lloyd MSS. (Winnetka).

[37] I, 203–206.

[38] "I might suggest that the Cleveland widow's wrong seemed to me the least obvious of any you described in your book. Under unrestricted Competition, she might have received even less." Charles B. Spahr of the *Outlook* to Lloyd, Oct. 13, 1895, Lloyd MSS. (Madison); certified copy, Affidavit of Mrs. F. M. Bachus, Nov. 4, 1880, Standard Oil Co. vs. Wm. C. Scofield *et al., ibid.;* Tarbell, I, 203–206, which contains not only Mrs. Bachus' first affidavit but refers also to corroborating but now missing affidavits from a bookkeeper and cashier of the Bachus Company which Lloyd, apparently, had also used. Lloyd's own narrative suggests that the minority stockholders of the Bachus Company, who negotiated its sale for Mrs. Bachus, were perhaps responsible for fixing the lower sale price. Professor Nevins argues with force that she received a fair price for her property, but in interpreting the circumstances that led to the sale he prefers affidavits secured by the Standard Oil or Mr. Rockefeller in 1903–1905, twenty-five years after the event. These, though corroborative of the generous treatment Mrs. Bachus received in the settlement, can hardly be accepted as establishing the conditions that led up to it in preference to more contemporary sources. In any case, John D. Rockefeller should not have been put under the imputation

checking, the exaggerated rumors in the Oil Region that told of numerous suicides, bank failures, cases of insanity, and defalcations that
resulted, supposedly, from the speculative frenzy that accompanied the
rise of the oil monopoly.[39]

In striking contrast with these lapses from accuracy are four chapters
(XVIII–XXI) in *Wealth against Commonwealth* that describe the famous
Buffalo criminal conspiracy trial of May, 1887.   In it three trustees of
the Standard Oil Trust and the president and vice-president of the
Vacuum Oil Company of New York were charged with having conspired
to blow up the works of a competitor and to injure its business in other
ways.   Lloyd's description of it is termed "one of the most dishonest
pieces of so-called history he has ever read" by Professor Nevins,[40]
whose own account is based upon the incomplete transcript of testimony
supplied to the House Committee of Manufacturers in 1888 by S. C. T.
Dodd, chief counsel for the Standard Oil.[41]   Lloyd used the complete
manuscript court stenographer's report, the Dodd transcript, the record
of several pertinent civil suits, the contemporary press, interviews with
public prosecutors and complainant, and data derived from the then
secret Trust Agreement and By-Laws of the oil monopoly.[42]   His account
presents, therefore, not only the evidence offered in the conspiracy trial
but also all knowledge pertinent to the issues involved.   It is, in consequence, the fullest description of the case extant.[43]   On three separate
occasions this lengthy narrative has been checked carefully and minutely
against the court records at Buffalo of the criminal case and against the
surviving records of the civil suits of the Buffalo Lubricating Oil Company against the Standard Oil and its subsidiaries.   It has been compared also with the contemporary Buffalo newspapers, other periodicals,

---

of having deliberately robbed Mrs. Bachus, since he departed in her case from his policy of
paying only appraisal value of works of competitors.   Nevins, II, 49–51, 722; Rockefeller,
Random Reminiscences, pp. 96–107; "Inglis Conversations," pp. 117–119, 1329–1332.

[39] Lloyd, pp. 43–44, 165.   Compare with "The Wrecked," *Petroleum Age*, II (Dec.,
1882), 413, and "Panic in the Petroleum Market," *ibid.*, II (Feb., 1883), 430.

[40] II, 336, n. 11.

[41] Nevins, II, 76, n. 24, but contrast with Lloyd, p. 244, n. 1.

[42] Possession of the complete court stenographer's report, secured from Charles B.
Matthews, the complainant and president of the Buffalo Lubricating Oil Company, gave
Lloyd access to evidence against the three Standard Oil Trustees that was excluded from
the printed court record by order of the court, after their directed acquittal, and to data
omitted from the Dodd transcript, some of which Lloyd identifies in his footnotes.   See
Wealth against Commonwealth, p. 244, n. 1; p. 267, n. 1; p. 275, n. 2; p. 298, n. 1.

[43] Contrast with Tarbell, II, 88–110, which adhers to the criminal case alone and is
founded upon the incomplete Dodd transcript; and with Nevins, II, 76–87.

and with pertinent contemporary correspondence.[44]   The result of this process has been the verification of Lloyd's treatment almost line for line, even to the extent of establishing a moral certainty that one or two of the Standard Oil trustees on trial were involved in at least one aspect of the conspiracy, if not others, through voluntary adoption of its benefits.   As for the president and vice-president of the Vacuum Oil Company, a three-quarters owned Standard Oil subsidiary, there can be no doubt that they were convicted primarily for conspiring to blow up the works of the Buffalo Lubricating Oil Company, as Lloyd contends.

Nevins' description of the case for the defense,[45] would be more convincing *if* he had not omitted the damaging admissions made by defense witnesses under cross examination again and again; *if* the defense had not resorted almost entirely to mudslinging tactics in the trial and refused to put either the Everests or the indicted Trustees of the Standard Oil on the witness stand; *if* the charge of Judge Haight to the trial jury had not emphatically stated that the question of the conspiracy to blow up the refinery of the Buffalo Lubricating Oil Company was *the central and most important issue* of the case; *if* the jury had not rendered a general verdict of guilty on all counts against the Everests, to which each juryman adhered when polled at the request of the defense attorneys as soon as the verdict was returned; *if* the appeal by the Everests from this verdict to the higher courts had not omitted all mention of the count in the indictment that they had conspired to blow up their competitors' works, as would surely have been done if the evidence on this, the most important

---

[44] The complete manuscript court stenographer's report of the People of the State of New York *vs.* Everest *et al.*, Court of Oyer and Terminer, Erie County, Feb., 1886, has long since disappeared.   There survive, in addition to various manuscripts, the printed *Bill of Exceptions* (Rochester, 1887) of the case and the so-called *Appeal Book* (1888) covering the appeal from the trial court by Hiram B. and Charles Everest.   Both contain a fuller report of the testimony than that supplied by Dodd to the House Investigation of Trusts in 1888 and reproduced in its *Report*, pp. 801–951.   The *Bill of Exceptions*, as the fullest report of the trial extant, although it did not contain all the testimony against the three trustees, has been carefully compared with Lloyd's narrative, as has been also the Dodd transcript in the *House Report on Trusts* of 1888.   In addition, the only local paper that seems to have been free from involvement in the local Standard Oil subsidiaries, the Buffalo *Express*, and the pro-Standard Oil dailies, the Buffalo *Daily Courier* and the Buffalo *Commercial* have been used to piece out the missing sections of the record in the *Bill of Exceptions* (see excerpt from Oil City *Blizzard* in the Buffalo *Express*, May 17, 1887, for the business affiliations of the Buffalo dailies).   Contemporary summaries of the trial in the *Petroleum Age* and the *Paint, Oil, and Drug Review*, respectively pro- and anti-Standard Oil in viewpoint, have been drawn upon to supplement the official record of the trial.   The Standard Oil Trust Agreement of 1882 and the By-Laws of the Trust, first published in the summer of 1888, have been compared with pertinent sections of Lloyd's account.

[45] II, 80–86.

part of the case, had been defective;[46] *if* as soon as the trial was concluded attempts had not been made to prepare the public mind for statements from the grand jury to the effect that the three Trustees had never been properly indicted, which would undoubtedly have resulted in the production of affidavits from some of the grand jurors if the falsity of the charge had not been promptly exposed by a judge of the Supreme Court;[47] *if* this did not give added support to the assertion of District Attorney Quinby that the affidavits from six trial jurors, presented to Judge Haight prior to the sentencing of the Everests, by the latter's lawyers, had not been secured with money;[48] *if* Judge Haight, in imposing a fine instead of imprisonment on the Everests, had not given as the decisive reason for this action the fact that the convicted Everests were also being sued civilly for large punitive damages by reason of the same overt acts that had convicted them in the criminal suit, and that it was the duty of the criminal court under the rules of law to impose in the circumstances only a nominal penalty and thus prevent double punishment for the same offense;[49] *if* the District Attorney, just before the imposition of sentence on the Everests, had not reminded Judge Haight that the act under which conviction had been secured contemplated the destruction of the works and business of a rival company.[50]

Lloyd, rather than Nevins, follows the evidence that won the case. Lloyd[51] exposes thoroughly the collapse of the case of the defense in the trial and the tampering by defense attorneys with witnesses, which the prosecuting attorney had first exposed before the jury by forcing admissions under cross examination from the witnesses concerned. The charge of blackmail raised against Matthews by the defense during the trial and now by Nevins was fully considered by the jury. It was never proved, and if it had been, was irrelevant to say the least. This accusation was raised again and again by the Standard Oil and its defenders against competitors who defeated them in the courts, notably against Scofield, Shurmer and Teagle, and George Rice, charges that are repeated in Nevins' biography.

Charles B. Matthews stated to Lloyd on October 12, 1886,[52] that the District Attorney, just after securing the indictment upon which the

[46] *Appeal Book*, pp. 14–15.
[47] Buffalo *Express*, May 19, 21, 1887.
[48] Tarbell, II, 106; Lloyd, p. 286.
[49] MS. Opinion, "Hon. Albert Haight, Justice, The People, &c. *vs.* Hiram B. Everest and Charles M. Everest, May 8, 1888." Erie County Clerk's Office, *Proceedings and Actions*.
[50] Buffalo *Express*, May 7, 1888.
[51] Pp. 279–284.
[52] Lloyd MSS. (Winnetka).

Everests and Standard Oil Trustees were to be tried, had stated to him that the oral testimony taken by the grand jury, together with the affidavits and other documents then on file, were ample to convict all five defendants. This would seem to dispose of Nevins' charge[53] that Matthews had induced the prosecuting attorney to indict the three trustees "without a shred of evidence that would bear examination in court."

So far as other specific charges by Nevins against Lloyd's account of the trial are concerned it may be stated that although Albert A. Miller's character was completely destroyed before he testified in the criminal suit, his testimony was hardly as worthless as charged. Otherwise, the Vacuum Oil Company officials, with apparent knowledge and consent of 26 Broadway, would hardly have secreted him in Boston and then for several years in California, and attempted finally to get him out of the country. Miller's testimony, incidentally, stood up well under cross examination, and he adhered to the same story before both grand and trial juries. In the light of the evidence given by attorney George Truesdale of Rochester, N. Y., the key witness for the prosecution, Lloyd was fully justified in saying that the Everests had "coolly debated with lawyers the policy of blowing up a competitor's works,"[54] although "a lawyer" instead of "lawyers" would have been more exact.[55] The Everests though technically president and vice-president of the Vacuum Oil Company, and owners of a quarter interest in this company which they had controlled formerly, were in reality "employees of the trust" as Lloyd said, since the evidence presented in the trial showed that they simply executed orders from 26 Broadway, where seventy-five per cent of the stock in the Vacuum Oil Company was held by the Standard Oil Trust. Lloyd, on page 252, was referring undoubtedly to the "explosion" that blew off the safety valve of the overheated still, since on pages 250–251 he had described carefully how the larger explosion intended to destroy the works of the Buffalo Lubricating Oil Company had failed to occur.[56]

If further comment were necessary it might be observed that if C. B. Matthews had abandoned his civil suit for $250,000 damages and had concentrated on the criminal action, the case for the people in the latter would have been considerably strengthened and might have led to the conviction of one or more Trustees, since under the rules of law the judge

[53] II, 84.
[54] Pp. 248–249.
[55] *Bill of Exceptions*, pp. 197–199.
[56] Compare Nevins, II, 336, n. 11.

had to exclude from the criminal case some evidence of importance secured in the civil suits. This, in any case, would probably have resulted in a prison sentence for the Everests, since the judge ruled as he did in imposing fines instead.[57]

The only other section of *Wealth against Commonwealth* under attack is that which (chapter XXVII) criticizes the United States Senate for refusing to investigate the election of Henry B. Payne. This passage is a carefully documented summary of the reasons offered by the state of Ohio to justify an investigation on the ground that the election had been secured corruptly by officials of the Standard Oil, and of the action taken by the Senate.[58] As such it has stood up extremely well under careful checking against the sources, with one exception. Lloyd's contention that the Senate Committee on Privileges and Elections erred in reporting against an investigation would have been strengthened had he analyzed also the reasons given by the Republican senators Logan, Teller, and Evarts for opposing the investigation instead of ignoring them and leaving himself open to the charge of having deliberately suppressed the fact of their opposition in order to make his case.[59] However, Lloyd used and cited Albert H. Walker's careful analysis of the entire question, which exploded the arguments and exposed the presumed motives of the three senators in question,[60] and felt, no doubt, that it would be pointless to waste space on this aspect of the question. Payne did not himself ask for an investigation by the Senate but actually opposed it.[61] The Standard Oil men charged with securing his election corruptly had kept out of Ohio during that state's limited investigation. Ohio legislators more than sufficient in number to have decided the election were seriously implicated by evidence offered in support of Ohio's request for an investigation. Together with evidence of continued Standard Oil control

[57] Adelbert Moot to C. B. Matthews, April 10, 1893, Lloyd MSS. (Winnetka), contains a considered condemnation by a competent attorney of Judge Haight's action in the trial in directing the jury to render a verdict of not guilty against the three trustees. Ida M. Tarbell's account of how H. H. Rogers tried to win her to the Standard Oil interpretation of the case is well told in "Would Miss Tarbell see Mr. Rogers?" *Harpers*, CLXXVIII (January, 1939), 142–144, and also in her autobiography.

[58] And not a collection of unfounded "inuendoes and accusations" against Payne as a "tool" of the Standard Oil as charged in Nevins, II, 336.

[59] Nevins, II, 102, n. 24.

[60] *The Payne Bribery Case and the United States Senate* (Hartford, 1886), *passim*. Walker shows, for example, that Logan and Teller had secured their own elections under circumstances that may very well have made them opposed to establishing a precedent for senatorial investigations into elections in which bribery was charged.

[61] Which Nevins, II, 102, mistakenly denies. Compare *Congressional Record*, 49 Congress, 1 Session, pp. 3861, 4706–4707, 7313–7314.

of the legislature that had elected Payne, and the expressed convictions
of informed leaders of both political parties in Ohio that the election had
been corruptly secured by the Standard Oil, this was more than sufficient
to justify the treatment contained in *Wealth against Commonwealth.*[62]

Save for the exceptions noted, the accuracy of *Wealth against Commonwealth's* factual basis may be regarded as beyond dispute. Lloyd's
deductions from the facts that he presented and the degree to which they
were accepted by competent, contemporary scholars must now be
examined. He was led at times into errors of judgment, because of the
unavailability of inside information on the policies, organization, and
economies of the Standard Oil. This accounts for the excessive emphasis
that he placed upon railroad rate favors and the piratical methods employed by it and its imitators as sources of the economic power and
wealth of the great combinations and their founders. It explains,
partially, his statement that the oil monopoly had contributed little or
nothing to the technology of the petroleum industry and his charge that
it was actually opposed to technical improvements. Yet, with the
possible exception of the Frasch process of purifying the Lima oils, he was
correct in stating that the basic processes and devices in use in the industry in 1894 came from pioneers and inventors outside of the combination.[63] On the other hand Lloyd's own investigation established his

[62] Cf. Flynn, pp. 255–257. Th. admission by Nevins, II, 103–104, that it is clear that
money was spent, probably corruptly, and "with inexcusable lavishness by the Payne
managers" would seem to clinch Lloyd's main contention. He may be forgiven, perhaps,
for failing to discover the distinction between Oliver H. Payne, the treasurer of the oil trust,
and Oliver H. Payne, the son of Henry B. Payne, and for failing to learn in which capacity
Oliver H. Payne was acting when he secured the election of his father to the United States
Senate with the active support of subordinates in the Standard Oil. Interesting confirmation of the position taken by Lloyd that the oil monopoly was heavily involved in Ohio
politics is found in a contemporary statement (Dec. 14, 1887) of ex-President Rutherford B. Hayes, who may be regarded as well informed on the hidden forces at work within
both major parties: "The Standard Oil monopoly . . . attempted to seize political power
and uzurp [sic] the functions of the State. It elected Hoadley Governor, elected Payne
Senator when the great mass of the Democrats hated him, and nine out of every ten wanted
either Thurman [Pendleton] or Ward; and attempted by outrageous frauds to steal the
Senatorship held by Sherman." Curtis W. Garrison, ed., "Conversations with Hayes: A
Biographer's Notes," *Mississippi Valley Historical Review,* XXV (Dec., 1938), 379–380.

[63] Cf. Stephen F. Peckham, "Production, Technology, and Uses of Petroleum and its
Products," *Twentieth Census of the United States,* 1880, X (Washington, 1884), for the au-
thoritative work on technology in petroleum that Lloyd relied upon. Both of Frasch's
inventions (Nevins, II, 7–8) had been perfected or initiated while he was not in the employ
of the Standard Oil, and the technical contributions made by the oil monopoly before 1894
seem to have been in the perfection and improvement of basic inventions or discoveries
made by others, such as in distillation, tank cars, pipe lines, tank steamers, lamps, paraffin
production, and the utilization of by-products.

contention that "the smokeless rebate," or railroad rate and service discriminations, was the chief weapon[64] employed in the creation of industrial monopoly in late nineteenth century America.[65] This conclusion was accepted by economists of the historical and welfare schools, such as John A. Hobson and Richard T. Ely,[66] who were not bewitched by the evolutionary hypothesis. It received full corroboration, in the case of the Standard Oil, from the Commissioner of Corporations in 1906,[67] and more recently from the account in Nevins' *Rockefeller*.

Lloyd's description of the evolution of monopolistic combination from the "corner," through the pool, trust, and holding company to the merger, and of the extension of its sphere of action from the national to the international field, has been accepted by virtually all students.[68] His assertion that this development by 1893 had resulted in the monopolization or attempts to monopolize most necessities of life in America has been cited in Ida Tarbell's more recent survey.[69] His analysis of monopoly price practices, made with the assistance of Byron W. Holt and E. Benjamin Andrews, discovered not only the greater rigidity of monopoly over competitive prices during periods of depression but it led him to assert that little if any of the reduction in costs that had characterized the oil industry since 1882 had been passed on to consumers by the Standard Oil, save during sporadic periods of competition. These conclusions have been confirmed by subsequent investigations.[70] John

[64] Chap. XXXIII, and particularly p. 492.

[65] In Europe, he confessed, other weapons were used, and he stated, furthermore, that if transportation discriminations were unavailable in America other devices and practices would be employed by the monopolists (p. 492). Sheer weight of capital resources he recognized as a factor of key importance in the Standard Oil's success in Europe. For a contrary view regarding the importance of railroad discrimination see "Inglis Conversations," p. 687.

[66] Hobson to Lloyd, Feb. 22, 1895 Lloyd MSS. (Winnetka); Ely to Lloyd, Mar. 23, 1898, *ibid.*; John A. Hobson, *Evolution of Modern Capitalism* (London, 1894), p. 133.

[67] *Report on the Transportation of Petroleum* (Washington, May 2, 1906), pp. xx–xxvii, 1, and *passim.* This report traces in detail the extraordinary rate favors and service discriminations that the Standard Oil enjoyed throughout the United States and declared, in the words of the Commissioner: "In almost every section of the country that company has been found to enjoy some unfair advantages over its competitors, and some of these discriminations affect enormous areas.

"Not only has this resulted in great direct pecuniary advantage in transportation cost to the Standard, but it has had the far more important effect of giving that company practically unassailable monopolistic control of the oil market throughout large sections of the country." *Ibid.*, p. 1.

[68] Cf. Hobson, pp. 128–130; Ripley, pp. ix–x; Ida M. Tarbell, *The Nationalization of Business, 1878–1898* (New York 1936,), chap. V.

[69] *Ibid.*; Lloyd, pp. 4–5, 537–544.

[70] Lloyd, pp. 430–431; Tarbell, *History*, II, chap. XVI; Nevins, I, 671–672; J. W. Jenks

A. Hobson's contemporary but independent researches confirmed Lloyd's deduction that the oil trust's monopoly price policy entailed curtailment of production below the competitive level.[71] That exorbitant profits were reaped by the Standard Oil from such a price policy is a conclusion in which Lloyd has the support of Allan Nevins.[72] The further deduction that the great American fortunes of his day came chiefly from monopoly was confirmed by a contemporary study published by John R. Commons.[73] The graphic description of the farflung investments and gigantic economic power of the Standard Oil group of millionaires, although admittedly incomplete, has been confirmed by such an investigator as Harold Faulkner.[74] Lloyd concluded, as did Thorstein Veblen a few years later, that American capitalism, so dominated and conducted as described in *Wealth against Commonwealth*, was still in the hawk stage, predatory and speculative.

While presenting an almost impregnable array of facts and the most penetrating analysis of monopoly capitalism yet made in America, Lloyd launched a devastating attack upon its philosophical and ethical foundations. He was convinced that the monopoly movement was receiving great impetus from the extreme individualism and materialism of the age. He advocated, therefore, no return to free competition nor simple trust busting to cope with what he termed the "greatest social, political, and moral fact" of his day. The great combinations, he declared, had been sired by competition. Orthodox economics, with its reliance on individual self-interest as a guarantee of social welfare, had proved to be nothing but "a temporary formula for a passing problem." Monopoly was merely competitive business "at the end of its journey," rewarding the "fittest" with the power of life and death over the necessities of life, to be wielded by the same "self-interest" that had wrested this power from the public.[75]

Lloyd knew, also, that for many a pragmatic American the business "success" of the Standard Oil had demonstrated the economic soundness of large scale organization.[76] He saw, too, that the "gospel of wealth,"

---

to Lloyd, June 11, 1896, Lloyd MSS. (Winnetka); J. W. Jenks, "Industrial Combinations and Prices," Industrial Commission, *Preliminary Report* (Washington, 1900), I, 48–53; "Digest of Evidence," *ibid.*, I, 125.

[71] *Op. cit.*, pp. 154–166.

[72] Nevins, I, 672–673; Lloyd, pp. 431, 457.

[73] *Distribution of Wealth* (New York, 1893), *passim*.

[74] Lloyd, pp. 460–461; Faulkner, *Quest for Social Justice, 1898–1914* (New York, 1931), pp. 43–44; Nevins, II, 359–426.

[75] Pp. 6, 494.

[76] This was the boast of S. C. T. Dodd in his book on *Combinations*. John D. Rockefeller

whose ostentatious piety and ever more widely advertised philanthropies Rockefeller practiced, cast a halo of sanctity about all that the oil monopoly did. Furthermore, it was clear that the official apology presented for Standard Oil by John D. Archbold and S. C. T. Dodd appealed to an urban reading public that was bewitched by the stereotypes of Social Darwinism.[77] By reason of some uncanny insight, Lloyd inferred, apparently, that Rockefeller himself secretly invoked the evolutionary philosophy of Herbert Spencer to justify his great raids upon the free enterprise system,[78] just as he seemed to find in the doctrine of stewardship divine sanction for his swollen fortune. Careful reading makes it clear that the pitiless exposure in *Wealth against Commonwealth* of the cruel and illicit methods employed by the oil monopolists was motivated by a desire to strike down all the philosophical supports[79] that the "Captains of Industry" relied upon to secure popular acceptance of the corporate business system. This is indicated by scores of allusions and illustrations in the book which Lloyd utilized to point up the grim contrast between the policies of monopoly and the philosophy and claims to public service professed by its adherents, between the religious philanthropies and prayer meeting attendance of the oil magnates and the Sabbath-breaking violation of the law by their natural gas subsidiary at Fostoria, Ohio.[80] In this manner Lloyd sought to destroy the popular belief that the trusts were the product of an evolutionary process in the true sense, that they or their wealthy managers represented the "survival of the fittest," or that their great wealth was the reward for either superior efficiency or greater moral worth. Thus in pillorying Rockefeller and the Standard Oil, *Wealth against Commonwealth* exposed the falsity of the "Gospel of Wealth of the Gilded Age,"[81] and the social evil

---

stated to Inglis that the Standard Oil pioneered alone, with limited help from Western Union, in establishing the feasibility of the great combination in industry.

[77] Namely, that the oil trust was the product of superior efficiency and business methods; that the charges against it came from the less efficient competitors; or were motivated by jealousy of the "success" of its founders; and that the inevitable rise of the large scale organization, itself a product of the evolutionary process, was accompanied by an inevitable reduction in the price of its products to the consumer.

[78] At least, his "Conversations with Inglis," pp. 97, 111–112, 736–737, offer Social Darwinism repeatedly as the ultimate justification of the history of the Standard Oil.

[79] Orthodox economics, Utilitarianism, Social Darwinism, the "gospel of wealth." Lloyd, chap. XXXIV. Cf. Lloyd to Thomas Davidson, Jan. 30, 1891, Thomas Davidson MSS. (Courtesy of Charles M. Bakewell, Yale University, New Haven, Conn.).

[80] Also by Lloyd's avowed purpose in writing the book. But see *Wealth against Commonwealth*, pp. 15, 21, 68, 127, 161, 165, 215, 341–349.

[81] Cf. Ralph H. Gabriel, *The Course of American Democratic Thought* (New York, 1940), chaps. XIII–XIV, to learn how accurately Lloyd aimed his barbed shafts at the central doctrines of Social Darwinism and the "gospel of wealth."

wrought by application of Darwinian principles to business. It demonstrated, also, how between the greatest oil magnate and Henry Demarest Lloyd the difference at bottom lay in the philosophy with which each confronted the problems of a business civilization.

Finally, Lloyd declared that the trust movement was developing in direct antagonism to the democratic heritage of America. The combination movement, he asserted, was destroying liberty. While it was closing one economic province after another to all but the privileged few, it was subject to the law that governed tyranny everywhere as it reached out to control the bench, manipulate legislatures, shackle the press, and pervert pulpit and classroom to its own purposes. Under this impulse America was moving toward an authoritarian system that recognized no moral standards and was evolving through industrial feudalism toward the rule of a single "corporate Caesar." By elevating "barbarians from below . . . into seats of power kings do not know" in America and Europe, monopoly capitalism was destroying civilization itself as the process of perfecting the race through promoting human welfare in an atmosphere of liberty.[82] Thus, whether judged by its methods, or ultimate consequences, or in the light of its philosophical defenses, the trust movement was a veritable Frankenstein.

Before democracy could subdue such a monster it must be equipped with ideological weapons adequate to the task in hand. Their fashioning was the work of the last chapters of Lloyd's book. For raw material he took three basic concepts: the widening community, the idea of civilization, and the Golden Rule. These he combined with a profound faith in humanity and a moving appeal to the democratic spirit of America. His fundamental postulate was the Golden Rule, the "irresistible power of brotherhood" whose "progressive sway" in "human affairs is the sole message of history" "as secular as sacred." This principle was the "applied means" that enabled men to live in society. It was the "original of every political constitution" and by its operation widened progressively the scope of social action.[83] By an almost Hegelian dialectic, Lloyd declared that the struggle between the individual and

---

It is clear from the "Conversations with Inglis" that the elder Rockefeller was sincere in his philanthropies and that he made no attempt to shield his business career and public acts behind either a reputation for piety or religious philanthropy. See especially page 1161, where, referring to Lloyd's quotation (p. 342) from the *National Baptist*, Rockefeller stated flatly that the oil men "have got to stand the test" of Milton's reply to the pleas urged in behalf of Charles I.

[82] Pp. 2, 297–298, 344–345, 500, 510–511, 531.
[83] Pp. 503–505.

society, and their harmonizing, was the progressive "line of conflict" that marked the path of progress.

Society thus passes from conflict to harmony, and on to another conflict. Civilization is the unceasing accretion of these social solutions. We fight out to an equilibrium, as in the abolition of human slavery; then upon this new level thus built up we enter upon the struggle for a new equilibrium, as now in the labor movement.[84]

As yet civilization, "the process of making men citizens in their relations to each other" had "reached only those forms of common effort which, because most general and most vital, first demanded its harmonizing touch."[85] Now, under the impulse of the "new morality" of universal brotherhood, democracy must perfect the new institutions and controls essential to subordinating industrial power and property to the general welfare. Institutions of wealth, monopoly itself, would thereby be molded into the co-operative commonwealth by liberty and the civilizing process of brotherly love. "The word of the day is that we are about to civilize industry," since "to be safe liberty must be complete on its industrial as well as on its political and religious side. This is the American principle." By applying the co-operative methods of the post-office and public school to monopoly, Americans would move upward to "a private life of a new beauty [as] commoners, travellers to Altruria."[86] Thus, as Albert Schweitzer was to plead twenty-five years later in his "philosophy of civilization,"[87] the development of a finer social ethics would enable civilization to master the machine age.

For the "Progressive mind" then shaping up in America during the "mauve decade," such a philosophy had a profound significance. It helped to develop the new theoretical approach essential to grappling with the economic, social, and political problems of the day.[88] Lloyd's plea for social justice, his elevation of human welfare above rugged individualism and wealth-making, his demand that democracy move forward to control and socialize monoply, his declaration that civilization and democracy both depend upon developing a more adequate social ethics, all struck responsive chords. Viewed from such perspective, the

[84] P. 506.
[85] " . . . the family . . . the club . . . the church . . . union . . . for self-defense" and the post-office (p. 497).
[86] Pp. 505, 517, 526, 534.
[87] Albert Schweitzer, *The Decay and the Restoration of Civilization, The Philosophy of Civilization*, Pt. I (London, 1923), pp. viii–xiii, and *passim;* Albert Schweitzer, *Civilization and Ethics, The Philosophy of Civilization,* Pt. II (London, 1923), *passim.* Cf. Charles A. Beard, *The American Spirit* (New York, 1942), pp. 438–442, for a lengthier presentation of Lloyd's doctrine of civilization.
[88] Alpheus T. Mason, *Brandeis and the Modern State,* (Washington, 1936), p. 118.

publication of *Wealth against Commonwealth* in 1894 was an event of first importance in American intellectual history. Its influence was decisive in awakening S. S. McClure, Ida M. Tarbell, and Charles Edward Russell to the journalistic possibilities of the literature of exposure.[89]   At the same time, the book confirmed the validity of a new method of analysis in which Lloyd's magazine articles had pioneered in the eighties, a method that subjected social and economic theories to the acid, pragmatic test, and which has become in the twentieth century an important part of the apparatus of both journalism and scholarship.[90] Allan Nevins has shown how, as a polemic, *Wealth against Commonwealth* created and perpetuated the stereotypes of an awakened antimonopolist spirit.[91]   This was a contribution of no mean importance in a day when thoughtful men and embattled farmers alike feared that monopolies would "take the place of Government of the people."[92]

Its constructive influence was such, however, that Lloyd's book must be viewed as a catalytic and directive influence of first importance upon the confused, angry, intellectual currents of the decade.   The profound influence that it exerted upon the thought of Louis D. Brandeis, who was groping for a new and constructive approach to contemporary problems,[93] the inspiration that it gave Samuel M. Jones of Toledo to embark upon his "Golden Rule" career as a manufacturer and municipal reformer,[94] the encouragement that it gave to Florence Kelley, Jane Addams, and Ethelbert Stewart[95] to pioneer in the interest of the consumer, social ethics, and labor are concrete indexes of this effect.   So is the strong appeal that *Wealth against Commonwealth* made to the Brotherhood of the Kingdom and other leaders among the clergy in the social gospel and Christian Socialist movements,[96] the unique position

[89] Lloyd MSS. (Madison), S. S. McClure to Lloyd, Apr. 8, June 16, 1894; Ida M. Tarbell, *All in the Day's Work* (New York, 1939), p. 204; Russell's introduction to Caro Lloyd, *Henry Demarest Lloyd* (New York, 1912), I, vi–viii.

[90] Here, of course, Lloyd was working in the same field and in friendly collaboration with Ely, John R. Commons, and Edward W. Bemis, who were all in constant correspondence with him in the nineties.

[91] II, 341.

[92] Garrison, p. 379, quoting ex-President Hayes; Hicks, pp. 78–80, 439–443.

[93] Mason, p. 27; Alfred Lief, *Brandeis* (New York, 1936), p. 64.

[94] *The Conservator*, Dec. 1903, pp. 151–152, quoting S. M. Jones's address at the Memorial Meeting in the Chicago Auditorium held in Lloyd's honor after his sudden death.

[95] All were personal friends and subject to Lloyd's continued influence.

[96] Numerous letters from George A. Gates, George D. Herron, B. Fay Mills, Leighton Williams, W. D. P. Bliss in the Lloyd MSS. (Madison and Winnetka), establish this beyond question.   Cf. James Dombrowski, *Early Days of Christian Socialism in America* (New York, 1936), pp. 121–124; Charles H. Hopkins, *Rise of the Social Gospel in American Protestantism, 1865–1915* (New Haven, 1940), pp. 131–132, 179, 196.

that it gained for Lloyd in the Populist movement, and the editorial support that he received for his views in a notable series of daily newspapers in Boston, New York, and the Middle West.[97] In the urban middle class, where views as radical as Lloyd's had long been anathema, *Wealth against Commonwealth* was of prime importance in shocking professional men, intellectuals, liberal clergy, and intelligent readers into a realistic attitude toward contemporary social and economic problems, and in opening minds to reform proposals that involved an enlargement of governmental powers.   This is more than indicated by the powerful endorsement and continued support that Lloyd and his book received from such molders of middle class opinion as the *Outlook*, the *Review of Reviews*, and the *New England Magazine*, and from the Congregational clergy in East and Middle West.[98]   Of almost equal importance, *Wealth against Commonwealth* played a significant role in popularizing and disseminating the non-Marxian, socialist ideas whose spread among workers, farmers, and the lower middle class was such an important phenomenon in the period.[99]   By linking them with the traditional antimonopolism, democratic faith, humanitarianism, and belief in civilization and progress, Lloyd made a unique contribution to the development of the "Progressive Mind."   Finally, the book established him as the outstanding publicist and champion of social democracy at the turn of the century, one who used his impeccable social standing and great reputation to bridge the gulf between wage earner and middle class and thus to pioneer in a new statesmanship.

[97] Especially the Springfield *Republican*, Boston *Globe*, Boston *Herald*, Boston *Transcript*; New York *World*, New York *Journal*, New York *Evening Post*; Chicago *Chronicle*, Chicago *Herald*.

[98] This is well established by Lloyd's correspondence with the editors of these periodicals, with clergy in many Protestant denominations, and by calls upon Lloyd for articles by the *Independent*, *Outlook*, *Atlantic Monthly*, and by numerous invitations to lecture before religious gatherings.

[99] This was supplemented, of course, by Lloyd's personal friendship with Thomas J. Morgan, Victor Berger, Eugene V. Debs, and A. M. Simons, with organizers of the co-operative movement, and by his influence on the leaders of the Christian Socialist movement.   Lloyd had circulated Fabian literature and arranged for lectures by members of the Fabian Society at the World Labor Congress, World's Columbian Exposition, Chicago, 1893.   His book was frequently quoted and his views supported by such socialist journals as the *Coming Nation* (Ruskin, Tenn.) and the *Appeal to Reason* (Girard, Kan.).

CHAPTER VIII

CONSUMMATION OF A LABOR-POPULIST ALLIANCE IN ILLINOIS, 1894*

IN 1894 the stage seemed set for a successful farmer-labor alliance in national politics. Nowhere were conditions more favorable to such a coalition than in the Old Northwest, where rural America and the new industrialism stood face to face. In Wisconsin,[1] Illinois, and Ohio,[2] serious attempts were made after the panic of 1893 to ally Populism with urban labor. These efforts and the subsequent attempt of urban radicals to capture the party's national organization are forgotten chapters in the history of the Populist revolt.

Illinois was the leading industrial and farming state of the Old Northwest. Chicago, its metropolitan center, was seemingly "the ideal place" to attempt a union of the radical wing of the labor movement with the embattled Populists.[3] There organized labor had fully recovered from the disastrous effects of the Haymarket Riot. A reasonable estimate in 1891 placed the number of unions in Chicago at 300, their membership at 60,000. Co-operation between them was facilitated by a Trades and Labor Assembly, the Building Trades Council and the Central Labor Union.[4] Downstate the movement extended to such towns as Joliet, Decatur, Peoria, Springfield, and East St. Louis, and into the coal-mining districts. The Illinois State Federation of Labor supplied the scattered unions with the means of common action.[5]

Powerful as it was, in Illinois organized labor was split into half a dozen schools of reform thought, each more or less antagonistic to the others. Aside from the declining Knights of Labor, there were Socialists, Anarchists, Single-Taxers, "simon pure" conservative trade-unionists, and members of the new industrial unions, the United Mine Workers,

---

* Reprinted from *The Mississippi Valley Historical Review*, XXVII (March, 1941), 589–602.

[1] Frank [Flower] to Spooner, [July], 1894, and enclosure, John C. Spooner MSS. (Library of Congress); *Chicago Daily Tribune*, September 7, 1893; *Chicago Searchlight*, June 14, 1894.

[2] *Cleveland Leader*, February 21, 1895, clipping in Henry D. Lloyd MSS. (Madison).

[3] Willis J. Abbott, "The Chicago Populist Campaign," *Arena* (Boston), XI, February, 1895, pp. 330–331.

[4] *Rights of Labor* (Chicago), February 7, 1891; William C. Pomeroy, *Official Labor Gazette, 1892* (Chicago, 1892), 15–29, 33, 47.

[5] *Official Labor Gazette, 1895* (Chicago, 1895), 127–129.

THE SITUATION WITH THOUSANDS OF WORKING PEOPLE

and the American Railway Union.[6]   Of these the Anarchists were but a shattered remnant eschewing violence, continually harassed by the Chicago police.   Chicago was also the stronghold of the Socialist Labor party in Illinois.   Iron discipline, Marxian doctrines, and foreign-born membership limited its influence and aroused fierce antipathies in other segments of the labor movement.   The Single-Tax faction was strong in "down-state" cities as well as in Chicago, where George Schilling supplied shrewd leadership and allied his followers to the rising star of John P. Altgeld.   Devoted followers of Henry George, whose panacea for social ills attracted support from millionaires while re-enforcing America's traditional individualism, the Single-Taxers waged unremitting war upon the Socialists.   More numerous than either, but less articulate politically were the trade-unionists.   Since 1886 they had shouldered aside the Knights of Labor, now retreating into small towns and rural areas, and they regarded the Socialists likewise with suspicion.

Both in the Chicago Trades and Labor Assembly and in the State Federation of Labor these elements were in constant conflict.   Common action, rare enough, occurred only when organized labor as a whole was seriously attacked, or when it engaged in a campaign that transcended ideological or organizational differences.   United political action, born of the employers' anti-union drive after Haymarket, had been wrecked by internal conflict between the Knights of Labor, Socialists, and corrupt labor politicians in 1887.[7]   In the place of the once powerful United Labor party, there appeared a succession of short-lived parties of little strength, engendered by emerging labor racketeers, who used them to extract political offices or direct subsidies from the major parties of Chicago.[8]   So powerful did these "labor skates" become that one clique headed by a joking, scheming Kentuckian, William Columbus Pomeroy, gained control of the Illinois State Federation of Labor and the Chicago Trades and Labor Assembly.[9]   The honest tradition of independent

[6] Abbot, "Chicago Populist Campaign," loc. cit., 330; Chicago Daily Tribune, August 30, September 18, 1891; Eugene Staley, History of the Illinois State Federation of Labor (Chicago, 1930), 61-64, 86, 97, 98.

[7] Knights of Labor (Chicago), April 9, 16, October 27, November 12, 1887; Chicago Inter-Ocean, January 8, 1888, clipping in the Thomas J. Morgan Scrap-books (Illinois State Historical Survey).

[8] Knights of Labor, February 2, May 18, 1889; Rights of Labor, September 27, 1890, October 10, 1891, October 22, 1892; Chicago Daily Tribune, March 19, September 24, 1891.

[9] Rights of Labor, September 24, December 17, 1892, January 21, February 18, April 8, 1893; T. J. Morgan to Lloyd, December 19, 1893, Lloyd MSS. (Madison); Staley, History of Illinois Federation, 89-91, 105-106.

political action was left to the advocacy of Thomas J. Morgan, leading spirit among the Chicago Socialists.[10]

Police persecution in Chicago,[11] together with a series of defeats suffered by the labor movement elsewhere, revived interest in independent politics in union circles in 1891–1892.[12] Henry Demarest Lloyd, well-to-do Chicago muckraker and Fabian Socialist, encouraged this tendency. His exposure of the trusts, together with the public support that he had given the labor movement since the execution of the Haymarket Anarchists, had endeared him to organized labor.[13] He was the most outstanding intellectual identified with the American labor movement in the early nineties, with the possible exception of Henry George. In June, 1893, he joined with the Populists in an abortive effort to commit the Chicago Anti-Trust Convention to government ownership of the coal mines.[14] By August, Chicago's neglect of the unemployed, whose numbers had been swelled by the panic and the World's Fair, led to great demonstrations on the "lake-front" and in the "loop," and to resolutions attacking "wage-slavery" and repudiating government by lawyers and millionaires.[15] Growing sentiment for political action crystallized in the Galesburg convention of the Illinois State Federation of Labor in October. There, an amendment to the constitution emphasized the "necessity for independent political action on the part of producers." Furthermore, the convention instructed the executive board to call a conference of all labor and farm organizations of Illinois within the next six months, with a view to securing "unity of action and singleness of purpose."[16]

To this movement for the organization of an independent labor party the Chicago convention of the American Federation of Labor gave added

[10] Letter of acceptance of the Socialist nomination for Mayor of Chicago, March 28, 1891' Thomas J. Morgan MSS. (University of Chicago); *Rights of Labor*, March 14, 28, April 4' 1891.

[11] Morgan to Lloyd, December 29, 1891, Lloyd MSS. (Madison); *Chicago Daily Tribune*, December 28, 1891, May 2, 1892.

[12] T. J. Morgan, "The Socialist Idea," Illustrated Supplement, Chicago *Inter-Ocean*, September 5, 1892; *Rights of Labor*, October 22, 1892; *Age of Labor* (Chicago), August 15, 1892.

[13] Lloyd to Samuel Gompers, February 18, 1891, American Federation of Labor Archives (Washington, D. C.); "Souvenir of the American Federation of Labor, December 14, 1891"; Gus Mohme to Lloyd, January 10, 1894, Lloyd MSS. (Madison).

[14] Ignatius Donnelly to Lloyd, May 30, 1893, Mrs. A. P. Stevens to Lloyd, June 7, 1893, *ibid.*

[15] Chicago *Daily Tribune*, August 21, 22, 1893; *Journal of the Knights of Labor* (Philadelphia), August 24, 1893.

[16] *Official Annual Labor Gazette, 1893* (Chicago, 1893), 42, 135–137.

impetus. Defeat by Pinkerton detectives in hard-fought strikes and adverse court decisions had left organized labor sore. Wage cuts, unemployment, and increasing vulnerability after the panic made the Illinois unions reluctant to strike against hopeless odds.[17] These conditions, together with the example set by the Independent Labour party in Great Britain, revived interest in the ballot. On December 14, 1893, the American Federation of Labor endorsed "the political action of our British comrades." By an overwhelming vote it referred British labor's political program and the subject of independent political action to its constituent unions with the request "that their delegates to the next annual convention . . . be instructed on this most important subject."[18]

Populists were few in Illinois. Crop specialization with major emphasis on corn and oats, hog production, cattle-feeding, and dairying made many farmers immune to the worst effects of western competition. Extensive tile drainage of the rich flat prairies so increased crop yields that land values rose steadily to 1896.[19] Far behind the moving frontier Illinois farmers escaped the spectacular boom of the middle eighties, the tragic collapse and long deflation that set Kansas to raising "hell" instead of corn. They did suffer, however, from the prolonged decline in the prices of farm products that characterized the period. The Illinois Bureau of Agriculture had reported in 1888 that for eight successive years the corn crop had netted a loss to the farmers.[20] Poorer farmers of central and northern Illinois were either crowded out by rising land values and falling prices for produce, or they were reduced to tenancy by the spread of landlordism. High rents, one year leases, and lack of leadership kept the renters inarticulate.[21] Save in the wheat raising counties of "Egypt" along the Wabash and Mississippi rivers, where

[17] W. E. Kell to Samuel Gompers, August 13, 1893, Chris Evans to Gompers, November 20, 1893, American Federation of Labor Archives; *Chicago Daily Tribune*, September 28, 1893; *Railway Times*, March 1, 1894.

[18] *Chicago Daily Tribune*, December 15, 1893. This was done on the motion of Thomas J. Morgan.

[19] *Prairie Farmer* (Chicago), May 9, October 31, 1885; *Western Rural* (Chicago), XXV, November 12, 1887, p. 735; *Chicago Daily Tribune*, March 23, 1889; *Report of the Statistics of Agriculture in the United States at the Eleventh Census: 1890* (Washington, D. C., 1895), 7–9, 12–13, 37, 92–95; Illinois Bureau of Labor Statistics, *Fifth Biennial Report* (Springfield, 1888), lvi–lvii; Illinois Farmers' Institute, *Annual Report, 1896* (Springfield, 1896), 25.

[20] *Farmers' Voice* (Chicago), December 15, 1888.

[21] *Chicago Daily Tribune*, February 17, 1890, March 19, 1892, March 30, 1893; *Western Rural*, LIII, January 24, 1895, p. 47; *Vanguard* (Chicago), June 4, 1892; Charles L. Stewart, *Land Tenure in the United States with Special Reference to Illinois* (Urbana, 1916), *University of Illinois Studies in the Social Sciences*, V, No. 3, p. 49.

land values were declining,[22] conditions essential to economic radicalism were lacking in rural Illinois.

The strength of the farmers' alliance movement, when it came, was found largely in the depressed wheat counties. Even there it was non-partisan in character. Efforts of professional third party leaders and radical farmers to dominate the state election of 1890 sent only three independents to the general assembly. These, it is true, held the balance of power between the major parties in a prolonged contest over the election of a United States Senator. Two of this so-called "Big Three," however, deserted Alson J. Streeter in the hour of victory, under most suspicious circumstances, for John M. Palmer, long an attorney of the Illinois Central Railroad.[23] This event led to the rapid decline of the Farmers' Mutual Benefit Association, the strongest farm organization in Illinois, and discredited the third party movement.[24] The departure of Herman E. Taubeneck,[25] who went to Washington, D. C., as national chairman of the People's party, and loss of the support of the *Farmers' Voice* when Montgomery Ward and Company dismissed its radical editor, robbed the Populists of effective leadership in Illinois. In the gubernatorial election of 1892, John P. Altgeld, a noted liberal, swept the state at the head of the Democratic ticket. The Populist vote was less than that of the old Greenback party of the seventies. It totalled only two and one-half per cent of the poll, a third less than that of the Prohibition party.[26]

The desire of agrarian leaders to enlist urban labor in their political ventures was as old as the Greenback Labor movement. An attempt to accomplish this in the guise of the Union Labor party of 1888 had met with little success.[27] From the dawn of the Populist movement, the party press in Illinois sought such an alliance. Lester C. Hubbard, while editor of the *Farmers' Voice*, agitated the subject ceaselessly. As first chairman of the Illinois State Central Committee, he set out to realize this ambition. Undaunted by his dismissal from the *Farmers' Voice*, he established the *Vanguard* in Chicago to woo the labor vote. This attempt proved abortive in 1892. The predominance of the Greenback element in the People's party in Illinois and the failure of the

---

[22] Illinois Bureau of Labor Statistics, *Fifth Report*, lvi; *Statistics of Agriculture, Eleventh Census*, 14.

[23] *Illinois State Register*, March 10, 1891; Joliet *Daily News*, March 13, 14, 1891; *Chicago Daily Tribune*, March 12, 1891.

[24] *Prairie Farmer*, April 18, 1891; *Farmers' Voice*, January 14, August 13, 1892.

[25] The one incorruptible member of the "Big Three."

[26] *Illinois Blue Book, 1899* (Springfield, 1899), 264.

[27] *Knights of Labor*, January 4, February 1, May 3, 1888.

Omaha platform "to say a word of any value for the workingmen's move-ment—nothing in favor of trade unions or the Eight Hour Day" made as bad an impression on labor circles in Chicago as they did on Samuel Gompers and Henry D. Lloyd.[28] Populist managers foolishly com-mitted their cause in Cook County to unknown candidates, the declining Knights of Labor, and discredited labor politicians.[29] Under such circumstances, it was impossible to wean the trades unions away from support of John P. Altgeld. In the urban centers of Illinois in 1892 the Populists polled less than half of one per cent of the poll. Thus Illinois illustrated the failure of the People's party to attract substantial support from either organized labor or the urban middle class in the states east of the Mississippi River.[30]

After the panic of 1893, the Populists sought to improve their dismal prospects in Chicago by courting the unemployed, aiding "General" Kelley's army of the Commonweal, and seeking association with Henry D. Lloyd.[31] Then, as labor's drift toward political action quickened and wage-earners began to join the party, Populist managers bestirred them-selves in the hope of capturing the labor vote.[32] A series of conferences with the Knights of Labor, the German-speaking Central Labor Union, and the Socialist Labor party was begun in April, 1894. They "resulted in harmony beyond all hopes." The conferences concluded on May 19, 1894, in a small convention representing the Cook County Farmers Alliance, Populists, Central Labor Union, Socialists, Bellamy National-ists, Single-Taxers, Free Silver organizations, prohibitionists, and several ward labor parties. They met to select delegates to the Populist state convention. A "crazy-quilt" platform, composed of planks advocated by the heterogeneous reform elements present, concluded with a state-ment that the convention's object "was to unite the farmers with the city laborers in one invincible political party."[33]

Meanwhile, the industrial conference authorized by the State Federa-

[28] H. D. Lloyd to Samuel Gompers, July 10, 1892, American Federation of Labor Archives; *Rights of Labor*, June 6, August 29, 1891, July 9, 1892; *Farmers' Voice*, August 6, 1892; *Chicago Daily Tribune*, February 26, 1892.

[29] D. Bruce Bird to Ignatius Donnelly, May 31, 1892, Ignatius Donnelly MSS.; *Rights of Labor*, August 13, 1892; *Farmers' Voice*, September 3, December 3, 1892.

[30] *Vanguard*, November 26, 1892.

[31] L. C. Hubbard to Lloyd, February 15, 1893, Lloyd MSS. (Madison); *Chicago Daily Tribune*, September 10, 1893, April 17, 1894; H. Vincent, *The Story of the Commonweal* (Chicago, 1894), 175.

[32] John Walsh to Donnelly, March 8, 1894, Donnelly MSS.; *Railway Times* (Chicago), February 15, 1894.

[33] *Chicago Daily Tribune*, May 20, 1894; *Railway Times*, May 1, 1894.

tion of Labor had been called by President M. H. Madden. It was to meet at Springfield on July 2–4 to consider the political program submitted by the American Federation of Labor and concert measures necessary for "independent political action."[34] To forestall the organization of a labor party in Illinois, William Hess of Milton, chairman of the Populist state central committee, at once called a "conference of all labor and farm organizations" to meet at Springfield, May 28, on the eve of the Populist state convention.[35] If harmony were achieved at this first industrial conference organized labor might be ushered bodily into the People's party on the following day.

The Populist conference met in Springfield as scheduled. In it were representatives from five farm organizations, the Knights of Labor, the State Federation of Labor, the Socialist Labor party, and various local trades assemblies together with individual Single-Taxers and some one hundred Populists. W. H. ("Coin") Harvey and H. S. Taylor represented Free Silver and prohibition, respectively. Twenty-two delegates came from the new coalition of Populists, trade-unionists, and urban radicals in Cook County. They were determined on united, independent political action. A platform was adopted whose avowed object was the union of "urban industrialists and agriculturalists in one harmonious political party." After endorsing the Omaha platform, it recommended the American Federation of Labor's political program to "the favorable consideration" of the Populist state convention of the morrow.[36]

"Plank 10" of the American Federation of Labor's program was the rock on which the projected alliance split. Its sponsor was none other than Thomas J. Morgan, who had offered the program to the American Federation of Labor the previous December. He was now leader of the Chicago delegation to the Populist convention. Morgan was an Englishman, a founder of the Chicago Trades and Labor Assembly. He was recognized as one of the most capable, honest, and best read leaders in the American labor movement. Short, broad-shouldered, and square-jawed, soft-voiced but combative, he was the leading spirit of the Socialist Labor party in Chicago.[37] "Plank 10," if endorsed by the Populists, would have committed them to socialism. It demanded "the collective ownership by the people of all means of production and

[34] *Eight-Hour Herald* (Chicago), May 10, 1894.

[35] *Chicago Daily Tribune*, May 29, 1894.

[36] *Illinois State Register*, May 29, 1894; *Chicago Daily Tribune*, May 29, 1894.

[37] T. J. Morgan to Lloyd, January 6, 1892, July 6, 1896, Lloyd MSS. (Madison); *Chicago Evening Post*, February 24, 1894, clipping in Morgan MSS.; *Rights of Labor*, April 4, 1891, clipping in Morgan Scrapbooks; Staley, *History of Illinois Federation*, 93–95.

distribution."[38]   Although Morgan was made chairman of the resolutions committee by the convention, the committee itself struck "Plank 10" out of the federation's program by a vote of three to one.   When Morgan carried the fight to the floor of the convention, Herman E. Taubeneck, chairman of the National Committee of the People's party, spoke for the agrarians, when he declared: "If this is what you came to the people's party for, we don't want you.   Go back from where you came with your socialism."   Amid "wild cheering" "Plank 10" was rejected by a vote of seventy-six to sixteen.[39]   Morgan went home disgruntled.   With this exception the convention endorsed organized labor's program, paying conspicuous attention to the "Mooney constitutional amendment" for the abolition of payment in truck and enforcement of "weekly pay."[40]   This action, however, failed to secure immediate support from the trades unions for the Populist ticket.   In spite of a genuine desire for political action on both sides, ideological differences derived from the deep-seated conflict between the agrarian movement and proletarian radicalism that characterizes modern times[41] had wrecked the Populist effort to recruit urban labor.

Simultaneously in the ranks of organized labor the conservative unions and the Single-Taxers developed increasing opposition to "Plank 10." The latter constituted a powerful faction in Chicago and down-state Illinois and, as has been observed, were inveterate enemies of Socialism. This fact boded no good for the industrial conference scheduled to meet at Springfield on July 2, under the aegis of the Illinois State Federation of Labor.   Neither did the increasing restiveness of the honest labor element of Illinois, which now sought to free both the State Federation and the Chicago Trades and Labor Assembly from the corrupt leadership of William C. Pomeroy.[42]   Meanwhile, all elements including the Populists prepared to send delegates to the conference.   Anticipating trouble, Henry D. Lloyd accepted appointment as delegate for Typographical Union No. 9 of Chicago.   He set to work upon the seemingly impossible task of reconciling the doctrinal differences of the diverse reform elements.[43]

[38] *Chicago Daily Tribune*, December 15, 1893.
[39] *Illinois State Register*, May 30, 1894.
[40] Joliet *Daily News*, June 2, 1894.
[41] Harry E. and Bernice M. Moore, "Problems of Reintegration of Agrarian Life," *Social Forces* (Chapel Hill), XV, March, 1937, pp. 385–387. Cf. *National Economist* (Washington, D. C.), March 3, 1894; *Chicago Daily Tribune*, June 1, 1894.
[42] Staley, *History of Illinois Federation*, 98, 122–125. To strengthen his position Pomeroy identified himself with the opposition to "Plank 10" and pledged his support to the attempt to unite the trade-unionists and the Populists. *Chicago Searchlight*, June 28, 1894.
[43] M. H. Madden to Lloyd, June 27, 1894, and draft preamble and platform for "The

Collapse of the desperate Illinois coal strike[44] and declaration of the famous Pullman boycott by the American Railway Union[45] on the eve of the Springfield conference added great impetus to the movement to unite the urban and agrarian radicals in a powerful third party. At the same time the Pullman strike deprived delegates to the conference of the necessary means of transportation. In consequence, the large Cook County delegation found itself stranded in Chicago. Finally it was compelled, not without permission from Eugene V. Debs, to board a special train run by a "scab" engineer.[46]

Every shade of labor and reform politics in Illinois was represented at the second Springfield conference. The Cook County delegation, for example, included representatives of the local prohibitionists, Populists, Anarchists, trades assemblies, Knights of Labor, Single Tax clubs, Socialists, and the American Railway Union. The United Mine Workers of Illinois sent their president, J. A. Crawford. A. L. Maxwell, chairman of the state central committee, led the down-state Populist delegation. The conference adjourned until July 3 to await the arrival of the Chicago contingent. Delegates from other cities attended also despite the Pullman boycott.[47] The railroad "blockade," incidentally, made it impossible for any to leave Springfield during the conference. The delegates remained for three full days in spite of the sharpest differences of opinion.

From the outset the proceedings were lively, as was to be expected from the heterogeneous character of the conference. Excitement was heightened by the injunctions issued against the officials of the American Railway Union by the United States District Court at Chicago, and by intervention of United States troops in the Pullman boycott. At the opening of the second day's session a sensation resulted from the announcement that William C. Pomeroy had telegraphed for funds to the Democratic Clerk of Cook County for the purpose of manipulating the gathering. Although the conference applied a thin coat of whitewash to him, Pomeroy's influence thereafter was at a low ebb.[48] The report of the platform committee furnished him with an opportunity, however,

---

People's Party Convention at Springfield, Illinois, July 4, 1894," Lloyd MSS.; *Chicago Searchlight*, June 21, 1894.

[44] John P. Altgeld to Lloyd, June 12, 1894, Lloyd MSS. (Madison); Joliet *Daily News*, June 14, 1894; *Illinois State Register*, April 24, May 27, 1894.

[45] *Railway Times*, August 15, 1894; Edgar A. Bancroft, *The Chicago Strike of 1894* (Chicago, 1895), 14–15.

[46] M. H. Madden to Lloyd, July 1, 1894, Lloyd MSS. (Madison).

[47] *Illinois State Register*, July 3, 4, 1894.

[48] *Ibid.*, July 5, 6, 1894; *Chicago Searchlight*, July 5, 1894.

to restore his tarnished prestige.   A. L. Maxwell, the Populist leader, presented the report.   He had come to the conference to secure the support of organized labor for the Populist state ticket.   The platform which he read was the product of an earnest effort to conclude a working agreement between the different schools of radical thought represented at the conference.   In the name of the wage-earners of Illinois it declared for "political action."   It contained the Populist financial, land, and transportation policies, an indefinite Single Tax plank, and every proposal of the American Federation of Labor's political program except "Plank 10."   Planks advocating government ownership of mines and municipal ownership of public utilities were included to placate the Socialists.[49]

The omission of "Plank 10," which he regarded as the heart of the Federation's political program,[50] and the platform's refusal to break decisively with the major political parties induced Thomas J. Morgan to offer a minority report.   This would have added "Plank 10" to the platform and attempted, also, to pledge the delegates present "never again to vote another Republican or Democratic ticket, never again to support politically any man or woman who refused to indorse the principles herein set forth."[51]   Morgan's report precipitated the withdrawal of Republican and Democratic politicians from the conference.   His attempt to write "Plank 10" into the platform, however, led to a prolonged and acrimonious debate.   In it Pomeroy attacked him again and again.   The Single-Taxers likewise attacked Morgan and countered with the proposal of an outright Single Tax plank to replace the vague expressions of the majority report.   Populists and orthodox trade-unionists likewise attacked the Socialists, who defended themselves doggedly.   Twice the conference had to be adjourned because of the extreme bitterness aroused by the debate.   Finally, on the morning of July 5, a speech by A. L. Maxwell nearly brought the Populists and Socialists to blows.In the roll call Morgan's minority report was defeated, 59 to 49, the Single-Taxers, Anarchists, conservative trade-unionists, and most of the farmer delegates voting against it.[52]

Morgan's defeat by so narrow a margin and the extreme bitterness provoked by the debate threatened the conference with immediate dis-

    [49] *Eight-Hour Herald*, July 10, 1894; *Chicago Searchlight*, July 5, 1894.
    [50] T. J. Morgan to Samuel Gompers, March 6, 1894, American Federation of Labor Archives.
    [51] *Illinois State Register*, July 5, 1894.
    [52] *Ibid.*, July 5, 6, 1894; *Eight-Hour Herald*, July 10, 1894; Abbot, "Chicago Populist Campaign," *loc. cit.*, 330–331.

ruption. At this juncture Henry D. Lloyd rose and spoke for an hour. His "remarks were received with marked courtesy and without interruption." Exerting to the utmost his great personal influence with all factions, he succeeded in obtaining the adoption of a compromise resolution by a majority of a single vote.[53] This was the limit to which the opposition would go to conciliate the Socialists. Lloyd's compromise recommended "independent political action" to the organizations represented at the conference. It recommended that "the officials of these bodies take immediate steps to hold a national convention to perfect plans for such political action." Pending organization of the new national party, members of the organizations represented at Springfield were urged to "vote for those candidates of the People's party at the coming election who will pledge themselves to the principle of the collective ownership by the people of all such means of production and distribution as the people elect to operate for the commonwealth."[54] Appended to the majority report these resolutions became an integral part of the platform of the Springfield conference. After their adoption the assemblage adjourned harmoniously.

The second Springfield conference, therefore, consummated the long sought alliance between the People's party and politically articulate labor in Illinois. Its platform was broad enough for all the diverse schools of radical thought in the state to stand upon. Its compromises were so deftly worded that none had sacrificed its cherished dogmas on the altar of political expediency. By means of the Lloyd compromise all factions had agreed to support the Populist state ticket in the coming election and local Populist tickets, where nominations had been made, provided that the candidates endorsed the Springfield platform. Elsewhere organized labor was to have a voice in naming the candidates. This was notably true of Cook County where the support of metropolitan labor was expected to bulk large in the fall campaign. Viewing this achievement, the *Chicago Searchlight*, edited by the well-known Henry Vincent, declared that "every loyal Populist" could now "cheerfully roll up his sleeves and enter into the work as laid out with the certain hope" of gaining control of the next legislature and with it a United States Senator.[55]

Sober second thought might have discerned that the Populists were

[53] *Chicago Daily Tribune*, July 6, 1894, quoted by Caro Lloyd, *Henry Demarest Lloyd* (New York, 1912), I, 243.

[54] *Eight-Hour Herald*, July 10, 1894.

[55] July 12, 1894.

pledged to participate along with the urban radicals in the establishment of a new national party. On this neither their own national organization nor Samuel Gompers might look with approval. Meanwhile, they had accepted a platform which permitted each radical faction in the Springfield coalition to campaign for its own peculiar dogmas, while supporting the Populist state and local tickets. On the other hand, the Populists themselves had given qualified approval to Socialism.[56]

Had the price paid for the urban alliance been too great? Could the coalition maintain harmony and tolerance of internal differences of opinion throughout a hard-fought campaign? Could it survive defeat? Would each school of radical thought forego the temptation to proselyte within the party? Would each compromise its cherished principles in the interest of permanent union? Could able leadership be found and used? Could candidates prominent enough to attract the floating voter be nominated? These insistent questions only the school of experience could answer.

[56] Down-state Populist leaders, such as State Chairman A. L. Maxwell, denied this. They interpreted the clause in the Lloyd compromise, "as the people elect to operate for the commonwealth," to mean a popular mandate attained through the initiative and referendum. On the basis of this interpretation they argued with poor grace that the party was not committed in any way to Socialism. Robinson *Argus*, July 25, 1894, quoted by Max L. Shipley, "The Populist Party in Illinois" (unpublished master's thesis, University of Illinois, 1927), 57-58. Irrespective of Maxwell's view the Socialists of Chicago took full advantage of the Springfield platform to campaign for Socialism within the People's party.

CHAPTER IX

THE LABOR-POPULIST ALLIANCE OF ILLINOIS IN THE ELECTION OF 1894

THE *rapprochement* between urban labor and the agrarian radicals that produced the labor-Populist coalition in Illinois was apparent elsewhere as early as April. Then the industrial armies of the Commonweal moved on Washington in ragged columns in the hope of forcing enactment of a program in full harmony with the Populist faith. "General" Jacob S. Coxey's demand for public works for the unemployed, to be financed by greenback inflation, and his lieutenant's denunciation of the banking system bespoke wage-earning support for the monetary antimonopolism of the Omaha platform. This involved acceptance, also, of the Populist canon that the powers of democratic government should be employed positively in behalf of the underprivileged. As a workingmen's movement, therefore, the armies of the Commonweal illustrated the loyalty of the unemployed and their working class sympathizers to the traditional, antimonopolist radicalism of the American masses.[1]

The collapse of the Commonweal was followed immediately by the great strike of the United Mine Workers in the central bituminous field from Pittsburgh to Illinois. No sooner had this ended, after a series of disorders and with little or no gain to the underpaid miners, than the Pullman boycott occurred with its catastrophic effect upon Eugene V. Debs' attempt to develop industrial unionism into an effective counterpoise for the great corporations. In these two struggles, as in the defeat of Coxey's armies, the intervention of federal courts, state militia, and federal troops played a decisive role. In each case the leaders of the beaten cause turned to Populism. Coxey ran for Congress at Massillon, to swell the Populist vote in his district fivefold[2] and lend prestige to a labor-Populist alliance in Ohio that extended as far south as Cincinnati. President John McBride of the United Mine Workers urged his following to support the Populist tickets in the fall elections,[3] as did Debs of the American Railway Union before he was sentenced to Woodstock jail.[4] The lieutenants of each labor leader ran for Congress on Populist tickets

[1] Donald L. McMurry, *Coxey's Army. A Study of the Industrial Army Movement of 1894* (Boston, 1929), 268–283.
[2] *Ibid.*, 286.
[3] *Illinois State Register*, August 10, 1894.
[4] Chicago *Searchlight*, August 2, 1894.

and gave full support to the Populist attempt to invoke the power of the democratic state to destroy corporate monopoly.

At the same time, the trades unions took under consideration the program of the British Independent Labour Party, referred to them in a formal referendum by the Chicago convention of the American Federation of Labor in December, 1893. The discussion of this program during the following summer and autumn quickened the drift of the craftsmen toward independent political action. Organized labor's entrance into the political arena was encouraged also by the neglect of the unemployed, by the reactionary policy of the federal government, and by the activities of the strong Socialist contingent within the Federation. Throughout the old Northwest the trades unionists were tempted to join the unemployed, the miners, and the railway workers in a *de facto* or formal alliance with the People's party.

Viewed against this background, the consummation of the labor-Populist alliance at Springfield, Illinois, was expecially significant. The Springfield Conference had grafted on to the Omaha platform, with its limited program of state ownership, nine of the planks of the political program of British labor, a vague single tax plank, and a modified version of "Plank 10," which endorsed the extension of collective ownership of the means of production and distribution as far as the voting public should approve through the initiative and referendum. Even apart from this last plank, which was to cause much controversy, the Springfield platform extended its application of the collectivist principle far beyond the Populist position. The new coalition, if victorious, was pledged to nationalization of the mines, municipal ownership of street railways, gas, and electric plants, employers' liability for occupational injuries and diseases, abolition of the sweating system, sanitary inspection of mines, factories, and homes, compulsory education, a legal eight-hour day, and confiscatory taxation of speculative land holdings.[5]

Antimonopolism, and an enlarged democratic collectivism in the interest of urban labor, as well as of small farmers, and petty businessmen, constituted the ideological foundation of the Populist campaign in Illinois. For the craft unions it represented either a shift toward Socialism or a distinct retreat from the new, autonomous trades unionist philosophy to the older labor reformism with its emphasis upon positive governmental action. At the same time, the new platform was the boldest attempt yet made to link the indigenous, antimonopolist radicalism of the United States to the unlimited collectivism then propagated by the

[5] Staley, *Illinois Federation of Labor*, 113 note 2, 115–118.

Bellamy Nationalists, the Marxians, and the advocates of the more congenial British Socialism that were then bidding for support among American liberals and laborers. Finally, the Springfield platform had been adopted with the expressed hope that it would facilitate extension of the newly formed labor-Populist alliance to the entire nation. The new program's success in the ensuing campaign in Illinois would gauge the calibre of its appeal on the larger political stage.

The economic situation in Illinois seemed to justify the most sanguine expectations of the labor-Populist allies. Distress was widespread. In the southern counties the drought of 1893 and the hard winter that followed had curtailed winter wheat acreage and reduced the fruit crop. Throughout the summer of 1894 the price of wheat declined, falling to fifty cents a bushel in September. Reports of the sale of crops under the sheriff's hammer and of grinding wheat for hog feed instead of corn appeared in the press.[6] In industrial centers, and especially in Chicago, widespread unemployment undermined the trades unions. Wage reductions, by early spring, averaged from ten to twenty per cent. Inadequate relief measures, despite the charity of soup kitchens and free lunches in saloons, made the lot of the jobless hard. During September, 1893, while the World's Columbian Exposition still drew tourists to the city, the unemployed had demonstrated, denouncing the rulers of society. Now, although the idle had diminished a little in numbers and summer weather eased suffering from exposure, conditions were still bad.[7]

A front page article in the Chicago *Searchlight* of August 2, based on a night excursion through the city, presented a moving picture of the sleeping unemployed. Five hundred men lay under the open sky on North Pier. Two hundred and fifty crowded the floors of a building on the Excursion Dock. Others lay on the dock itself, many of them of respectable antecedents. Numberless men slept in alleys, vacant lots, hallways, and wagons. The viaducts and rights of way of the "L" roads were lined for miles with the sleeping bodies of "honest toilers suffering from intolerable legislative and monopolistic wrongs," as the Populist editor described them. Thousands lodged at five cents a night each in noisome cellars amid vermin and foul air. This account verified the portrait of the City Hall at night published recently by W. T. Stead in *If*

[6] McCormick Harvesting Machine Company MSS., Alexander Keady to the Company, August 3, 1893; *Prairie Farmer*, September 9, 16, 1893; *Chicago Daily Tribune*, April 11, 1894, January 1, 1895; *Illinois State Register*, April 4, 5, 1894; *Farmer's Voice*, September 8, 1894.

[7] American Federation of Labor Archives, Charles H. Davis to Chris Evans, November 20, 1893; W. E. Kell to Samuel Gompers, August 15, 1893; *Railway Times*, March 1, May 1, 1894; *Chicago Daily Tribune*, September 28, 1893.

By the National Reform Press Association.

ADVICE TO STRIKERS.

The Best Way to Win a Strike is at the Ballot Box—Elect the Candidates of the People's Party Next November and There Will Be No More Cause for Strikes—Government Ownership of Railroads and All Other Public Conveniences is Coming and the Sooner You Make Up Your Mind to Vote the People's Party Ticket the Sooner Will Redress Be at Hand.

ADVICE TO STRIKERS

Christ Came to Chicago. In that public building every inch of floor space in the halls and on the stairs was covered by sleeping mechanics, sailors, engineers, and former mates of lake craft. As for the vagrants and those technically liable to the charge of vagrancy, Captain Harnett of the Harrison Street police station declared them "too many for us." The whole situation, he confessed, was deplorable.

To distress was added bitter discontent. Of the strikes waged in defense of living standards painfully acquired during years of industrial conflict, two had an important effect upon the political situation in the State. The first of these was the the great coal strike. It had been deliberately provoked in Illinois, it was told in high places, by a World's Fair Director who, as a big operator, had made half a million from the sale of his surplus stocks during the scarcity that ensued.[8] Called in the face of almost certain defeat to stop competitive wage cutting, the strike had been punctuated by occasional outbreaks of violence where operators were especially ruthless. Although not entirely a failure, the struggle left many miners bitter against the Democratic officials of the state and federal governments, because of hostile court action, intervention of the militia, and the shooting of two miners in Spring Valley by United States troops. This led officials of the United Mine Workers to take an active part in the Springfield Conference and the subsequent campaign.[9]

Much greater impetus to the independent political movement in Illinois came from the Pullman Strike. This was to be expected, since Chicago was the center of that epic struggle. Against its dramatic background, the labor-Populist coalition had been formed at the state capital. There the indignation of all elements in the Conference at the judicial and presidential intervention on the side of the railroads had been an undoubted factor in producing agreement. In Chicago, as the Cook county delegates returned from Springfield, the arrival of United States troops precipitated extensive rioting. Then the pent up bitterness of the floating population against the railroads and a national government patently subservient to the eastern "money power" resulted in considerable destruction of railroad property. Thoroughly informed by the *Chicago Times* of the open alliance between the White House, the United States

[8] Walter Q. Gresham MSS. (Library of Congress), R. M. Johnson to Gresham, July 24, 1894. Cf. Illinois Bureau of Labor Statistics, *Eighth Biennial Report* (Springfield, 1895), 441–442.

[9] *Ibid.*, 435–462; *Chicago Times*, May 1–June 18, 1894; Lloyd MSS. (Madison), John F. Powers to Lloyd, May 30, 1894, Governor J. P. Altgeld to Lloyd, June 6, 12, 1894, H. D. Lloyd to Altgeld, June 2, 1894; Harvey Wish, "The Administration of Governor John Peter Altgeld of Illinois, 1893–1897" (Ph.D. Dissertation, Northwestern University), 142–178; *Illinois State Register*, May 27, July 4, 1894; Joliet *News*, November 8, 1894.

District Court, and the General Managers Association, the trades unions in Chicago were antagonized even more by the hostility of General Nelson A. Miles to the strikers and by the flagrant, anti-labor bias of the bulk of the metropolitan press.   As the propertied elements and many of the middle class were swept by panic and fear into extreme antipathy for organized labor, the trades unionists felt obliged to consider the advisability of a general, sympathetic strike.   This was prevented by the sudden collapse of the Pullman boycott when Eugene V. Debs and the Directors of the American Railway Union were arrested for conspiracy under the Sherman Act by the United States Marshall.[10] When this was followed shortly by contempt proceedings against the strike leaders for violation of an earlier federal court injunction, it intensified the bitterness of wage-earners and middle class liberals against the national government.

Judging from the correspondence of Secretary of State Walter Q. Gresham,[11] and the labor and metropolitan press, Chicago and its neighboring cities were as bitterly divided in their attitude toward organized labor as they had been eight years earlier after the Haymarket Riot. Wrecked by the lockout imposed by the victorious railroads, the American Railway Union openly threw its support to the Populists.[12]   In Chicago all articulate elements in the labor movement identified themselves with the proposal to nominate a complete slate of county and legislative candidates on the Populist ticket.   A great ratification meeting in Brick-Layers Hall was attended by 2,500 trade unionists, American Railway Unionists, Knights of Labor, Socialists, Single-Taxers, and Populists. This gathering endorsed the Springfield platform and renounced allegiance to the old parties.   Declaring for independent political action, the throng pledged itself to make "a straight fight under the banner of the people's party."[13]

Thus, during late July, the enthusiasm of organized labor for the People's party reproduced the desperate unity of the autumn and winter of 1886–1887.   Then the employers' anti-union drive, the hostility of the business class, and the unfair trial of the Anarchist leaders had forced united, political action upon the warring factions of the labor movement. Now, a sense of equal urgency led union locals to resolve themselves into Populist clubs after adjournment of business meetings.   Typographical

[10] Almont Lindsey, *The Pullman Strike* (Chicago, 1942), 90–279.
[11] Gresham MSS., John N. Jewett to Gresham, July 12, 1894; R. U. Johnson to Gresham, July 24, 1894.
[12] *Railway Times*, August 15, September 1, 15, 1894; Chicago *Searchlight*, August 2, 1894.
[13] *Ibid.*, July 19, 1894.

Union No. 16, containing some of the most influential trades unionists in the city, selected delegates to the county convention. The Knights of Labor, whose strength had increased rapidly during the great strike, announced their support. Enthusiasm among the craft unions for the People's party was such that the Chicago Trades and Labor Assembly broke all precedents in permitting a candidate for office to address it. This was Howard S. Taylor, attorney and Populist nominee for Congress in the first district. After Taylor and the Populist State Committee Chairman, A. L. Maxwell of Flat Rock, had urged a united front, the Assembly elected delegates to the Populist county convention and sent recommendations to its platform committee. In the second congressional district, a harmonious convention placed John Z. White, an outstanding Single-Taxer, on a platform containing Single Tax and Socialist planks. The *Searchlight*, the party organ, opened columns devoted to "Labor Notes" and the "Single Tax," and boasted of the harmony that existed within the coalition.[14]

The unity of the party, however, was more superficial than real. It was threatened with disruption almost from the beginning by the recalcitrance of Thomas J. Morgan, leader of the Socialists. Long experience with local labor politics and the devious methods of William C. Pomeroy led him to suspect that the independent movement would be "sold out" once more by the "labor skates." Morgan also feared that the more conservative elements in the party might repudiate the modified "Plank 10" recently adopted at Springfield. Shortly after his return from that turbulent conference, he announced in the Trades Assembly that he would not speak at the ratification meeting or participate in the movement "unless it could first be taken out of the hands of the corrupt element."[15] Immediately thereafter he set out to unite the Socialists into an auxiliary group that could be used to force the other factions to remain loyal to the Springfield platform. These actions, predicated upon the assumed motives of the "Pomeroy push" and the presumed bad faith of the trades unionists, Knights of Labor, and Single-Taxers could not but be disastrous if pursued. Some labor leaders, at least, believed that on this occasion Pomeroy was sincerely working for the success of the independent cause. At any rate, he was too powerful to antagonize while Morgan was too articulate and influential to be ignored.

An appeal was made to Henry D. Lloyd at once in the hope that he

---

[14] *Ibid.*, July 26, August 2, 4, 9, 16, 1894; *Eight-Hour Herald*, August 10, 1894; Chicago *Evening Post*, August 2, 1894.

[15] Lloyd MSS. (Madison), S. Woodman to Lloyd, July 15, 1894, T. J. Morgan to Lloyd, August 3, 1894.

could persuade Morgan to adopt a more reasonable course. Lloyd was now at his spacious summer home at Sakonnet Point, Rhode Island, where he had gone from Springfield. Friendly relations made it possible for him to induce Morgan, by letter, to moderate his stand. Lloyd's report to Typographia No. 9, which he had represented at Springfield, and the inclination of the Chicago *Arbeiter Zeitung* to follow his advice in political matters no doubt facilitated this adjustment. Admitting that the Populists were a middle class party, and that a permanent union of workingmen with them might prove to be unprofitable, he argued forcefully that a temporary coalition might make possible a closer union of the wage-earners with the more enlightened farmers. These last, he declared, the unions should endeavor to draw to common action by every possible means.[16]   Persuaded by such arguments, Morgan and his followers plunged energetically into preparations for the county convention of August 18, not without misgivings over its unwieldy size and the danger of subterranean interference by the major parties. At the same time, the leaders of the Pomeroy faction withdrew from conspicuous participation in the movement. The danger of an open schism in the People's party seemed to have passed.[17]

Meanwhile, Henry Lloyd besought Samuel Gompers to take the initiative in extending the labor-Populist alliance to the entire nation. By telegram and in successive letters, the mid-western antimonopolist urged the cautious President of the American Federation of Labor to convoke a national, delegate convention which should unite trades unionists, Single-Taxers, Socialists, and Populists in a common front in the autumn state and congressional elections.[18]   In this manner, Lloyd hoped to develop in American politics a counterpart of the Independent Labour Party of Great Britain. Two years earlier, immediately after the Omaha Convention, Lloyd had urged upon Gompers without avail the "importance to the workingmen that the farmers should be made their allies."[19]   His appeals to Gompers now were equally fruitless. During the preceding months, Gompers had wavered in his adherence to a strict, non-partisan, craft union program. Now, the total defeat of the American Railway Union and the divisions introduced into the labor movement by the *de facto* alliance with the Populists led him to withhold support

[16] *Arbeiter Zeitung*, August 2, 1894.
[17] Lloyd MSS. (Madison), Florence Kelley to Lloyd, August 1, 1894; T. J. Morgan to Lloyd, August 3, 1894.
[18] *Ibid.*, Lloyd to Gompers, July 30, August 14, 1894.
[19] American Federation of Labor Archives, Lloyd to Gompers, July 10, 1892.

from Lloyd's proposal.   Eventually he warned new union officials of the dangers of subordinating the trades unions to party politics.[20]

Privately, Gompers prophesied that the venture of the trades unionists into independent politics would prove "not an unmixed evil." First hand experience with the bitter rivalries and disruptive effects of political action would lead laborers to re-examine the desirability of sponsoring an independent party on a national scale.   Although the possibility of such action had been envisaged in the Chicago Convention, when the political program was referred to the unions, Gompers now felt that those locals which experimented with independent politics in 1894 would send delegates to the Denver Convention in December who, in the light of their own experience, would "save the general movement" from involvement in partisan politics.[21]   Thus, despite his respect for Lloyd's views, Gompers was determined clearly to restrict and terminate the alliance between organized labor and Populism.

The fiasco in the Cook County Populist convention of August 18, 1894, was an undoubted factor in strengthening Gompers' determination to free the craft unions from politics.   Intoxicated by the prospect of support by every *bona fide* trades union, the Populist leaders decided that the party should nominate a county ticket, instead of confining itself to the legislative field as the *Eight-Hour Herald* and the friendly *Times* advised.[22] This decision offered every inducement to the corrupt organization of the Democratic Mayor, John P. Hopkins, to pack or disrupt the convention. The wage-earners had long been the backbone of Democratic supremacy in Chicago that dated from the first mayoralty of Carter Harrison, the elder.[23]   Any considerable defection of the laborers from the Democratic party was certain to restore the Republicans to power locally, as well as throughout the State.   Thus the Hopkins ring, which closed its term of office with a notorious franchise steal,[24] was bound to resent every attempt to coax its labor following into the independent movement, the more so because Hopkins and the Chicago police had been friendly to the strikers during the Pullman strike.

The Populist city committee was soon alarmed by rumors that Hopkins ward heelers were filtering into the independent camp by organizing

[20] *American Federationist*, I (October, 1894), 172.

[21] Joseph A. Labadie MSS. (Labadie Collection, University of Michigan), Samuel Gompers to Joseph Labadie, September 13, 1894.

[22] *Eight-Hour Herald*, August 10, 1894; *Times*, August 18, 1894.

[23] Claudius O. Johnson, *Carter Henry Harrison I* (Chicago, 1928), 181, 182–185.

[24] Cf. Lincoln Steffens, *The Struggle for Self-Government* (New York, 1906), 45–52, for the character of the Hopkins organization.

bogus unions and district Populist clubs. Less extensive attempts at infiltration by Republicans served only to complicate the situation. Fearful lest the third party fall into the hands of either of its rivals, or slip under the control of the Pomeroy gang, whose strength in the Building Trades made it peculiarly close to the City Hall, Populist managers resorted to arbitrary precautions. A disproportionately large delegation was assigned to the old Populists, to the American Railway Union, and the Socialists. The Single-Taxers received but ten delegates and the trades unions were given less than a majority, although they were to supply most of the votes relied upon for victory in November. Since membership was the basis of representation for each union, and there was no settled way of determining the exact number of legitimate delegates it was entitled to, a committee of three was appointed to pass upon credentials in advance of the county convention. Composed of Robert Lindblom, local chief of the Knights of Labor, Charles G. Dixon, a former Knight, and Thomas J. Morgan, it contained no representative of the craft unions. Under these circumstances, the committee's refusal to admit delegates from forty-two unions was regarded as unfair by wage-earners who questioned the right of old-line Populists, Knights, railway men, and Socialists to dominate the proceedings.[25]

Despite these precautions and a door guard of fifty Populists at West Twelfth Street Turner Hall, the Populist County Convention was packed by a "political crowd." Hopkins heelers, City Hall employees, Clark Street "toughs," and Pomeroy henchmen seized tickets from accredited delegates as they approached the entrance. They gained admittance by assaulting the door in the sight of the indifferent police, or entered after Pomeroy personally had relieved the harassed Populist door guard. The meeting was in an uproar from the start. It proved impossible to elect permanent officers for the Convention. Finally, after seven and a half hours of pandemonium, it was adjourned by the temporary chairman. Thereupon the Populists, Socialists, and many honest labor delegates left the hall, taking the credentials with them and turning off the lights.[26] Removal of the credentials prevented the Pomeroy gang from assuming control, and the rump delegates also went home.[27]

[25] *Times*, August 14, 17, 18, 1895; *Chicago Daily Tribune*, August 14, 15, 1894; *Chicago Herald*, August 17, 1894; *Eight-Hour Herald*, August 25, 1894.

[26] *Ibid.*; *Chicago Daily Tribune*, August 19, 20, 21, 1894; *Times*, August 19, 1894; Abbot, "Chicago Populist Campaign," *loc. cit.*, 332; *Searchlight*, August 23, 1894.

[27] Abbot, *op. cit.*, 332–333. According to the *Times* and the *Eight-Hour Herald*, the bitterness of the trades unionists at being deprived of a proportionate delegation was a factor in the fiasco. Andrew B. Adair denied, however, that the Populists had combined to de-

Immediately after leaving the Convention Hall, the delegates of Typographical Union No. 16, led by Andrew B. Adair, chief compositor of the Chicago *Daily News*, proceeded to the Briggs House. That evening, on their invitation, delegates from the American Railway Union, Machine Wood-Workers, Telegraphers, Cigar-Makers, Metal Polishers, Machinists, Knights of Labor, Single-Taxers, Socialists, and Populists joined in an informal conference. At this Briggs House meeting, it was decided that an auxiliary committee of twenty-five should be appointed by the labor unions sincerely attached to the third party. This committee should meet with the Populist county committee. Together they would call a new convention based upon a fairer apportionment of representation. The Typographical Union also published an address. This attributed the fiasco at West Twelfth Street Turner Hall primarily to the "labor skates" in the pay of the City Hall. Note also was made of the unwieldy size of the gathering and the "haste and imperfection of the preliminary arrangements." It concluded with the demand that the "proper officials" of the People's party call another, smaller convention to nominate a county ticket "at once" under adequate precautions against "fraudulent and violent invasion."[28]

This action secured for the honest, politically independent labor leaders control of the labor-Populist alliance in Cook County. The Briggs House committee, headed by Andrew B. Adair, proposed that Pomeroy be excluded from the new convention, which was to be reduced by two-thirds in size, and that representation be restricted to the "bona fide unions and parties . . . represented at the Twelfth Street Turner Hall." The Populists immediately appointed a second committee of twenty-five, on request, to work with the first in arranging details. Since this second committee contained some labor leaders, control of the joint committee of fifty and of the People's party in Chicago passed definitely to organized labor.[29]

The date of this second Populist convention was hurriedly advanced to August 25, at Uhlich's Hall, in order to forestall the Pomeroy faction which threatened to call a meeting of its own under the Populist label.

feat the trades unions, and declared that the Populist candidate for temporary chairman, C. G. Dixon, had been entirely satisfactory to the trades unionists. Chicago *Daily News*, August 20, 1894.

[28] Chicago *Inter Ocean*, August 19, 1894; Chicago *Herald*, August 19, 1894.

[29] *Inter Ocean*, August 21, 1894. L. W. Rogers, J. Schwerzgen, and Keliher of the American Railway Union, J. P. Weldon of the Allied Printing Trades, Paul Ehrmann, John Berlyn, and Jesse Cox of the Socialists, Charles Dold, head of the local Cigar-Makers Union, and President Lindblom of the Knights of Labor were also members of the Briggs House Committee. *Times*, August 21, 1894; *Searchlight*, August 23, 1894.

Nevertheless, numerous trades unionist delegations to the Uhlich's Hall convention were assured, including one from the Steam Fitters Union, despite the fact that its head, J. J. Ryan, was President of the Building Trades Council and a leading lieutenant of the Pomeroy gang.   To pre-

UNITED STATES POSTAL SAVINGS BANK

vent a repetition of the fiasco of the previous convention, the City Hall was requested pointedly not to send policemen.   Instead, forty uni-formed, armed Turners guarded the stairs at Uhlich's Hall effectively against assaults of the "gang."   Upstairs, each of the seventeen sections had its chairman to take the roll and collect funds.   Populists and Social-ists sat in front on either side of the center aisle.   Behind were ranged blocks of Single-Taxers, delegates from the American Railway Union, Knights of Labor, sixty-eight trades unions, four Turner clubs, four In-dustrial Legions, and three reform clubs.   This arrangement, though admirable for preservation of order and a guarantee of legitimate attend-ance, symbolized the continuance of ideological differences.   Of the 313 delegates, representatives of organized labor were greatly in the majority.[30]

[30] *Ibid.*, August 30, 1894; *Times*, August 24, 1894.

The radical temper of the Uhlich's Hall Convention was expressed by the fiery address of Director L. W. Rogers of the American Railway Union. The object of the coalition, he declared, was to "turn upside down our whole industrial system." The immediate objective of the gathering, he declared, was the organization of a new party pledged to the accomplishment of this end. The leaders of the American Railway Union would not be deterred from participating in such a movement despite threats from high Democratic officials that they would do well "to keep out of politics" in view of their approaching trial for contempt, and for conspiracy under the Sherman Act as well.[31]

Thomas I. Kidd, of the Machine Wood-Workers presided over the Convention. The Populists were compensated by being given control of the resolutions committee. They produced a platform containing a lengthy exposition of "Why We are Populists," and a statement of Populist financial principles in addition to general endorsement of the Omaha, Illinois, and Springfield platforms. No specific mention was made of Socialism. Thomas Morgan rose at once to demand insertion of Lloyd's modified "Plank 10." A lively debate ensued. The State Chairman, A. L. Maxwell, W. H. ("Coin") Harvey, and H. S. Taylor led the opposition to this proposal. Nevertheless, Morgan's amendment was added to the platform by an overwhelming majority, "amid wild cheering from the socialist section." In the nomination of the county ticket the labor contingent again demonstrated its ascendancy. Aside from three important offices, one of which Morgan had first rejected although it was offered him by acclamation, the nominations went entirely to wage-earners. Labor again predominated in the newly elected county committee, although here the orthodox Populist contingent received far more than its proportionate strength. L. W. Rogers was made county chairman. After adjournment, the Uhlich's Hall Convention received high praise from the Republican *Inter Ocean* and the Democratic *Times*, both of which declared that it represented the reputable labor element of Chicago. Although it regarded the inclusion of the modified "Plank 10" in the platform as a blunder, the *Times* declared that neither this document nor the nominees of the new party were to be "set aside with contempt."[32]

The *Searchlight* rejoiced over the harmony that prevailed within the People's party of Chicago. The Convention, it declared, had "represented the solid unanimous vote in the majority of cases, of local unions, the district unions, and the central bodies, every shade of labor organization from top to bottom."[33] It overlooked the fact that only sixty-eight

[31] *Searchlight*, August 30, 1894.
[32] *Ibid.*; *Times*, August 26, 1894; *Inter Ocean*, August 25, 1894.
[33] August 30, 1894.

of some 260 trades unions in the City had been represented, and that the
Trades and Labor Assembly had sent no delegation to Uhlich's Hall because its representatives had been excluded earlier from the Turner Hall
Convention and no apology for this action had been forthcoming.[34]   The
influential *Eight-Hour Herald* had pointedly demanded that the Populists
concentrate solely on the legislative ticket so as to gain the balance of
power in the General Assembly.   This craft union journal was to support only a few candidates on the third party county ticket in November.[35]

Nevertheless, the independent campaign in Cook County was "in all
essentials" a labor movement, conducted largely by representatives of
unions affiliated with the American Federation of Labor.   Its Populist
façade deceived no one.   Despite the disproportionate influence that the
old Populist organization retained in the new county organization, the
chief impulse and support came from organized labor.[36]   If further evidence on this point were required, it was supplied by the active participation of many leading trades unionists in the campaign.   Led by Typographical Union No. 16, the Cigar-Makers, Machine Wood-Workers,
Seamen, Bricklayers, and American Railway Union sponsored a great
meeting of trades unionists to "ratify" the actions taken at Uhlich's
Hall.[37]   Not the least active in the independent movement were the
unions of the Building Trades' Council although its President, Ryan, had
joined with Pomeroy in the organization of a fourth party, the People's
Party Populists.

This rival movement held its convention shortly after that at Uhlich's
Hall.   It adopted the platform recently formulated by the People's
Party, upon which were nominated Democrats who were candidates for
nomination also by the approaching Democratic Convention.[38]   Ryan's
action in heading up this separatist movement was repudiated publicly
by the Building Trades' Council in a great mass meeting that pledged its
participants to support the regular Populist ticket.[39]   At the same time,
a formidable revolt developed in the Trades and Labor Assembly against
the leadership of "Billy" Pomeroy.[40]   As the result of these developments, the People's Party Populists failed to attract a following.   Even-

[34] *Eight-Hour Herald*, August 25, 1894.

[35] *Ibid.*, August 25, October 10, 25, 1894.   The editor maintained shrewdly that a large
vote on the Cook county ticket that fell short of victory would have no real significance.

[36] Abbot, *op. cit.*, 330; *Times*, September 17, October 1, 1894.

[37] *Ibid.*, September 11, 1894.

[38] *Ibid.*, September 2, 1894; *Chicago Daily Tribune*, September 2, 1894.

[39] *Times*, October 14, 1894; *Searchlight*, October 17, 1894.

[40] *Times*, October 28, 1894.

tually, on the eve of the election, its ticket was withdrawn. In the interim, however, the Cook County People's party was forced to fight hard to win recognition as the regular organization from the State Central Committee and from the county and state boards of review.[41]

Other difficulties beset the leaders of the labor-Populist alliance. The Hopkins-Sullivan machine continued its interference, attempting to control district conventions in Cook County and to trade for support in the congressional field.[42] The Chicago *Herald*, the most influential Democratic newspaper, worked sedulously to precipitate a split between the Socialists and trades unionists in the third party.[43] The same tactic was pursued by the *Inter Ocean*,[44] organ of the traction magnate, Charles T. Yerkes, whose interests would be jeopardized by a powerful, local antimonopoly movement.

In addition, there was the stubborn fact that many labor leaders held appointive offices under Democratic administrations in Chicago and Springfield. From this vantage point within the ruling party they had secured real favors for their unions in the friendly attitude of the Chicago police and of Governor Altgeld during the strikes of the spring and summer. Control of the Illinois Bureau of Labor Statistics was enjoyed by George A. Schilling, the Secretary, who was leader of the powerful Single Tax element and a close friend of the honest, downstate, anti-Pomeroy leaders in the Illinois State Federation of Labor. Schilling was Altgeld's advisor on labor questions, and no doubt held a substantial number of liberal, politically articulate laborers firm in their allegiance to the Democratic party. If more had been needed to accomplish this, it was supplied by Altgeld's pardon of the surviving Haymarket Anarchists, by his stinging criticism of George M. Pullman and of the absentee, corporate owners of the Spring Valley coal mines, and of Grover Cleveland's intervention in the Pullman Strike. Added to this was the unprecedented labor legislation and system of factory inspection that Altgeld had secured from the General Assembly in 1893 with the aid of Hull-House and Henry D. Lloyd.[45] Just as Altgeld's administration diminished the force of the agrarian revolt in rural Illinois, so it lessened the ability of Andrew B. Adair and his associates to draw the bulk of the labor vote away from the Democratic party. Operating in the same direction, in the re-

[41] *Ibid.*, October 10, 11, 13, 24, 25, 27, 30, 1894.

[42] *Ibid.*, September 18, 1894; *Inter Ocean*, August 24, 1894.

[43] August 23, October 22, 1894.

[44] September 24, 1894.

[45] Lindsey, *op. cit.*, 180–183; Wish, *op. cit.*, *passim*; Harry Barnard, "*Eagle Forgotten*," *The Life of John Peter Altgeld* (Indianapolis, 1938), chs. XXVII–XXXII; Staley, *op. cit.*, 97–98, 100–105.

trospective opinions of Clarence S. Darrow and T. P. Quinn,[46] an Irish Knight of Labor, was the reluctance of Catholic wage-earners to support an independent movement in which Socialism figured as prominently as it did in the Cook county Populist campaign.

Despite these handicaps the Cook county Populist campaign proved to be "a model for all independent movements."[47]   First returned by such an experienced observer as Willis J. Abbot, editor of the *Times*, this verdict was justified by the effective organization and brilliant leadership developed by labor-Populist alliance during the canvass.   Since the new county chairman, L. W. Rogers, was involved in the litigation growing out of the Pullman strike, direction of the campaign was delegated promptly to J. A. Copeland, a Nationalist, with the title of Campaign Manager.   He was an admirable selection, in part because he occupied an ideological position midway between that of the Populists and Knights and the proletarian collectivism of Tommy Morgan's following. Copeland labored, with support from the State Executive Committee, to hold campaign speakers to the Omaha and Springfield platforms.   At the same time he pushed the organization of People's Party Clubs and Industrial Legions vigorously in the wards and precincts of Chicago.   An active woman's auxiliary was also established.[48]   An adequate campaign fund resulted from frequent appeals for money to meet customary political expenses, including the cost of circulating the petitions that were required of political parties that had cast less than two per cent of the vote in the preceding election before their tickets could be placed on the official ballot.   Aside from generous contributions from a few well-to-do sympathizers such as Henry D. Lloyd, Populist funds in Cook County came from "workingmen, the clerks and small business men."   They were sufficient to finance the campaign on a scale commensurate with the activities of the party.[49]

For a third party, the labor-Populist alliance in Cook County enjoyed exceptional press support.   The *Railway Times*, organ of the American Railway Union, and the *Chicago Workman* labored to rally wage-earners to the ticket.   The party received strong editorial support from Henry Vincent, one of the famous journalistic expounders of Populism, on the *Searchlight*.   In this ably conducted journal, which appeared twice or

[46] Interviews.

[47] Abbot, *op. cit.*, 334.

[48] *Searchlight*, July 26, August 2, 4, 16, 23, 1894; *Times*, September 7, 11, 18, 21, 25, 26, October 13, 1894; *Eight-Hour Herald*, August 10, 1894.

[49] Lloyd MSS. (Madison), Henry J. Vaupel to Lloyd, October 11, 1894; Fanny Kavanaugh to Lloyd, October 30, 1894; *Searchlight*, September 6, 1894; *Times*, October 19, 24, 1894; *Inter Ocean*, November 4, 1894.

three times weekly and achieved a circulation of 20,000, every effort was made to harmonize all factions. Union compositors and eventual recognition as a union pressroom strengthened the *Searchlight's* influence with organized labor.[50] Considerable though not always disinterested publicity was given the independents by the metropolitan press. Republican dailies were zealous in defending them from the encroachments of the Hopkins machine, assuming no doubt that any increase in Populist strength would draw largely from the Democrats.[51]

Due to exceptional circumstances, also, the independent canvass received friendly publicity and counsel from the *Chicago Times*. Formerly the property and powerful tool of Carter H. Harrison the elder, this paper was part of his unliquidated estate. It was managed by the two Harrison sons, who in local politics were completely at odds with the dominant Hopkins faction, in part because it had refused to nominate Carter Harrison, II, for County Treasurer, an office that would bring a large share in the public printing to the *Times*.[52] Willis J. Abbot, editor of the *Times*, was a well-known liberal who later became editor of the *Christian Science Monitor*. Given a free hand by the Harrison sons, who wished to build up the paper by a frank appeal to the discontented wage-earners, he had been able to display marked sympathy with the United Mine Workers and the striking Pullman laborers and the American Railway Union. One hundred per cent increase in circulation resulted. One hundred and one thousand daily sales in mid-July[53] made the Harrisons hopeful of finding a purchaser for the paper that would relieve them of the burden of meeting its annual deficits. This prospect was dimmed somewhat by the boycott of their advertising columns imposed by the State Street merchants, whose antagonism to Debs and the railway workers extended to an open attempt to coerce the recalcitrant *Times* into a policy more agreeable to the business interests of Chicago.[54] At the same time, the two-cent dailies forced their carriers and dealers to stop handling the one-cent *Times*.[55] Nevertheless, the Harrisons and Abbot continued their outright "underdog" policy with such effect that embittered workingmen and Populists of the Middle West and as far east

[50] *Searchlight*, September 20, October 17, November 1, 1894.

[51] *Chicago Daily Tribune*, September 2, 4, 1894; *Inter Ocean*, September 3, October 24, 27, 1894; *Daily News* September 3, 1894.

[52] Carter H. Harrison, *Stormy Years* (Indianapolis, 1935), 194-196.

[53] Lloyd MSS. (Madison), W. H. Burke to Lloyd, July 10, 1894, W. J. Abbot to Lloyd, July 14, 1894.

[54] *Ibid.*, Abbot to Lloyd, July 14, 1894.

[55] *Searchlight*, August 9, 1894.

as Pennsylvania came to regard it as "the only great paper that bore a semblance" of friendship to "their cause."[56]

The fifth page of Bliss's *Populist Compendium* appeared in bold face type at the head of the editorial page of the *Times* during the Pullman strike.[57] Early in August, Abbot declared that a "strong Populist minority, or indeed, a third party majority, in the state legislature or the national Congress would be a good thing for the cause of industrial progress." The Democratic party had fallen so completely under the control of eastern moneyed interests that it was incapable of "just and intelligent legislative action."[58] The *Times* complimented the German-speaking, Socialist unions for their decision to withdraw from the first county convention "if it should be captured by corruption,"[59] and then continued to give the third party warm support despite Populist refusal to accept advice to drop "Plank 10" and keep out of the county election. Abbot supported the People's party in its contest with Pomeroy for a place on the official ballot. He placed three outstanding Populist congressional candidates, White, Taylor, and Henry D. Lloyd, the independent nominees for county clerk, clerk of county court, and most of the Populist candidates for county commissioners on the *Times'* own ticket. The brother of the chief compositor of the *Times*, it may be noted, was none other than Andrew B. Adair.[60]

Perhaps because the Harrison estate was negotiating for a time in the hope of disposing of the paper to Henry D. Lloyd,[61] Abbot was able to make it temporarily the vehicle of that well known radical's views. In a series of able editorials, Abbot laid out the common ideological ground upon which he urged all elements in the labor-Populist alliance to stand. Trades unions, he declared, had to go into politics in order to succeed in collective bargaining. Abbot argued that "socialism," in opposition to laissez faire, had lost its meaning in the light of such governmental undertakings as the post office, the Interstate Commerce Commission, and municipally owned water works. The *Times* urged extension of the principle of public ownership and operation to the express, telegraph, and railroads, as well as to municipal gas and electric plants, street and elevated railways. The people were blind who could not see how steadily and inexorably public opinion was moving toward public ownership of "every natural monopoly," Abbot declared. This, rather than a vague,

[56] *Ibid.*, February 28, 1895.
[57] *Ibid.*, July 19, 1894.
[58] Quoted in *ibid.*, August 9, 1894.
[59] Quoted in *ibid.*, August 2, 1894.
[60] *Times*, September 23, October 25, 28, 1894; Harrison, *op. cit.*, 196.
[61] Lloyd MSS. (Madison), Clarence S. Darrow to Lloyd, May 20 [1894], night letter, Jessie Bross Lloyd to H. D. Lloyd, September 8, 1894.

modified "Plank 10" was a more practical, commendable position for the labor-Populist allies to assume.[62]   Thus Abbot emphasized the anti-monopolism common to all elements in the coalition.   By demanding public ownership and operation of all natural monopolies he appealed to the Populists and Knights of Labor, to whom the Omaha platform had already defined banking, transportation, and communication as proper fields for the application of this principle, and also to the Single-Taxers who followed Henry George in demanding public ownership of natural and franchise monopolies.[63]   The Nationalists and Socialists regarded municipalization of utilities and nationalization of railroads and tele-graphs as important "immediate" steps on the road to their respective utopias.   A limited program of government ownership, applicable to all monopolies, carried an undoubted appeal to all elements in the Cook County People's Party.

The extent to which Willis Abbot was able to impose this program upon the independent movement can be seen in an address by Thomas I. Kidd, delivered at Battery D, October 31, before a mass meeting of Populist trades unionists.   Kidd contemplated, clearly, the extension of Popu-list, antimonopolist collectivism to the municipal field.

We are not afraid nor ashamed to advance principles which must eventually bring about industrial emancipation to the masses. . . .   This form of trades unionism is intended to take the place of the old.   It has the indorsement and support of such men as John Burns of England and Eugene V. Debs here at home.   If we can get the ownership of the railroads in the hands of the government there will be no more Pullmans nor Vanderbilts.   We want the initiative and the referendum, and when we get them there will be no more valuable franchises given away by city councils to street railway magnates and privileged monopo-lies.   None of the rights of the people of this great metropolis will go away from them with-out their consent or without adequate compensation.

It is only by the ballot that we can get municipal ownership of the street railways, elec-tric lights, gas plants, and similar institutions which should belong to the people as a whole.[64]

It is not surprising, therefore, that the *Searchlight* thanked the *Times* for its service in "sharply defining the lines of reform as represented by the People's party movement from those injected into it by representatives of various isms."[65]

The composite character of the People's party in Chicago was reflected in the wide variety of literature circulated during the campaign.   Fa-vorite tracts were *Coin's Financial School*, *The Story of the Commonweal*, *The Dogs and the Fleas*, and S. F. Norton's *Ten Men of Money Island*.

[62] *Searchlight*, August 30, 1894; Joliet *Daily News*, October 2, 1894; *Commonwealth* (New York), II, No. 3 (January 19, 1894), 4–5; each quoting extracts from the *Times*.

[63] Henry George, *Progress and Poverty* (New York, 1938), 412.

[64] *Times*, November 1, 1894.

[65] October 17, 1894.

Tens of thousands of leaflets containing the platform and ticket were distributed.[66]   In addition, Thomas J. Morgan enlisted Henry D. Lloyd's assistance in gathering information on British labor's venture into politics, for distribution in Chicago.   One of Morgan's productions was a large, four or five page circular entitled, "The International Political Labor Movement," that was distributed in successive editions.   It presented the platform of the Independent Labour Party, the Trades Union Congress' recent act favoring independent political action, articles by Keir Hardie, Tom Mann, and Justin McCarthy, together with the political program of the American Federation of Labor and Lloyd's modification of "Plank 10," while the collectivist aspects of the Omaha platform were duly emphasized.   Edited by Lloyd before publication, this pamphlet indicates the reliance of the English speaking, Chicago Socialists upon the example and principles of the British labor movement for justification of the non-Marxian, Socialist principles interjected into the Cook County Populist campaign.[67]   Even the *Searchlight* portrayed graphically the "equal share to all" of the "Socialistic Republic" along with impressive cartoons depicting such orthodox Populist demands as inflation, government banking at two per cent interest, and public ownership of railways.[68]

The campaign in Chicago was exceptionally well managed, save for the error in nominating an opponent of Congressman August E. Gans, a sincere friend of labor.[69]   The People's party was fortunate in possessing a coterie of brilliant men, "radical in thought and intolerant of the restrictions imposed on them by old party ties."[70]   They were Henry D. Lloyd, Lyman Trumbull, Clarence S. Darrow, Thomas J. Morgan, John Z. White, Howard S. Taylor, Andrew B. Adair, Eugene V. Debs.   More than a score of less well known but able labor leaders joined them in the canvass.   In addition, notable speakers were imported to encourage the different elements in the party, Ignatius Donnelly of Minnesota, Father McGlynn of New York, the Single Tax priest, and Governor Davis H. ("Bloody Bridles") Waite of Colorado, the champion of free silver. Henry George was also invited to speak in the expectation that he would enhance the enthusiasm of the Single-Taxers for Populism.

[66] *Searchlight*, July 19, August 2, September 27, 1894; *Chicago Daily Tribune*, October 21, 1894.

[67] Lloyd MSS. (Madison), T. J. Morgan to Lloyd, September 8, 15, October 20, 1894, and copies of the circular.

[68] August 2, 16, 23, September 20, 1894.

[69] Lloyd MSS. (Madison), August E. Gans to Lloyd, October 9, November 15, 1894; *Times*, September 17, 1894.   This action antagonized Gans, who had earlier offered his support to Copeland in aid of Henry D. Lloyd's congressional campaign.

[70] Abbot, *op. cit.*, 334.

During the early weeks political rallies were staged in outlying districts. Campaign Manager Copeland husbanded his resources and arranged a series of downtown demonstrations for the last five weeks of the canvass.[71] This "Loop" campaign was opened on September 29 by a gigantic torchlight procession that initiated one of the largest political jamborees that Chicago had seen for years. Ignatius Donnelly and Eugene V. Debs spoke to a monster mass meeting at Central Music Hall that night, which was so well attended that three overflow rallies were held.[72] Debs' appeal to labor to support the People's party was very effective, but the announcement that aged, ex-Senator Lyman Trumbull would speak under Populist auspices from the same platform a week later created a sensation. Trumbull was justly famous for his discriminating patriotism during the Civil War and Reconstruction, and for his attachment to the principle of equal rights. He had broken with the Republican party and supported the Liberal Republican movement of 1872. Thereafter he had joined the Democrats whom he had led in 1880 as the Illinois gubernatorial candidate. Until 1894 Trumbull had remained in the Democratic fold, sympathetic with the common people and the free silver movement. His divergence from the Cleveland Democracy of the day had already been indicated by his association with Clarence Darrow in the defense of the indicted leaders of the American Railway Union.[73]

This second Populist meeting in Central Music Hall proved to be the high point in the independent campaign.[74] Clarence Darrow presided and Father McGlynn sat on the platform, but Trumbull and Henry D. Lloyd were the main speakers. Darrow's popularity was great with the cheering 3,000 that packed the hall, because of his resignation as chief counsel of the Chicago and Northwestern Railroad to defend Debs.[75] The young lawyer's graceful opening speech, concluded by a poem from William Morris, the English poetic champion of medieval art and modern Socialism, set the tone of the meeting.

Lyman Trumbull, who followed, was greeted with the greatest enthusiasm. He declared that the "underlying cause" of popular discontent was the poverty and suffering of the laboring masses, whose inadequate pay contrasted glaringly with the concentrated wealth of a few millionaires and wealthy corporations. Neither strikes, nor violence, nor government con-

---

[71] *Searchlight*, September 20, 1894; *Times*, September 22, 1894.
[72] Donnelly MSS., Eugene Smith to I. Donnelly, September 18, 1894; *Times*, September 30, 1894; *Railway Times*, October 15, 1894.
[73] *Times*, October 4, 6, 1894; Chicago *Herald*, October 5, 1894; Horace White, *The Life of Lyman Trumbull* (Boston, 1913), 377–388, 412–414.
[74] Lloyd MSS. (Madison), C. S. Darrow to C. L. Withington, November 9, 1905.
[75] Clarence S. Darrow, *The Story of My Life* (New York, 1932), 49–62.

AT CENTRAL MUSIC HALL.

THE GREAT POPULAR DEMONSTRATIONS CONTINUE.

LYMAN TRUMBULL AND H. D. LLOYD

Send Forth Addresses that Ring from Ocean to Ocean.

The Venerable Statesman-Jurist at the Age of Eighty Years Starts a New Chapter in Political History—Declaration for Reform More Radical and Far-Reaching than the Platform of Any Party.

SUPREME COURTS ARE NOT OMNIPOTENT.

Human Rights and Human Liberties Take Precedence Over the Rights of Property or the Caprice of Corporations.

Who wrote the Thirteenth Amendment providing that "neither slavery nor involuntary servitude shall exist within the United States."

AT CENTRAL MUSIC HALL

trol of railroads and corporations, he declared, could remedy this evil. If the concentration of wealth continued it would "make the masses dependent upon the generosity of the few for the means to live." Only united, independent political action by labor and the middle class could apply the remedy. Once in control of Congress and the state legislatures, the coalition should make wages the first charge against industry, a proposal that was crystallized a half century later in the automobile industry in the demand for an annual wage. The victorious Populists, Trumbull declared, should not only curb the giant corporations by law, but they should also limit the right to bequeath property to a total of $500,000, diverting the balance of great fortunes to the state.   In addition, he demanded curtailment of the power of the federal courts, which, he asserted, now claimed the right to

take possession of and run the railroads of the country, to issue injunctions without notice, and to punish for contempt by fine and imprisonment anyone who disputes their authority.

Such judicial usurpation, if unchecked, would undermine the very "pillars of the constitution."[76]

Lloyd followed. His presence together with Darrow on the platform led the Chicago *Record* to declare that although "Judge Trumbull" was mingling there in "new and unaccustomed society," still it was "entirely respectable . . . even by the worldly standards of wealth and culture." As for Lloyd, he was not only

a social reformer (not to say socialist); he is also, like Bebel and Liebknecht, the social democratic leaders of the German reichstag, a man of substance, a scholar and a philanthropist.

It would not do to call him, or Trumbull, or Darrow, or William Morris, "demagogues or to denounce the movement they have espoused as a passing fad."[77]

Lloyd spoke as the chief architect of the labor-Populist alliance. His address was clothed in the striking, epigrammatic style and pitched on the high moral and intellectual plane that characterized all his literary productions. He sought to identify the People's party with the new parties of the left then emerging in Britain, Germany, France, and Australia as the result of the awakening of the masses. This development, he asserted, was "the great political fact of our times." At the same time he reached back as far as Jefferson for an analogy between the efforts of this new democratic movement "to demonetize the millionaire" and the great Virginian's attempt to overthrow the planter aristocracy of 1776. Lloyd thus sought to define the common meeting ground of the

[76] *Chicago Daily Tribune*, October 7, 1894.
[77] October 8, 1894.

old, antimonopolist democratic tradition of America with the newer, non-Marxian Socialism of the British Fabians and labor leaders, and of such American writers as Edward Bellamy and Lawrence Gronlund. He attempted, in other words, to harmonize the limited Populist collectivism with its program of state ownership and intervention in finance, money, transportation, communication, and land, with the progressive conquest of industrial and monopoly capitalism by the democratic state as envisaged by the Nationalists and Socialists of all types. To accomplish this Lloyd postulated no Marxian theory of class and civil strife, of materialism and dictatorship. Instead he invoked the traditional hostility of American democracy to privilege and concentrated corporate power, and its underlying concepts of liberty, equal rights, and brotherhood.

Here Lloyd interjected into the political arena the conclusions that he had just presented to the reading public in *Wealth against Commonwealth*. Drawing upon this study of monopoly capitalism, he painted a vivid picture to the crowd in Central Music Hall of the disastrous effect that the combination movement had had upon popular government in the United States. While liberals were still talking of "the coming revolution" and hoping that it would be peaceful, a revolution opposite to their hopes had already taken place. Government "by campaign contributions" had delivered city, state, and national governments over to

the trusts, and armor-plate contractors, and the whisky ring, and the subsidized steamship companies, and the street railways and railroads buy the privilege of running these governments to enrich themselves and send troublesome leaders of the people to jail, to keep themselves out of jail.

This revolution had already perverted popular government to "the enrichment and aggrandizement of a few" through abuse of the right of eminent domain and control of the highway. This revolution had created railroad, national bank, bond, tariff, land-grant millionaires. It had transferred control of the city streets to street railway, gas, telephone, and electric power syndicates. It had perverted the antitrust law into a weapon against organized labor while letting "the presidents, and managers, and owners of the railroads and trusts go free of all punishment for the crimes they are committing." It had made bread dear, and clothing and coal scarce. It was restricting the free movement of goods to consumers.

The Populists and their labor allies, Lloyd declared, were participants in a world-wide "counter revolution," in which workingmen everywhere were joining with consumers, farmers, and small capitalists. Its object was the overthrow of monopoly capitalism and its governments of privilege. Its ultimate purpose was to establish the "co-operative commonwealth" in which industrial liberty would be regained and secured through the collective ownership and operation of as many of the means of production and distribution as the public desired. This objective was made possible, therefore, by the modified "Plank 10" of the Springfield platform.

So viewed, the "co-operative commonwealth," Lloyd asserted, was the legitimate extension of the republican principle, that power should rest on the "consent of the governed," from government into business. It could be accomplished only by the People's party since the Republicans had long since put the "white man on the auction block of the money power to be sold to the lowest bidder under the iron hammer of monopoly." The Democrats, on the other hand, had surrendered their states rights defense of individual liberty to "centralized corporate despotism" under the leadership of Grover Cleveland. It was the People's party that would use the public powers of eminent domain, of borrowing, and monetary control to introduce the "co-operative commonwealth." It would enfranchise women, institute a postal telegraph, a parcels post, and postal savings and insurance. Municipal ownership of street cars and other public utilities would eliminate from American city governments the notorious "political corruption, boss rule, and boodle" that sprang "mainly from the intrigues and briberies of syndicates." Finally, production for use in an economy of plenty would abolish unemployment. All should work "when the people come in."[78]

The great enthusiasm that greeted Lloyd's address indicated clearly how far to the left politically independent labor in Cook County had swung after the Pullman strike. Now federal prosecution of Eugene V. Debs and his associates had raised unrest to fever heat. Trumbull's and Lloyd's addresses were printed and circulated in large numbers in Chicago.[79] Until the close of the campaign large crowds listened enthusiastically to the gospel of the "co-operative commonwealth," whether presented by Lloyd or other spokesmen.[80] Freed from Marxist connotations by the tactful borrowing of Lawrence Gronlund's inoffensive phrase,[81] and harmonized verbally with the indigenous radical

---

[78] *The Wealth Makers* (Lincoln, Nebraska), October 25, 1894.

[79] Lloyd MSS. (Madison), W. S. Timblin to Lloyd, October 18, 1894; *Times*, November 4, 1894.

[80] Lloyd MSS. (Madison), Timblin to Lloyd, October 18, 1894.

[81] *The Cooperative Commonwealth* (1884), which had had a wide sale. As the first systematic attempt to adapt socialist thought to the American radical tradition, it presented Socialism from an evolutionary rather than a revolutionary viewpoint.

tradition, it bade fair to supply the ideological basis for an extension of the labor-Populist alliance to the entire nation.   Such was undoubtedly Lloyd's hope now, in early October, as his address was published in full in such widely separated Populist papers as the *American Noncon-formist* at Indianapolis, the *Wealth Makers*, in Lincoln, Nebraska, and the *Searchlight* of Duluth.   C. P. Somerby, a Socialist publisher in New York who was circulating Thomas Blatchford's *Merrie England* with great success, reprinted Lloyd's Music Hall address in the *Common-wealth* and then distributed it in pamphlet form with the expectation of selling 100,000 copies before election day.[82]

Meanwhile, in Chicago, the followers of Tommy Morgan were so gratified with the Populist campaign that they virtually suspended activity as the local branch of the Socialist Labor party.   Similarly, the Single-Taxers worked whole-heartedly for the third party, ignoring Henry George's advice of 1892 to remain free from the Populist move-ment.   Their action paralleled that of the Socialists, who had broken away from Daniel DeLeon's leadership, and of the trades unionists, who were ignoring Samuel Gompers' coolness to their venture into independ-ent politics.   In each case, participation in the People's party involved repudiation of New York leadership, and willingness to surrender ideological autonomy for fusion on the basis of drastic extension of the antimonopolist collectivism of the Populist revolt.

This development of an integrated radical party was checked midway in the campaign in Illinois by two not unrelated incidents.   The first was an address by Henry George in Chicago under the auspices of the Single Tax Club on October 10, 1894.   The second was the meeting of the Illinois Federation of Labor at Belleville on October 10–12.   Henry George's contribution to this *dénouement* is easily explained.   He spoke at Central Music Hall to a great, mixed throng that had met to pledge support to John Z. White and Walter F. Cooling, respectively Single-Taxer candidates of the People's party on the congressional and county tickets.   Under the circumstances, the audience expected from Henry George a hearty indorsement of the labor-Populist alliance.   It was keenly disappointed.   He avowed, instead, his "indifference, or even hostility" to the Omaha platform and the resolutions more recently adopted at Springfield.   He ranked the Populists no higher ethically than either major party.   He disavowed any desire to awaken enthusi-asm for their cause.   Instead, he presented coldly and "scientifically" the case for the Single Tax.[83]

[82] Lloyd MSS. (Madison), C. P. Somerby to Lloyd, October 20, 1894; *Commonwealth* (New York), October 27, 1894.

[83] *Times*, October 12, 1894, editorial, "Mr. George and the People's Party."

This address had profound implications for the future of the labor-Populist alliance. Since the Single-Taxers in Peoria had already set up a local ticket independently of the Populists, and Henry George went there to speak again solely in behalf of the Single Tax,[84] he can hardly be acquitted of having used his great personal influence with his Illinois following to disrupt its newly formed coalition with the other radical elements in the state. The downstate Single-Taxers, who remained close to Altgeld by virtue of George Schilling's influence, needed no more encouragement than this and the recollection of Henry George's known antipathy for Socialism to discard their alliance with Tommy Morgan. Hostile as downstaters to all elements in the Chicago labor movement, and eager to free the State Federation from the corrupt dominance of William C. Pomeroy's racketeers, the Single-Taxers at the Belleville convention resolved, after learning of Henry George's stand, to play Pomeroy off against Tommy Morgan. By thus capitalizing on the antipathy between the two men, they hoped to destroy Socialism's influence within the State Federation and at the same time seize control of it for themselves.

This coup was completely successful. Helpless as long as the powerful Socialist and Single-Taxer wings of the Federation remained allied in support of the Springfield platform, Pomeroy had offered no opposition to the convention's endorsement of this document at Morgan's instance during the first day's proceedings. On the next day the situation changed abruptly. Re-enforcements for Pomeroy's "push" hurried down from Chicago, while the redoutable Kentuckian agreed to the hard proposals from the downstaters that would enable him to wreak vengeance for the ouster of his City Hall faction from the People's party in Cook County. Thus, as leader of the "pure and simple" trades unionists of Chicago, spokesman of their dislike of Socialism, and, as local organizer of the American Federation of Labor, the ally of Samuel Gompers, Pomeroy agreed to surrender control of the state offices in exchange for a concerted attack upon "Plank 10." On the last day of the convention the Pomeroy-Single-Taxer combination substituted a statement against land monopoly for the original "Plank 10," voted down Lloyd's modified version when offered as a substitute, and instructed the State Federation's delegate to support the remainder of the political program of the American Federation of Labor at the Denver Convention in December. Then the offices in the Illinois Federation were filled with downstate Single-Taxers.[85]

[84] Henry George MSS. (New York Public Library), Henry George to William L. Garrison, October 5, 1894.

[85] *Searchlight*, October 17, 1894; Staley, *op. cit.*, 122–124.

Morgan's discomfiture was complete. Pomeroy and his following returned to Chicago in high glee, singing

> Whoopla! Whoopla! Whoopla, ho!
> We are the people from Chicago.
> We are the people—we are the men,
> We are the people who killed Plank Ten.
> They were easy—just like wax;
> We knocked them out with the Single Tax.[86]

These events threatened the labor-Populist alliance in Illinois with immediate disruption. It was plain now to all leaders of the third party in Cook County that the Pomeroy "labor skates" would continue their opposition to the independent movement to the last. To Morgan, the action of the Belleville convention in repudiating "Plank 10" was a body blow, not only to himself but also to the Socialist movement within the American Federation of Labor. The one plank in the political program of the Federation that mattered most to the Socialists had been repudiated in the state of its sponsor. In Illinois, furthermore, the participation of the Socialists in the People's party rested upon the good faith with which the trades unions, Single-Taxers, and agrarians adhered to Lloyd's compromise "Plank 10." Its repudiation by the downstate Single-Taxers and the conservative, Chicago trades unionist following of "Billy" Pomeroy was bound to raise suspicions regarding the future attitude toward Socialism of the Cook County Single-Taxers, Populists, and the trades unionists that remained within the People's party there. This question was of more than local significance, also, since Victor L. Berger and the Wisconsin Socialists had entered the Populist movement in their state under a similar arrangement,[87] and fusion of trades unionists and Socialists with the People's party was being attempted in Ohio.

To prevent an open split between the Socialists and Single-Taxers in Cook County became an object of immediate concern to the Populist leaders. The *Times* was stinging in its castigation of Henry George for his refusal to work for immediately realizable ends in the independent movement. These ends, Willis Abbot declared to be free coinage of silver, the eight hour day, full recognition of the labor movement, government ownership of railroads and "municipal ownership of local natural monopolies." Declaring his respect for the prophet from San Francisco, Abbot concluded by doubting his "political wisdom" in setting aside "the struggle against corporate encroachments upon governmental power, against trusts, against gang rule—. . . the whole program of the

---

[86] *Ibid.*, 124, republished by permission of the University of Chicago Press.
[87] Klotsche, *op. cit.*, 383.

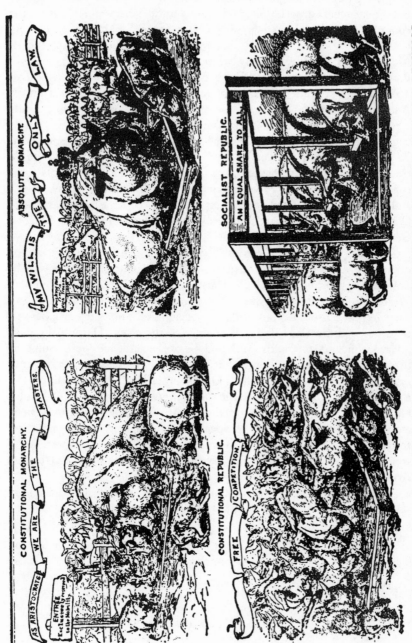

CONSTITUTIONAL MONARCHY; ABSOLUTE MONARCHY; CONSTITUTIONAL REPUBLIC; SOCIALIST REPUBLIC

people's party" for single-minded agitation of the Single Tax.   Instead, the *Times* recalled both "Single-Taxers and Socialists" forcefully to the common purposes of the labor-Populist alliance.   Abbot charged flatly that Pomeroy had deliberately tried to wreck it through humiliation of Morgan at Belleville, and by whipping up the "covert antagonism" between "the Georgeites and the Morganites."[88]   Finally, he called attention to appeals for harmony from Henry Lloyd and Andrew B. Adair that were published on the same editorial page.   While Adair stressed the common antimonopolism of all elements in the party, Lloyd urged that they adopt the slogan, "an end to all private use of social powers—from land to trusts," and copy John Z. White's admirable championship of the whole party program announced from the platform that he shared with Henry George in Central Music Hall.   Thus Lloyd, Abbot and Adair exerted their great influence with the wage-earners of Cook County to counteract the disruptive effects of the tactics of Henry George and William C. Pomeroy.[89]

The independent campaign in Cook County continued to be one of great thoroughness and enthusiasm.   Thousands attended the weekly downtown meetings at which Darrow, Father McGlynn, Governor Waite and other figures spoke.   Noon meetings at headquarters on 121 Fifth Avenue drew large crowds.   One hundred and forty speakers in all addressed meetings in every quarter of the city.   Despite the misgivings of headquarters, the rank and file of the audiences were willing to listen to the pleas for Socialism that Tommy Morgan insisted on presenting after his defeat at Belleville.   On the other hand, Morgan supported the Populist program, while the *Searchlight* gave space to Socialist arguments.   All parts of the orthodox state Populist platform were emphasized at the gatherings.   Speaker after speaker, however, turned to the fundamental problem with which farmers and laborers were alike concerned.   As Clarence Darrow put it to a mass meeting at Battery D. Armory:

The question is, shall the people who produce the wealth, who toil and spin, continue to do so that a few may grow rich while the masses remain in poverty and want?[90]

This was the central issue of the Cook County campaign.[91]   Even Henry Vincent, original Populist from Kansas, worked for "The establishment of the Co-Operative Commonwealth" as the remedy.[92]

[88] October 12, 14, 1894.
[89] October 14, 1894.
[90] *Times*, November 1, 1894.
[91] *Ibid.*, addresses by E. G. Bell and D. M. Fulwiler; *ibid.*, October 4, 1894.
[92] *Searchlight*, November 1, 1894, editorial.

The Populist campaign in Chicago concluded with a remarkable demonstration on the evening of November 3, when a monster torchlight parade of 7,000 voters entered the "Loop." Knights of Labor, Socialists, Turners, Single Tax clubs, and trades unions carried banners, flags, and "transparencies" of every imaginable description, some bearing quotations from Emerson, Henry George, and the local press. To these Tommy Morgan's followers added red ribbons and a profusion of red fire along the entire line of march. The candidates of the party marched on foot at the head of the procession and were cheered continuously by sympathizers lining the streets. After traversing the business section the marchers turned south to Tattersall's, a great ampitheatre on the South Side. There the scene "when the parade arrived was well-nigh indescribable." Between 12,000 and 15,000 marchers and sympathizers crowded into the building. An estimated 5,000 were "unable to get seats or standing room to hear the speakers." Jammed to the doors, cheering and yelling for half an hour before Chairman L. W. Rogers could quiet it sufficiently to introduce the speakers, the enthusiastic crowd listened in succession to Reverend W. H. Carwardine of Pullman, William Hogan of the Seamen's Union, Thomas Morgan, Henry D. Lloyd, Clarence Darrow, and Jesse Cox. Morgan's outspoken advocacy of "Plank 10" and of the ballot as the proper means of achieving the "co-operative commonwealth" was cheered again and again. Lloyd, on his part, proclaimed the new party's intention to make the Golden Rule and the brotherhood of all men in industry practical issues by organizing the government as a "people's syndicate." This would deny the "use of public powers or public property to private profit," and assert the people's right to "use public powers for the public welfare to any extent the public demands."[93] Thus conceived, the modified "Plank 10" that he had written into the Springfield platform was but the application, through politics to economic life, of the "New Self Interest" and the philosophy of civilization that he had formulated in *Wealth Against Commonwealth*.[94]

While the Cook County Populist campaign drew to a close in an atmosphere of hope and excitement,[95] amid considerable anxiety on the part of old-party managers,[96] the downstate Populists were concluding a desultory canvass. In spite of rosy expectations for the legislative

[93] *Times*, November 4, 1894.
[94] Chapters XXXIV–XXXV.
[95] Lloyd MSS. (Madison), Willis Abbot to Lloyd, November 5, 1894.
[96] *Daily News*, October 29, 1894; *Inter Ocean*, October 25, 1894; *Searchlight*, November 1, 1894; *Farmers' Voice*, September 22, 1894.

ticket,[97] the State Executive Committee was so handicapped by lack of funds that its fond hopes for 100,000 votes in November with the balance of power in the General Assembly and possibly a United States Senator[98] were little short of chimerical. By mid-September the State Chairman, A. L. Maxwell, lacked funds to maintain campaign headquarters at Springfield. Having exhausted his personal resources, he was forced to call for aid upon Henry Lloyd, with whom he had differed radically at the Springfield Conference.[99]

Although the Chicago Fabian extricated Maxwell from this dilemma, the state organization continued in straitened circumstances. No money was available for literature, save a small supply of the platform. The filing of petitions was so expensive that the State Chairman was obliged to borrow on his personal credit. Finding it impossible to raise funds from the county and district committees, he was reduced as a last resort to another appeal to Lloyd, already the largest contributor. Finally, after the election, Maxwell submitted to him a statement of receipts and expenditures. Out of the pitifully small sum of $1,177.64 spent, but $69.75 had gone to campaign literature, some of which had been sent to the local branches of the United Mine Workers on November 2, almost too late to be of assistance to the Populist ticket. Only $135.15 had been spent on speaker hire. Total contributions left a "NET DEFICIENCY" of $259.04 which, by implication, Maxwell hoped Lloyd would defray.[100] It is evident that the earlier expectation of electing ten Populist legislators from downstate had been utopian indeed. The activity of local Populist organizations, outside of Chicago, hardly made up for the failure to set up a vigorous, well-financed state headquarters. Conventions met and tickets were nominated in most districts and many counties. Customary farmers' basket picnics, accompanied by political harangues, were held in the rural districts. In Hancock county an unsuccessful effort was made to bring Ignatius Donnelly in to speak at a "contemplated mass meeting."[101] Among the farmers, however, there were few indications of an "impending revolution."

Organized labor, by contrast, was somewhat more active in the downstate cities and towns, although even here the People's party failed to take full advantage of the favorable situation created by the great strikes. At Joliet, Samuel Leavitt, veteran reform journalist from

---

[97] Joliet *News*, June 30, 1894; *Chicago Daily Tribune*, October 10, 1894.
[98] Lloyd MSS. (Madison), A. L. Maxwell to Lloyd, September 5, 1894.
[99] *Ibid.*, Maxwell to Lloyd, September 13, 1894.
[100] *Ibid.*, Maxwell to Lloyd, October 18, November 1, 3, 23, 1894, January 5, 1895.
[101] Donnelly MSS., Dr. A. E. McNeall to Donnelly, October 8, 1894.

Peter Cooper's *Advocate*, worked on the *News*, ran for Congress, and spoke in adjacent districts.[102] There, in addition to open air meetings, larger demonstrations were staged, at which T. J. Morgan, G. W. Howard of the American Railway Union, Clarence Darrow, and Robert Schilling of Milwaukee occupied the platform. Yet in Joliet the Populist campaign expenditures totalled but $125. There was "no thorough enrollment of voters, no personal solicitations, no carriages, no special favors of any kind, and no fireworks." Throughout the county the organization was justly termed "exceedingly primitive."[103] Similar activity was evident among the wage-earners at Bloomington, where Father McGlynn was brought to speak.[104] In important coal mining districts, an effort was made to enlist the miners. J. A. Crawford, State President of the United Mine Workers, was nominated for Congress by the Populists in the Springfield district, while other miners were nominated for the legislature at Spring Valley and Belleville.[105] Yet even among the thoroughly receptive coal miners, the lack of funds and want of thorough organization stood in the way of maximum results. Elsewhere, the influence of Governor Altgeld with the downstate labor leaders, and the hostility of the rural Populists and alliance farmers to the Socialists and Single-Taxers of Chicago operated still further to diminish the prospect that the People's party would accomplish anything substantial at the polls.[106]

Among the major parties, the aggressive campaign of the Republicans more than recovered the ground lost in 1892. They were assisted by Governor William McKinley of Ohio, Thomas R. Reed of Maine, and the propaganda of the American Protective Tariff League. Wage-earners were won over in large numbers to the tariff for the first time as the Republican party reaped the harvest of unrest sown by the panic, the great strikes, the Wilson-Gorham tariff fiasco, the repeal of the Sherman Silver Act, and the attack upon the farmers' organizations by J. S. Morton, Cleveland's Secretary of Agriculture.[107] The lack of harmony

---

[102] Joliet *News*, June 29, August 13, 28, 1894.

[103] *Ibid.*, September 12, 17, October 20, November 1, 7, 1894.

[104] *Ibid.*, November 2, 1894.

[105] *Farmers' Voice*, June 9, 1894; *Searchlight*, July 19, 1894; *Chicago Daily Tribune*, June 12, 1894.

[106] A. L. Maxwell in the Robinson *Argus*, July 25, 1894, quoted by Shipley, *op. cit.*, 57–58; *Chicago Dispatch*, February 4, 1895; interview with J. D. Hess, Pittsfield, Illinois.

[107] Grover Cleveland MSS. (Library of Congress), Thomas Keady, Secretary, Illinois State Grange, to Cleveland, January 20, 1894; Spooner MSS., Cornelius N. Bliss, President, American Protective Tariff League, to Spooner, January 12, February 12, 1894, W. F. Wakeman, Secretary, to Spooner, December 18, 1894; *Chicago Daily Tribune*, October 15, 1894.

within the Democratic party in Illinois also aided the Republicans. The sound money, Cleveland faction was forced to muster its utmost strength in the State Convention to defeat the free silver contingent from southern and western Illinois, which enjoyed the support of the *State Register*.[108] Yet, the radical anti-trust position of the Illinois Democrats, their advocacy of municipal ownership of electric light plants,[109] and the popularity of Governor Altgeld with the masses made recruiting Democrats for the People's party difficult indeed. Finally, the Prohibition party managed to keep its ranks fairly intact in spite of Populist bids for fusion.[110]

Notwithstanding these numerous handicaps, the Populist vote in Illinois outside of Cook County in November increased to 26,100 from barely twenty thousand two years before. In no downstate county did the election returns give the People's party as many as a thousand votes on the state ticket.[111] The slight over-all increase was due probably to support from the American Railway Union and the United Mine Workers. In Bureau county, which cast the heaviest Populist vote, 700 out of 973 ballots came from the mining community of Spring Valley.[112] In LaSalle and St. Clair counties, the large Populist poll was due in all probability also to the support of the coal miners. In Will county, most of the relatively large Populist vote was credited to the "railroad men of Joliet."[113] The railroad labor vote was responsible for the strength of the party in Peoria and Rock Island counties. In McLean, where Father McGlynn had spoken in an attempt to hold the Single Tax craft unionists faithful to the People's party, the Populist vote was small, a fact that supports the inference that this powerful downstate wing of the labor movement had deserted the Springfield platform after the Belleville convention of the Illinois Federation of Labor.

In the rich farming districts that surrounded the railroad towns and coal mining communities of central Illinois the Populist vote was negligible. The greatest rural strength mustered by the People's party in Illinois was in Pike county and in the tier of wheat-raising counties running south from Christian and Shelby to Johnson.[114] This had been the stronghold of the party in 1892.

[108] Cleveland MSS., Lambert Tree to Cleveland, June 27, 1894; *Illinois State Register*, February 17, 28, March 5, April 12, July 3, August 12, 1894.

[109] *Ibid.*, February 21, March 10, 1894.

[110] *Ibid.*, May 4, 1894; Joliet *News*, November 19, 1894.

[111] *Illinois Blue Book, 1899* (Springfield, 1899), 403–404.

[112] Joliet *News*, November 8, 1894.

[113] *Ibid.*, November 7, 1894.

[114] *Illinois Blue Book, 1899*, 403–404; John M. Stahl, *The Real Farmer* (Quincy, [1910]), 53.

In Chicago, as elsewhere, "the people turned to the republicans for relief from hard times . . . with a unanimity . . . scarcely ever . . . paralleled in the political history"[115] of the nation. Under these circumstances, the 34,000 to 40,000 votes polled by the People's party in Cook County was a creditable but not a remarkable showing. When its brilliant campaign and the great potential political strength of labor in the metropolitan area were taken into account, the results were "wholly disappointing."[116] This was especially so in the "distinctively working-men's districts" of the city. In none of the thirty-four wards did the Populist vote approach 2,000. In only seven did it exceed 1,000. In the most favorable Congressional district, John Z. White received only 8,000, less than half the strength of the successful Republican candidate. In the Seventh District along the north shore, a Republican stronghold bulwarked by the Chicago and Northwestern Railroad, Henry D. Lloyd received a personal tribute of nearly 7,000 votes. This was a remarkable achievement for one of his radical views in an area characterized by a "fearfully conservative if not reactionary voting population."[117] No other congressional candidate of the People's party did nearly so well in Cook County, comparatively. None were elected to office, a lot shared by every legislative and county nominee on the ticket.

A variety of reasons can be offered to account for the disappointing results of the labor-Populist campaign in Cook County. First among them, undoubtedly, was the band wagon pull of the Republican victory, whose appeal to the discontented labor vote was helped by the slogan, "the full dinner pail." In addition to this was the contest between the independents and Pomeroy's People's Party Populists over their status on the official ballot, which must have confused and alienated otherwise sympathetic voters. Apart from its racketeering proclivities in politics, the hostility of Pomeroy's following to Tommy Morgan, whether because of attachment to "pure and simple trades unionism," or Roman Catholic antipathy to Socialism, meant that a large section of labor would withhold support from a third party in whose campaign Morgan's ideas were prominent.[118] The more conservative Single-Taxers undoubtedly followed a similar course of action, especially in view of Henry George's opposition to Populism. August E. Gans, who was perhaps not com-

[115] *Eight-Hour Herald*, November 10, 1894.

[116] Abbot, *op. cit.*, 335. The voting strength of labor in Chicago was estimated at 235,000 by August E. Gans to Lloyd, October 9, 1894, Lloyd MSS. (Madison).

[117] Abbot, *op. cit.*, 335; *Searchlight*, November 8, 1894; *Chicago Daily Tribune*, November 22, 1894.

[118] *Eight-Hour Herald*, November 10, 1894; *American Federationist*, I (November, 1894), 182; interview with Clarence S. Darrow.

pletely objective in his criticisms, blamed the large number of unknown men on the county ticket, some nonentities in the congressional field, and the refusal of the Populist managers to work with genuine friends of labor in the Democratic party for the loss of "fully 30,000 votes." Gans predicted that if the existing management of the party were continued for another campaign, including Thomas J. Morgan whose "intolerance and envious stupidity" he singled out for especial condemnation, it would wipe out "about half of the present Labor vote of the People's Party" in Cook County.[119]

Certain other factors had an undoubted effect in keeping the Populist vote from rising to a strength equivalent to that registered by the United Labor party in Chicago in 1887. The sale of the *Times* to a Democrat in mid-October was a body blow to the Populist cause. To this Dr. Bayard Holmes, when Populist mayoral candidate a few months later, attributed a major share of the party's disappointment in November.[120] The immediate toning down of the *Times'* "underdog" policy, after the change in ownership, deprived the labor-Populist allies of its most valuable press support just when Willis Abbot was doing his utmost to heal the schism between the Socialists and Single-Taxers. Abbot sympathized heartily with the independent cause and did his best privately to keep it from losing momentum before election day.[121] The letdown that followed the loss of the *Times'* outright support was such that it gave considerable impetus to an abortive attempt to establish a national Populist daily newspaper in Chicago under the direction of Henry D. Lloyd and one of Abbot's assistants.[122]

Finally, there is some evidence that the election returns were manipulated in a manner that artificially reduced the Populist poll. Acknowledging that complaints after defeat would be discounted heavily, the *Searchlight* published a lengthy account of election incidents and outrages. These exhibited a settled determination on the part of local politicians of the older parties to exclude third party watchers from the polls, to intimidate independent voters, and to refuse the People's party a fair count.[123] Willis Abbot, in his review of the campaign for the

[119] Lloyd MSS. (Madison), Gans to Lloyd, October 9, November 15, 1894.

[120] Campaign circular, "What the People's Party Means," in "People's Party Pamphlets" (State Historical Society of Wisconsin); Joliet *News*, October 19, 1894.

[121] Lloyd MSS. (Madison), Abbot to Lloyd, November 5, 1894; *Times*, October 25, 1894.

[122] Lloyd MSS., C. S. Darrow *et al.* to Lloyd, November 22, 1894, Abbot to Lloyd, November 5, 1894, B. O. Flower to Lloyd, October 21, 1894; Donnelly MSS, F. J. Schulte to Ignatius Donnelly, October 3, 1894.

[123] November 8, 1894.

Arena concurred in this judgment.[124] Since the election commissioners were forced to appoint election judges from the People's party before the mayoral election the following April, a privilege denied the Populists in November, some weight must be attached to the claim that twenty-five per cent of the labor-Populist vote in Cook County was not recorded in the final returns. If fully accepted this claim would raise the real Populist voting strength in Chicago in November, 1894, to 45,000 to 50,000. This was the estimate placed on the potentiality of the third party movement by the *Times* just after Lyman Trumbull and Clarence Darrow had joined it.[125]

When all allowances by independent apologists were made, however, the fact remained that the most strenuous efforts had failed to elect a single candidate to office. Combined with an empty treasury and un-resolved factional differences within the movement, this presented a gloomy prospect to the champions of a permanent farmer-labor, radical alliance in American politics. The political upheaval in Illinois had swept the Democrats from control of the General Assembly and defeated them in all but two Congressional districts. It left the labor-Populist allies with little more than seven per cent of the official vote in the State.[126] Only in Cook County had the new coalition exhibited evidence of enthusiastic popular support and aggressive leadership. It remained to be seen there whether the Chicago Populists could carry their strength unimpaired into the approaching mayoral contest. It had yet to be demonstrated whether the diverse elements in the coalition could be welded into a harmonious, stable, radical party on the basis of the Springfield platform. Finally the national organization of the People's party had yet to approve this document with its application of the collectivist principle to fields undreamed of by the formulators of the Populist creed.

[124] P. 336.

[125] *Times*, October 9, 1894. D. W. Fulwiler, a trades unionist candidate on the Populist ticket received 40,519 votes, far more than A. B. Adair, candidate for county clerk, who polled only 33,368. *Searchlight*, November 8, 1894.

[126] Hicks, *op. cit.*, 337.

Chapter X

"THE REVOLUTION IS HERE"[1]

Henry Demarest Lloyd's address at Central Music Hall in Chicago on October 6, 1894,[2] was omitted from the speeches and papers that were published posthumously by his sister Caro and intimate friends. Although it appeared in a number of Populist papers at the time, and excerpts can be found in the Chicago press, the speech has escaped the notice of all students of the Populist revolt. Its character is such that it justifies re-publication here, because of its bearing on the labor-Populist alliance.

The philosophical character and general significance of the document have been indicated in the preceding essay. Only first-hand examination, however, will reveal how skilfully Lloyd harmonized the Lockean political doctrines of the Jeffersonian tradition and the antimonopolist Populist faith with the collectivist principle. The document makes it clear, furthermore, that Lloyd was offering the Springfield platform not only as the basis of the Cook County campaign but also as the foundation of the nation-wide labor-Populist alliance that he sought to consummate. Already, as he observed, there was a clearcut drift toward an extension of the coalition into other localities. In Wisconsin this had been apparent as early as September, 1893, when the Wisconsin Labor Congress endorsed independent political action and the platform of the People's party.[3] At Milwaukee, on July 4, 1894, after the Wisconsin State Federation of Labor had "declared in favor of the Populists,"[4] the Wisconsin People's Party Convention adopted the entire political program of the American Federation of Labor, including "Plank 10," in addition to the Omaha platform, as the basis of a labor-Populist alliance whose position was slightly farther to the left than that consummated at Springfield, Illinois, on the same day.[5] This brought Victor Berger's

[1] The title given Lloyd's address by the Duluth (Minnesota) *Searchlight*, October 26, 1894.

[2] The original manuscript of this address has not appeared among either collection of Lloyd papers. Probably the most accurate version, since there is a possibility that Lloyd read the proofs, is the one republished in No. 2 of *The Commonwealth Library* (October, 1894, Commonwealth Company, New York), pp. 13. Cf. C. P. Somerby to H. D. Lloyd, October 20, 1894, Lloyd MSS. (Madison).

[3] *Chicago Daily Tribune*, September 7, 1893.

[4] Chicago *Searchlight*, June 14, 1894.

[5] Undated, unidentified clippings from a Lacrosse Newspaper, enclosures, Frank [Flower] to John C. Spooner, "Friday," [July 5], 1895, Spooner MSS.

Socialist following in Milwaukee into the People's party of Wisconsin, where Berger remained until after the St. Louis convention of 1896. In New York, where Charles B. Matthews of Buffalo, a redoubtable antagonist of the Standard Oil, headed the state ticket, a similar alliance was formed.[6] In St. Louis, an abortive attempt was made to bring the Socialists and Populists together before the election of 1894.[7] In Minneapolis and St. Paul, however, trades unionists and Socialists joined the Populist movement in such numbers that they swelled its poll far beyond that of 1892, and so decimated the Socialist Labor party there that De Leon had to begin again from the bottom when he launched his organizing campaign in 1895.[8]

Viewed in this setting, Henry Lloyd was entirely correct in presenting the Cook County Populist campaign as the spearhead of the movement to transform the People's party into the American counterpart of the Independent Labour Party. The wide circulation and friendly reception accorded his Central Music Hall address in Populist circles suggested that such a development would not be incompatible with indigenous Populism. Incidentally, the speech brought Lloyd into even greater repute in Minnesota and the Dakotas whence came invitations to speak at Populist encampments that had been listening already to the Christian Socialism of George D. Herron.

REVOLUTION.
THE EVOLUTION OF SOCIALISM.
By Henry Demarest Lloyd.

*An Address delivered in Central Music Hall,
Chicago, Ill., October 6, 1894.[9]*

All our parties are Reform parties. The democracy has been lowering the tariff ever since the government was established. They have done so well that their rates are higher in 1894 than they were in 1842. The republicans have been "saving the union" for thirty years, and the

[6] Lloyd MSS. (Madison), C. B. Matthews to Lloyd, September 27, 1894.

[7] *Illinois State Register*, August 7, 1894.

[8] Socialist Labor Party MSS. (State Historical Society of Wisconsin), F. A. Cowell to *The People*, January 5, 1895, George B. Leonard to *The People*, March 5, 1895, George B. Leonard to Daniel De Leon, January 27, 1896, April 23, 1897; *The People*, April 7, 1895; Maude Gernes, "The Influence of the Labor Element in the Populist Party" (Typewritten MS., June 9, 1924, Minnesota Historical Society).

[9] This is the heading from the *Commonwealth Library* edition, from which the text is reproduced.

tramp, tramp, tramp, of a million men on the march still sounds through the country—the tramp of the tramp. The appearance at the polls of a new party, which was not known in 1888, and in 1892, in its first presidential campaign, cast over 1,000,000 votes, is a hint that a new conception of reform is shaping itself in the minds of our fellow citizens. They want reform that will reform, and they want it now. Reform that is reform, and reform in our time, not in our great-grandchildren's, is what the people need and what they mean to have.

Lafayette said in 1791 that it would take twenty years to bring freedom to France; in two years feudalism was dead. Our great Emerson said in 1859—within four years of the emancipation proclamation—"We shall not live to see slavery abolished." Jefferson, the young delegate in the house of burgesses of Virginia, in one year abolished entail, and primogeniture, and the whole fabric of aristocracy, in that colony. The patricians pleaded for delay, for compromise. "Let our oldest sons inherit by law at least a double portion." "Not unless they can do twice as much work and eat twice as much as their younger brothers," was the reply of this first great social democrat, and he finished his reform at the same session at which he began it.

No great idea is ever lost. The greatest of human ideas is democracy. It has often disappeared, but it has never been lost. We have democratized religion, and the humblest men have equal rights with all others to find the Almighty within themselves, without the intervention of a privileged class. We have nearly finished democratizing kings, and we are now about to democratize the millionaire. Under absolutism the people mend their fortunes by insurrection. Under popular government they start a new party. All over the world, wherever popular government exists with its provisions for peaceful revolution instead of violent revolution, the people are forming new parties—in England, France, Germany, Australia, as well as in this country. This is the great political fact of our times. Some of these, like the distinctively workingmen's parties, are class movements. They are the natural and inevitable reaction from class movements against the workingmen. These parties all have practically the same object—to democratize the millionaire, and, as Jefferson did when he democratized the provincial patricians of Virginia, to do it as nearly as possible at one sitting.

THE EVILS OF CONCENTRATED WEALTH

A broad view of the reforms demanded by the new parties rising in Europe and America and Australia shows the substance of them all to be the same. There is nothing, Lowell says, that men prize so much as some kind of privilege, even though it be only the place of chief mourner at a funeral. In all the great industries a few men are building themselves up into the chief places, not as mourners themselves, but to make their fellow citizens mourners. The millions produce wealth; only the tens have it. There is the root of the whole matter. The first and last political issue of our time is with its concentrated wealth. Not with wealth, but with its concentration. "Far-seeing men," says James Russell Lowell, "count the increasing power of wealth and its combinations as one of the chief dangers with which the institutions of the United States are threatened in the not distant future." This concentration of wealth is but another name for the contraction of currency, the twin miseries of monoply [sic] and pauperism, the tyranny of corporations, the corruption of the government, the depopulation of the country, the congestion of the cities, and the host of ills which now form the staple theme of our novelists and magazinists, and the speeches of the new-party orators.

Those faithful watchers who are sounding these alarms are ridiculed as calamity howlers. When strong, shrewd, grasping, covetous men devote themselves to creating calamities, fortunate are the people who are awakened by faithful calamity howlers. Noah was a calamity howler, and the bones of the men who laughed at him have helped to make the phosphate beds out of which fertilizers are now dug for the market. It was a calamity howler who said, "Sweet are the uses of adversity," and another averred that "Man was born to trouble, as the sparks fly upward." There are thirty-two paragraphs in the Declaration of Independence; twenty-nine of the thirty-two are calamity howls about the wrongs and miseries of America under British rule.

The contraction of the currency is a terrible thing, but there is another as terrible—the contraction of commodities and work by stoppage of production, lockout, the dismantling of competitive works, the suppression of patents, and other games of business. The institutions of America were founded to rest on the love of the people for their country; we have a new cement now to hold society together—injunctions and contempt of court.

And we see materializing out of the shadows of our great counting-rooms a new system of government—government by campaign contribution. The people maintain their national, state, city, and local governments at a cost of $1,000,000,000 a year; but the trusts, and armor-plate contractors, and the whisky ring, and the subsidized steamship companies, and the street and other railways, buy the privilege of running these governments to enrich themselves, to send troublesome leaders of the people to jail, to keep themselves out of jail. By campaign contributions of a few millions is thus bought away from the people the government which cost the people $1,000,000,000 a year. There are many marvels of cheapness in the market, but the greatest counter bargains in modern business are such as the sugar trust got when, by contributing a few hundred thousand dollars to both parties, it bought the right to tax the people untold millions a year.

THE COMING REVOLUTION IS HERE

We talk about the coming revolution and hope it will be peaceful. The revolution has come. This use of the government of all for the enrichment and aggrandizement of a few is a revolution. It is a revolution which has created the railroad millionaires of this country. To maintain the highways is one of the sacredest functions of a government. Railroads are possible only by the exercise of the still more sacred governmental power of eminent domain, which when citizens will not sell the right of way takes their property through the forms of law by force— none the less by force because the money value is paid. These sovereign powers of the highway and of eminent domain have been given by you and me, all of us, to our government, to be used only for the common and equal benefit of all. Given by all to be used for all, it is a revolution to have made them the perquisite of a few. Only a revolution could have made possible in the speech of a free people such a phrase as a railroad king.

It is a revolution which has given the best parts of the streets that belong to all the people to street-railway syndicates, and gas companies, and telephone companies, and power companies. It is a revolution which has created national-bank millionaires, and bond millionaires, and tariff millionaires, and land-grant millionaires, out of the powers you and I delegated to the government of the United States for the equal good of every citizen. The inter-state commerce act was passed to put into prison the railroad managers who used their highway power to rob the people, to ruin the merchants and manufacturers whose business they wanted to give to favored shippers. The anti-trust law was passed to put into prison the men who make commerce a conspiracy, to compel the people every day to pay a ransom for their lives. It is a revolution which is using these inter-state commerce and anti-trust laws to prosecute the employes of the railways for exercising their inalienable rights as free men to unite for defense against intolerable wrong. It is a revolution which lets the presidents, and managers, and owners of the railroads and trusts, go free of all punishment for the crimes they are committing; which sends out no process against any of the corporations or corporation men in the American Railway Association, while it uses all the powers of the attorney-general of the United States to prosecute, and, if possible, to send to prison, the members of the American Railway Union. It is a revolution which is putting the attorneys of corporations into ermine on the bench to be attorneys still.

It is a revolution by which great combinations, using competition to destroy competition, have monopolized entire markets, and as the sole sellers of goods make the people buy dear, and as the sole purchasers of labor make the people sell themselves cheap. The last and deepest and greatest revolution of all is that by which the mines, machinery, factories, currency, land, entrusted to private hands as private property, only as a stewardship, to warm, feed, clothe, serve mankind, are used to make men cold, hungry, naked, and destitute. Coal mines shut down to make coal scarce, mills shut down to make goods scarce, currency used to deprive people of the means of exchange, and the railways used to hinder transportation.

COUNTER REVOLUTION OF THE PEOPLE

This is the revolution that has come. With local variation it is world-wide, and against it the people are rising world-wide in peaceful counter revolutions, in people's parties. It begins now to be seen generally what a few have been pointing out from the beginning, that the workingmen in organizing to defend themselves have been only pioneers. The power which denied them a fair share of their production was the same power which is now attacking the consumer, the farmer, and even the fellow capitalist. In organizing against modern capitalism the workingmen set the example which all the people are now driven by self-preservation to follow. The trades union of the workingmen was the precursor of the farmers' alliance, the grange, and the people's party.

Chicago to-day leads the van in this great forward movement. Here the workingmen, capitalists, single-taxers, and socialists have come together to join forces with each other and with the farmers, as has been done in no other city. Its meetings are attended here by thousands, as you see to-night. It is the most wonderful outburst of popular hope and enthusiasm in the recent politics of this country. Chicago thus leads in numbers and in enthusiasm and promises of success, because it has led in boldness and sincerity and thoroughness of reform doctrine. The workingmen of Chicago at the Springfield conference, which was the fountainhead of this tidal wave, stood firm as a rock for the principle without which the industrial liberties of the people can never be established—the principle that they have the right at their option to own and operate collectively any or all of the means of production, distribution, and exchange. They already own some; they have the right to own as many more as they want. This is the mother principle of the government we already have, and it covers the whole brood of government railroads, telegraphs, telephones, banks, lands, street railways, all the municipalizations and nationalizations in which everywhere the people are giving utterance to their belief that they are the only proper and the only competent administrators of the wealth which they create.

The Declaration of Independence of 1776 declared that the people felt themselves able to manage for themselves the government, all of whose powers sprang from them. This declaration of 1894 is the proclamation of the next step in independence. The people have done so well that they will move forward again and manage for themselves some more departments of the commonwealth all of whose powers spring from them. The democratization of government, the democratization of collective industry—they are parts of one great upward emancipation. The American idea, says Emerson, is emancipation. The co-operative commonwealth is the legitimate offspring and lawful successor of the republic. Our liberties and our wealth are from the people and by the people and both must be for the people. Wealth, like government, is the product of the co-operation of all, and, like government, must be the property of all its creators, not of a privileged few alone. The principles of liberty, equality, union, which rule in the industries we call government must rule in all industries. Government exists only by the consent of the governed. Business, property, capital, are also governments and must also rest on the consent of the governed. This assertion of the inherent and inalienable right, and ability, of the people to own and operate, at their option, any or all of the wealth they create, is the fundamental, irrepressible, and uncompromisable keynote of the crisis, and with this trumpet note you can lead the people through any sacrifice to certain victory.

THINGS THE PEOPLE HAVE LEARNED

Jefferson, one of his biographers tells us, was one of the most successful politicians of his time because he kept his ear close to the bosom of the people. If we will do the same we will hear the great heart of the common people beating the world over with this new hope of coming to own their means of production and the fruit of their labor, and so for the first time in history owning themselves. The people always think quicker and straighter than the philosophers, because while the philosopher simply meditates the people suffer. The people here to-night have learned in their marketing, in their cut wages, in their lockouts and search for employment, in the prices they pay for sugar, and coal, and matches, and meat, and hundreds of other things, that all the other reforms—of the tariff, the banks, the land system, the railroads, and the currency—would leave them still the slaves of syndicates which hold the necessaries of life and means of production in absolute right as private property, beyond the reach of all these reforms, and with wealth which puts them beyond competition. Herein is the inner citadel of monopoly and "plank 10" is the battering-ram which will bring down its walls.

This cardinal principle, to which every candidate of the people's party of Cook county who seeks the support of the workingmen must subscribe, has been adopted in substance by the party in New York. The party in Connecticut in their last platform show themselves ready for it. It will without doubt be adopted overwhelmingly by the next national convention of the people's party, and under the banner of this principle— which is as big as the crisis—the party will move into the presidency, perhaps as soon as 1896. It is not to the parties that have produced the pandemonium of intermittent panic which is called trade and industry that the people can look for relief. To vote for them is to vote for more panics, more pandemoniums. Both these parties have done good work, but their good work is done. The republican party took the black man off the auction block of the slave power, but it has put the white man on the auction block of the money power, to be sold to the lowest bidder under the iron hammer of monopoly. The democratic party for a hundred years has been the pull-back against the centralization in American politics, standing for the individual against the community, the town against the state, and the state against the nation. But in one hour here last July it sacrificed the honorable devotion of a century to its great principle and surrendered both the rights of states and the rights of man to the centralized corporate despotism to which the presidency of the United States was then abdicated.

There ought to be two first-class political funerals in this country in 1896, and if we do our duty the corpses will be ready on time. "Are you going to the funeral of Benedict Arnold?" one of his neighbors asked another, "No, but I approve of it." We will not go to the republican and democratic funerals, but we approve of them. There is a party that the people can trust because in the face of overwhelming odds, without distinguished leaders, money, office, or prestige, it has raised the standard of a principle to save the people. The continual refrain of Mommsen, the great historian of Rome, is that its liberties and prosperity were lost because its reformers were only half reformers, and none of its statesmen would strike at the root of its evils. By that mistake we must profit.

It is a fact of political history that no new party was ever false to the cause for which it was formed. If the people's party as organized in Cook county is supported by the country, and the people get the control of their industries as of the government, the abolition of monopoly will as surely follow as the abolition of slavery followed the entrance of Abraham Lincoln into the white house in 1861. Then we will have the judges and the injunctions, the president and the house of representatives. There will be no senate; we will have the referendum, and the senate will go out when the people come in. The same constitution that could take the property of unwilling citizens for the railroads for rights of way can take the railroads, willing or unwilling, to be the nation's property when the people come in. Then the national debt, instead of representing the waste of war, will represent the railroads and other productive works owned by the people and worth more, as in Australia, than the bonds issued for them. The same constitution that could demonetize silver can remonetize it, or demonetize gold for a better money than either. The honest dollar will come in when the people come in, for it will not be a dollar that can be made scarce, to produce panics, and throw millions of men out of work, and compel the borrower to pay two where he received only one.

WOMEN MUST VOTE NOW

Women will vote, and some day we will have a woman president when the people come in. The post office will carry your telegrams and your parcels as well as your letters, and will be the people's bank for savings, and their life and accident insurance company, as it is elsewhere already. Every dark place in our cities will be brilliant with electricty, [sic] made by the municipalities for themselves. Working men and women will ride for 3 cents and school children for 2½ cents, as in Toronto, on street-car lines owned by the municipalities, and paying by their profits a large part of the cost of government now falling on the tax-payer. When the people come in, political corruption, boss rule, and boodle will go out, because these spring mainly from the intrigues and briberies of syndicates to get hold of public functions for their private profit. We will have a real civil service, the inevitable and logical result of the demands of the people's party, founded, as true civil-service reform must be, on a system of public education which shall give every child of the republic the opportunity to fit himself for the public service. The same constitution which granted empires of public lands to create the Pacific railroad kings will find land for workingmen's homes and land for co-operative colonies of the unemployed.

There will soon be no unemployed when the people come in. They will have no shoemakers locked out or shoe factories shut down while there is a foot unshod, and all the mills and mines and factories the needs of the people require the people will keep going. Every man who works will get a living and every man who gets a living shall work, when the people come in. These are some of the things the people's party of Cook county means. At the coming election let every man and woman vote—for the women must vote through the men until they vote themselves—let every man and woman vote for those, and only for those, who accept this grand principle of the liberation of the people by themselves. Let this platform get a popular indorsement at the polls next November that will advertise to the world that the people have at last risen in their might, not to rest until another great emancipation has been added to the glorious record of the liberties achieved by mankind.

CHAPTER XI

FREE SILVER VS. COLLECTIVISM: DISINTEGRATION OF THE LABOR-POPULIST ALLIANCE IN ILLINOIS

For the development of American democratic radicalism, the labor-Populist alliance in Illinois was fraught with unusual significance. Populism, as indicated earlier,[1] was at bottom a re-elaboration of the Jeffersonian tradition in an attempt to meet the problems produced by corporate monopoly and the urban-industrial age. Its antimonopolism, insistence on equal rights, labor-cost theory of wealth, hostility to finance capitalism and the money power, and the assertion of a community of interest between rural and urban producers were concepts in a pattern that is clearly discernible in the writings of John Taylor of Caroline and the journalistic productions of William Leggett.[2] Grafted into this radical ideology were other concepts and proposals that re-oriented it from political negation to positive but limited state intervention in the economic field. As a product of this process, Populism desired to restore and consolidate the regime of small, self-employing enterprisers which Jefferson had worked to establish. Viewed in this light, Populism was but the projection into the "mauve decade" of the native, radical tradition of the democratic masses of the United States.

The long sought alliance with urban labor, when it came, presented Populist leaders with several dilemmas. I. As advocates of the limited collectivism of the agrarian movement, were they willing to extend it into the fields of industrial relations and municipal utilities so as to make it of genuine advantage of wage-earners? The answer was "Yes," in 1894 in a considerable number of localities and even in several states.[3] A substantial increment in the Populist poll resulted in November.[4] II.

---

[1] *Supra*, Chapter I.

[2] John Taylor, *An Inquiry into the Principles and Policy of the Government of the United States* (1814), Chapter I and *passim*; Eugene Tenbroeck Mudge, *The Social Philosophy of John Taylor of Caroline* (New York, 1939), 151–192; Theodore Sedgwick, Jr., ed., *A Collection of the Political Writings of William Leggett* (New York, 1940), I–II, *passim*; Richard Hofstadter, "William Leggett, Spokesman of Jacksonian Democracy," *Political Science Quarterly*, LVIII (December, 1943), 581–594.

[3] *Supra*, Chapter IX.

[4] As in California and Minnesota, with significant but numerically moderate increases in Illinois, Wisconsin, Indiana, Michigan, and Iowa. It should be conceded, however, that some of the greatest gains were made in the cotton states, and that there was a sharp reduc-

Where a substantial labor following materialized, should control of the party machinery be surrendered to the newly developed urban wing? This was done in Cook County, Illinois, where the orthodox Populists reserved for themselves, however, a disproportionately large minority voice in the county committee. III. Could the party program be adapted to the specific aspirations of the urban elements that had now entered the party? This involved the harmonizing of the newer schools of urban radicalism with the traditional system of agrarian Populism and labor reform. This Henry Lloyd had attempted in his Central Music Hall address.

To a certain extent, as Samuel Gompers had observed, the basic interests of owner-operator farmers and wage-earning laborers were in opposition. Yet, both small farmers and urban craftsmen might well have profited from a limited program of state action that was restricted to cheap credit, cheap transportation, cheap communication and utility rates, and a minimum program of protective labor legislation, together with the destruction of monopolies and the reduction of great fortunes through taxation shifted somewhat from the shoulders of the masses.

Complicating the situation was the growing popularity among a minority of wage-earners, of the Single-Tax movement and of Socialism. Both of these schools of urban radicalism were biased toward independent political action. Both had ventured into it far more boldly than the bulk of the trades unionists. Both movements possessed a disciplined following and zealous leadership that would be invaluable to a labor-farmer alliance in politics. But each possessed a complete ideology more or less at odds with Populist agrarianism. As has been observed earlier in this series of essays, the single-minded zeal of Henry George, and the alliance of his disciples with the Cleveland and the Altgeld Democrats made a permanent coalition between the Populists and Single-Taxers almost out of the question. Common hostility to land monopoly, and a common demand for government ownership of natural or franchise monopolies, however, made possible a temporary coalition between the Populists and the more radical Single-Taxers, such as those who followed Father McGlynn. This was accomplished in Illinois in 1894 with results that have been appraised. It remained to be determined whether the left wing of the Single Tax movement could be attached longer to the People's party.

The problem presented by the mid-western Socialists was far more seri-

tion in the Rocky Mountain area, where fusion was abandoned. Hicks, *op. cit.*, 263, 337; Gernes.

ous. Their willingness to join the People's party on condition that it endorse "Plank 10" or Lloyd's modification of it, with the implication that they would be free to agitate for its acceptance within the coalition, offered a major dilemma to Populist leaders. Quite apart from the bitter antagonism that existed between Single-Taxers and Socialists, which introduced internecine strife into the People's party when both elements were admitted, was the sharp challenge that Socialism presented to Populism as a system of radical thought. To the Populists, as noted above, collectivist methods were simply a legitimate means of restoring free enterprise and small, competitive capitalism. The Socialists, on the contrary, advocated collectivism for its own sake, as a means of overthrowing the free enterprise system and of establishing a completely different economic and social order. This was founded upon an alien, materialistic, proletarian philosophy entirely antagonistic to that of American craftsmen and farmers. Its alien character was symbolized by the foreign languages and slum *enclaves* of immigrant-perpetuated foreign culture in the rapidly growing cities of the Middle West. It was this conflict between Marxism and Populism, between immigrant and American culture, and not just the uncompromising leadership of Daniel De Leon that made an alliance between the Socialist Labor party and the People's party impossible.[5]

By contrast, friendly relations existed between the Nationalists and the Populists. The native born, middle class followers of Edward Bellamy avoided a direct clash with Populism by their willingness to work for such partial measures as government ownership of railroads, which the antimonopolist and evolutionary character of their utopia made possible without the necessity of stressing at all points the desirability of a complete collectivism. Neither materialism nor class warfare was a part of the Nationalist system. For these reasons it had been possible to leave the Nationalists more or less in control of the eastern wing of the People's party, where the lack of vigor of Bellamy and his disciples and the paucity of their following presented no threat to western, agrarian control of the national organization

The English-speaking Socialists of Chicago, Tommy Morgan, Jesse Cox, and Paul Ehrman, Victor L. Berger of Milwaukee, and native-born radical labor leaders like Eugene V. Debs and John McGuire were another matter. In Chicago, furthermore, the *Arbeiter-Zeitung* had de-

[5] *The People* (New York), July 17, 1892, November 13, 1892, March 10, 1895; Joseph R. Buchanan, *Story of a Labor Agitator* (New York, 1903), 449-457; George H. Knoles, "Populism and Socialism, with Special Reference to the Election of 1892," *Pacific Historical Review*, XII, 295-304.

liberately induced the foreign-speaking Socialists to repudiate De Leon's leadership. Instead, the editors persuaded their readers to follow Henry D. Lloyd and the local English-speaking Socialists into the labor-Populist alliance on the basis of the Springfield platform.[6] Lloyd, furthermore, had attempted, systematically, a harmonization of the indigenous, agrarian radicalism with the collectivist principle that had shorn it of its Marxist and alien characteristics. Although this had received a wide and friendly hearing, it remained to be seen whether outright collectivism, even when clad in the terminology of American radicalism, could be superimposed upon Populism as its final goal.

The relations of the mid-western "individualist" Socialists[7] to the People's party were complicated by still another matter. They were the spearhead of the movement to commit the American Federation of Labor to a program of independent political action. The great popularity of this proposal among the craft unions early in 1894 and their widespread participation in third party politics had given the Populists their long-sought opportunity to win a working-class following. For the Populists to repel the overtures of the English-speaking Socialists, before the Denver Convention of the American Federation had acted finally on the political program, might jeopardize the newly formed labor-Populist alliance.

As matters stood, at the close of 1894, the Chicago Socialists had already joined the People's party. They had abandoned the separate, proletarian movement devoid of appeal to the American mind. In exchange, they had gained the right to agitate for unlimited collectivism within the Populist movement, subject to the practical operation of the initiative and referendum. They had won also Populist endorsement of the "immediate" demands of the Socialists for public ownership of public utilities. The Populists, on their side, enjoyed the prospect that continued acquiescence in the Springfield compromise might secure the permanent adherence of the non-Marxian Socialists and of the radical, politically self-conscious wing of the American labor movement. This was certainly the hint contained in the post-election statement of John McBride, President of the United Mine Workers, who predicted an extensive independent labor vote in the next two years on the basis of Lloyd's modified "Plank 10."[8] The presence of Victor Berger's following in the Wisconsin People's party and the infiltration of Socialists

[6] Lloyd MSS. (Madison), Edmund Deuss to Henry D. Lloyd, May 1, 1895.

[7] This term was applied by De Leon and *The People* to the mid-western Socialists that repudiated New York leadership and joined the People's party.

[8] *Commonwealth*, II, No. 2 (January 12, 1895), 7.

elsewhere into the Populist movement, when added to the Nationalist influence already within it, made Lloyd's hope that the entire party could be committed to an extensive, democratic collectivism as its ultimate goal less chimerical than it may seem in retrospect.

The perpetuation of the labor-Populist alliance in Illinois, then, and its extension to the national plane depended upon a variety of factors. On the one hand it rested upon a continuing willingness of the mid-western craftsmen, Single-Taxers, and Socialists to surrender autonomous status, their mutual antipathies, and extreme ideological pretensions in the interest of a united front with the farmers. It depended on the other hand upon the willingness of the national leaders of the People's party, and their following, to accept some such extension of the Omaha platform as was contained in the Springfield platform and Lloyd's subsequent interpretations. In the third place, much hung upon the outcome of the contest over the political program of organized labor at the Denver Convention. Endorsement of it in entirety, including the original or modified "Plank 10," would have made it extremely hazardous for the Populists to retreat from the Springfield agreement lest they witness at once the organization of a competing, labor party. Endorsement at Denver of independent political action and of all the demands in the program save "Plank 10" would have made it still possible, theoretically, to consummate a firm farmer-labor alliance but impossible, for lack of reference to the collectivist principle *per se*, to include the Socialists.

Herman E. Taubeneck of Illinois, chairman of the National Executive Committee of the People's party, and the Populist congressional delegation were quick to publish their opposition to the Springfield platform. They knew that the great mass of discontented farmers in the South and West had already refused to endorse the limited collectivism of the subtreasury plan and the railroad-telegraph plank of the Omaha platform. The swift decline of the farmers' alliance movement everywhere after the left wing had imposed these demands on the People's party was ample evidence to this effect. Although the great depression had intensified unrest to a point where wider acceptance of the Omaha platform might have been expected, the Democrats and Republicans had successfully invoked the free silver issue to prevent the discontented but more moderate farmers from joining the Populist revolt. As a result of this situation, and of Populist rejection of fusionist proposals, the People's party had actually lost ground seriously in the Rocky Mountain, silver mining states,[9] while it had failed to make appreciable

[9] Hicks, *op. cit.*, 301, 333. Cf. C. Van Woodward, Tom Watson, *Agrarian Rebel* (New

gains in the great corn belt that stretched from eastern Kansas to central Ohio.

The set back in the Rocky Mountain area threatened, also, to jeopardize the finances of the Populist national organization. These had depended heavily upon contributions from the silver interests.[10] It was not to be expected that the American Bi-Metallic League would support a labor-Populist alliance on the basis of the Springfield platform when effective champions of silver could be found among the western Republicans and Democrats. This situation suggested to Taubeneck the advisability of a retreat from the specific collectivist proposals in the Omaha platform to a single-minded championship of free silver, even though this entailed public repudiation of the opposition to such a step that he had expressed as recently as 1893.[11] Assuming that eastern interests would continue to dominate both major parties, Taubeneck could hope to regain control of the Rocky Mountain States by such a course, and clinch financial support from the silver interests. He could hope to win over to the People's party the free silver Republicans and Democrats while appeasing the antimonopolist Populists with the prospect of smashing Wall Street's "money power" with silver. Such tactics, if successful, might well bring victory in the presidential election of 1896. They would have the additional advantage, from Taubeneck's viewpoint, of stopping at once the infiltration of Socialism into the People's party which he and his rural supporters had originally blocked in the Illinois State Populist Convention on May 28, 1894.[12]

The new departure in Populist tactics and ideology was first announced by Senator William A. Peffer of Kansas, shortly after the November election. Predicting that the free silver men in both major parties would be forced to bolt and consider the organization of a new party, Peffer declared that he and the Populists generally would be "perfectly willing to unite" in the formation of "a new party" that would "make free silver the single issue of the campaign" in 1896, provided that it would also support the general principle that "all public functions must be performed through public agents."[13] This last proviso was a sop to the radical, antimonopolist, and Bellamy wing of the People's party,

York, 1938), 285 and *passim*, for invocation of free silver by Southern Democrats in order to prevent the spread of Populism.

[10] Donnelly, MSS., H. E. Taubeneck to Ignatius Donnelly, July 27, 1892, July 8, December 18, 1893.

[11] H. E. Taubeneck to the Editor, *National Spectator*, August 18, 1893, clipping in H. E. Taubeneck Scrapbook.

[12] *Supra*, Chapter VIII.

[13] *The People*, November 18, 1894.

who might be expected to continue to give it their support on such a
basis for want of anywhere else to go.

Following this announcement, the National Executive Committee
sent out from three to four hundred invitations to leading Populists,
from which were excluded many of the more radical leaders,[14] to meet in
a mass conference at St. Louis, Missouri, on December 28–29, 1894.
The invitation declared that the gathering would be the "most important
meeting held since the Omaha Convention."[15]   In a statement given
simultaneously to the press, Taubeneck declared that the People's party
would have an opportunity at St. Louis "to make known the fact that
it has outgrown many of the 'isms' that characterized its birth and early
growth, and take a stand on the financial question that will make it
worthy of the support of those who have looked askance at the acts of
Wait and Lewelling, and have not cared to support the party on account
of its wild theories."   Taubeneck hinted, also, that "the sub-treasury
and kindred ideas" would be entirely eliminated from the party's program at the St. Louis conference.[16]

Peffer's trial balloon had already provoked caustic comment from
Daniel De Leon. He had observed in *The People*[17] that the wage-
earners furnished the bulk of Populist support in the East and considerable backing in the West. Recruited by the Populists on the
ground that they could secure remedial action through the People's
party, and at the same time escape the odium attached to Socialism,
the laborers in the movement were now "to be sold out to a combination
of silver Democrats and Republicans" whereby "Populist farmers are
to get free silver at 16 to 1, so that they may pay their debts with depreciated money and thus become capitalists; the Populist politicians
will get the spoils of office, while the Populist wage workers will mop
their foreheads and rub their empty stomachs with a glittering gen-
erality."

While Taubeneck's maneuver encouraged De Leon to launch a
vigorous campaign in the old Northwest to win laborers away from
Populism to the Socialist Labor Party, it alarmed the Nationalists, the
antimonopolists, the radical labor element, and the Socialists within the
People's party. Henry R. Legate, Bellamy's lieutenant in Massachusetts, set out to rally opposition to Taubeneck's plan in advance of
the St. Louis meeting, and procured a letter of protest from Edward

[14] Lloyd MSS. (Madison), George H. Gibson to Lloyd, December 19, 1894.
[15] *Ibid.*, H. E. Taubeneck to Henry D. Lloyd, December 10, 1894.
[16] *The People*, December 9, 1894.
[17] *Ibid.*, November 18, 1894.

Bellamy for presentation there.[18]   George Howard Gibson, editor of the
Lincoln, Nebraska, *Wealth Makers*, joined Legate in warning Henry D.
Lloyd of the attempt that Taubeneck's associates would make at St.
Louis, backed by a strong Colorado delegation, to "eliminate or shelve
the socialistic planks in our party . . . the land, railroad, telegraph, and
government-loans-to-the-people questions."[19]

Lloyd was already in consultation with his friends on the question of
the St. Louis Conference when he received the warnings from Legate and
Gibson.   Indignation at Judge William A. Wood's action in sentencing
Debs and the other American Railway Union defendants to Woodstock
jail for contempt sharpened his perception of the issue at stake in
Taubeneck's maneuver.   Lloyd was convinced that the reactionary
forces in America opposed to Populism were "growing radical much more
rapidly than we, . . . adding aggression to aggression, and doctrine to
doctrine."   Aware that Taubeneck's group intended to "throw the
radicals in the party overboard," Lloyd warned the publisher of the
American Non-Conformist that "Revolutions never go backward.   If
the People's Party goes backward it will prove that it is not a revolution,
and if it is not a revolution, it is nothing."[20]

Lloyd was determined not to retreat an inch from the Springfield platform.   He was convinced that the Socialists could and should be kept
within the People's party, and that this involved no sacrifice of Populist
principles, since they were collectivist, as he felt all democratic movements had to be.   Besides, in Chicago, the Socialists had in his estima-
tion been the best workers of the labor wing of the party.[21]   To make
it possible for them to remain in the Populist movement and to defeat
the silverites Lloyd sought to unite the agrarian and urban radicals in a
vigorous attack upon monopoly, upon government by injunction and
standing armies.   After consultation with local leaders and Debs he
took to the St. Louis Conference a set of resolutions whose authorship
he attributed to Lyman Trumbull.

The St. Louis Conference was attended by 250 leading Populists.
Although its proceedings were sketchily reported in the press, it is evident
that the gathering split sharply.   The faction anxious to shelve the
Omaha platform and concentrate on the silver issue found itself in the
minority to its dismay and indignation.   On the first day, Thomas F.

---

[18] Lloyd MSS. (Madison), Henry R. Legate to Lloyd, December 19, 1894.   Legate declared: "I feel that this is the most critical period in the history of the People's party."
[19] *Ibid.*, George H. Gibson to Lloyd, December 19, 1894.
[20] Lloyd MSS. (Winnetka), Henry D. Lloyd to C. A. Powers, December 16, 1894.
[21] *Ibid.*, Lloyd to Clarence S. Darrow, November 23, 1894.

Byron, editor of the influential *Farmers Tribune* of Des Moines, Iowa, forced James Baird Weaver so to alter the agenda that the conferees were permitted to express themselves "by states and to appoint a committee on address from the floor, instead of leaving Taubeneck the power to pack that committee for silver, given him by the passage of Weaver's motion just before dinner."[22] This gave the varied elements anxious to retain or extend the Omaha platform their opportunity. They rallied around Henry D. Lloyd, whose speech met with marked favor when he urged that the address to be adopted by the Conference contain declarations so vitally affecting the wage-earners that they would be drawn into the party as their defender and champion.[23]

Trumbull's resolutions, which Lloyd presented, forced a showdown. Their adoption by a majority vote[24] was a clear victory for both the agrarian radicals and the advocates of the labor-Populist alliance. Much of the appeal that the Trumbull resolutions made to the Conference must be attributed to their skillful use of the ancient shibboleths of American liberalism. "Human brotherhood and equality of rights," they declared, were fundamental to democracy, as were the ancient freedoms of the press and labor and "trial by jury." The resolutions invoked, also, the traditional hostility of American liberals to arbitrary government, monopoly, concentrated wealth, special privilege, and the misuse of judicial power and the standing army. Upon this basis Trumbull and the St. Louis Conference extended the Populist platform to include: limiting the size of fortunes that could be acquired through inheritance; free silver; and public ownership and operation "under civil service rules" of all monopolies "affecting the public interest." "Down with monopolies and millionaire control. Up with the rights of man and the masses!" was the slogan adopted by the triumphant radicals at St. Louis.

Lloyd's "great service at St. Louis in the work of keeping the People's Party train from derailment,"[25] as Henry Legate put it, won him the esteem and friendship of eastern Nationalists, leading midwestern Populists, and several Populists in the South.[26] He returned to Chicago

---

[22] Lloyd MSS. (Madison), Thomas F. Byron to Lloyd, April 8, 1895.

[23] *Ibid.*, J. C. Manning to Lloyd, February 16, 1895.

[24] *Western Rural*, LIII (January 10, 1895), 17; *Searchlight*, January 24, 1895. Hicks, *op. cit.*, 343–344, contains only a brief notice of the St. Louis Conference and mistakenly dates it early in 1895.

[25] Lloyd MSS. (Madison), Henry Winn to Lloyd, February 14, 1895.

[26] *Ibid.*, O. D. Jones to Lloyd, January 14, 1895, Paul Van Der Voort, Commander-in-Chief of the National Industrial Legion, to Lloyd, January, 1895, Phoebe W. Couzins to Lloyd, December 30, 1894, J. C. Manning to Lloyd, February 16, 1895, John H. Cherry to Lloyd, February 13, 1895.

to resume the arduous work of welding the diverse elements in the movement there into a compact, harmonious radical party.

In the seven weeks that had elapsed since the November election, only
the most strenuous efforts had sufficed to prevent the coalition in Cook
County from dissolving into its component parts. To counteract the
inevitable discouragement born of defeat, the county committee had
issued a manifesto immediately after the election which sounded the
"advance" and predicted that the "deluded masses" would turn to the
People's party after a few months of "republican prosperity."[27]   A
sharp struggle for control of the organization then ensued. On November 26, in the absence of Lloyd and Darrow, before the trades unionist
and Socialist delegates arrived at a meeting of the county committee, the
old line Populists led by H. S. Taylor seized control.[28]   Taylor had
indicated his dissatisfaction with the prominence given to the "Co-
operative Commonwealth" in the preceding campaign in a speech before
the Sunset Club immediately after the election.[29]

At the same time, a difference of opinion over party strategy had developed between Darrow and Lloyd that temporarily deprived the
majority element of its best leaders. A few days before the meeting of
November 26, Darrow had declared privately his unwillingness "to
help run another Socialist movement under the guise of 'The Peoples
Party.' "[30]   Lloyd's rejoinder throws considerable light on the purposes
that led him to attend the St. Louis Conference a month later. He first
attempted to rally Darrow from the pessimism inspired by the conviction of the American Railway Union men in Chicago and San Francisco in the federal courts, declaring "Events must be our leaders, and
we will have them. I am not discouraged. The radicalism of the
fanatics of wealth fills me with hope." Lloyd then urged that Darrow
give "sympathetic attention" to the course of the Chicago Socialists,
who, contrary to all their past practice and the threats of the New York
leaders, had given up their separate identity and worked more whole-
heartedly for the success of the Populist ticket than any other element
in the coalition during the autumn campaign. He then asserted:

The People's Party platform is socialistic, as all democratic doctrine is. No question of
principle is involved in the admission of all the Socialists as full and regular members of
the People's Party. They are the most intelligent, most energetic, most reliable workers
we have. To shut them out would be to repeat the blunder Henry George made at the
State convention in Syracuse some years ago. They were willing to co-operate with him,

[27] *Railway Times*, December 15, 1894.

[28] Harvey (Illinois) *Citizen*, December 15, 1894; T. J. Morgan to Lloyd, November 27,
1894, Lloyd MSS. (Madison).

[29] Sunset Club, *The Meetings of 1894–95* (Chicago, 1895), 50–51.

[30] Lloyd MSS. (Madison), C. S. Darrow to Lloyd, November 22, [1894].

but to save himself the odium of "socialistic" affiliations he excluded them from the convention—and he has never been heard of since as a political force.

Our cue is to get the Socialists of other states to do as the Chicago Socialists have done. That makes Chicago the intellectual and political leader of this movement. If we come out for a good budget of municipalizations and nationalizations in our platform, and a general principle like Peffer's—"Public ownership of public utilities,"—or something similar, the Socialists will "jine" as they say in Kentucky, and we will get up a head of steam possible in no other way. . . . We must unite our dissimilar elements in the face of a common danger greater than that of the Spanish Armada. What we ought to have at once is a conference of the most active reformers from all over the country to bring about this co-operation of all. But if we begin to read each other out of the ranks for differences of opinion we are lost.[31]

Darrow replied that Lloyd did not understand his position:

I never did and never will believe in barring any one out of any thing least of all the Socialists, of whom I am one. My only suggestion was as to whether we could claim to commit the peoples party to Socialism.

I think it was done too much in the last campaign—for instance all the literature circulated at the meeting[s] was intensely socialistic such as the "People's party" would not indorse and as it was under their auspices it ought not to have been such as was antagonistic to a large portion of the party. . . . I am inclined to think that I would be willing to support a straight Socialistic movement and perhaps that is best, but if we intend to work with the great National "Peoples party" we must keep in line with it, leaving each person to have their own views & express them but not seeking to commit the party to anything they do not wish to indorse. I believe the Socialists are the best Radicals we have and I always hav[e] and always will support and defend them. I only insist that we ought to make the movement stand for just what it pretends or we can not keep it together.[32]

A weekend at Winnetka no doubt strengthened Darrow's friendship for the Lloyds and did much to convince Henry Lloyd of the validity of his colleague's point of view, with direct influence on the tactics followed later at the St. Louis Conference. Meanwhile, their temporary inactivity in the local organization of the party left the initiative to the orthodox Populists. The immediate effect of the seizure of control by this element was the withdrawal of the Socialists and the trades unionists led by Adair. The Socialists threatened to revive their independent organization.[33] Confronted with this split in the labor-Populist movement in Chicago, Lloyd promptly joined hands with Morgan, Adair, and Jesse Cox. At the December meeting of the county committee, they overturned the old guard and restored control to those in sympathy with the collectivist tendencies of the party.[34] In the meantime, the dependence of the State Central Committee on Chicago for funds and intellec-

[31] *Ibid.*, Lloyd to Darrow, November 23, 1894. Italics mine.
[32] *Ibid.*, Darrow to Lloyd, "Saturdy."
[33] *Ibid.*, Morgan to Lloyd, November 27, 1894.
[34] Harvey *Citizen*, December 15, 1894.

tual leadership was such as to ensure, seemingly, co-operation from A. L. Maxwell and the downstate leaders.[35] This position made it possible for Lloyd to represent the cause of the labor-Populist alliance at St. Louis with especial force.

The organization of a Radical Club in Chicago at the close of 1894 was intended to strengthen the position of the left wing of the local Populists. It was sponsored by Henry and Jessie Bross Lloyd, Darrow, Andrew B. Adair and J. H. Schwerzgen; the noted Populist advocate of the alliance with urban labor, Lester B. Hubbard, and the Socialists, Jesse Cox, the Thomas J. Morgans, and Paul Ehrmann. The Club's ostensible purpose was to provide the radicals with opportunities for social, educational, and political intercourse on a continuous, informal basis.[36] Its ideological bent was socialistic, although more akin to the British Fabians than the Marxism of Daniel De Leon and the foreign-language-speaking Socialists. Lloyd, himself, preferred "Fabian" as the name of the organization, but gave way to the majority who desired the less definitive term, "Radical."[37]

While the Chicago Radicals consolidated their position and the action of the St. Louis Conference made them the spearhead of the movement to enlist laborers and Socialists from other states in the People's party, the cause of independent political action in the labor movement received a severe and unexpected defeat at Denver. Judging from available evidence it seems clear that the supporters of the political program, including "Plank 10," had won the referendum among the trades unions in advance of the Convention. Whether because of extraordinarily poor leadership on their part, or because Gompers in desperation joined hands with Pomeroy and the racketeer fringe in order to defeat the Socialists, the advocates of independent politics were completely outgeneralled in a two day fight. By piecemeal consideration of the political program, thereby gaining support from elements generally in favor of it while opposing specific provisions, Gompers and the supporters of a non-partisan policy succeeded in striking out the preamble, and in substituting a vague anti-land-monopoly plank for "Plank 10." This struggle was accompanied, incidentally, by a bitter, running fight between the conservative craftsmen and the Socialists. The maneuvers against the political program, which duplicated those of Pomeroy and the

---

[35] Lloyd MSS. (Madison), A. L. Maxwell to Lloyd, November 13, 23, December 4, 1894, T. J. Morgan to Lloyd, November 13, 1894.

[36] *Ibid.*, circular letter from R. H. Howe, *et al.*, November 13, 1894.

[37] *Ibid.*, Lloyd to Rev. W. D. P. Bliss, May 4, 1895; *Union Workman* (Chicago), January 18, 1896.

Single-Taxers in the Illinois Federation of Labor a month earlier, received support from the painters' delegates and from some of those sent by the mine workers, iron and steel workers, tailors, and lasters, who had all been instructed to vote for the entire document. Finally, after all the remaining planks had been approved separately, a declaration to endorse the amended program was killed by the votes of the pure and simple trades unionists and the embittered Socialists. Then, on the last day of the Convention, the anti-Socialist coalition revoked the charter of the International Machinists' Union, of which Thomas J. Morgan was a member.[38]

Before this, the Socialists had joined hands with the supporters of John McBride of the United Mine Workers and elected him President of the Federation in place of Gompers. Friendly to independent political action, and equally favorable to the labor-Populist alliance, McBride sought to resuscitate the political program by declaring, after the Convention, that since each plank save "Plank 10" had been adopted separately, the program and independent political action had both been approved.[39]

Despite McBride's efforts, the action at Denver was little short of disastrous in its effect upon the labor-Populist alliance in Chicago. Enthusiastic approval of the political program would undoubtedly have given a "powerful impulse . . . to the third party movement," as the Eight-Hour Herald had predicted in advance of the Denver Convention.[40] Now, as Lloyd observed in a letter to John Burns in London, the defeat of "Plank 10" at Denver "threatens to make it impossible to get our workingmen into any kind of political action outside the old parties."[41] The first fruit in Chicago of the defeat of the Socialists at Denver was the disruption of the Trades and Labor Assembly. In this body the advocates of the labor-Populist alliance had been slightly stronger than the Pomeroy faction. Even on the question of "Plank 10" the Assembly

---

[38] Thomas J. Morgan MSS., "Report of R. Pohle, Delegate to the National Convention of the American Federation of Labor from the International Machinists Union"; *Western Rural*, XXXII, 827; Commons, *Hist. of Labour*, II, 512–513; Staley, *op. cit.*, 127.

[39] Commons, *op. cit.*, II, 513.

[40] November 10, 1894. After a bitter fight over "Plank 10" in the Trades and Labor Assembly after the election of the delegate, and perhaps because of pressure from Gompers the *Eight-Hour Herald* declared during the Denver Convention that that body could confer no more lasting benefit on organized labor than to forever debar "the discussion of political questions in trade union meetings . . . nothing has ever had so demoralizing an effect on our local organizations as has the introduction of political discussions." December 10, 1894.

[41] Lloyd MSS. (Winnetka), Lloyd to Burns, February 6, 1895.

had been so evenly divided that Pomeroy had been able to defeat the
motion to instruct that body's delegate to support it at Denver only on a
Sunday when Tommy Morgan was absent.[42]

Now, on their return from Denver, the fury of the Socialists passed all
bounds. They were joined by the politically independent unions, when
these learned of Pomeroy's prominent role in the defeat not only of
"Plank 10" but also of independent politics at the Convention. Together with the Knights of Labor these elements withdrew from the Trades
and Labor Assembly. Led by Andrew B. Adair, Thomas I. Kidd and
other opponents of the "labor fakir" element in the Chicago labor movement, they established a new central labor organization.[43] It was
entitled the Chicago Trade and Labor Congress, and applied promptly
to John McBride for a charter from the American Federation of Labor.
This that friend of independent labor politics and honest unionism was
unable to grant owing to the Federation's regulations against the recognition of dual labor organizations.[44] Composed of "the purest element
of the trade union movement" in Chicago, as Thomas I. Kidd asserted,[45]
the Labor Congress for the next two years was the stronghold of opposition to the rule of the "labor skates" in the local labor movement[46]
and of support for the labor-Populist alliance.[47]

The existence of a pure, sympathetic central labor body in Chicago
might have been an even greater asset to the local Populist movement
had not the actions of the Denver Convention put the Socialists on the
defensive and discouraged labor participation in the independent move-

[42] *Eight-Hour Herald*, November 10, 1894.

[43] *American Federationist*, I (February, 1895), 286, II (March, 1895), 17.

[44] American Federation of Labor Archives, copybook XII, 316, John McBride to George
Manns, Secretary, Chicago Labor Congress, August 8, 1895. Ultimately, after Gompers
was restored to power in the Federation, he forced both wings of the Chicago labor movement to unite in the Chicago Federation of Labor, from whose proceedings partisan politics
was completely barred. *American Federationist*, III (November, 1896), 188; Staley, *op.
cit.*, 139 note.

The program of the Chicago Trade and Labor Congress indicates clearly its bias toward
political action of the type advocated by the left wing of the local Populists. Aside from
specific labor legislation, the Congress demanded abolition of the United States Senate, direct election of President and Vice-President, nationalization of railroads, telegraphs, and
telephones, municipalization of public utilities, judicial reform, the initiative and referendum, and abolition of stock speculation. Ultimately it looked to the establishment of the
"co-operative commonwealth." The exclusion from the Congress of delegates not actually
working at their trades or devoting their entire time to the work of their labor organizations
was clear evidence of its determination to exclude the "fakirs" from its proceedings.

[45] Lloyd MSS. (Madison), Thomas I. Kidd to Lloyd, June 27, 1895.

[46] *Union Workmen*, November 2, 1895.

[47] Chicago *Times-Herald*, March 19, 1895.

ment, generally. Within the third party, the defeat of "Plank 10" at Denver encouraged the conservatives to renew their opposition to Socialism and its sympathizers. Thus the defeat of the Socialists at Denver tended to cancel the gains that Henry Lloyd had won at St. Louis. In Chicago the developing issue between the party's left and right wings was sharpened by Henry Vincent's resentment against the Typographical Union, which had ruled against permitting the enlarged *Searchlight* to use free material from the *Times* as filler, under a printing contract that he had negotiated with Willis Abbot. Previously doubtful of the wisdom of the extreme position taken by some radicals in the party, and now discouraged by the defeat of the attempt to develop his paper into the much needed Populist daily, Vincent held all advocates of "Plank 10" save Lloyd responsible for the failure of his plans.[48] Abandoning the role of mediator between the Single-Taxers and Socialists, Vincent joined Willis Abbot in urging the necessity of restricting the party's program to the radicalism which the public might be expected to approve. He also depreciated the contribution that organized labor had made in the recent campaign.

On January 9, 1895, the *Searchlight* published a symposium entitled "Were the Trade Unions with us?" The contributors maintained that a very large vote had been secured from small tradesmen, professional men, and others not in the labor movement, while the trades unionists by comparison had definitely let the People's party down. A week later Vincent editorialized bluntly on "Socialism and the People's Party." This was a vigorous, thinly veiled attack on Thomas J. Morgan, whose views were carefully differentiated from those of Lloyd. Instead, Morgan was identified with the intransigeant, ultra-Marxist position of the Socialist Labor Party, whose organization had just been revived in Chicago on the initiative of De Leon. To Morgan's prominence in the local Populist movement, Vincent now attributed the disappointing vote it had received in November and a supposed decline in "the farmer vote in counties hitherto strong and active against the old parties." Even the defeat of "Plank 10" at Denver he ascribed to personal antipathy of the delegates to "the cold-blooded attitude of its principal champion." Now the time had come for plain speaking. Henry Lloyd and Edward Bellamy, in contrast to Morgan and the New York Socialists, were doing much "to advance the great middle classes" toward a variety of Socialism that contemplated taking "all natural monopolies, such as railroads, telegraphs, telephones, street car lines, gas, electric lighting, mines, etc.,

[48] Lloyd MSS. (Madison), Henry Vincent to Lloyd, November 11, December 6, [1894].

from individual or corporate ownership" and placing them under government ownership and operation. This, Vincent declared, was "the
socialism that can be accepted in America today." But he asserted,

There is another degree of socialism for which the American people are not ready, and
which has cost the reform movement unmeasured losses for having to carry it. It is not
an American product. It is born and nursed under monarchical conditions. It knows but
little of American institutions and cares infinitely less.

Vincent quoted Lloyd's expressed opinion of the unwisdom of those
Socialists who insisted upon "attaching the German construction of their
demands to conditions as they existed here" and particularly to the
Springfield platform. It was Lloyd's modified "Plank 10," which
subjected all collectivist proposals to the initiative and referendum, that
was the most advanced position on the issue that the public could be
expected to support. Vincent then concluded with the frank warning
that there were "mutterings and widespread dissent throughout the
great mass of all classes who are looking to the new party, especially in
Chicago, over just the features pointed out in this article." Thus
Vincent and the *Searchlight* championed the older, developing radicalism
of the agrarian and labor reform tradition against the infiltration of the
alien, Marxist system. He concluded:

It is not that the party desires to disconnect from the socialists, but they emphatically do
dissent from the construction placed upon this movement by some of the Socialist leaders. For so long as such tactics are pursued there will be no union of action between the
city and country. . . . The farmer is a socialist on the question of the great natural
monopolies. When it comes to socializing the land, of course he is not yet that far along.
Concede the time will come, when he will learn that the land question must come up for
readjustment, but since the people are not ready for it, why nauseate them with unpalatable presentations of phrases and conditions that effect no good? . . . In other words, the
American people can tolerate the socialism of its Lloyds, its Bellamys, and its Waylands.
Anything more radical they will not, at least for a time.[49]

For a few months longer, Henry Vincent worked with Henry Lloyd in
the attempt to persuade all elements in the party to co-operate on the
basis of the Address adopted at the St. Louis Conference. An interview
given by Lloyd to the press in Boston, was reprinted by the *Arbeiter-
Zeitung* with obvious approval of his assertion that wage-earners must
be not less radical than the middle class in combating the great corporations, the exploitation of labor, the concentration of wealth, and that a
policy of strikes without support of the People's party would prove unproductive.[50] Vincent also published the interview and reported to

[49] January 17, 1895.
[50] January 15, 1895.

Lloyd that it "has taken splendidly" in Chicago where the Populist ward clubs circulated the number of the *Searchlight* containing Lloyd's remarks as propaganda.[51] This educational work was badly needed. The Populist organization was so incomplete, or its support so concentrated in special districts, that it was unable to nominate election judges in 203 out of 932 precincts in the city when called upon by the Board of Election Commissioners.[52] Nevertheless, the increased activity of the ward and district clubs indicated that the party would participate seriously in the spring mayoral election.

The apportionment of delegates to the Populist nominating convention however, opened a Pandora's box of troubles. Wary after the disruptive effect of partisan politics upon labor organizations during the preceding autumn, the active labor leaders in the party now regarded the direct assignment of ninety-one delegates to the unions as a serious mistake. In addition, the allocation of a delegate each to the several Socialist and Single Tax organizations provoked outspoken indignation from the followers of Henry George. Their large club under this arrangement would be far outnumbered by the Socialist sections, whose total membership was probably no greater than the number of Single-Taxers in Chicago. Unless this arrangement was adjusted more equitably, the leaders of the Chicago Single Tax Club threatened to bolt.[53] The proposal that all delegates and each candidate named by the convention be required to renounce all idea of fusion with the major parties also met with considerable opposition in the county committee. The empty treasury of the city committee added another to the unsolved problems of the third party movement.[54]

As the convention date, Washington's Birthday, approached it became more and more apparent that a bitter conflict over "Plank 10" was likely to divide the Populist convention. A. L. Maxwell, the State Chairman, wrote from Flat Rock to Lloyd to express the hope that the action of the gathering would be "judicious as very much depends on it."[55] In writing to President Benjamin Andrews of Brown University, Lloyd admitted that as in the Springfield Conference of the previous summer "the only issue" in the convention would be "Plank 10 as relating to municipal life." He predicted that all elements in the party would

[51] Lloyd MSS. (Madison), H. Vincent to Lloyd, January 25, 1895; *Searchlight*, January 24, 1894.

[52] *Ibid.*, January 17, 1894; *Chicago Daily Tribune*, January 20, 26, 1895.

[53] *Times*, January 31, 1895.

[54] *Inter Ocean*, February 5, 1895.

[55] Lloyd MSS. (Madison), Maxwell to Lloyd, February 20, 1895.

unite on a platform demanding "municipalization of all public services, monopolies, and . . . municipal employment of the unemployed." The wage-earners, he declared, would work with the Populist party if it "goes their way, and . . . their way grows more radically socialistic every day."[56]

Despite Lloyd's optimism, Clarence Darrow had instituted a series of meetings among the party's leaders in advance of the convention. His purpose was to prevent an open fight over "Plank 10."[57] At his suggestion Lloyd drafted a short platform to replace it, which was acceptable to Howard S. Taylor, leader of the conservatives,[58] and to Thomas Morgan after Lloyd had assured him that a municipal campaign should turn on municipal issues alone.[59] Drawn up with this in view the municipal platform of the party should not involve endorsement or rejection of "Plank 10."

The document contained a shrewd appeal to the general dissatisfaction in Chicago with the inefficient, costly service dispensed by the street railway companies and the Chicago gas trust. It capitalized also upon the apprehension produced among small shop keepers by the rise of the State Street department stores. As drafted by Lloyd, the platform envisaged eventual municipal ownership of utilities, with franchises withheld in the interim unless adequate, annual compensation was paid to the City from gross earnings, while the utilities themselves were to revert absolutely to the municipality after twenty years. To this was joined the demand that Chicago itself "erect and own a down-town loop for the elevated railways," which Charles T. Yerkes and other traction magnates were then constructing. Reform of the system of tax assessment, application of the merit system to the police and clerical staff of the city, and direct municipal responsibility for public improvements without employment of contractors were all designed to remedy specific abuses. Finally, commendation of the Civic Federation for its promotion of municipal reform, and a pledge that the People's party would be its "surest ally" in this work, suggests that Lloyd and his associates intended to bid directly for middle class as well as for labor support in the campaign.[60]

When the convention met on the afternoon of February 22, Darrow

[56] February 19, 1895, *ibid.*

[57] *Ibid.*, Darrow to Lloyd, February 15, 1895.

[58] *Ibid.*, Taylor to Lloyd, February 21, 1895, which thanked him for the present of a book describing municipal experiments in Europe.

[59] *Ibid.*, Morgan to Lloyd, February 21, 1895.

[60] *Ibid.*, MS. draft platform, corrected in Lloyd's hand.

had the situation well in hand. Lloyd was present as delegate at large despite his residence in Winnetka. As Temporary and then Permanent Chairman, Darrow named the committees and mustered sufficient support to prevent any serious deviation from the course of action that he had planned. Lloyd was made chairman of the platform committee, from which representatives of the Socialists and Single-Taxers were excluded. Two trades unionists, H. S. Taylor, and a physician, Bayard Holmes, completed its membership. Both of the excluded elements protested vigorously against this arrangement. S. S. Vaughn, Socialist chairman of the Northside organization where the German-speaking colony was situated, moved to substitute a committee of nine composed of two each from the city's three Divisions and one each from the Socialists, Single-Taxers, and trades unions. This was laid on the table. Then W. F. Cooling, a prominent Single-Taxer, urged that the resolutions committee be composed so as to represent the different schools of economic thought in the coalition rather than geographic districts. As a concession, Darrow added Cooling and J. H. Schwerzgen to the committee and then was upheld by the delegates when Morgan appealed from this ruling.[61]

When the convention reconvened after supper, it voted down Cooling's minority report and then adopted Lloyd's platform almost unanimously. To the original draft had been added endorsement of the Omaha and Springfield platforms, municipalization of harbor facilities, abolition of the slums, and approval of the principle of public ownership of all monopolies in addition to municipal home rule. Eschewing the extremes of "Plank 10" and outright endorsement of the Single Tax, the majority report drew heavily upon Albert Shaw, the outstanding American authority on municipal reform, in its search for a solid municipal program for the labor-Populist alliance.[62] The indebtedness of the platform to the municipal Socialism of the new Liberals, the Fabians, and the Independent Labour Party of Great Britain is also apparent.[63]

The candidates named by the convention were undistinguished. The nominee for mayor was Dr. Bayard Holmes, Professor of Surgery at the College of Physicians and Surgeons. A native of Vermont, forty-two years old, he had been a resident of Chicago since 1861. He was an inveterate reformer, a sympathizer and participant for some years past in local reform movements. In addition to the platform, he advocated a variety of educational reforms, including special schools for defec-

[61] *Inter Ocean*, February 23, 1895; *Searchlight*, February 28, 1895.

[62] Lloyd MSS. (Winnetka), Lloyd to Albert Shaw, April 6, 1895.

[63] W. D. P. Bliss, *Encyclopedia of Social Reform* (New York, 1897), 166, 658, 828–830.

tives and incorrigibles, free text books, and free meals for children attending night schools. Inconspicuous in the political history of Chicago, he represented the awakening social conscience of the urban professional and middle class, which combined the traditional American antagonism to monopoly and special privilege with a positive program for the amelioration of city life.[64]

The aldermanic candidates were selected from the wage-earners and small businessmen, native and immigrant. H. O. Wilson, a carpenter and Methodist native of New York, was named by the thirteenth ward. In the fourteenth, O. Krabol, a Norwegian who had risen from factory worker to head of the Automatic Folding Bed Company, was the candidate. The twenty-first ward selected Benno Koerner, native of Saxony and for twenty-two years resident of the United States, a turner who had distinguished himself guarding the door of Uhlich's Hall the previous August. He was engaged in the art reproduction business. J. S. Kirkpatrick of the thirty-first ward had come from an Ohio farm to work as a bricklayer before rising to the position of a leading contractor. James Lawler of the fifth ward was a New Yorker and a street railway conductor before he had set up his grocery and meat market.[65] W. W. Weaver, President of the International Aluminum Company, was named for City Treasurer. When he declined, he was replaced by Robert Lindblom. A printer was named for City Clerk, and lawyers necessarily for City Attorney and Circuit Judge.[66]

The leaders, platform, and candidates that found favor with the city convention all indicated how far toward the center the People's party in Chicago had moved from the radical, labor leadership of the previous November. Open championship of the "co-operative commonwealth" was hardly to be expected after "Plank 10" had been subordinated and the party's collectivism restricted to natural monopolies and a program of immediate reforms beneficial to the entire consuming public in the city. Yet, the relatively moderate program of the party was founded upon a realistic appreciation of the relationship between the privately owned utilities and the notorious corruption of the Common Council. Even this was considerably in advance of the political intelligence of most middle class Chicagoans of the day. This Populist awareness of the close connection between franchise monopoly and urban misgovernment was clearly implied in Henry Lloyd's summary of what the independent movement offered to Chicagoans:

[64] *Searchlight*, February 28, 1895.
[65] *Ibid.*, March 14, 1895.
[66] *Inter Ocean*, February 23, 1895.

The People's Party is pledged to regain control of all the franchises already granted for the existing gas, street railways, and other public monopolies; and to make them the absolute property of the City. Its aldermen will insist that the terminal loop be built as a municipal enterprise. To have reform the people must do more than elect "good men," they must abolish the bad system of private monopolies in our streets. The People's party is the only one which strikes at the root of boodle.[67]

Viewed from this standpoint the Populist municipal campaign in Chicago was but the beginning of a movement that was to revive again in 1897 and gather strength with each succeeding year of agitation against the corrupt alliance of Charles T. Yerkes, the all-powerful traction magnate of the North and West Divisions, with the bipartisan majority of "boodlers" in the Common Council. It was perhaps the earliest attempt to invoke the traditional hostility to special privilege and monopoly of the American democratic, radical tradition, to gain support for a comprehensive municipal reform program.[68] It represented also an attempt to invoke this indigenous heritage, that Populism itself symbolized, to gain support for reform projects borrowed from the social democratic movement of European cities.

For their own day, the Chicago Populist leaders intended that their platform should be a model for the application of the St. Louis Address of December, 1894, to the problems of city life and thus facilitate the extension of Populism into the urban world. They were seeking, in other words, to hammer out in practical politics the necessary "unity of belief" upon which "unity of organization" between agrarian and urban radicals could be founded. This Mason A. Green of the *Greater Boston Magazine* identified as the unique contribution of Henry D. Lloyd's leadership to the Populist revolt.[69] When Populist conventions in other cities, Cleveland, New York, and Boston followed the example of the Chicago movement, the American correspondent of the London *Labour Leader* reported to Keir Hardie:

The People's party is becoming Socialistic, and even the Socialists, who have hitherto worked on the narrow, jealous lines of the Socialist Labour party (led in the United States mainly by Germans) are now coming to the People's party. The recent platforms of this party, adopted in Chicago, Cleveland, New York City, and Boston, and other cities, are out and out Collectivism. The effort to narrow down the People's party to a mere Silver party has utterly failed. Only one People's party paper has declared for the so-called Sil-

[67] Lloyd MSS. (Winnetka), MS. note.

[68] The preceding discussion of the natural gas pipe-line controversy in Toledo indicates that the traditional antimonopoly stereotypes were invoked by the advocates of the municipal pipe-line there. In Detroit, at the same time (1889–1896), Hazen S. Pingree was waging single-handed his successful campaign for a municipal electric light plant. Bliss. *op. cit.*, 1011. In neither city, however, was a comprehensive program of economic and social reform presented as it was in Chicago by the Populists in 1895.

[69] Lloyd MSS. (Madison), Green to Lloyd, February 3, 1895.

ver party. This means that the People's party will win the Collectivist city vote and the farmer's currency vote. It means that the People's party 1,800,000 votes will soon increase to 3,000,000, and be cast for Socialism.[70]

Whatever the potential merit possessed by such a program as that sponsored by Henry Lloyd and Clarence Darrow may have been, its prospects in Chicago and elsewhere were wrecked on the rocks of irreconcilable, ideological opposition. Taubeneck, the Populist congressional delegation, and Nelson A. Dunning, editor of the *National Watchman*, refused to accept as final the defeat which Lloyd and his supporters had inflicted upon their one-plank, free-silver movement within the party. Joined by James B. Weaver, the party's presidential nominee in 1892, and by the secretary of the National Executive Committee, they published a manifesto a week before the Chicago Populist Convention. This document urged Populists everywhere "to concentrate their entire force" upon the silver issue and to invite "the aid and co-operation" of all persons favoring "the immediate free coinage of silver at the ratio of 16 to 1."[71] Supported vigorously by the *National Watchman*, this repudiation of the action of the St. Louis Conference aroused a storm of protest from the left wing elements who had committed the party, they thought, to public ownership of all monopolies as its distinguishing objective. Ignoring these protests, the *National Watchman* attacked the supposedly prominent position of the Socialists in the party organization in Chicago, in an obvious attempt to discredit the leading champions of the labor-Populist alliance.[72]

Henry Vincent defended the silverites in the party from the charge of treachery leveled at them by the victors at St. Louis. He also corrected Dunning's mistaken impression of the strength of the Socialists in the Chicago movement. He did this, however, in terms that exhibited little good will toward this extreme element:

The Watchman has also had something to say about the prominence taken by the socialists of Chicago in their effort to capture the party and the movement. Again we can remark that very much can be charged along that line, and not exaggerate the facts, but as for capturing the movement at large, or even having controlled the St. Louis conference, they have not yet become quite so all powerful. But the tendency of their leaders prompts the observation right here, that the Socialists in their arrogant assumption are looking upon the People's party with much the same contemplation that a boa constrictor looks upon the beast he is shadowing for an early morning meal. This much by way of a gentle reminder, and it may call for radical treatment in the near future.[73]

---

[70] *The* (London, England) *Labour Leader*, May 4, 1895, p. 11, "Labour Echoes from Afar. America."

[71] *Searchlight*, February 21, 1895.

[72] *Ibid.*, March 7, 1895.

[73] *Ibid.*

The attack in the *Watchman* and the cold hostility of the *Searchlight* proved to be more than the Chicago Socialists could bear. Reconciled to the municipal platform and candidates by the general endorsement of the Springfield platform and the prominence of Lloyd and Darrow in the movement, Thomas J. Morgan had been excluded from the new city committee. Its chairman was now Henry S. Taylor, whose orthodox Populist views and professional position as an attorney had won him the leadership of the conservatives. Only Jesse Cox represented the Socialists. Charles Dold of the Cigar-Makers, Lloyd and Darrow were prominent members. John Z. White had been added to appease the dissatisfied Single-Taxers.[74] Every prominent figure in the labor-Populist alliance but Morgan, therefore, was included within the inner leadership of the municipal campaign.

The subordination of "Plank 10" Morgan had found especially difficult to accept, since he regarded its agitation as essential to the propagation of Socialism.[75] Owing to his admiration for Lloyd, however, he had been willing to accept a minor role for the present and to restrict his speaking engagements to the near North Side and along Milwaukee Avenue in the German-speaking districts. He was sensitive, nevertheless, to personal slights and the growing coolness to Socialism of his associates in the Radical Club. Added to all this was not only the hostility of the *National Watchman* and the Chicago *Searchlight* but also the stinging ridicule of Daniel De Leon, which was pointed at all Socialists who had compromised with Populism only to find themselves reduced now to fighting the one-plank silver scheme within the party.[76] And finally, A. L. Maxwell, State Chairman, had pointedly informed Morgan in advance of the municipal convention that Socialists weren't wanted in the party.[77] Provoked beyond endurance, the Socialists attacked Henry S. Taylor. At a meeting of the city committee, the members from the fifteenth ward, a Socialist stronghold, declared that Taylor had advocated fusion with the Democrats and charged him with having refused to preside at a Debs protest meeting in the Auditorium.[78] Although Darrow promptly addressed a letter to the city committee that completely vindicated Taylor from the charge of disloyalty to either the

[74] *Times*, February 24, 1895. According to Willis Abbot the old-line Populists and trades unionists were well satisfied with the platform and the ticket.

[75] Lloyd MSS. (Madison), Morgan to Lloyd, February 21, 1895.

[76] *The People*, March 10, 1895.

[77] Lloyd MSS. (Madison), Morgan to Lloyd, July 6, 1896.

[78] *Searchlight*, March 7, 1895.

party or the cause of labor, he was unable to close the breach in the coalition's ranks.[79]

Taylor made his reply on March 11. Candidly reviewing his political activities of the past months, he confessed to having proposed fusion with the Democrats in order to avoid the heavy expense of a hopeless municipal campaign. He then turned bitterly upon the Socialists who, he asserted, were attacking him because of his opposition to "Plank 10." He denounced Morgan as the Socialist "Bishop" of Chicago. He charged him with participating in the Populist movement with the sole object of capturing it for the Chicago "Commune." Then, after carefully distinguishing between the antimonopolist, democratic program of Populism and the proletarian collectivism of the Socialists,[80] he literally read them out of the party. In the future, "and on every occasion," Taylor promised to

oppose Plank 10 and its supporters, publicly and privately and always, as being not only not in harmony with the People's party, but radically opposed to it, and if permitted to continue in association with it, utterly destructive of it.

After this all that was needed to complete the breach between the orthodox Populists and the Socialists was an assault upon Henry Vincent by T. P. Quinn, an Irish Knight of Labor of radical views, after the *Searchlight* had attacked his character and principles viciously.[81]

Despite this breach with the Socialists, the Populist municipal campaign in Chicago was conducted with considerable ability. Although the managers were handicapped by inadequate funds and a hostile metropolitan press,[82] the situation was not entirely hopeless. Organization had been perfected. It ranged upward from precinct and ward clubs to three Division Conferences and the city executive committee with its active naturalization bureau and campaign committee. The party now possessed election judges in three fourths of the precincts and a number of speakers acceptable to immigrant and Negro elements. To both of these particular attention was paid.[83]

On the other hand, ebbing of the excited indignation born of the Pull-

[79] *Ibid.*, March 14, 1895.

[80] "The People's party is a party opposed to monopolies and in favor of special privileges to none and equal rights for all, but they do not dream of a commonwealth founded upon the primary principle of confiscation of legitimate property or the spoliation of legitimate proprietors; ..." *Ibid.*

[81] *Ibid.*, March 7, 28, 1895.

[82] *Ibid.*, March 14, 1895.

[83] *Searchlight*, February 28, March 7, 1895; *Daily News*, March 19, 1895; MS. resolution adopted by the campaign committee, March 9, 1894, Lloyd MSS. (Madison).

man strike and the subsequent imprisonment of its leaders deprived the independents of much of the dash and spirit of the previous autumn. After the indifference or hostility to independent political action exhibited by the Denver Convention, organized labor was disinclined to increase its support of the Populist movement.[84]   Yet, an ugly scandal in the Common Council a month before the election offered a golden opportunity to a party advocating municipal ownership of public utilities as a means of driving the corruptionists from public life.   Facing almost certain defeat in April, the Hopkins-Sullivan "boodler" ring voted itself two highly valuable franchises. One of these, the Ogden gas franchise, authorized the establishment of a company to compete with the extremely profitable, but equally unpopular gas "trust," just as the People's Gas and Coke Company was about to merge its constituent members into a single company.   The stockholders in the new Ogden Gas Company, according to Carter Harrison, Jr., were headed by none other than Mayor John P. Hopkins and Roger Sullivan, the two "bosses" of the City Hall machine.   Opposed bitterly in the Council by the representatives of the public and of the vested interests concerned, the Ogden and its accompanying Cosmopolitan electric franchise had been openly "boodled" through.[85]

This notorious franchise steal precipitated an outburst of public wrath. It culminated in a great protest meeting at Central Music Hall under the aegis of the Civil Federation.   The gathering was presided over by Lyman J. Gage, President of the First National Bank, and founder of the Federation.   Invited to speak as Chicago's greatest authority on monopolies, Henry D. Lloyd did his utmost to turn the meeting from a witch hunt to a realistic appreciation of the forces at work behind Chicago's corrupt politics.   The "Gas Trust" was even then seeking a perpetual franchise from the General Assembly, he declared, while it sought the repeal of the new ordinances with the aid of the indignant public. There could be no real purification of politics, Lloyd claimed, until the citizens of Chicago followed the lead of the "progressives" in the London County Council in Great Britain.   There slum clearance and municipalization of street railways was the order of the day.   Chicagoans might examine with profit also the precedent set by eleven American cities that manufactured their own gas in municipally owned works.   No reform could come to Chicago until its citizens banded together on bi-partisan

[84] Henry D. Lloyd, "The American Labour Movement," (London) *Labour Leader*, May 11, 1895.
[85] Steffens, *Struggle for Self-Government*, 49–52; Barnard, *op. cit.*, 406–407; Harrison, *op. cit.*, 192–194.

lines and established the principle that public powers and public property should be administered solely by the city in the public interest.   Otherwise, the Ogden gas steal would only serve to pave the way for an even greater fraud on the city, accompanied by even greater corruption, of the terminal loop proposed for the elevated railroads then under construction.[86]

This was a shrewd forecast, both of how Charles T. Yerkes was to gain the franchise for the elevated loop, and of the methods Chicagoans would be forced to resort to in order to wrest control of the city from the traction interests.   Eloquent though Lloyd's plea was, he was overborne by the more moderate civic and religious leaders who spoke from the same platform that afternoon.   They organized a movement whose purpose was to drive the corruptionists from public office.   It produced a Municipal Voter's League. Led by George E. Cole and William Kent it published the records of the "boodlers" in the Common Council and succeeded in defeating twenty-five of them in the April election.   This was but the beginning of a middle-class reform movement that was to do much to elevate the tone of public life in Chicago in years to come.[87]   It was not until several years later, however, that the leaders of the Municipal Voter's League awakened to full appreciation of the ramifications of the corrupt alliance between Charles T. Yerkes and the leadership of both major parties.

The Populists, meanwhile, made all the political capital they could out of the Ogden and Cosmopolitan franchises.   Four days after the great protest meeting their mayoral candidate, Dr. Bayard Holmes, declared in his letter of acceptance that the "civic scandal" emphasized the need for drastic reform.   As long as the municipality employed contractors on public work and allowed public franchises to be granted to "private parties," the public must not "be surprised or shocked at a corrupted council, a system of courts made tardy and uncertain by jury bribing, and executive officers and assessors discriminating in the performance of their duties."   Civic purity and freedom from monopoly exploitation of the city's streets could be secured only by municipally owned and managed utilities and public works.   To accomplish this the support of every wage-earner, professional man, and all who suffered from the misdeeds of the trusts, department stores, and usurers was needed.[88]

[86] *Inter Ocean*, March 4, 1895.
[87] Steffens, *Self-Government*, 51–54; Lincoln Steffens, *The Shame of the Cities* (New York, 1904), 240–248.
[88] *Searchlight*, March 14, 1895.

An intensive canvass followed. Fifty-five Populist speakers sought to reach the voters in nightly meetings throughout the city. Ably drawn broadsides informed voters that "Boodlers Live on Boodle," and "What the People's Party Platform Means." "A Political Primer" held out the inducement of a tax free city that derived its revenue from "The Rental value of Public Franchises." "Cheap gas and well-lighted streets," "cheap fares and a seat for every one who pays for it," clean streets, the abolition of the sweating system and child labor, public works for the unemployed, a municipally owned and operated terminal elevated loop, and purification of public life would follow the installation of a Populist administration devoted to "the general welfare."

Friendly assistance came from Willis J. Abbot, now managing editor of the *Times-Herald*, who contributed funds and opened his columns to Populist news. This broke the "conspiracy of silence" of the metropolitan press.[89] Professor Edward W. Bemis, a well-known exponent of the historical, welfare school of economic thought and member of the extension staff of the University of Chicago, contributed an article to the *Searchlight* supporting the Populist demand for a municipally owned gas plant.[90] Even Thomas J. Morgan quietly furthered the interests of the Populist campaign in the Labor Congress and offered advice on the proper approach to the labor vote, although he refrained from active participation by request.[91] Henry Lloyd circulated literature on the London County Council and Albert Shaw's book on municipal reform to key figures, including Jane Addams.[92] He did not, however, publicize his discovery that the municipally owned and operated Brooklyn Bridge in New York was currently milked of millions from operating receipts for alleged new construction by Tammany officials protected from exposure by the Platt Republican machine at Albany, New York.[93]

A mass meeting at Central Music Hall on March 15 was the high point of the Populist canvass. Although well attended it drew a smaller crowd than the huge gathering there in early October in the previous campaign. Lyman Trumbull was absent, though scheduled to speak. The addresses, though spirited and aggressive, were on a lower plane than those in which he and Lloyd had laid the ideological basis of the

---

[89] *Times-Herald*, March 10, 1895; Lloyd MSS. (Madison), Abbot to Lloyd, March 23, 1895.

[90] *Ibid.*, Bemis to Lloyd, March 24, 1895.

[91] *Ibid.*, Morgan to Lloyd, March 19, 1895, June 15, 1896.

[92] *Ibid.*, E. Moore to Lloyd, March 4, 1895, Jane Addams to Lloyd, March 11, 1895.

[93] *Ibid.*, H. L. Bridgman to Lloyd, March 25, 1895, Lloyd to Bridgman, March 27, 1895.

labor-Populist alliance five months earlier. An especial object of attack was the recent decision of the Supreme Court of Illinois in Ritchie v. The People. This had invalidated the safeguards thrown about women's work by the Factory Act of 1893 and was a bitter blow to the Chicago Populists, because of the implications that the decision carried for their program.[94]

Lloyd's address at this gathering measured his own indignation at the decision in the Ritchie case. The state Supreme Court, he declared, was the bulwark of plutocracy, against the rising tide of democracy in Chicago. He then alluded bitterly to the Michigan Avenue Armory as the "Bastille" of those who "refused to arbitrate because they had the power to subjugate." This provoked great applause and was especially well received by the Socialists.[95] Tremendous applause greeted his concluding threat to use the "terminal loop for the elevated railroads" as "a halter to hang all the boodlers of Chicago," if the Common Council should boodle it off instead of building it for the City. More in harmony with Lloyd's long range purpose of developing an adequate ethical foundation for democracy in the machine age was his assertion that the growing demand for "regeneration of the cities" might lead to the economic, humanitarian, and political rehabilitation of the urban world. This would counteract the "growing hatred between classes" that was such an ominous characteristic of the age. Municipalization of utilities, therefore, should be sought not only for the cheap transportation and gas that was essential to urban prosperity, but also because it promised to recover true democracy and civic morality.[96]

At the same meeting Robert Lindblom and John Z. White denounced the ramshackle North Division cable cars and the corrupt means by which the West Division traction system had secured its franchises. Lindblom was particularly biting in his references to Yerkes, who controlled both systems.[97] Thus the Populists attempted to develop the traction issue into a campaign theme second only in importance to the elevated loop that they demanded Their opinion of the traction issue's potential vote-getting appeal was indicated by their attempt to persuade Mayor Hazen S. Pingree of Detroit to assist them in the Chicago campaign. This Republican champion of municipal ownership in electric

[94] Illinois Bureau of Labor Statistics, *Eighth Biennial Report*, 436–471; *Times-Herald*, March 16, 1895.

[95] *Arbeiter Zeitung*, March 16, 1895.

[96] *Ibid.*; *Times-Herald*, March 16, 1895.

[97] *Ibid.*; *Chicago Daily Tribune*, March 16, 1895.

lighting replied that he dared not leave Detroit for a single day lest his own corrupt city council boodle off a series of franchise steals in a special session during his absence.[98]

None of this was sufficient to stay the disintegration of the labor-Populist alliance in Chicago. At the most, Adair and Lloyd, respectively Campaign Chairman and Secretary, hoped to poll the same percentage of votes as the party had secured in November. These expectations must have been built in part at least upon the more conservative tactics of the party, and upon the hope of arousing popular interest in the traction issue, so as to gain support for the party's comprehensive reform program. The factional conflict between H. S. Taylor's following and the Socialists,[99] and the declining interest of the wage-earners in independent politics all militated against the achievement of so modest an objective.

In addition, the well-financed organization of George B. Swift, Republican nominee for Mayor, was particularly successful in drawing laborers and even labor Populists into its ranks. Hard times had left the trades unions with empty treasuries and many unemployed members with dues in arrears. A party whose candidates had to bear their own expenses and which could offer neither the hope of office nor election funds to compensate its "heelers" for their efforts was particularly vulnerable to the raids of the Swift machine.[100] Swift was backed by business and political elements "as vicious and dangerous as ever grouped about a candidate in this city,""the Times had declared on Washington's Birthday. Despite this, the needy labor leaders affiliated with the Peoples party found it "hard to refuse" the offers that came from the Republican mayoral candidate. Charles G. Dixon, John B. Clark, and H. A. Hamilton abandoned the Populist cause for the Republican ticket.[101] The first two had been congressional candidates of the third party only five short months before. To the consternation caused by these desertions was the demoralizing effect upon the Populist coalition of the resort to the hostile press of its embittered factions in their eagerness to attack one another as well as those directing the campaign.[102]

Under such circumstances, the independents polled some 15,000 for

[98] Lloyd MSS. (Madison), Pingree to A. B. Adair, Chairman, H. D. Lloyd, Secretary, March 25, 1895.

[99] Lloyd, "American Labour Movement," loc. cit.; The People, April 7, 1895.

[100] Inter Ocean, March 30, 1895; Times, February 24, 1895; Daily News, March 19, 1895.

[101] Times-Herald, March 23, 1895.

[102] Chicago Daily Tribune, March 22, 1895; Lloyd MSS. (Madison), R. H. Howe to Lloyd, April 5, 1895.

their aldermanic candidates.   Dr. Holmes, the Populist mayoral candidate, received only 12,308.   Since Swift was elected by 143,207 votes to 102,284 cast for the Democratic nominee, the independent movement did not even hold the balance between the major parties.   The most favorable computation gave the People's party but a bare five per cent of the popular vote.   In only four of the thirty-four city wards did its aldermanic candidates receive over 1,000 votes.   In none did a candidate get as many as fifteen hundred.   Not a single alderman was elected by the Populists.[103]

Disappointing as the results of the campaign were to Adair, Lloyd, and Bayard Holmes, they were received with joy and derision by both Daniel De Leon and the Populist national headquarters.   In a long editorial *The People* declared that the decline of Populism in Chicago proved the falsity of the belief that radical reforms could be accomplished by a political movement without a revolutionary program.   Collapse of the labor-Populist alliance in the mid-western metropolis, De Leon declared, would leave the field there clear at last for the development of a revolutionary movement "squarely planted upon the platform and under the banner of international Socialism."[104]

Ten days before the Chicago election the *National Watchman*, as spokesman for the silver wing of the Populist party, had insinuated that Lloyd and the mid-western antimonopolist editors of the *Non-Conformist*, *Farmers Tribune*, *Advocate*, and *Wealth Makers* were about to launch a new movement "to be known as the socialist labor party."[105]   This oblique attack was accompanied by severe pressure upon the aged proprietor of the *Farmers Tribune* from James B. Weaver and the silver men in an attempt to get him to remove its editor, Thomas F. Byron, and to abandon the St. Louis and Omaha platforms.[106]   Now that the labor-Populist coalition in Chicago had suffered a stunning defeat, the *Watchman* rejoiced exuberantly.   On April 12, at the head of its editorial page, it declared

If Mr. Lloyd can run a Populist conference, he failed most sadly to run a socialistic election.

The Platform of 1896 will not be broadened to meet socialistic ideas.   Let us thank God and the recent election at Chicago for that fact.

Who is on top now, Chairman Taubeneck or the great socialistic leader, Mr. Lloyd.   As evidence, we refer to the late disaster at Chicago. . . .

[103] *Chicago Daily Tribune*, April 3, 1895.
[104] April 14, 1895.
[105] March 22, 1895; Chicago *Express*, April 6, 1895.
[106] Lloyd MSS. (Madison), Byron to Lloyd, April 8, 1895.

> Populism and socialism have parted company. For proof of this see the returns from the Chicago elections.
>
> The Omaha platform will not be broadened. . . .

Instead, the *National Watchman* declared that the Chicago election had vindicated those who wished to narrow the Populist platform to the silver issue. With his subscription list doubled since November, Dunning concluded that there was "no use fooling away any more time or labor in the cities, the workingmen will not vote as they march. It is the country and smaller towns that must be depended upon to vote for reformers." Then with Weaver's aid, the silver men were now able to oust Byron from the *Farmer's Tribune* and deprive the antimonopolist defenders of the Omaha platform of one of their most doughty journalistic champions.[107]

As late as March, just before the Chicago election, Henry D. Lloyd had felt it possible to write Keir Hardie in London that the People's party was growing more radical, with some prospect of becoming in America the equivalent of the Independent Labour Party. This Lloyd dared to hope for despite the coldness of most craft unions to the labor-Populist alliance, and the effect that fear of losing police protection and the advantage of having henchmen in the City Hall under major party auspices had upon reducing the appeal of the independent movement to labor organizations.[108] Now, as letters poured in from Populist sympathizers in the Middle and Far West, where alarm was felt at the renewed activity of the silverites within the party,[109] Lloyd and his associates witnessed the final collapse of their coalition.

The Socialists were the first to act. Having withdrawn earlier from the People's party, they now organized the Chicago Socialist Federation composed of "individualist Socialists" and De Leon's small following.[110] At the same time, Lloyd's friends lost control of the *Arbeiter-Zeitung*.[111] Far more disastrous to the prospects of an independent movement in Chicago along the lines laid down at the St. Louis Conference, was the cleavage that developed within the Chicago movement between the conservatives and the radical, non-Marxian trades unionists and professional men who had played such an important part in the organization

[107] *Ibid.*, Byron to Lloyd, May 5, 28, 1895.

[108] Lloyd, "American Labour Movement," *loc. cit.*

[109] Lloyd MSS. (Madison), Phoebe W. Cousins to Lloyd, April 25, 1895, Eugene Higgins to Lloyd, May 7, 1895, T. P. Benedict to Lloyd, January 7, 1896.

[110] *Ibid.*, T. J. Morgan to Lloyd, April 6, May 16, 1895; *The People*, April 7, 1895; *Chicago Daily Tribune*, June 9, 1895.

[111] Lloyd MSS. (Madison), Edmund Duess to Lloyd, May 1, 1895.

and leadership of the party. Headed by Thomas I. Kidd, Adair, Lloyd, and Darrow, backed by the Radical Club, the Labor Congress, and the *Union Workman*, this wing of the party had furnished most of the voting strength of the coalition. If harmony had prevailed, this radical element might have continued to work effectively within the local, state, and national Populist organization in the attempt to extend the Omaha platform toward an antimonopolist collectivism congenial to urban, non-Marxian radicals. This was not to be.

Deprived now of the financial support which the party's left wing had provided, Henry Vincent merged the *Searchlight* with the Chicago *Age*. Immediately after the city election, he identified the editorial policy of the new paper with that of the *National Watchman*. Vincent now declared that Lloyd had been involved in a Marxian plot to destroy the Populist party and throw the Omaha platform overboard by boring from within.[112] The *Age and Chicago Searchlight* then opened its columns to an appeal from Howard S. Taylor. He urged the Populists, Single-Taxers, and trades unionists to join together to oust the "Communists" who, Taylor alleged, had gained control of the party in Chicago by playing the other factions off against each other. This had "dislocated" the "relation to the National People's party" of the Populist movement in Chicago. Following this manifesto, Vincent published an appeal from James B. Weaver in behalf of the one plank, free silver platform and asserted that thousands of votes in Chicago and elsewhere had been lost because "of utterances of mouthing socialists who claim to control the organization." At the same time, Vincent joined with Taylor, the Single Tax leaders, Charles Dold of the Cigar-Makers, and other conservatives in organizing an Omaha Club that pledged fidelity to the policy of the "National People's party."[113]

Thereafter, the rift between the radicals and conservatives widened into an open breach in the Cook County movement. This development came to a head in September during preparations for the county election. Then, during the visit of Keir Hardie to Chicago under the auspices of the Labor Congress, the Taylor faction packed and held a county convention that repudiated the Springfield platform. It also nominated the Colonel of the Seventh Regiment of the Illinois National Guard for drainage trustee,[114] an action that was particularly obnoxious to the trades unionists and radicals of the party. The left wing voiced its

[112] *Age and Chicago Searchlight*, April 13, 1895.

[113] *Ibid.*, April 27, 1895.

[114] Lloyd MSS. (Madison), Thomas I. Kidd to Lloyd, September 16, 1895, T. J. Morgan to Lloyd, September 9, 1895.

protest and indignation through the city committee.[115] Thereupon the
conservatives and radicals read each other out of the Populist movement, clinging respectively to the county and city committees and
claiming to represent the national People's party in the metropolitan
area. At the end of the year Thomas I. Kidd instituted conferences
between the radicals and the trades unionists in an effort to revive their
zeal for a genuine labor-Populist alliance based upon the Springfield
platform. Taylor, on the other hand, joined forces with William H.
("Coin") Harvey in setting up a secret, free silver organization that
excluded wage-earners entirely from the councils of the party. Both
factions looked forward to 1896 and the Populist national convention for
recognition and vindication.

Meanwhile, the disruption of the labor-Populist alliance in Chicago
had destroyed its ability to exert any significant influence upon the
political strategy of the national organization. Thus the failure to
recruit a numerous following in Illinois for the broader collectivism which
the Chicago radicals had added to the Omaha platform had a negative
effect upon the attempt of the agrarian antimonopolists and eastern
Nationalists to block the silver movement within the People's party.
The last act in the drama, whose first scene had been staged at the
Springfield Conference of July, 1894, was to be witnessed at the St. Louis
Convention two years later. In the meantime, the fate of the attempt
to graft an alien collectivism into the traditional pattern of American
democratic radicalism had been clearly foreshadowed in Chicago.

[115] *Ibid.*, Morgan to Lloyd, September 10, 17, 26, 1895; Chicago *Chronicle*, September 24,
October 2, 8, 1895.

INDEX

Abbot, Willis J., appraises Chicago Populist campaign, 190; pro-labor policy, 191; urges government ownership of monopolies on Labor-Populists, 192–93; castigates Henry George, 202–04; tries to prevent Socialist-Single-Taxer schism, 210; contracts with Henry Vincent, 236; aids Populist mayoral campaign, 248.

Absolute Money, 64.

Adair, Andrew B., denies trades unionist disaffection, 184 n. 27; leads Briggs House conference, 185; influence with labor weakened by Altgeld, 189; brother, 192; appeals for harmony, 204; vote for, 211 n. 125; leads bolt, 232; joins Radical Club, 233; organizes Trade and Labor Congress, 235; mayoral campaign chairman, 250; defeated, 251; leader of radical Populists, 253.

Adams, Charles Francis, 60.

Addams, Jane, 160, 248.

Advocate, 251.

Age and Chicago Searchlight, 253.

Alarm, 82.

Alexander, Jesse P., 62.

Allen, Senator William V., of Nebraska, 30.

Alliance, 72.

Altgeld, John P., pardons Anarchists, 189; Single-Taxer backing, 13, 164, 201, 223; elected governor, 167; popularity with labor, 168, 189, 207; and farmers, 208.

Altruria, 20, 159.

American Bimetallic League, 30 n. 83, 227.

American Commonwealth, 135–36, 140.

American Co-operative Union, 21.

American Federation of Labor, Socialist infiltration, 102; Chicago convention, 165; endorses British independent labor politics, 166; votes referendum on political program, 166; Illinois Populists endorse, save "Plank 10," 172; Springfield Conference adopts with modified "Plank 10," 172–73; program published, 194; Illinois Federation adopts, except "Plank 10," 201; Wisconsin Populists endorse, 212; referendum encourages independent political action, 176; affiliated unions lead Chicago Populists, 188; Populist policy dependent on fate of referendum, 225–26; program wins, 233; despite Gompers' opposition, 182–83; defeated at Denver Convention, as are Socialist sponsors, 233–34, 236; who help elect McBride President, 234; he tries to revive political program, 234; refuses charter to Chicago Labor Congress, 235.

American Free-Trade League, invokes Locofoco stereotypes, 5; western branches, 5–6; stimulates western antimonopoly and Liberal Republican movements, 6–7; trains Lloyd, 11, 137.

"American monetary system" (See Kelloggism), 57, 63, 74.

American Nonconformist, 69, 200, 229, 251.

American Protective Tariff League, 207.

American Railway Association, 217.

American Railway Union, 21, 164, 171, 175, 180, 184–88, 190, 207–08, 217, 229, 231.

"American System of Finance," 60.

Anarchism, 15, 95.

Anarchism, American, 78–80, 82.

Anarchists (Communist-Anarchists), attack Kelloggism, 74; European, 26; invited to Pittsburgh Congress, 78, 80; Bakuninist, 79; factionalism, 89, 162; beliefs, 90; desert Buchanan, 104; eschew violence, 164; oppose "Plank 10," 172.

Andrews, E. Benjamin, 155, 238.

Anti-industrialism, 50, 76.

Antimonopolism, of Locofocos, 3; of Henry George, 12; single tax movement, 223; in Populism, 17–18, 25, 212, 220, 222–23, 236–37, 245, 251, 254; "middle-of-the-road" Populists, 21; in free trade agitation, 5, 23; invoked, 27–28; in Kelloggism, 53–55, 61; in Alliance movement, 67; Knights of Labor a stronghold of, 104; in Fostoria, 106; invoked in Toledo pipeline controversy, 112, 114, 116–17, 242 n. 68; of *Wealth Against Commonwealth*, 138,

255

central issue in campaign, 242, 247, 249–50; Brooklyn Bridge, 248.

Munn v. Illinois, 11.

National Anti-Monopoly Cheap Freight Railway League, 4, 6.

National banking system, 23, 33–35, 43, 56–57, 64, 76.

National Direct Legislation League, 24 n. 63.

National Economist, 69–71.

National Farmers' Alliance, 14, 69–70.

National Farmers' Alliance and Industrial Union, 70.

National Grange, 70.

National Greenback Party, 8, 27 n. 71, 61, 63–65.

Nationalism, 14, 16, 18, 224.

Nationalists, 14, 20–21 n. 50, 24 n. 63, 30, 168, 177, 190, 193, 198, 224, 228–30, 254.

Nationalization (see Government Ownership).

National Farmers' Alliance, 8–9, 69.

National Labor Union, participates in anti-monopoly movement, 4; accepts labor-cost theory, 25; vehicle of post-bellum labor reformism, 50–51; Baltimore Convention, 56 n. 62; Chicago Congress, 56 n. 62, 57, 60 n. 90; adopts Kelloggism, 8, 56 n. 62, quoted, 57; New York Convention, quoted, 58; zeal for co-operation, 9, 51, quoted, 57; trades unions withdraw, 59; recommends formation of a labor party, 58–59; monetary system urged on farmers, 61; contributes leadership to Greenback party, 63; Knights of Labor inherit philosophy, 66.

National Transit Company, 110.

National Watchman, 243–44, 251–52.

Natural gas, 105; waste of, 106, 132; conservation of, urged in Ohio, 107, 110; "free gas," 106–08, 112, 115, 133; Indiana field, 107; popular theory of inexhaustibility, 106–07, 112.

Nevins, Allan, 146; reverses opinion of *Wealth against Commonwealth*, 140–41; errors in own use of, 141–42 n. 16–17; indictment of, 142, 145, quoted, 141, 149;

account of Buffalo conspiracy trial analyzed, 150–52; supports Lloyd on Standard Oil profits, 156; attests to influence of *Wealth against Commonwealth*, 160.

"Newcastle Program," 31.

"The New Conscience," 137.

"New Departure," 46–47.

New England Magazine, 161.

"New Liberalism," 30, 240.

New York Advocate, 63–64, 74, 207.

New York Evening Post, 5, 48–49.

New York Herald, 41.

New York Tribune, 41, 49, 62.

New York World, 41, 46, quoted, 41 n. 59.

Norris, George W., 31.

North American Review, 29, 137.

Northwestern Ohio Natural Gas Company, forced out of Fostoria and Tiffin by municipal gas, 107, 112; Standard Oil gains control of, 108–09; franchise secured in Toledo, 109; quarrel over rates, 109–10; rates analyzed, 111–12; service to industry, 111, 118; public relations policy, 112–13, 119; popular dissatisfaction with, 111–12; gas territory, 109; extended to block Toledo pipe-line, 124, 126, 129; protective drilling, 126; opposes Griffin bill, 118–19; stock-watering charged against, 123; and credit mobilier methods, 122–23; absorbs Toledo Natural Gas Company, 124; suspends service to Toledo municipal institutions, 132; final victor over Toledo, 134; management changed, 134.

Norton, S. F., 15, 68, 73, 76, 193.

Oberholzer, E. P., 44.

O'Day, Daniel, 110, 113, 121, 127–28.

Ogden Gas Company, 246.

Oglesby, D., 68.

Ohio General Assembly, 114, 118–19, 121, 131, 142 n. 16–17, 153–54.

"Ohio idea," 43.

"Ohio rag baby," 7, 49.

Oil City Derrrick, 125, 134.

Oil Region, 4, 141 n. 16, 146–47, 149.

Ohio State Republican Convention (1867), 36.

DATE DUE

GAYLORD   PRINTED IN U.S.A.